# PARALLEL ALGORITHMS

## DESIGN AND ANALYSIS

## PRANAY CHAUDHURI

*University of New South Wales*
*Australia*

**Prentice Hall**  New York  London  Toronto  Sydney  Tokyo  Singapore

Acquisitions Editor: Andrew Binnie.
Production Editor: Fiona Marcar.

Typeset by Monoset Typesetters, Strathpine, Qld.

Printed in Australia by Impact Printing, Brunswick, Victoria.

1 2 3 4 5 96 95 94 93 92

ISBN 0 13 351982 1.

**National Library of Australia**
**Cataloguing-in-Publication Data**

Chaudhuri, Pranay, 1951–
   Parallel algorithms.

   Bibliography.
   Includes index.
   ISBN 0 13 351982 1.

   1. Parallel processing (Electronic computers).
   2. Computer algorithms. I. Title.

004.35

Library of Congress Cataloging-in-Publication Data are available from the publisher.

Prentice Hall, Inc., *Englewood Cliffs, New Jersey*
Prentice Hall Canada, Inc., *Toronto*
Prentice Hall Hispanoamericana, SA, *Mexico*
Prentice Hall of India Private Ltd, *New Delhi*
Prentice Hall International, Inc., *London*
Prentice Hall of Japan, Inc., *Tokyo*
Prentice Hall of Southeast Asia Pty Ltd, *Singapore*
Editora Prentice Hall do Brasil Ltda, *Rio de Janeiro*

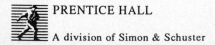 PRENTICE HALL

A division of Simon & Schuster

*To my Mother,*
*and*
*in memory of my Father*

# Contents

# CHAPTER 2

## Models of Parallel Computation   19

# CHAPTER 3

## Complexity of Parallel Algorithms   45

# CHAPTER 4

## Merging and Sorting  61

# CHAPTER 5

## Selection and Searching  118

# CHAPTER 6

## Matrix Computations   156

# CHAPTER 7

# Algorithms for Unweighted Graphs   194

## CHAPTER 8
## Algorithms for Weighted Graphs    255

## CHAPTER 9
## Updating Algorithms for Graphs    287

# Preface

There has been considerable interest in the development of parallel algorithms, even before parallel computers became available. Commercially available parallel computers have provided further impetus to the research on the design of efficient parallel algorithms for solving various problems. This book is about the design of fast and efficient algorithms for parallel computers and the analysis of their complexities.

The book is intended as a text for a course on parallel algorithms normally offered at the final-year undergraduate or graduate level in computer science, electrical engineering, and mathematics. In addition, it may be used as a reference for computer professionals. It is expected that the reader possesses the background usually provided by an introductory course on the design and analysis of algorithms.

After a discussion of the computational models and complexity-related issues, the text is restricted to the design and analysis of parallel algorithms for a few important classes of problems. Efforts have been made to provide sufficient material on each of the problem areas covered so that it will be useful not only to senior undergraduate/graduate students but also to the research workers and readers interested in investigating a particular topic more thoroughly. The text deals with some important problems on lists and sequences (e.g., merging, sorting, selection, and searching), matrix computations, and graph theory. My motive was to concentrate more on the depth of the treatment of the topics covered rather than the breadth of the book in terms of the number of topics.

To make the text comfortable for the reader, besides an Introduction, Chapter 1 provides some architectural and mathematical background which is often required to study such a book. Chapter 2 deals with the computational models, whereas Chapter 3 is concerned with the complexity-related issues and paradigms for parallel computation. Two closely related problems on lists and sequences, namely merging and sorting, are treated in Chapter 4. Chapter 5 is devoted to two other related problems (i.e., selection and searching). Parallel algorithms for matrix computations are investigated in Chapter 6. During the past several years a vast amount of research has been centered around parallel graph algorithms. In recognition, in this text the last three chapters have been devoted to covering this area. Specifically, algorithms for unweighted graphs have been studied in Chapter 7. Chapter 8 considers the algorithms for weighted graphs and finally, parallel updating algorithms for graphs are discussed in Chapter 9.

This text is based primarily on the research papers published in the field of parallel algorithms over the past twenty years. Every effort has been made to cite as many references as possible, including the latest available papers, on each of the topics/problems covered. However, there are many important works which I have not been able to cite simply because the literature is too rich and the space in the text is too limited. I express my indebtedness to all the authors whose works I have referred to and used as the main sources of various ideas; and apologize to the other authors for not being able to cite their works in the text.

I am grateful to my revered teacher Sukumar Ghosh, University of Iowa, for his encouragement and inspiration, without which it would have been difficult to complete this work. I am also grateful to my elder brother Pranab for his unfailing support throughout my career.

Thanks are due to Ratan Ghosh, Indian Institute of Technology, for many stimulating discussions during the past several years leading to various ideas, some which have been reflected in the text. I wish to thank Jiannong Cao, James Cook University, for reviewing a large portion of the manuscript and providing valuable suggestions. I also acknowledge several helpful comments made by my graduate students at the University of New South Wales.

Special thanks are due to Maurice Clint, Queen's University of Belfast, for thoroughly reviewing the manuscript. His constructive criticism and suggestions on an early draft have improved the book considerably. I also thank Richard Brent, Australian National University, for several helpful comments. Finally, I appreciate very much the friendly support provided by Andrew Binnie, Prentice Hall Australia, during the entire period of this work.


Pranay Chaudhuri

Email: pranay@cs.unsw.oz.au
Sydney, Australia

# CHAPTER 1

# Introduction and Background

## 1.1 INTRODUCTION

This book is concerned with the design and study of parallel algorithms. More precisely, it is about methods for solving problems on parallel computers and the costs of using those methods (usually in terms of the running time and the number of processors required).

An algorithm is a step-by-step method for solving a problem. Algorithms have two characteristic properties in common. The first is that the algorithm must have a finite textual representation. Elementary components of this text are termed "steps." The second property is that each of these steps must be mechanically performable in a finite time. We also append the requirement that the algorithm must come to an end in a finite number of steps for any input. It is important to specify the executor of an algorithm at least implicitly. Algorithms that are executed by a computer are referred to as computer algorithms. In the context of this book the executor of all algorithms is assumed to be a computer (machine) and the terms "algorithm" and "computer algorithm" will be used synonymously.

Execution of an algorithm takes time (computation time). Algorithms for some problems can be executed quickly while those for others take a very long time. People have always been interested in designing better algorithms for solving different problems by discovering faster ways for their solution. Since the computation time also depends on the processing speed of the computer executing the algorithm, efforts have been made to increase the speed of computers. Over the past four decades, increases in processing speed have been achieved by using inherently faster electronic components in the same basic hardware organization for the computer. The developments in the basic components

1

occurred mainly in four phases. From vacuum tubes and relays to discrete diodes and transistors to small and medium scale integrated (SSI/MSI) circuits to large and very large scale integrated (LSI/VLSI) circuits. But it appears that the future may not witness as great a rate of increase in speed of the basic components as in the past. The reason is that an increase in computation speed can be attained both through increased circuit density (thereby reducing propagation delay) and increased switching speed. But circuit densities are fast approaching the limits of optical resolution (Stone 1980). Thus, even if switching times become instantaneous, distances between circuit components may not become small enough to reduce propagation delays enough to make a considerable increase in computation speed.

There are many scientific and industrial problems which require enormous processing or computing power (measured in terms of a certain number of operations per unit time, such as one million multiplications of 16-bit integers per second, etc.). In some cases, huge amounts of data must be processed to produce usable results, and in others, large numbers of calculations must be performed on relatively smaller sets of data. Examples of some of these computations are weather forecasting, aerodynamic studies, satellite collected imagery analysis, biomedical image processing, simulation studies in nuclear and plasma physics, robot vision, and seismic data processing. Very powerful computer systems are needed to solve these problems in order that the results are available in a reasonable time (e.g., calculation of weather forecast for 24 hours in less than 24 hours to make it worthwhile). The current demands for high-speed computing cannot be satisfied only by using faster hardware components. It appears that this demand can be satisfied only by parallel processing. Parallel processing means performing independent operations simultaneously so that the overall computation time is reduced. In a conventional (serial) computer there is only one processing unit and hence it can only perform operations strictly serially, i.e., one at a time. Therefore, in order to achieve parallel processing we need a computer which has a number of processing units. Such a machine is referred to as a parallel computer. The basic requirement is that the single task must be partitionable into a number of mutually independent subtasks. If it is not possible then obviously it will be a fruitless effort to attempt to process such a task in parallel. However, many scientific and industrial problems can be solved very fast by parallel processing.

The subject of parallel processing is a comparatively new field of study. But it is expanding very fast relative even to other areas of computer science and has become, within a decade, a mainstream computer science subject. The prime reason for this is that, with the advent of VLSI technology, the cost of hardware has been steadily decreasing, making it increasingly feasible to assemble a large number of processing units or processors with which to build parallel computers. The advance of hardware technology and greater computational requirements motivated hardware designers to develop parallel computers, as a result of which a number of parallel computers are now commercially available. However, parallel computers present a great challenge to algorithm designers. Algorithms are designed with a view to the particular computer on which they are to be executed. Algorithms used on conventional (serial) computers are referred to as serial algorithms. In order to solve a problem using a parallel computer we need to develop a parallel algorithm. For some problems this can be done easily by parallelizing a corresponding serial algorithm. However, for many problems, this is not an effective way and we need to design parallel algorithms "from scratch." For serial algorithms, the running time and the space utilization are the main measures of complexity. These two measures are also important for parallel algorithms. There are some additional measures of complexity for parallel algorithms, the most important of which is the number of processors required. Some problems are hardly parallelizable even if an infinite number of processors are available. The reason is that the computational steps involved in solving these problems are inherently serial.

Introduction of parallelism in most of the computations does indeed enhance the speed of execution. However, the degree of speedup is limited. There are two reasons for this. First, the difficulties caused by the need for intensive interprocessor communication and for simultaneous memory access. Second, even if one assumes a parallel computation model which has no restriction due to interprocessor communication or memory access there will still exist lower bounds to the computational time and these are due to the intrinsic complexity of the problems concerned. Thus it is important to study parallel algorithms within an idealized unrestricted parallel computation framework in order to gain a deeper insight into the inherent complexity of various problems. On the other hand, it is also important to study the performance of parallel algorithms under certain constraints, such as that imposed by the limited number of processors available. In such cases, the processors must be used effectively to improve the performance of the algorithm. Another important issue is communication among the processors. The time required to exchange data between two processors is usually more than that required to perform simple operations on the data. Moreover, the distances between the different pairs of communicating processors can also vary. Synchronization is yet another important problem when constructing algorithms that run on independent machines connected by some communication network. Such algorithms are usually referred to as *distributed algorithms* and will not be considered in this book. We shall restrict ourselves mainly to computational models that assume full synchronization.

The rest of this chapter provides some background material which will be useful in the study of this book. More specifically, architectural developments and classification are briefly presented in Section 1.2. Some mathematical preliminaries, including the concepts related to sets, data structures, order notation, etc. are discussed in Section 1.3. However, these are not prerequisites to reading this book and a reader who is familiar with these definitions and concepts may start directly with Chapter 2.

## 1.2 ARCHITECTURAL BACKGROUND

A variety of architectural developments increased the performance of computers. In this section we briefly review these developments. A widely used architectural classification scheme is then presented.

### 1.2.1 Developments to Enhance Speed of Computation

Computational speed has increased by orders of magnitude over the past four decades. Most of these developments are attributable to inherently faster electronic components. Any further increase in computation speed from new device technology is less likely and it appears that the only alternative to enhance overall computational speed is by increasing the number of operations that may take place concurrently either through pipelining or parallelism. In this section, we briefly highlight the architectural advancements that have taken place in the past four decades.

Early first-generation computers used bit-serial main memory and a bit-serial central processing unit (CPU). Each bit of a word was read individually from memory and arithmetic was performed on a bit-by-bit fixed-point basis. Bit-parallel arithmetic became possible after bit-parallel memory was developed. Magnetic core memory was first developed as bit-parallel memory and used on a commercial basis in 1955 in the IBM 704 (Hayes 1978).

The introduction of input/output (I/O) processors was an important development in computer systems architecture and allowed main CPU to be exploited more effectively. In the first-generation computers, the I/O instructions were executed by the CPU. This was a main reason for poor performance since the electromechanical I/O devices were much slower than the data manipulation rate of the electronic CPU. This problem was solved by using an independent I/O processor to handle I/O operations. Upon receiving I/O instructions from the CPU, the I/O processor (also called the channel) worked independently, freeing the CPU to do other computational tasks.

The next phase of architectural advance was due to the development of interleaved and cache memory. In interleaved memory, a memory unit is partitioned into a number of modules. Each memory module has its own addressing circuitry and all modules can be accessed simultaneously. Memory interleaving enables a relatively slow memory to interface with a relatively fast processor. If the memory is partitioned into two memory modules, then the memory unit can supply two successive words to the CPU in one memory cycle period since both the modules can be accessed simultaneously. A cache memory is a small fast memory placed between the CPU and the main memory. The cache memory acts as a high-speed buffer and reduces the time the CPU must spend waiting for data to arrive from the slower main memory. Both of these features exist in some of the late second-generation machines such as the IBM 7094 (Hayes 1978).

A further increase in computational speed is achieved by using multiple functional units, and through instruction and data pipelining. The early computer systems had only one arithmetic and logic unit (ALU) in its CPU and the ALU could perform only one function at a time. In practice, a set of specialized functional units (e.g., adder, multiplier, shifter, etc.) can be used to perform the functions of the ALU. These functional units are independent of each other and can operate simultaneously. Examples of computers that use multiple functional units are the CDC 6600 and the IBM 360/91 (Hwang and Briggs 1984). Instruction pipelining allows more than one instruction to be in some stage of execution at the same time. Execution of each instruction can be divided into various phases such as instruction fetch, instruction decoding, operand fetch and then arithmetic-logic execution. In a nonpipelined computer these four phases must be completed before the next instruction is fetched. In contrast, in a pipelined computer successive instructions are executed in an overlapped manner. Thus the instruction execution cycle is effectively reduced to one-fourth of the original cycle time by using a four-stage linear pipeline processor. A vector computer allows operations on both vectors and scalars. In the case of vector instruction execution, vectors are streamed from memory into the CPU, where pipelined arithmetic units perform the operation. Examples of some pipelined vector computers are the Cray-1, Cyber-205 and Fujitsu-200 (Hwang and Briggs 1984). An alternative way to implement vector computers is by using a synchronized processor array so that the processors are capable of performing the same operation on different data at the same time.

All of the computers mentioned so far are called *control flow computers* because the order in which instructions are to be executed is controlled by a program counter. *Data flow architectures* which have been proposed in recent years eliminate the program counter. The execution of an instruction is enabled whenever its required operands are available. The computations are data-driven. The instructions in a program are not ordered and instruction initiation depends on data availability. The data dependency constraint determines the execution order and, theoretically, maximal concurrency in a program may be exploited by such a machine.

## 1.2.2  Classification of Computer Architectures

A typical CPU operates by fetching instructions and operands from main memory, executing instructions, and finally storing the result in memory. The instructions can be viewed as forming an instruction stream flowing from memory to the CPU, while the operands form the data stream flowing between the memory and the processor.

Several classification schemes for computer systems have been proposed (see e.g., Flynn 1966; Feng 1972; Handler 1977). The classification scheme due to Flynn is the most popular one and is presented in this section. This classification is based on the number of simultaneous instruction and data streams seen by the processor during program execution. Let $n_i$ and $n_d$ denote the number of distinct instruction and data streams, respectively, which can be actively processed at the same time in a computer. These are referred to as the instruction and data multiplicities of the computer and measure its degree of parallelism. According to Flynn, computer systems can be classified into four distinct classes based on the values of $n_i$ and $n_d$.

*Single instruction stream, single data stream* (SISD): In SISD computers $n_i = n_d = 1$. Most conventional computers with one processor containing a single ALU capable only of scalar arithmetic belong to this class.

*Single instruction stream, multiple data stream* (SIMD): In SIMD computers $n_i = 1$, $n_d > 1$. This class includes machines with a single program control unit and multiple ALUs. In such computers many data items may be accessed from the memory and processed simultaneously by a single instruction. Array processor machines fall into this category.

*Multiple instruction stream, single data stream* (MISD): In MISD computers $n_i > 1$, $n_d = 1$. A number of processors execute distinct instructions over the same data stream. This mode of operation is generally unrealistic and there are no computers which fit into this category.

*Multiple instruction stream, multiple data stream* (MIMD): For MIMD machines $n_i > 1$, $n_d > 1$. The machines that fall into this class are capable of executing several independent programs simultaneously. Most multiprocessor systems and multiple computer systems fall into this category. An MIMD computer is referred to as tightly coupled if the degree of interactions among the processors is high; otherwise it is loosely coupled.

# 1.3  MATHEMATICAL PRELIMINARIES

In this section, we will begin by reviewing the concepts of sets, relations, and functions. Then we will discuss briefly the concepts of data types and data structures. We will also present the notions of order notation necessary for analyzing algorithms. Finally, by considering some common algorithm segments we will show how to express, using order notation, the time complexity of an algorithm.

## 1.3.1  Sets, Relations, and Functions

A *set* is a collection of distinct objects which are called its *elements* or *members*. Sets are usually represented in one of two ways. The first way uses a pair of braces to enclose all elements of a set. The elements are separated by commas. The other way is to specify a set in terms of a characteristic property of its elements. For example, consider the set X containing all prime numbers less than 8. Set X can be represented either by X = {1, 2, 3, 5, 7}, or by X = {p | p is a prime number and p < 8}. If x is an element of a set X, then we say that x belongs to X. This is denoted by $x \in X$. Alternatively, $x \notin X$ denotes that x does not belong to X. A set consisting of no elements is called the *empty set* or *null set* and is represented by symbol $\emptyset$. The *size* or *cardinality* of a set X is the number of elements it contains. A set is finite if its cardinality is finite, otherwise it is infinite.

Given two sets X and Y, the set X is said to be a *subset* of Y if every element of X is an element of Y. X is said to be a proper subset of Y if X is a subset of Y and there is at least one element of Y which is not in X. The statement "X is a subset of Y" is denoted by $X \subseteq Y$ or $Y \supseteq X$. The statement "X is a proper subset of Y" is denoted by $X \subset Y$ or $Y \supset X$. If X is a subset of Y, then Y is said to be the superset of X. Two sets X and Y are equal (denoted by X = Y) if and only if $X \subseteq Y$ and $Y \subseteq X$. If X is any finite set, then the power set P(X) of X is the set of all subsets of X including itself and the empty set, $\emptyset$. Thus $P(X) = \{A \mid A \subseteq X\}$.

We now consider different operations on sets which allow us to construct new sets from given sets. If X and Y are sets, then their union $X \cup Y$ is defined by $X \cup Y =$ {a | a ∈ X or a ∈ Y or ( a ∈ X and a ∈ Y)} and their intersection $X \cap Y$ is defined by $X \cap Y = \{a \mid a \in X \text{ and } a \in Y\}$. In general, if $X_1, X_2, \ldots, X_n$ are sets then their union is the set of all elements which belong to at least one of them, and is denoted by $X_1 \cup X_2 \cup \ldots \cup X_n$, or $\cup_{1 \le i \le n} X_i$. The intersection of n sets $X_1, X_2, \ldots, X_n$ is the set of all elements which belong to every one of them, and is denoted by $X_1 \cap X_2 \cap \ldots \cap X_n$, or $\cap_{1 \le i \le n} X_i$. Two sets X and Y are said to be *disjoint* if they have no element in common. Thus, X and Y are disjoint if $X \cap Y = \emptyset$.

If X and Y are sets then the *difference* of X and Y written as X − Y, is the set consisting of all those elements of X which do not belong to Y, i.e., X − Y = {a | a ∈ X and a ∉ Y}. If Y is a subset of X then X − Y is called the *relative complement* of Y with respect to X.

An *ordered pair* is a pair of elements in a fixed order. The ordered pair of elements x and y with x as the first element and y as the second element is denoted by (x, y). Two ordered pairs (x, y) and (u, v) are said to be equal, denoted by (x, y) = (u, v), if and only if x = u and y = v.

The *Cartesian product* of two sets X and Y, denoted by $X \times Y$, is the set of all ordered pairs (x, y) such that $x \in X$ and $y \in Y$. That is, $X \times Y = \{(x, y) \mid x \in X$ and $y \in Y\}$. In general, the Cartesian product of n sets $X_1, X_2, \ldots, X_n$ is given by $X_1 \times X_2 \times \ldots \times X_n = \{(x_1, x_2, \ldots, x_n) \mid x_i \in X_i, 1 \leq i \leq n\}$. The expression $(x_1, x_2, \ldots, x_n)$ is called an ordered n-tuple. If $X_1 = X_2 = \ldots = X_n = X$, then the *n-ary* Cartesian product $X \times X \times \ldots$ (n times) is written as $X^n$.

Given two sets X and Y, a *binary relation* R from X to Y is a subset of $X \times Y$, i.e., for every element $r \in R$ there exist $x \in X$ and $y \in Y$ such that $r = (x, y)$. In the particular case where $X = Y$, we say R is a binary relation on X. An n-ary relation is a subset of the Cartesian product on n sets $X_1, X_2, \ldots, X_n$.

Let R be a binary relation from X to Y. The set of all x which are in relation R with some y is called the *domain* of R and is denoted by *dom R*, i.e., dom R = $\{x \mid x \in X$ and $(x, y) \in R$ for some $y \in Y\}$. On the other hand, the set of all y, such that for some x, x is in relation R with y, is called the *range* of R and is denoted by *ran R*. That is, ran R = $\{y \mid y \in Y$ and $(x, y) \in R$ for some $x \in X\}$. Clearly, dom R is the set of first elements of all ordered pairs in R and ran R is the set of second elements of all ordered pairs in R. The *field* of R is the set dom R $\cup$ ran R.

We sometimes write xRy instead of $(x, y) \in R$ and say that x is in relation R with y if xRy holds. Let R be a binary relation on a set X. Relation R is *reflexive* if xRx for all $x \in X$; *anti-reflexive* if xRx for no $x \in X$; *symmetric* if xRy implies yRx; *anti-symmetric* if xRy and yRx together imply $x = y$; and *transitive* if xRy and yRz together imply xRz. A relation R on a set X is called a *pre-ordering* of X when it is reflexive and transitive. Relation R is called an *equivalence relation* when it is reflexive, symmetric and transitive; R is called an *ordering* of X when it is reflexive, anti-symmetric and transitive.

Let X and Y be two nonempty sets. A *function* from X to Y, denoted by F, is a relation from X to Y such that dom F = X and for all $x \in X$ both $(x, y) \in F$ and $(x, z) \in F$ imply $y = z$. It is commonly expressed as F: $X \rightarrow Y$ and we say F is a function (or mapping) from X to Y. In other words, a function F from X to Y is a rule which associates with each element in X a unique element in Y. If $(x, y) \in F$, then y is called the *image* of x and is written as $y = F(x)$. Function F is said to be *one-to-one* if $F(x_1) = y$ and $F(x_2) = y$ implies $x_1 = x_2$. F is *onto* if ran F = Y. There exists a one-to-one correspondence between sets X and Y if F is a one-to-one and onto function and a many-to-one correspondence otherwise. If a function F : $X \rightarrow Y$ is a one-to-one correspondence, then the inverse relation $F^{-1} = \{(y, x) \mid (x, y) \in F\}$ from Y to X is called the *inverse function* of F.

Let N be the set of natural numbers, i.e., N = $\{0, 1, 2, \ldots, \}$. A function F: $N \rightarrow N$ is said to be *monotonically increasing* if for all $n_1, n_2 \in N$, $n_1 > n_2$ implies $F(n_1) \geq F(n_2)$. Similarly, it is *monotonically decreasing* if $n_1 > n_2$ implies $F(n_1) \leq F(n_2)$. F is said to be *strictly increasing* if $n_1 > n_2$ implies $F(n_1) > F(n_2)$ and *strictly decreasing* if $n_1 > n_2$ implies $F(n_1) < F(n_2)$. Two functions $F_1$: $N \rightarrow N$ and $F_2$: $N \rightarrow N$ are said to be *polynomially related* if there exist two polynomials $P_1(x)$ and $P_2(x)$ such that for all $n \in N$, $F_1(n) \leq P_1(F_2(n))$ and $F_2(n) \leq P_2(F_1(n))$.

A *binary operation* on a set X can be defined as a function from $X \times X$ to X. In general, an *n-ary operation* on a set X is a function from $X^n$ to X. Sometimes we refer to such functions as *operators* and the applications of operators are called *operations*. A *Boolean operator* is one of the binary operators *OR*, and *AND*, or the unary operator

*NOT*, or an operator defined in terms of these. The operands for the Boolean operators can have a value of either 1 or 0, representing "true" or "false" respectively; i.e., in this case X = {0, 1} or {true, false}. Note that NOT is a unary operator and hence it is a function from X to X. The operator OR is often symbolized by ∨, AND by ∧, and NOT by ′ (e.g., complement of a Boolean variable B is denoted by B′). The operators ∨ and ∧ can be applied to binary numbers of the same length by applying them to corresponding pairs of bits; i.e., bit vectors. For instance, if $b_1$ = 100011 and $b_2$ = 000111, then $b_1 \wedge b_2$ = 000011.

## 1.3.2  Data Types and Data Structures

The term *data* (or data items) refers to objects which constitute the inputs and outputs of an algorithm and also the objects constructed by the algorithm and used during its execution. Data can be of various kinds. The term *data type* is used to refer to the set of values that a variable may assume in a programming language. Some data types in Fortran are integer, real, logical, complex, etc.; in Pascal integer, real, Boolean, character, etc. Some programming languages allow the construction of composite data types, such as record in Pascal and structure in Cobol.

If the data type of a variable is fixed during the lifetime of a program then the data type is said to be static. This is the case in Fortran, Pascal, PL/I, etc. In contrast, there are some programming languages (e.g., APL, Lisp) in which variables have no fixed data type. Instead their types are determined by the types of their current values. In such cases the data type is said to be dynamic.

In some cases, the data type is not important when designing algorithms. Instead it is important to specify a fixed set of operations on a set of data items. For example, consider the waiting line of customers in a bank which is simply a first-in-first-out queue. In this waiting line no one is allowed to join in the middle or leave from the middle of the line. Thus the set of operations on a queue is fixed; i.e., addition at the back of the line and removal from the front of the line. An *abstract data type* refers to a set of data items or variables of similar or different data types together with a set of operations defined on them.

Data structures are used to organize data items in ways that enable the performance of the set of operations defined on the data items. The basic component of data structures is the cell, usually drawn as a box, representing a variable. Variables correspond to memory or storage in an algorithm. A collection of cells with some fixed connections among them, and some fixed access pattern, is a data structure. Arrays are the simplest way of structuring data. Let us consider a situation where it is necessary to refer to many data items randomly. This requires the construction of a list of variables such that any item in the list can be accessed with equal ease. This can be done by arranging the items in a *one-dimensional array,* also called a *vector*. A vector X of n elements consists of n variables X[1], X[2], . . . , X[n] which are stored in n consecutive locations. A variable is used to index the vector and different index values refer to the contents of different elements of the vector. For example, X[i] represents the content of the ith element of X. This variable can assume a value between 1 and n for the vector described above.

It is quite often necessary to arrange data in the form of a table. The data structure corresponding to a table is called a *two-dimensional array* or a *matrix*. In this case an array element is referred to by using two index variables, one for row and the other for column. Thus, a two-dimensional array Y consisting of n rows and n columns is represented by Y[i, j], $1 \leq i, j \leq n$, or by Y[1 : n, 1 : n]. In many cases, the data cannot be arranged exactly in a rectangular format because different rows may contain different numbers of elements. In such a case an array may be used whose size is determined by the size of the row with the maximum number of elements, and the size of the column. Obviously in this case there will be many empty elements in the array. This can be avoided by effectively compressing each row separately to contain only the nonempty elements. The compressed rows constitute a set of vectors of varying length. Then a vector of length n can be used such that each of its elements points to the beginning of each of the n vectors of different lengths. Such a data structure is usually referred to as *vector of vectors*.

In many applications a list is used in which the elements of the list can be accessed only in some fixed ways. *Queue*s and *stack*s are such lists. In the case of a queue, elements can be added at one end and removed from the other end. No element can be added or removed from the middle of a queue. A queue is also referred to as a first-in-first-out or FIFO store. A stack, on the other hand, is a list in which addition and removal of elements is allowed only at one end. Therefore, a stack is a last-in-first-out or LIFO store. In practice, we consider queues and stacks as distinct data structures rather than as special kinds of lists. This is important since explicitly defined operations are only permissible on data structures of a particular type. For example, in the case of a queue we can use elementary operations *Enqueue(q, Q)* and *Dequeue(Q)* which add element q to the back of the queue Q and remove the front element of the queue, respectively. Such explicitly defined operations relieve an algorithm designer from looking for formulations involving indices to perform these operations. Similar elementary operations on stacks are *Push(p, S)* and *Pop(S)* which respectively add the element p on the top of stack S and remove the top element of the stack.

The tree is one of the most important data structures and it provides a way of arranging a set of items in a hierarchical structure. A tree consists of a set of elements called nodes (one of which is distinguished from all others known as the root) and a "parent-of" relation which assigns to each node another node which is its immediate predecessor or parent (the parent of the root node is usually assumed to be itself). Normally, trees are drawn with the root at the top level and other nodes below it; nodes are drawn as circles and denote data items or elements. The level of each node is its distance from the root, assuming the root to be at level zero.

We say that there exists a path from node $a_1$ to node $a_k$ in a tree if there is a set of nodes $\{a_1, a_2, \ldots, a_k\}$ in the tree such that $a_1$ is parent of $a_2$, $a_2$ is parent of $a_3$, $\ldots$, $a_{k-1}$ is parent of $a_k$. If there is a path from node a to node b, then a is said to be a *predecessor* (or *ancestor*) of b, and b is said to be a *descendant* (or *successor*) of a. A predecessor (descendant) of a node other than the node itself is said to be a proper predecessor (descendant). A node with no proper descendant is referred to as a *leaf* of the tree. Information or data can be stored in the leaves as well as in the other nodes of a tree.

The basic data structures discussed in this section are illustrated in Figure 1.1.

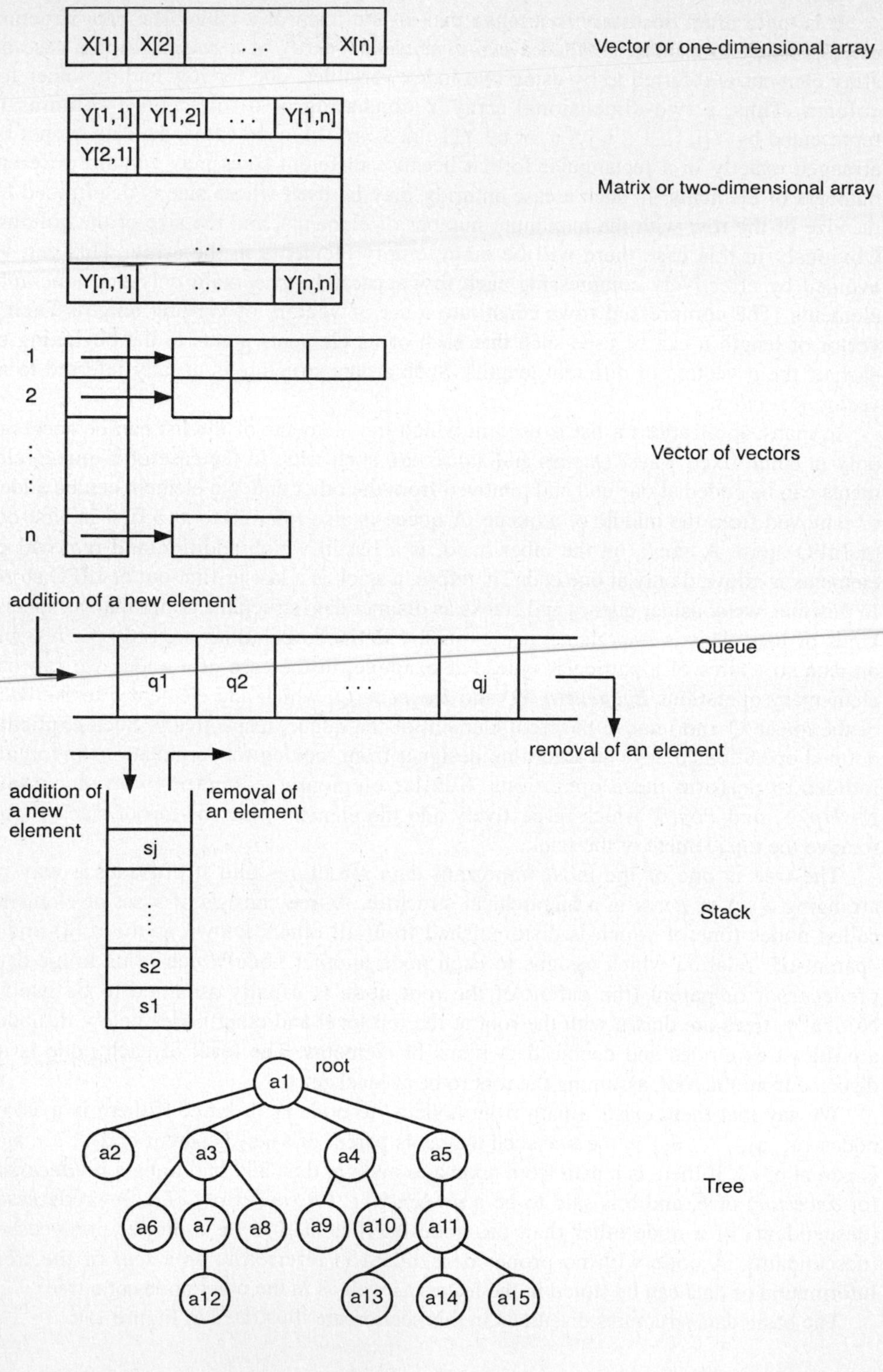

| X[1] | X[2] | . . . | X[n] |
|------|------|-------|------|

Vector or one-dimensional array

| Y[1,1] | Y[1,2] | . . . | Y[1,n] |
|--------|--------|-------|--------|
| Y[2,1] | . . . | | |
| | | | |
| . . . | | | |
| Y[n,1] | . . . | | Y[n,n] |

Matrix or two-dimensional array

1

2

:

:

n

Vector of vectors

addition of a new element

| | q1 | q2 | . . . | qj | |
|--|----|----|-------|----|--|

Queue

removal of an element

addition of
a new
element

removal of
an element

| sj |
| : |
| s2 |
| s1 |

Stack

root

a1

a2  a3  a4  a5

a6  a7  a8  a9  a10  a11

a12  a13  a14  a15

Tree

## 1.3.3  Graphs

An undirected *graph* G = < N, E > consists of a finite, nonempty set N of nodes and a set E ⊆ N × N of edges, such that each edge of the graph is identified with an unordered pair of nodes. Thus, in an undirected graph the pairs (x, y) and (y, x), for x, y ∈ N, represent the same edge. The number of nodes |N| and the number of edges |E| are denoted by n and e, respectively.

A *directed graph* (also known as a *digraph*) is defined in the same way as an undirected graph, except that the edges are ordered pairs of nodes. Therefore, in a digraph, the pairs (x, y) and (y, x) represent two different edges. These edges are drawn with an arrowhead, one pointing toward node y and the other pointing toward node x, respectively.

Among the various types of data structures used for representing and storing graphs in a computer, the simplest and most popular are the *adjacency matrix* and the *adjacency list*. The adjacency matrix corresponding to an n node graph G is a two-dimensional n × n array, say A, with the property that A[x, y] = 1 if and only if (x, y) ∈ E. A[x, y] = 0 if there is no such edge in G. The adjacency matrix for an undirected graph is obviously symmetric since (y, x) ∈ E, if and only if (x, y) ∈ E. The adjacency matrix of a digraph need not be symmetric. In the adjacency list representation of a graph, a list is constructed for each node x that consists of all the nodes adjacent to x. Thus an n node graph can be represented by n adjacency lists, one for each node (similar to a vector of vectors). Figure 1.2 shows an undirected graph with four nodes and a digraph with five nodes. The corresponding adjacency matrix and the adjacency lists for the two graphs are also shown.

A *path* P in a graph G is a walk from one node of G to another, where at each step the walk uses an edge of the graph. A *directed path* refers to a path in a digraph in which each edge is traversed in the direction of the arrowhead. Formally, a path is a sequence $x_1, x_2, \ldots, x_k$ of nodes of G such that $(x_i, x_{i+1}) \in E$, for i = 1, 2, . . . , k − 1. A path P is *simple* if all of its nodes are distinct; *Hamiltonian* if it is simple and visits every node exactly once; and *Eulerian* if it uses every edge of G exactly once.

A *cycle* is a closed path; i.e., a path in which $x_k = x_1$. A cycle is *simple* (also referred to as a *circuit*) if $x_1$ is the only repeated node in it. Similarly, Hamiltonian and Eulerian circuits of a graph G are the circuits of G that visit, respectively, every node or every edge of a graph G.

A digraph G is *acyclic* (i.e., directed acyclic graph, or DAG for short) if, for all i ∈ N, there exist no directed paths of length more than one starting with and ending at node i. *Self-loops* are defined as edges from a node to itself. It is assumed that an undirected graph does not contain multiple edges (i.e., more than one edge connecting the same pair of nodes) and self-loops. Similarly, a digraph does not contain parallel edges (i.e., directed edges having the same start and end nodes) and self-loops.

A *complete* graph is one in which every pair of distinct nodes is connected by an edge. A *subgraph* G' = < N', E' > of a graph (undirected or directed) G = < N, E > is a graph such that N' ⊆ N and E' ⊆ E. An undirected graph G is *connected* if, for every pair of nodes x, y ∈ N, there exists at least one path joining x and y in G. A digraph G is *strongly connected* if every two nodes are mutually reachable through directed paths of length greater than one, and *weakly connected* if every two nodes are connected by a path

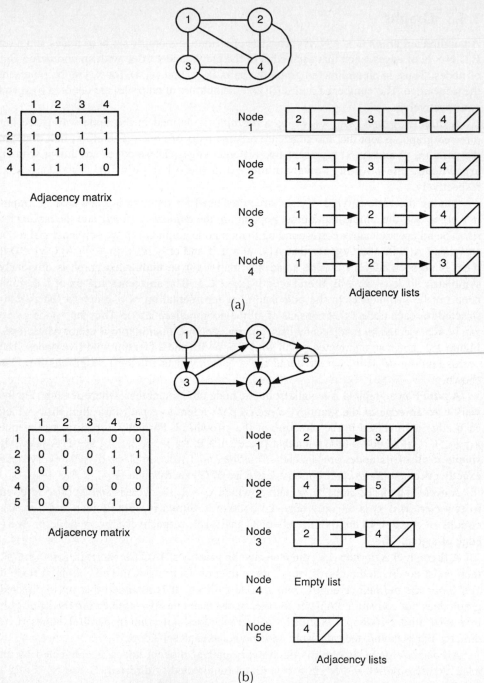

**Figure 1.2** (a) An undirected graph together with corresponding adjacency matrix and adjacency lists; (b) a diagraph and corresponding adjacency matrix and adjacency lists.

in which the direction of each edge is ignored. The graph of Figure 1.2a is, in fact, a complete graph. The digraph of Figure 1.2b is weakly connected. However, the addition of an extra edge from node 4 to node 1, i.e., (4,1) makes it strongly connected.

A graph G with n nodes is called a *tree* if (i) G is connected and has no cycles, or (ii) G is connected and has n − 1 edges, or (iii) G has n − 1 edges but no cycles, or (iv) there is a unique path between every pair of distinct nodes. Let T = < N', E' > be a digraph. If the underlying undirected graph of the digraph T is a tree, then T is referred to as a directed tree. If T is a subgraph of a digraph G = < N, E > and N' = N, then T is referred to as a spanning tree in G. Moreover, if the underlying undirected graph of T is a subgraph of an undirected graph G = < N, E > and N' = N, then T is a directed spanning tree in G.

## 1.3.4  Order Notation

An algorithm must terminate in a finite number of steps for any input (finiteness) and it must produce the required output every time it is executed (correctness). To compare two algorithms which solve the same problem, we need to have some measure of their running or execution times. The evaluation of the exact running time of an algorithm is very difficult because it depends on the instruction execution speed of the computer on which the algorithm is executed, and on the way the algorithm has been implemented. However, these factors can affect the running time of an algorithm by a constant factor. Our approach will be to ignore constant factors when evaluating the running time of an algorithm. That is, we are only interested in the rate of growth of the running time for larger and larger instances of a problem. An instance of a problem is a set of actual parameters corresponding to the set of formal parameters. Suppose we have designed an algorithm for finding the smallest integer of a set N of integers. Now, if N is given as {5, 7, 2, 3, 9} then this set is an instance of this problem. The rate of growth of the running time of an algorithm is normally expressed as a function of the size of the instance considered. The size of the problem (or instance) is measured in terms of the amount of input data. For example, in the minimum finding problem the cardinality of the set N of integers of which the smallest integer is required is the size of the problem. The size of a graph theoretic problem may be the number of its nodes or the number of its edges.

To evaluate and express the rate of growth of the running time of an algorithm, we introduce a special notation. A function f is $O(t)$ for another function t (read as "big oh of" or "order of"), if there exist two constants k and N such that for all $n \geq N$, $f(n) \leq kt(n)$. If we write $f(n) = O(t(n))$, it means that f certainly does not grow at a faster rate than t. That is, for sufficiently large n, $f(n)$ is no more than a constant times $t(n)$. This definition also allows $f(n)$ to become even sufficiently smaller than $t(n)$. Thus, the "O notation" bounds $f(n)$ only from above; i.e., it gives the upper bound of $f(n)$. For example, we can write $f(n) = O(n^3)$ and at the same time write $f(n) = O(n^4)$, for a function $f(n) = 2n^3 + n^2 + 7n$ because one can easily find two pairs of constants $k_1, N_1$ and $k_2, N_2$ such that $f(n) \leq k_1 n^3$ for $n \geq N_1$ and $f(n) \leq k_2 n^4$ for $n \geq N_2$. If a function t is such that the running time of a given algorithm $A$ can be expressed as $O(t)$ then we say that the *time complexity* of algorithm $A$ is $O(t)$. It is clear that this function does not define the running time precisely. Of course we will try to find an expression that is as close to the actual running time as possible. Thus, if we say that the time complexity of an algorithm is $O(n^3)$, it means that the running time $t(n)$ of this algorithm is expressible in the form $t(n) = c_3n^3 + c_2n^2 + c_1n + c_0$. All other terms except the highest order term and all the constants of proportionalities are assumed to be absorbed within this "big oh" notation. The time complexity of an algorithm expressed by this order notation will not be affected by the way the algorithm is implemented or by changing the computer and thus the instruction execution speed. The reason is that these factors only affect the constants of proportionalities $c_0$, $c_1$, etc., but not the order of the running time. A function $f(n)$ is said to be $O(1)$ if and only if $f(n) \leq k$ for some constant $k$ and for all $n$. Thus, if the running time of an algorithm is constant and independent of the problem size, then we say that its time complexity is $O(1)$. The "O notation" is very convenient and widely used as a measure of the worst-case time complexity of an algorithm.

There are several other notations used to express the rates of growth of functions. These are "o" (read as "little oh of"), "$\Omega$" (read as "omega of"), and "$\Theta$" (read as "theta of"). The definitions of these are given below.

A function $f$ is $o(t)$ if $\lim_{n \to \infty} f(n)/t(n) = 0$. That is, $t(n)$ grows faster than $f(n)$ for large n. For example, $2n^2 = o(n^3)$, $n^2/\log n^* = o(n^2)$, but $n^2/5 \neq o(n^2)$.

A function $f$ is $\Omega(t)$ if there exist constants $k$ and $N$, such that for all $n \geq N$, $f(n) \geq kt(n)$. Informally, $f$ grows at least as fast as $t$. If we say that $O(t)$ corresponds to the "$\leq$" relation then $\Omega(t)$ corresponds to the "$\geq$" relation. This notation is used to handle the lower bounds of functions ignoring the constants.

A function $f$ is $\Theta(t)$ if there exist constants $k_1$, $k_2$, and $N$, such that for all $n \geq N$, $k_1t(n) \leq f(n) \leq k_2t(n)$. Alternatively, we say that $f$ is $\Theta(t)$ if it satisfies both $f = O(t)$ and $f = \Omega(t)$. That is, $f$ and $t$ both grow at the same rate; only the multiplicative constants may be different. Therefore, "$\Theta$" gives more precise information about the rate of growth of functions. The time complexity of an algorithm expressed in terms of any of these notations is, in general, referred to as *asymptotic time complexity* because they reflect the behavior of the algorithm (i.e., rate of growth of the running time) for sufficiently large values of the problem size.

We will now describe some important properties of the "O notation" and some commonly used functions which will be used to compute the time complexities of various algorithms.

P1: The rate of growth of the sum of two functions is given by the rate of growth of the faster growing function. That is, if $f = O(u)$ and $t = O(v)$ then $f + t = O(\max(u, v))$.

P2: The rate of growth of a polynomial function is given by the rate of growth of its leading term. That is, if $f(n)$ is a polynomial of degree $k$, then $f = O(n^k)$.

P3: If $f$ grows faster than $t$ and $t$ grows faster than $x$, then $f$ grows faster than $x$. That is, if $f = O(t)$ and $t = O(x)$, then $f = O(x)$. The relation represented by "O" is transitive.

P4: The upper bound for the product of two functions is given by the product of upper bounds for these two functions. That is, if $f = O(u)$ and $t = O(v)$, then $f.t = O(u.v)$.

P5: Exponential functions grow faster than polynomial functions. That is, for all monotonically growing functions $f(n)$, $f^a = O(b^f)$ for all $a > 0$, $b > 1$.

---

* All logarithms used in this book are to the base 2 unless otherwise specified.

P6: Logarithmic functions grow more slowly than polynomial functions. That is, $\log_b n = O(n^c)$ for all $b > 1$, $c > 0$.

## 1.3.5 Algorithm Analysis

The design of an algorithm for the solution of a problem usually begins with an informal description of the problem. This description is refined to obtain a more formal specification of the problem and then the data structures for input, output, and intermediate storage of data are selected. Finally, the design process ends by expressing the various steps involved in solving the problem in some algorithmic language. The analysis of an algorithm mainly refers to the determination of the time complexity of the algorithm.

In order to obtain the time complexity of an algorithm we need to count the number of elementary operations performed at each step of the algorithm. An elementary operation may be defined as an operation whose execution time is bounded from above by a constant. Thus, the time complexity of an elementary operation is $O(1)$. In an algorithm, different steps may consist of different numbers of elementary operations. We therefore concentrate only on the major step of the algorithm, i.e., the step that has the maximum number of elementary operations. The reason is that the time complexity of the major step will determine the time complexity of the algorithm. Thus, if $O(t)$ is the bound for the number of elementary operations in the major step of an algorithm then the time complexity of the algorithm will also be $O(t)$.

In addition to time complexity, the space complexity of an algorithm is also used to determine its efficiency. The space complexity refers to the amount of temporary storage required during the execution of the algorithm. The storage required by the input, output and the program corresponding to the algorithm are, in general, not included in the space complexity. Like time complexity, a similar notation is used to express space complexity as an asymptotic function of the problem size. In general, estimation of space complexities are straightforward and are not discussed here.

The determination of time complexities of algorithms by identifying the major steps and counting the number of operations in them is not always simple. There is no procedure for obtaining the time complexity of an algorithm. Estimation of time complexity for a given algorithm largely depends on intuition and experience. In the rest of this section, we consider several arbitrary algorithm segments with some commonly occurring patterns and determine their time complexities.

Consider an algorithm segment (Figure 1.3a) consisting of k elementary operations, where k is an integer independent of the problem size n. If each of these k operations is executed only once then we say that the time required by this algorithm segment is constant; in other words, the time complexity is $O(1)$.

The algorithm segment of Figure 1.3b consists of a simple loop. Since the set of k elementary operations is to be executed n times, the time complexity of this segment is $O(kn) = O(n)$.

The nested loop structure of Figure 1.3c indicates that the inner loop whose time complexity is $O(n)$ is to be executed n times. Therefore, this segment has time complexity $O(n^2)$.

In Figure 1.3d, another nested loop is shown where the number of executions of the inner loop depends on the value of the outer loop variable. More precisely, the inner loop

```
      do                              for i = 1 to n do
         { ... }                         for j = 1 to i do
      od                                     { ... }
                                          od
                                      od
```

(a)                                (d)

```
   for i = 1 to n do               i := 1
      { ... }                      while i < n do
   od                                 { ... }
                                      i := 2*i
                                   od
```

(b)                                (e)

```
   for i = 1 to n do               for i = 1 to n do
      for j = 1 to n do               j := 1
         { ... }                      while j < n do
      od                                 { ... }
   od                                    j := 2*i
                                      od
                                   od
```

(c)                                (f)

**Figure 1.3** Some commonly occurring algorithm segments.

will be executed once for i = 1, twice for i = 2, and so on, finally n times for i = n. Therefore, the time complexity of this segment is given by the expression $1 + 2 + 3 + \ldots + n = n(n + 1)/2 = O(n^2)$. It seems that the number of elementary operations to be performed by the algorithm segment of Figure 1.4d is nearly half of that by the segment of Figure 1.3c, assuming that the sets of elementary operations in both of the inner loops are identical. But, asymptotically, there is no difference in running time and hence they are indistinguishable in "O notation."

The while-loop of Figure 1.3e indicates that the set of elementary operations will be executed each time i assumes a value 1, 2, 4, 8, and so on until it reaches or exceeds n. Clearly, the loop will be executed $\lfloor \log n \rfloor$* + 1 times. Hence the time complexity of this algorithm segment is O(log n). Figure 1.3f shows an algorithm segment whose time complexity is O(n log n).

In the case of parallel algorithms, the number of processors used to execute a parallel algorithm is almost as important as time complexity. There are also several other measures of performances of parallel algorithms in addition to time and space complexities. All complexity-related concepts for parallel algorithms are discussed in Chapter 3.

---

* Throughout this book $\lceil x \rceil$ (ceiling of x) denotes the least integer equal to or greater than x, and $\lfloor x \rfloor$ (floor of x) denotes the greatest integer equal to or less than x.

# 1.4 BIBLIOGRAPHIC NOTES

The evolution of computers and the division of computers into generations are discussed in great detail in many well-known texts on computer architectures such as Baer (1980), Hayes (1978), Hwang and Briggs (1984), and Stone (1980). There are several classification schemes for computer systems of which the most popular one due to Flynn (1966) is discussed in this chapter. The other classification schemes can be found in papers by Feng (1972), and Handler (1977). The need for parallel computers has been discussed in several books and articles. These include Baer (1980), Bernhard (1982), Hwang and Briggs (1984), Schaefer and Fisher (1982), and Quinn (1987).

There are a large number of useful texts in which the mathematical preliminaries discussed in this chapter can be found explained in much greater detail, but in a distributed manner. In particular, there are several texts that deal only with set theory, such as Devlin (1979), Halmos (1960), Hrbacek and Jech (1978), and Monk (1969). All the basic material related to sets, relations, functions, etc. may be found in any of these texts and in any other texts on graphs and discrete mathematics, like Carre (1979), and Skvarcius and Robinson (1986).

There are many good books on data structures from which much more information about data types, data structures and graphs can be obtained. Knuth (1973a and 1973b) contain a wealth of information about data structures and algorithms. Other relevant texts include Aho et al. (1983), Horowitz and Sahni (1976) Reingold and Hansen (1983), Smith (1987), and Wirth (1986).

The asymptotic notation is widely used for measuring algorithm efficiency. Two useful references on this are De Bruijn (1961), and Knuth (1976). Several books on discrete mathematics and combinatorics (e.g., Brualdi 1977; and Graham et al. 1989) also cover the techniques for evaluating summations, recurrence relations, etc. which are useful for analyzing algorithms. The books by Knuth (1973a), Green and Knuth (1982), and Purdom and Brown (1985) are devoted entirely to algorithm analysis. A brief account of the behavior and properties of the order notation are also available in the introductory chapters of some recent texts on algorithms, such as Brassard and Bratley (1988), Cormen et al. (1990), Smith (1989), and Wilf (1986).

# 1.5 BIBLIOGRAPHY

Aho, A., Hopcroft, J., and Ullman, J. (1983). *Data Structures and Algorithms.* Addison-Wesley, Reading, Mass.

Baer, J. L. (1980). *Computer Systems Architectures.* Computer Science Press, Potomac, Md.

Bernhard, R. (1982). Computing at the speed limit. *IEEE Spectrum* 19, 26-31.

Brassard, G., and Bratley, P. (1988). *Algorithmics: Theory and Practice.* Prentice Hall, Englewood Cliffs, NJ.

Brualdi, R. A. (1977). *Introductory Combinatorics.* North Holland, NY.

Carre, B. (1979). *Graphs and Networks.* Oxford University Press, Oxford.

Cormen, T. H., Leiserson, C. E., and Rivest, R. L. (1990). *Introduction to Algorithms.* McGraw-Hill, NY.

De Bruijn, N. G. (1961). *Asymptotic Methods in Analysis.* North Holland, Amsterdam.

Devlin, K. J. (1979). *Fundamentals of Contemporary Set Theory.* Springer-Verlag, NY.

Feng, T. Y. (1972). Some characteristics of associative/parallel processing. *Proceedings of the 1972 Sagamore Computer Conference,* Syracuse University, NY, pp. 5-16.

Flynn, M. J. (1966). Very high speed computing systems. *Proc. IEEE* 54, 1901-9.

Graham, R. L., Knuth, D. E., and Patashnik, O. (1989). *Concrete Mathematics.* Addison-Wesley, Reading, Mass.

Green, D. H., and Knuth, D. E. (1982). *Mathematics for the Analysis of Algorithms.* Birkhauser, Boston.

Halmos, P. R. (1960). *Naive Set Theory.* Van Nostrand, NY.

Handler, W. (1977). The impact of classification schemes on computer architectures. *Proceedings of the 1977 International Conference on Parallel Processing,* IEEE Computer Society, Washington, DC, pp. 7-15.

Hayes, J. P. (1978). *Computer Architecture and Organization.* McGraw-Hill, NY.

Horowitz, E., and Sahni, S. (1976). *Fundamentals of Data Structures.* Computer Science Press, Potomac, Md.

Hrbacek, K., and Jech, T. (1978). *Introduction to Set Theory.* Marcel Dekker, NY.

Hwang, K., and Briggs, F. A. (1984). *Computer Architecture and Parallel Processing.* McGraw-Hill, NY.

Knuth, D. E. (1973a). *The Art of Computer Programming vol. 1: Fundamental Algorithms.* Addison-Wesley, Reading, Mass.

Knuth, D. E. (1973b). *The Art of Computer Programming vol. 3: Sorting and Searching.* Addison-Wesley, Reading, Mass.

Knuth, D. E. (1976). Big omicron and big omega and big theta. *SIGACT News* (April-June) 18-24.

Monk, J. D. (1969). *Introduction to Set Theory.* McGraw-Hill, NY.

Purdom, P. W., and Brown, C. A. (1985). *The Analysis of Algorithms.* Holt, Rinehart & Winston, NY.

Quinn, M. J. (1987). *Designing Efficient Algorithms for Parallel Computers.* McGraw-Hill, NY.

Reingold, E. M., and Hansen, W. J. (1983). *Data Structures.* Little, Brown, Boston, Mass.

Schaefer, D. H., and Fisher, J. R. (1982). Beyond the supercomputer. *IEEE Spectrum* 19, 32-7.

Skvarcius, R., and Robinson, W. B. (1986). *Discrete Mathematics with Computer Science Applications.* Benjamin/Cummings Publishing Co., Calif.

Smith, H. F. (1987). *Data Structures, Form and Function.* Harcourt Brace Jovanovich, Calif.

Smith, J. D. (1989). *Design and Analysis of Algorithms.* PWS-KENT Publishing Co., Boston, Mass.

Stone, H. S. (1980). *Introduction to Computer Architecture.* (Ed. H. S. Stone), SRA, Chicago.

Wilf, H. S. (1986). *Algorithms and Complexity.* Prentice Hall, Englewood Cliffs, NJ.

Wirth, N. (1986). *Algorithms & Data Structures.* Prentice Hall, Englewood Cliffs, NJ.

# Models of Parallel Computation

## 2.1 INTRODUCTION

A parallel computer consists of a large number of processing elements* dedicated to solving a single problem at a time. This new breed of computing machine is capable of executing, simultaneously, either the same instruction on different data sets or different instructions on different data sets. Two distinct classes of parallel machines arise from the two different execution strategies, namely, the single-instruction stream, multiple-data stream (SIMD) and multiple-instruction stream, multiple-data stream (MIMD) computers (discussed in Chapter 1). An SIMD machine consists of an array of processing elements connected in a network and controlled by a main processor. The main processor broadcasts the instructions to be executed by the processing elements. In the case of MIMD machines, no single processor owns any subset of resources such as memory, I/O devices, etc.; instead, the resources are shared by the processors. Each processor in an MIMD machine may be simultaneously executing independent or related programs without time sharing or multiprogramming.

In addition to these two standard classes of parallel computers, another class of machines, which has the potential to be efficiently realized in very large-scale integration (VLSI) technology, has been used extensively for designing parallel algorithms for various problems. This class of machines is known as systolic machines (Kung and Leiserson 1978).

As a result of the emergence of large-scale parallel computers in the past decade, a variety of algorithms have been designed which can gainfully exploit various parallel

---

*A processing element is essentially an arithmetic logic unit (processor) with registers and a local memory.

computer architectures. The underlying model of computation used has a fundamental role in the design and analysis of algorithms because the design and performance of an algorithm depends very much on the architecture of the machine. In serial computation, there are standard models of computation such as Random Access Machine, Random Access Stored Program Machine, and Turing Machine. All of these three models are equivalent in computing power, i.e., they are polynomially related (Aho et al. 1974; Mehlhorn 1984). For parallel algorithms there are a considerable number of very different models related to the three classes of parallel computers mentioned above. These range from special-purpose array processors to loosely coupled networks of processors. It is essential to keep the model of the target machine in mind when designing parallel algorithms.

In this chapter, we first introduce some basic models for parallel computation and then present a taxonomy for parallel algorithms. Finally, we describe the notation which will be used to present parallel algorithms later in this book.

## 2.2  BASIC MODELS OF PARALLEL COMPUTATION

The parallel machine models that are examined may be divided into three major categories:

- Array processor (SIMD) machines
- Multiple CPU (MIMD) machines
- Systolic machines

According to Flynn's classification (Flynn 1966) of computers, the array processor machine falls into the single-instruction stream, multiple-data stream (SIMD) category. On the other hand, multiple central processing unit (CPU) machines fall into the multiple-instruction stream, multiple-data stream (MIMD) category. Throughout this book, we shall use the terms array processors (respectively, multiple CPU machines) and SIMD machines (respectively, MIMD machines) synonymously.

SIMD machines are studied more extensively than MIMD machines in the context of parallel processing. This is because the problems that arise in the design, construction and application of MIMD machines are much more complicated than those that occur in SIMD machines.

A systolic machine consists of a set of special-purpose processors, each capable of performing some simple operation. The data in a systolic machine flows from the memory in a rhythmic fashion, passing through many processors before it returns to memory, like the circulation of blood to and from the heart.

### 2.2.1  Array Processor (SIMD) Machines

The most popular model of parallel computation is the array processor (SIMD) machine. It consists of a set of identical processing elements (PEs), capable of simultaneously performing the same operation on different sets of data. The execution of the instructions is synchronous in the sense that each PE executing the instruction in parallel must be allowed to finish before the next instruction is taken up for execution.

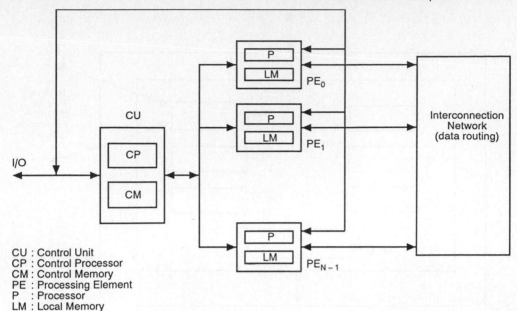

CU : Control Unit
CP : Control Processor
CM : Control Memory
PE : Processing Element
P    : Processor
LM : Local Memory

**Figure 2.1**  Block diagram of an SIMD computer.

SIMD models can vary in two respects. One is in terms of the number of processors which may be fixed (i.e., limited) or unlimited. The other is in terms of the data-routing mechanism among the PEs. The PEs may communicate with each other via a common or shared memory or through an interconnection network.

A typical SIMD machine is depicted in Figure 2.1. It consists of a control unit (CU), N PEs and an interconnection network. We assume that $N = 2^k$, i.e., $\log N = k$ in order to facilitate future illustrations. We also assume that the PEs are numbered $0, 1, \ldots, N-1$. Each PE consists of a processor (P) with a set of registers and a local memory (LM). The CU broadcasts a single instruction to all the PEs at the same instant. The PEs execute the same instruction simultaneously (i.e., single-instruction stream). Because each PE executes the instruction on data stored in its associated memory module LM, a multiple-data stream results. This model has been implemented in the widely publicized ILLIAC-IV computer (Barnes et al. 1968; Kuck 1968). Although the PEs execute instructions simultaneously, they may suitably be programmed to ignore a particular instruction using masking mechanisms (Siegel 1979; Quinn and Deo 1984; Hwang 1984) as discussed below.

In addition to a set of fast access registers denoted by $R_1, R_2, R_3$, each processor P of an SIMD machine has a status flag SF, an arithmetic logic unit (ALU), an address register ADDR, and a data-routing register DRR. A typical PE is shown in Figure 2.2. The DRR of each PE is connected to the DRRs of the other PEs via the interconnection network. When data transfers occur among PEs the contents of the DRRs of the PEs involved are transmitted. The register ADDR contains the address (i.e., PE number) of the PE to which data is to be transmitted.

Each PE is either in active or inactive mode during each instruction cycle. If a PE is in active mode it executes the instructions broadcast to it by the CU. Alternatively, if a

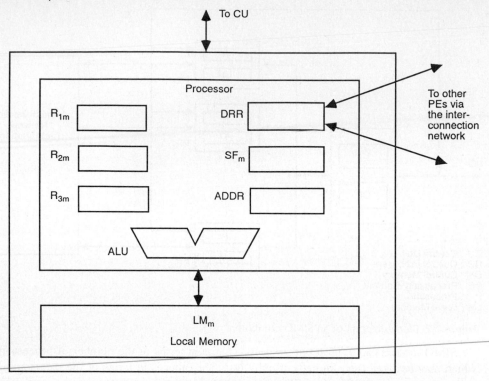

**Figure 2.2** A processing element, $PE_m$ (m = 0, 1, . . . , N − 1).

PE is in inactive mode it does not execute the instructions broadcast to it. The masking schemes used to select a set of PEs which will be active are specified by the status flag $SF_m$ of each $PE_m$, m = 0, 1, . . . , N − 1. It is assumed that if $SF_m$ = 0 (reset) then $PE_m$ is active; if $SF_m$ = 1 (set) then $PE_m$ is inactive.

Two distinct masking schemes are: PE address masking and data conditional masking. A typical *PE address masking* scheme (Siegel 1979) uses a k-position mask to specify which PEs are to be activated. It is assumed that, in the CU, there is a k-bit masking register M. The contents of M are broadcast to the PEs when a mask is to be set. Each position of the mask containing either a 0, 1, or x ("don't care") corresponds to a bit position in the addresses of the PEs. Those PEs whose addresses match with the mask (i.e., 0 with 0, 1 with 1, and either 0 or 1 with x) are activated.

A *data conditional mask* is the implicit result of performing a conditional branch depending on local data of the PE concerned. For example, suppose a conditional branch instruction provides two alternatives: branch if the accumulator contains zero, otherwise do not branch. What should happen if the accumulators of some but not all PEs contain zero? The instruction stream should ideally be split into two streams, one for the set of PEs with zeros in their accumulators and the other for the set of PEs with non-zero accumulator contents. But an SIMD computer cannot support two independent instruction streams simultaneously. The two cases must, therefore, be handled sequentially. This is indicated in Figure 2.3. It is clear that the effective parallelism is approximately halved by this process.

Formally, an SIMD machine S can be represented as the 4-tuple

$$S = <N, F, I, M>$$

where (i) N is a positive integer, representing the number of PEs in the machine; (ii) F is the set of interconnection functions, where each function determines the communication links among the PEs; (iii) I is the set of machine instructions; and (iv) M is the set of masking schemes, where each mask partitions the set of PEs into two disjoint sets of active (enabled) PEs and inactive (disabled) PEs.

Different models of SIMD computers are obtained by choosing different interprocessor communication strategies. The most commonly used SIMD machine models can be classified as: (1) Shared memory (2) Mesh connected (3) Cube connected (4) Perfect shuffle and (5) Tree connected.

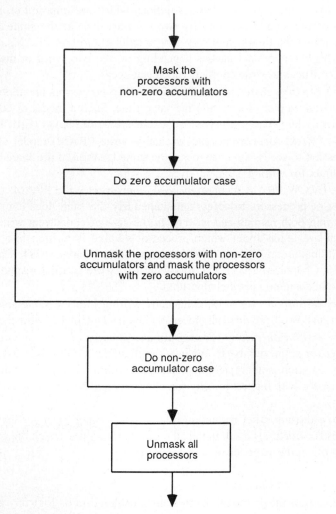

**Figure 2.3** A data conditional masking example.

### 2.2.1.1　Shared Memory SIMD Computer

The interprocessor communication in the shared memory SIMD model is established through a shared (also referred to as common or global) memory. This model can be obtained simply by replacing the interconnection network of Figure 2.1 by a shared memory. PEs can store integer numbers in the (shared) memory, load them into their own registers and perform arithmetical and logical operations.

We also assume that: (a) any memory location can contain an arbitrary integer; and (b) all arithmetical and logical operations as well as memory read and write cycles require one time unit.

These conditions are a straightforward generalization of the properties of the Random Access Machine defined for serial algorithms (Aho et al. 1974). In fact, the shared memory SIMD model can be viewed as a parallel variant of the Random Access Machine. Such a model is more commonly referred to as Parallel Random Access Machine (PRAM) in the literature. The restrictions which are imposed on access to the same location of the shared memory by two or more PEs at the same instant have significant impact on the time complexity of a parallel algorithm. PRAMs are classified into the following three distinct classes depending on the two types of memory access conflicts (read conflict and write conflict) which can occur.

(a) In the most restrictive shared memory model, no two processors are allowed to access the same shared memory location at the same time. Such a model of computation is more commonly known as exclusive read, exclusive write PRAM (EREW PRAM).

(b) The CREW PRAM (concurrent read, exclusive write PRAM) model allows two or more processors to access simultaneously the same location of the shared memory for reading, but not for writing.

(c) Finally, the CRCW PRAM (concurrent read, concurrent write PRAM) model allows any number of processors to access simultaneously the same location of the shared memory during both reading and writing. In the case of concurrent writing, different assumptions are made about which processor's value is written into the memory location (Shiloach and Vishkin 1981; Kucera 1982; Vishkin 1984; Chaudhuri and Ghosh 1986; Chaudhuri 1987). The following two write conflict resolution rules are widely used in designing parallel algorithms:

(1) *Equality resolution rule* — Simultaneous writing into the same shared memory location is allowed, provided all processors involved attempt to write the same value.

(2) *Priority resolution rule* — Processors are linearly ordered according to their priorities (or serial numbers). When a simultaneous writing into the same shared memory location is attempted, the memory location receives the value written by the processor with highest priority (or, alternatively, the one with the lowest serial number).

In addition, a third conflict resolution rule which is much stronger than the above-mentioned rules is sometimes used. In this, the sum of all values which the processors are attempting to write in the same location is stored there.

### 2.2.1.2　Mesh Connected Computer

In the mesh connected SIMD model the PEs are considered to be logically arranged as a d-dimensional array $A[n_{d-1}, n_{d-2}, \ldots, n_0]$, where $n_i$ is the size of the ith dimension. Thus the total number of processors in the array is $N = n_{d-1} \times n_{d-2} \times \ldots \times n_0$. The PE at location $A(i_{q-1}, \ldots, i_0)$ is connected to the PEs at locations $A(i_{q-1}, \ldots, i_u \pm 1, \ldots, i_0)$ where $0 \leq u < q$, provided they exist. Interprocessor communication is established through these connections and data may be transmitted from one PE to another only through this interconnection pattern. For example, consider a two-dimensional mesh connected array consisting of 16 processors. This array can be represented as $A[4, 4]$, where the locations of the individual PEs are $A(0, 0)$, $A(0, 1)$, ..., $A(3, 3)$. Therefore, the PE at location $A(2, 1)$, say, is connected to the PEs at locations $A(2, 2)$, $A(2, 0)$, $A(3, 1)$, and $A(1, 1)$ whereas the PE at location $A(2, 0)$ is connected to the PEs at locations $A(2, 1)$, $A(3, 0)$, and $A(1, 0)$ since there is no PE at location $A(2, -1)$. Clearly the mesh connected SIMD model requires at most $2k$ connections per PE. The interconnection scheme for a 16 PE mesh connected computer with $d = 2$ is shown in Figure 2.4. This model of parallel computation has been used extensively for solving various numerical and non-numerical problems.

Some variants of the mesh connected network allow wraparound connections between processors on the edge of the mesh. In such cases every PE is connected to the same number of other PEs. The mesh connected network implemented in the ILLIAC-IV computer with $N = 64$, $d = 2$ has four connections per PE. In particular, each $PE_i$ is connected to $PE_{i+1}$, $PE_{i-1}$, $PE_{i+r}$ and $PE_{i-r}$, where $r = \sqrt{N}$. For the ILLIAC-IV, $r = \sqrt{64} = 8$. Formally, the four interconnection or routing functions for the ILLIAC network can be characterized as follows:

$$I_{+1}(i) = (i + 1) \bmod N$$
$$I_{-1}(i) = (i - 1) \bmod N$$
$$I_{+r}(i) = (i + r) \bmod N \qquad \text{(A)}$$
$$I_{-r}(i) = (i - r) \bmod N$$

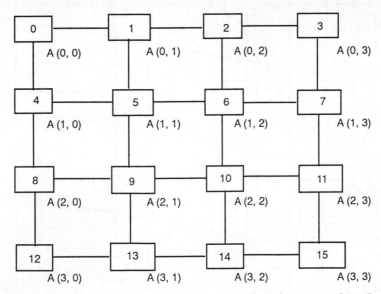

**Figure 2.4** The interconnection pattern of a two-dimensional mesh connected SIMD computer with 16 PEs.

where $r = \sqrt{N}$ and $0 \leq i \leq N - 1$. In practice, N is taken to be a perfect square, e.g., N = 64 in the ILLIAC-IV network.

A mesh connected network for N = 16, based on the interconnection functions given by equation (A), is illustrated in Figure 2.5. This network is a partially connected network, i.e., no PE can transfer data to all remaining PEs in a single step. It is clear from the network of Figure 2.5 that four PEs can be reached from any PE in a single step, seven PEs in two steps, and eleven PEs in three steps. In general, a mesh connected network with N PEs, based on the interconnection functions of equation (A), requires at most $(\sqrt{N} - 1)$ steps to route data from $PE_i$ to $PE_j$, $0 \leq i, j \leq N - 1$. It is obvious that, if we increase the connectivity of the network then this upper bound can be lowered at the expense of providing more hardware.

The interconnection functions of equation (A) can be expressed in terms of permutation cycles as follows. The indices of the PEs in each row form a linear circular list governed by the two permutations $I_{+1}$ and $I_{-1}$ defined below, where each permutation consists of a single cycle of order N.

$$I_{+1} = (0 \ 1 \ldots N - 1)$$

$$\text{(B)}$$

$$I_{-1} = (N - 1 \ldots 1 \ 0)$$

The permutation cycle $(0 \ 1 \ldots N - 1)$ stands for the permutation 0 1, 1 2, ... , N − 2 N − 1, N − 1 0.

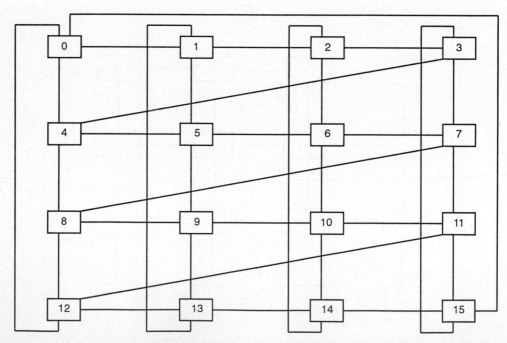

**Figure 2.5** The mesh connections as used in ILLIAC-IV computer with 16 PEs.

The interconnections among the PEs of the different columns are characterized by the following two permutations, each with r cycles of order r each.

$$I_{+r} = \prod_{0 \le i \le r-1} (i \; i+r \; i+2r \; \ldots \; i+N-r)$$

(C)

$$I_{-r} = \prod_{0 \le i \le r-1} (i+N-r \; \ldots \; i+2r \; i+r \; i)$$

For the example given in Figure 2.5

$I_{+1} = (0 \; 1 \ldots 14 \; 15)$

$I_{-1} = (15 \; 14 \ldots 1 \; 0)$   (D)

$I_{+4} = (0 \; 4 \; 8 \; 12) \; (1 \; 5 \; 9 \; 13) \; (2 \; 6 \; 10 \; 14) \; (3 \; 7 \; 11 \; 15)$

$I_{-4} = (12 \; 8 \; 4 \; 0) \; (13 \; 9 \; 5 \; 1) \; (14 \; 10 \; 6 \; 2) \; (15 \; 11 \; 7 \; 3)$

When either the $I_{+1}$ or $I_{-1}$ interconnection function is used, data is routed through all the PEs as defined by equation (B), provided that all the PEs in the cycle are active. Likewise, when the interconnection function $I_{+r}$ or $I_{-r}$ is executed, data is routed as defined by equation (C), provided that all the PEs numbered $i + kr$ (where $k = 0, 1, \ldots, r - 1$) are active for each i. For example, the cycle $(0 \; 4 \; 8 \; 12)$ in the permutation $I_{+4}$ shown above will not be executed if one (or more) of $PE_0$, $PE_4$, $PE_8$, and $PE_{12}$ is disabled by masking.

### 2.2.1.3 Cube Connected Computer

Let us assume that $N = 2^k$ and let $i_{k-1} \; i_{k-2} \ldots i_0$ be the binary representation of i for $0 \le i \le N - 1$. Let $i^{(b)}$ be the integer whose binary representation is $i_{k-1} \; i_{k-2} \ldots i_{b+1} \; i_b' \; i_{b-1} \ldots i_0$, where $i_b'$ is the complement of $i_b$, for $b = 0, 1, \ldots, k - 1$. In a cube connected SIMD model the ith PE is connected to the $i^{(b)}$th PE, for $b = 0, 1, \ldots, k - 1$. Clearly, each PE requires $k = \log N$ connections. Thus the interconnection or routing functions, $I_b$, for a cube connected network can be specified as follows:

$$I_b(i_{k-1} \ldots i_1 i_0) = i_{k-1} \ldots i_{b+1} \; i_b' \; i_{b-1} \ldots i_0 \quad \text{for } b = 0, 1, \ldots, k - 1. \quad \text{(A)}$$

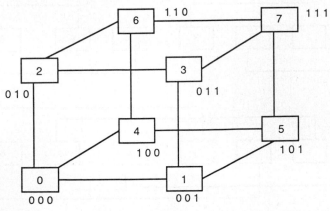

**Figure 2.6**  A cube connected network for N = 8.

In the k cube, each PE located at a corner is directly connected to k neighbors. The indices of neighboring PEs differ in exactly one bit position. For illustrative purposes, let us consider a cube network with N = 8. The number of connections per PE is k = log 8 = 3. Figure 2.6 shows the complete interconnection pattern.

The interconnection function $I_b$, b = 0, 1, . . . , k − 1 for the cube connected network corresponds to performing the following permutation on N PEs:

$$\prod_{0 \le j \le N-1} (j\, I_b(j))$$

(B)

where the bth bit of j is zero and $PE_j$ and $PE_{I_b(j)}$ are both active. For example, the interconnection function $I_1$ applied to a 3-cube network corresponds to the following permutation on eight PEs:

$I_1$ = (0 2) (1 3) (4 6) (5 7).

The interconnection functions for a 3-cube network is illustrated in Figure 2.7.

### 2.2.1.4  Perfect Shuffle Computer

The *shuffle* refers to the interconnection pattern shown in Figure 2.8a. On the left in the figure is a vector of components with indices 0, 1, . . . , N − 1, where N = $2^k$ for some integer k. The components are connected to the vector on the right of the figure through an interlaced interconnection pattern. This network corresponds to perfectly shuffling a deck of N cards. Let A = $a_{k-1}a_{k-2} \ldots a_1a_0$ be a PE index. Then the shuffle function S is defined as

$$S(a_{k-1}a_{k-2}\ldots a_1a_0) = a_{k-2}a_{k-3}\ldots a_1a_0a_{k-1}$$

(A)

Interconnection
function

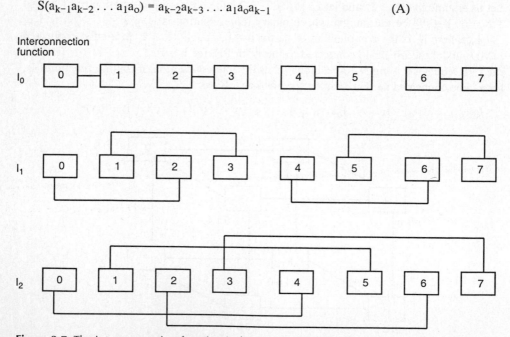

**Figure 2.7**  The interconnection function $I_b$, b = 0, 1, 2 for the cube network with N = 8.

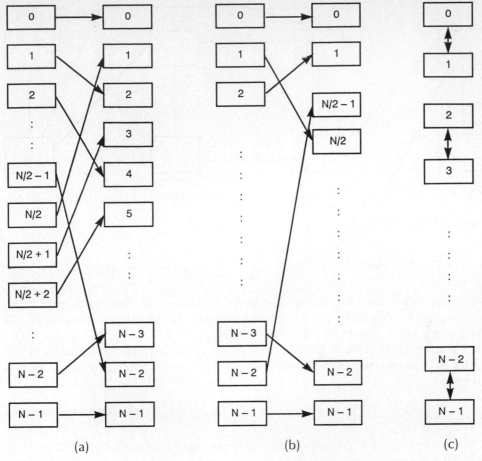

**Figure 2.8** (a) The shuffle; (b) the unshuffle; and (c) the exchange, for an N element vector.

The function S performs cyclic shifting to the left of the bits in A through one bit position. The *unshuffle* function undoes the effect of *shuffle* to restore the original ordering. Another function, called the *exchange* routing function (E) is defined as follows:

$$E(a_{k-1}a_{k-2} \ldots a_1 a_0) = a_{k-1} a_{k-2} \ldots a_1 a_0'$$  (B)

The exchange function thus indicates that two adjacent PEs should be connected for data exchange. The unshuffle and exchange interconnection patterns are shown in Figures 2.8b and 2.8c, respectively. In the perfect shuffle SIMD computer the PE interconnection is based on the shuffle, unshuffle and exchange functions. Figure 2.9 shows a perfect shuffle computer with 8 PEs.

In order to express the interconnection functions in terms of permutations on the N PEs, suppose that $S^i(u)$ denotes i applications of the shuffle function S to u. The shuffle function S of equation (A) then corresponds to the permutation cycles:

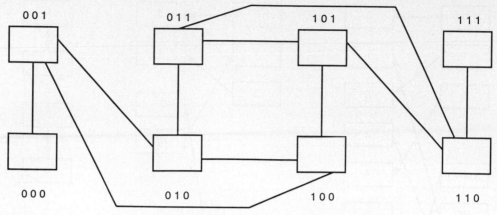

**Figure 2.9** The perfect shuffle network for N = 8 PEs.

$$\prod_{0 \le u \le N-1} (u \; S(u) \; S^2(u) \; \ldots \; S^{k-1}(u)) \tag{C}$$

where, for each cycle, u has not appeared on any previous cycle. The largest cycle in the permutation (C) has order k = log N. For example, the shuffle function for N = 8 corresponds to the permutation (0) (1 2 4) (3 6 5) (7).

The exchange function E, given in equation (B), can be expressed as a product of N/2 cycles of order two, provided the index is even. Thus the corresponding permutation is given by

$$\prod_{0 \le u \le (N-2)/2} (2u \; 2u + 1) \tag{D}$$

The exchange function obviously results in the permutation function (0 1) (2 3) (4 5) (6 7) for N = 8.

### 2.2.1.5  *Tree Connected Computer*

In a tree connected computer the processors form a complete binary tree. Such a tree has h levels, numbered 0, 1, . . . , h − 1, and N = $2^h$ − 1 nodes. Each node represents a processor and the edges of the tree represent two-way communication links. There is a distinct processor called the root processor whose level is 0. The root has no parent but has two child processors. The processors at level h − 1, which are called the leaf processors, have no child processors. However, each of them has a parent processor. With the exception of the root and leaf processors every other processor at level i is connected to a single parent processor at level i − 1 and to each of its two child processors at level i + 1. Figure 2.10 illustrates the interconnection of a tree connected computer for N = 15 processors and h = 4. The root and leaf processors are the only processors that have an interface with the outside world and are thus used to handle input and output. The number of processors needed on the machine and the computing and storage capabilities of each processor vary depending on the particular application in hand.

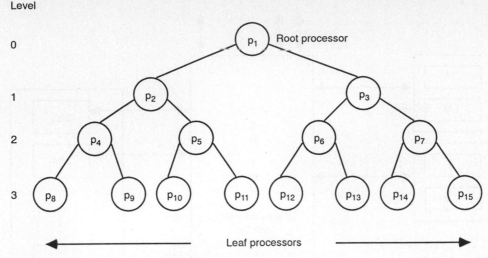

**Figure 2.10** Tree connected computer with 15 processors.

## 2.2.2 Multiple CPU (MIMD) Machines

Multiple CPU or MIMD machines consist of a number of PEs, which may be individually indexed. In addition, each PE knows its index and has some local memory where both data and program can be stored. The PEs are fully programmable and each PE is capable of executing its own program. Three important attributes which distinguish different MIMD models are: (i) the number of PEs may be fixed or unlimited; (ii) the PEs may be synchronous or asynchronous; and (iii) the interconnection patterns used may be different. In an asynchronous MIMD model, different PEs execute different instructions at any time. The PEs communicate results among themselves during computation. In some MIMD models the time required to communicate data from PE to PE dominates the overall complexity of the algorithm. Several interconnection patterns are used for MIMD machines. In general, MIMD machines may be divided into two distinct classes. One class includes tightly coupled MIMD machines (TC-MIMD) and the other loosely coupled MIMD machines (LC-MIMD).

**TC-MIMD Computer**

In a TC-MIMD, all the PEs operate through a central switching mechanism (interconnection network) to access a shared main memory. The inter-PE communication is established by means of the shared memory. Each PE may have a small local memory. Figure 2.11 shows the block diagram of a TC-MIMD computer model. The shared memory consists of a set of memory modules. The cost involved in the switching process in a TC-MIMD machine becomes the dominant factor as the number of PEs increases. It is thus impractical to build large systems of this type and, consequently, architectures based on this model have a rather limited number of processors (Stone 1980). The best-known example of a TC-MIMD machine is the C.mmp system which has only 16 PEs. The interconnection network used in C.mmp is called the crossbar switch in which, for

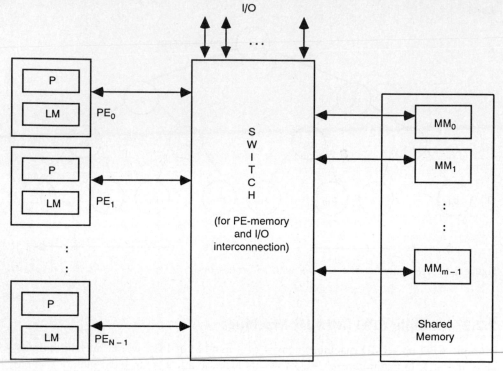

**Figure 2.11** Block diagram of a TC-MIMD.

every PE, there is a separate path available for each memory module. A crossbar switch that interconnects N PEs with m memory modules is shown in Figure 2.12. The important requirements of a machine utilizing a crossbar interconnection matrix are: (i) the simplicity of the switch to functional unit interfaces; and (ii) the ability to support simultaneous transfers for all units. In order to accommodate these features, the hardware capabilities of the switch must be increased. Each cross point must not only be capable of switching parallel transmissions, but must also be capable of resolving the conflicts among multiple requests for access to the same memory module which occur during the same memory cycle. These memory access conflicts are usually resolved on a pre-determined priority basis.

The hardware required to implement such a facility in the switching network obviously becomes quite complicated and increases the cost of the system, which is proportional to the product of the number of PEs and the number of memory modules.

### LC-MIMD Computer

LC-MIMD systems do not generally suffer from the problem of memory access conflicts associated with TC-MIMD systems. In these systems, each processor has a set of I/O

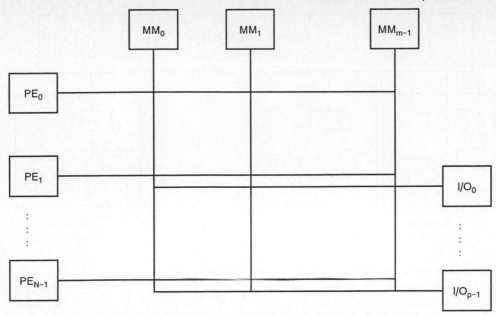

**Figure 2.12**  Crossbar switch system organization for TC-MIMD models.

devices and a large local memory where instructions and data are usually stored. We call this processor, together with its local memory and I/O interfaces, a computer module. Communication between two processes which are being executed by two different computer modules is achieved by exchanging messages through a message passing system (MPS). The degree of coupling in an LC-MIMD system is determined by the communication topology of the associated MPS. In general, LC-MIMD systems are efficient when the amount of interaction among the various processes executed by the computer modules is minimal.

Figure 2.13 shows the logical block diagram of an LC-MIMD system. Each computer module consists of a processor (P), a local memory (LM), local I/O devices and an interface to other computer modules (e.g., a channel and arbiter switch (CAS)). The CAS is responsible for resolving the MPS access conflicts when two or more computer modules attempt to access a part of the MPS simultaneously, by choosing one of the simultaneous requests according to a given service discipline. It is also responsible for delaying other requests until the servicing of the selected request is finished.

The best-known example of an LC-MIMD system where the computer modules are connected in a hierarchical fashion is Carnegie-Mellon's Cm*. Each computer module of the Cm* system consists of a processor (P), a local memory (LM), local I/O devices and a local switch (LS). The LS is somewhat similar to the CAS of Figure 2.13. All processor references to I/O or LM go through the LS. If an access is local, the reference is directed to the LM or local I/O devices. Nonlocal references are directed to the rest of the processors through a map bus (Figure 2.14a). A cluster is formed by combining several computer modules which share a single map bus. Competition for the map bus is limited to the set of computer modules which are in the same cluster. Clusters are connected via

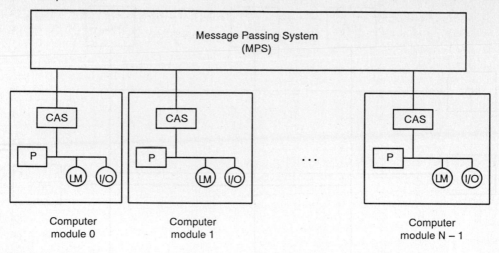

**Figure 2.13** Block diagram of a typical LC-MIMD system.

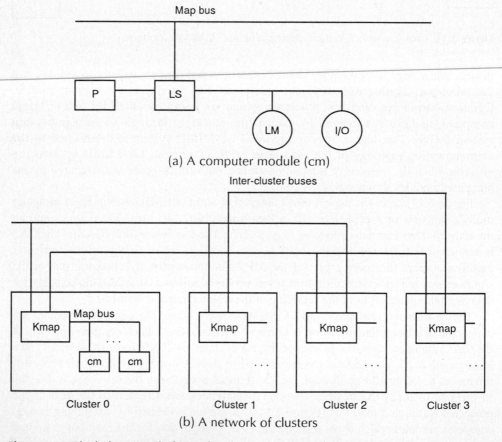

**Figure 2.14** Block diagram of a hierarchically structured LC-MIMD system.

inter-cluster buses. The map controller (call it Kmap) upon detecting a memory reference to another cluster redirects the reference via an inter-cluster bus to another Kmap, which places the reference on its own map bus. Figure 2.14b shows a network of clusters. Since the LC-MIMD system does not require a centralized switching mechanism, a relatively large number of processors may be connected together. For example, Cm* has 50 processors (Haynes et al. 1982).

## 2.2.3 Systolic Machines

A systolic machine consists of a set of synchronized, special-purpose, rudimentary PEs with a fixed interconnection network. Each PE regularly pumps data in and out, each time performing some simple computation, in order to sustain a regular flow of data in the network. The function of each PE and the type of interconnection scheme usually depend upon the problem being solved.

The simplicity of the PEs and the uniformity of the interconnection pattern allow systolic machines with a large number of PEs to be implemented on a single chip using VLSI technology (Foster and Kung 1980; Kung 1982).

Computational tasks can be divided into two classes: compute-bound computations and I/O-bound computations. If, in a computation, the total number of operations is more than the total number of input and output operations, then the computation is compute-bound, otherwise it is I/O-bound. For example, the standard matrix multiplication algorithm represents a compute-bound task because it has $O(n^3)$ multiplication and addition operations whereas there are only $O(n^2)$ I/O elements. In contrast, the addition of two matrices is an I/O-bound task, since there are $n^2$ addition operations and $3n^2$ I/O operations. Speeding up I/O-bound tasks requires an increase in memory bandwidth,* which is difficult using current VLSI technologies. On the other hand, a compute-bound task may often be speeded up by using systolic machines. The basic structure of a systolic machine is shown in Figure 2.15. In place of a single PE, a one- or two-dimensional array of PEs can be used to increase the computation throughput without increasing the memory bandwidth. The systolic machine differs from the conventional von Neumann machine because of its highly pipelined computation. When a data item is extracted from memory it may be used at each cell it passes along the array. Such machines are

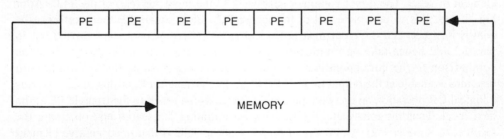

**Figure 2.15** Basic configuration of a systolic machine.

---

* The memory bandwith is defined as the maximum rate in bits per second at which information can be transferred to or from the main memory.

particularly attractive for a wide class of compute-bound problems, where multiple operations are performed on each data item in a repetitive manner. Thus, systolic machines do not suffer from the classic memory access bottleneck problem, due to the slow processor-memory interconnection, commonly encountered in von Neumann machines.

In summary, a systolic machine may be defined as a computing network possessing the following features:

(i) Simplicity and regularity: The machine consists of a large number of simple modular PEs with fixed homogeneous interconnections.

(ii) Synchrony: The data are rhythmically computed under the discipline of a global clock and passed through the network.

(iii) Pipelining: The machine exhibits a linear rate speedup, i.e., it should achieve an O(N) speedup with N PEs, where speedup is the ratio between the processing time required by a single processor and the processing time required by the N PE machine.

Systolic machines are used as high-speed special-purpose functional units attached to general-purpose computers. The tree-structured computer (TSC) of Bentley and Kung is a noteworthy example of a systolic machine (Bentley and Kung 1979). The TSC consists of a large number, say O(N), of three types of nodes connected in a mirrored binary tree as shown in Figure 2.16. The types of nodes are: (i) circles — which are capable of broadcasting data they receive; (ii) squares — which store data and compute; and (iii) triangles — which are capable of combining their inputs in an elementary way; for example, the operations they perform on the corresponding inputs might include finding their maximum or minimum, their sum, or performing elementary logical operations. A small conventional computer (driver) is assumed to reside between the output PE ($t_{out}$) and the input PE ($c_{in}$) whose purpose is to drive the tree machine. It is also assumed that one unit of routing time is required to perform data transmission or broadcasting from one level of the TSC to the next.

To illustrate the operation of a TSC, let us consider the problem of searching for an element k in a set S of N elements. Let us assume that each of N square PEs holds an element of set S. The driver computer supplies k to the input PE ($c_{in}$) of the TSC. After log N steps this value reaches all of the square PEs. Each square PE then performs the comparison between the element it holds and k. All N comparisons are carried out in parallel and hence take only unit time. Every square PE then sends the result of its comparison to the corresponding triangle PE. After log N steps the required result becomes available at the output triangle PE ($t_{out}$). Each triangle PE, in this case, performs a logical OR operation on its two inputs and broadcasts the result to the triangle PE at the next level. Thus the total elapsed time between initiating the search and obtaining the result is ($2 \times \log N + 2$). An important property of the TSC is that m successive element searches can be pipelined to run in ($m + 2 \times \log N + 1$) time. Likewise, it can be verified that finding the maximum or minimum of a set S of N elements can be achieved by a TSC in O(log N) steps if it is assumed that each of the N square PEs holds an element of set S.

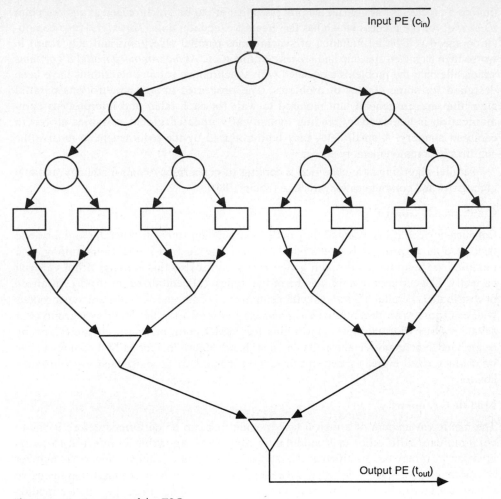

Input PE ($c_{in}$)

Output PE ($t_{out}$)

**Figure 2.16** Structure of the TSC.

## 2.3 TAXONOMY FOR PARALLEL ALGORITHMS

A parallel algorithm can be viewed as a set of p independent task modules or processes that can be executed concurrently and cooperatively to solve a given problem. Clearly, for a serial algorithm p = 1. During the execution of a parallel algorithm, different processes interact by synchronizing and exchanging data. Thus, in a task system, there may be some points where the tasks or processes communicate with other processes. These points are referred to as the *interaction points*. A process may be divided into a number of stages based on the interaction points so that at the end of each stage a process may communicate with some other process(es) before the next stage of computation is initiated. As a result of the interactions between the processes, some may be blocked at certain times. A parallel algorithm in which processes have to wait for some events to occur in some other processes is called a *synchronous algorithm*. Since the execution time of a process is variable all the processes that are to be synchronized at a given point must wait for the process which has the greatest execution time. This worst-case computation speed is a basic limitation of synchronous parallel algorithms and may result in worse than expected speedup and processor utilization. *Asynchronous parallel algorithms* which alleviate the problems associated with synchronous parallel algorithms have been designed for some classes of problems. The processes in an asynchronous parallel algorithm are, in general, not required to wait for each other and interprocess communication is achieved by reading dynamically updated global variables stored in common memory. A small delay may be introduced by the requirement to resolve the conflicts in common memory access.

Parallel algorithms are classified according to concurrency control strategy, module granularity and communication structure (Kung 1980).

## Concurrency Control

Concurrency control is essential for parallel computation since, in general, more than one task module or process is executed at a time. The desired interactions among task modules are maintained through concurrency control so that the algorithm can run correctly. Concurrency control may be of two types: (a) centralized, or (b) decentralized or distributed. Parallel algorithms with centralized concurrency control are synchronous whereas those with decentralized concurrency control may be either synchronous or asynchronous. For example, algorithms for SIMD computers are characterized by centralized synchronous control. On the other hand, algorithms for MIMD computers can be characterized either by decentralized synchronous or decentralized asynchronous control.

## Module Granularity

The maximum amount of a typical task module that can be performed before it has to communicate with other task modules in a parallel algorithm is referred to as its granularity. It may be quantified as the ratio of the amount of computation to the number of communication events. Whether a parallel algorithm will be communication intensive or not can be determined from its module granularity. More precisely, smaller module granularity implies more communication among the task modules and larger module granularity implies less communication. For example, algorithms for systolic machines have small module granularity whereas the algorithms for MIMD machines have large module granularity. Algorithms for SIMD machines could have small or large module granularities.

## Communication Structure

Parallel algorithms may also be classified according to the topology of the network used for interprocessor or processor-memory intercommunications. Figure 2.17 shows some possible communication structures. The leaves of this classification tree represent the space of the communication structures. For example, the leaf labeled "square" represents communication structures that correspond to regular two-dimensional square arrays.

Based on these three main attributes the space of the parallel algorithms could be represented as all possible combinations of concurrency control, module granularity and communication structure. For example, some possible combinations of concurrency

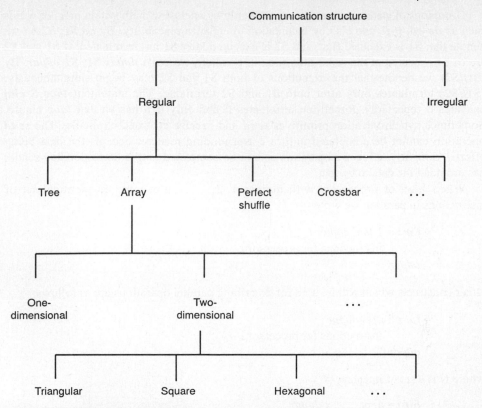

**Figure 2.17** Different types of communication structures.

control and module granularity correspond to systolic machines, some to SIMD machines and some to MIMD machines. The most important subspace of parallel algorithms could be described as the Cartesian product between the two sets {systolic machine, SIMD machine, MIMD machine} and {communication structure}. Clearly, some of the members of this subspace are systolic algorithms using a triangular array if the computational model used is a systolic one where the communication structure used is a triangular array, algorithms for crossbar MIMD machines, etc.

## 2.4 NOTATION FOR PRESENTING PARALLEL ALGORITHMS

In describing algorithms, we shall take the liberty of combining English with the standard constructs of structured programming languages like Algol or Pascal. Constructs used include the *if-then-else*, *for* and *while*, which will be assumed to have their usual semantics. The standard Boolean logical operators OR($\lor$), AND($\land$), and NOT($'$) are also used.

Groupings of statements are shown explicitly by enclosing them within pairs of words such as *do-od*, *if-fi*, and also by indentation to enhance readability. By *do* S1; S2 *od* we denote that S1 is executed first, and S2 is executed after S1 has terminated. If S1 and S2 are to be executed at the same time (i.e., in parallel), we write *dopar* S1; S2 *odpar*. By (S1//S2) we denote that the executions of both S1 and S2 may begin simultaneously. (S1//S2) terminates only after both S1 and S2 terminate. The statement *loop* S *end* executes S repeatedly. Repetition terminates if and only if S has an *exit loop* clause. Sometimes synchronization primitives *send* and *receive* are used explicitly. The *send* operation cannot be completed until a corresponding receiver accepts the data being offered. Similarly, a *receive* operation cannot be completed until a corresponding sender has provided the data to be sent.

When a set of processors with indices 1, 2, . . . , n execute an identical set of instructions in parallel, we write:

> *for* i = 1 *to* n *dopar*
> > instructions for processor i
> *odpar*

Other constructs which will be used for describing parallel operations are as follows:

> *for* all i∈N *dopar*
> > instructions for processor i
> *odpar*

where N is a set of integers, or

> *for* i = a, b, . . . , x *dopar*
> > instructions for processor i
> *odpar*

where the values assumed by integer i are enumerated.

## 2.5   BIBLIOGRAPHIC NOTES

Random access machine and random access stored program machine models are presented in detail in Aho et al. (1974), and Mehlhorn (1984). Details of the ILLIAC-IV are available in Barnes et al. (1968), Kuck (1968), and Falk (1976). Interconnection networks for SIMD models are discussed in detail in Siegel and Hsu (1988), Siegel (1984), and Feng (1981). A comparison of various interconnection networks for SIMD machines is presented in Siegel (1979). Mesh connected and cube connected SIMD computers are also discussed in Nassimi and Sahni (1979, 1981), and Hwang and Briggs (1984). Preparata and Vuillemin (1981) have proposed another interconnection scheme called cube connected cycles. This model has the additional advantage that the corresponding VLSI layout is more compact and regular, and it can emulate the cube connected and perfect shuffle SIMD models. The perfect shuffle network was introduced by Stone (1971) and further references on shuffle exchange networks include those by Lang and Stone (1976), and Siegel (1979). The investigation of Galil and Paul (1981,

1983) concerns a universal parallel model which can simulate every reasonable parallel computational model.

The computational models discussed in this chapter include those which are commonly used for designing parallel algorithms. Pipelined architectures are not covered in this chapter. However, interested readers are referred to, for example, Dasgupta (1989), Hayes (1988), Hwang and Briggs (1984), and Kogge (1981). It may be noted that there is some disagreement among authors as to whether pipelined architectures should be regarded as SIMD or SISD computers. For example, machines like Cray-1, a pipelined vector processor, is regarded as an SIMD machine by Hockney and Jesshope (1981). In Hwang and Briggs (1984), and Dasgupta (1989) the Cray-1 is considered to be an SISD machine, since it does not have multiple processing elements. On the other hand, Krishnamurthy (1989) describes pipelined architectures as MISD computers.

An overview of a number of commercially available multiprocessors in addition to the C.mmp is given in Satyanarayanan (1980). Additional references to C.mmp include Oleinick (1978), Mashburn (1979), and Wulf and Harbison (1978). Cm* is described in Stone (1980), Swan et al. (1977), Haynes et al. (1982), and Hwang and Briggs (1984).

Systolic arrays for VLSI computation were introduced by Kung and Leiserson (1978). A survey of systolic architectures can be found in Kung (1982). A substantial amount of information about systolic machines is available in Kung (1980), Foster and Kung (1980), and in the book by S. Y. Kung (1988). A classification of parallel algorithms based on architectures is available in Kung (1980).

## 2.6 EXERCISES

2.6.1   It has been the goal of more recent computer architects to eliminate the von Neumann bottleneck, which refers to the fundamental speed limitation in the von Neumann style of architectures.

(a)   Briefly describe the fundamental features of the conventional von Neumann architecture.

(b)   Explain the term "von Neumann bottleneck." Can you suggest some ways to overcome this bottleneck?

2.6.2   Assuming that all elementary operations, like, $+$, $-$, $*$, $/$, etc. take an identical time to compute, a computation may be partitioned into a sequence of stages. Within each stage all elementary operations can be evaluated independently of each other and every elementary operation at stage x requires at least one operand which is computed at stage x $-$ 1. If there are $p_x$ elementary operations at stage x, then $p_x$ is said to be the *instantaneous parallelism* at stage x. The number of parallel steps required by the computation is simply the number of stages as defined above. With this background, determine the instantaneous parallelism at various stages, and the number of parallel steps required to perform the following computations.

(a)   $A := ((u + v) * (w - x))/((x + y) * (y - z))$

(b)   $B := x * x$;   $C := y * y$;   $D := z * z$;   $E := (B + C)/(2 * C - D)$

(c)   $S := \sum_{1 \le i \le n} x_i$,   n is a power of 2.

2.6.3    Show how an N-processor CRCW PRAM can compute the OR of N Boolean values in constant time.

2.6.4    Assume that in a shared memory SIMD machine simultaneous writing is allowed only to selected memory locations which can contain only the numbers 0 or 1. Moreover, the processors writing simultaneously in the same memory location must write the value 1. Explain how this conflict resolution rule may be implemented by an existing hardware (Kucera 1982).

2.6.5    Show that the write conflict resolution rule as described in Exercise 2.6.4 is strong enough to simulate both equality and priority resolution rules of Section 2.2.1.1 (Kucera 1982).

2.6.6    Study Preparata and Vuillemin's *cube connected cycles* SIMD computer with particular reference to its capability of emulating the cube connected and perfect shuffle SIMD computers (Preparata and Vuillemin 1981).

2.6.7    Show that cube connected cycles may be considered as an efficient general purpose network (Galil and Paul 1981, 1983).

2.6.8    How many steps are required to broadcast an element from one PE to all other PEs using the following interconnection patterns, assuming that the total number of PEs N (say) is a power of 2?
(a) Cube connection;
(b) Shuffle-exchange connection assuming that in each step either the shuffle or the exchange step can be performed.

2.6.9    Considering an array of size N, where N is a power of 2, show how many shuffles will be required to bring all the elements back to their original position.

2.6.10   Distinguish between an MIMD machine and a computer network.

2.6.11   Discuss the major differences between the LC-MIMD and TC-MIMD machines. List the advantages and disadvantages if it is required to move from an LC-MIMD to a TC-MIMD model.

## 2.7  BIBLIOGRAPHY

Aho, A., Hopcroft, J., and Ullman, J. (1974). *The Design and Analysis of Computer Algorithms.* Addison-Wesley, Reading, Mass.

Barnes, G. H., Brown, R. M., Kato, M., Kuck, D. J., Slotnick, D. L., and Stokes, R. A. (1968). The Illiac IV computer. *IEEE Transactions on Computers* C-17, 746-57.

Bentley, J. L., and Kung, H. T. (1979). A tree machine for searching problems. *Proceedings of the 1979 International Conference on Parallel Processing,* IEEE Computer Society, Washington, DC, pp. 257-66.

Chaudhuri, P. (1987). An O(log n) parallel algorithm for strong connectivity augmentation problem. *Intern. J. Computer Math.* 22, 187-97.

Chaudhuri, P. and Ghosh, R. K. (1986). Parallel algorithms for analyzing activity networks. *BIT* 26, 418-29.

Dasgupta, S. (1989). *Computer Architecture: A modern synthesis.* vol. 2, John Wiley and Sons, NY.

Falk, H. (1976). Reaching for the gigaflop. *IEEE Spectrum* 13, 64-70.

Feng, T. Y. (1981). A survey of interconnection networks. *Computer* 14, 12-27.

Flynn, M. J. (1966). Very high speed computing systems. *Proc. IEEE* 54, 1901-9.

Foster, M. J., and Kung, H. T. (1980). Design of special-purpose VLSI chips — Example and opinions. *Computer* 13, 26-40.

Galil, Z., and Paul, W. J. (1981). An efficient general purpose parallel computer. *Proceedings of the 13th Annual Symposium on Theory of Computing,* ACM, NY, pp. 247-62.

Galil, Z., and Paul, W. J. (1983). An efficient general purpose parallel computer. *J. ACM* 30, 360-87.

Hayes, J. P. (1988). *Computer Architecture and Organization.* McGraw- Hill, NY.

Haynes, L. S., Lau, R. L., Siewiorek, D. P., and Mizell, D. (1982). A survey of highly parallel computing. *Computer* 14, 9-24.

Hockney, R. W., and Jesshope, C. R. (1981). *Parallel Computers: Architectures, Programming and Algorithms.* Adam Hilger, Bristol, England.

Hwang, K., and Briggs, F. A. (1984). *Computer Architectures and Parallel Processing.* McGraw-Hill, NY.

Kogge, P. M. (1981). *The Architecture of Pipelined Computers.* McGraw-Hill, NY.

Krishnamurthy, E. V. (1989). *Parallel Processing: Principles and Practice.* Addison-Wesley, Australia.

Kucera, L. (1982). Parallel computation and conflicts in memory access. *Inform. Process. Lett.* 14, 93-6.

Kuck, D. J. (1968). Illiac IV software and application programming. *IEEE Transactions on Computers* C-17, 758-70.

Kung, H. T. (1980). The structure of parallel algorithms. In *Advances in Computers*, vol. 19, M. Yovits, ed. Academic Press, NY, pp. 65-112.

Kung, H. T. (1982). Why systolic architectures? *Computer* 15, 37-46.

Kung, H. T., and Leiserson, C. E. (1978). Systolic arrays (for VLSI). *Sparse matrix Proc.*, Duff, et al., eds. Society of Industrial and Appl. Math., Philadelphia, pp. 245-82.

Kung, S. Y. (1988). *VLSI Array Processors.* Prentice Hall, Englewood Cliffs, NJ.

Lang, T., and Stone, H. S. (1976). A shuffle-exchange network with simplified control. *IEEE Transactions on Computers* C-25, 55-6.

Mashburn, H. H. (1979). *The C.mmp/Hydra project: An architectural overview.* Tech. Rep., Dept. of Computer Science, Carnegie-Mellon University, Pittsburgh, Pa.

Mehlhorn, K. (1984). *Data Structures and Algorithms 1: Sorting and Searching.* Springer-Verlag, Berlin.

Nassimi, D., and Sahni, S. (1979). Bitonic sort on a mesh-connected parallel computer. *IEEE Transactions on Computers* C-28, 2-7.

Nassimi, D., and Sahni, S. (1981). Data broadcasting in SIMD computers. *IEEE Transactions on Computers* C-30, 101-7.

Oleinick, P. (1978). The implementation of parallel algorithms on an asynchronous multiprocessor. Ph.D. dissertation, Dept. of Computer Science, Carnegie-Mellon University, Pittsburgh, Pa.

Preparata, F. P., and Vuillemin, J. (1981). The cube-connected cycles: a versatile network for parallel computation. *Comm. ACM.* 24, 300-9.

Quinn, M. J., and Deo, N. (1984). Parallel graph algorithms, *Computing Surveys* 16, 319-48.

Satyanarayanan, M. (1980). *Multiprocessors.* Prentice Hall, Englewood Cliffs, NJ.

Shiloach, Y., and Vishkin, U. (1981). Finding the maximum, merging, and sorting in a parallel computation model. *J. Algorithms* 2, 88-102.

Siegel, H. J. (1979). A model of SIMD machines and a comparison of various interconnection networks. *IEEE Transactions on Computers* C-28, 907-17.

Siegel, H. J. (1984). *Interconnection Networks for Large-Scale Parallel Processing: Theory and Case Studies.* Lexington Books, Lexington, Mass.

Siegel, H. J., and Hsu, W. T. (1988). Interconnection networks. In *Computer Architecture: Concepts and Systems*, V. M. Milutinovic, ed. Elsevier Science Publishing Co., pp. 225-64.

Stone, H. S. (1971). Parallel processing with perfect shuffle. *IEEE Transactions on Computers* C-20, 153-61.

Stone, H. S. (1980). Parallel computers. In *Introduction to Computer Architecture*, H. S. Stone, ed. Science Research Associates, Chicago, chap. 8.

Swan, R. J., Bechtolsheim, A., Lai, K. -W., and Ousterhout, J. K. (1977). The implementation of the Cm* multi-microprocessor. *Proceedings of the National Computer Conference,* AFIPS Press, Reston, Va., pp. 645-55.

Vishkin, U. (1984). An optimal parallel connectivity algorithm. *Discrete Math.* 9, 197-207.

Wulf, W., and Harbison, S. P. (1978). *Reflections in a pool of processors.* Tech. Rep., Dept. of Computer Science, Carnegie-Mellon University, Pittsburgh, Pa.

# CHAPTER
# 3

# Complexity of
# Parallel Algorithms

## 3.1 INTRODUCTION

In this chapter we will discuss the concepts related to the complexity of parallel algorithms and the programming paradigms underlying the design of efficient parallel algorithms. Although in serial algorithms the performance is measured in terms of time and space complexities, in parallel algorithms a number of additional measures of performance are often used. Moreover, the time complexity of a parallel algorithm cannot be determined simply by counting the number of elementary operations involved in the computation, as is the case for serial algorithms. Instead, it depends on how these elementary operations can be implemented on a P-processor computer, where $P > 1$. The processor complexity of a parallel algorithm is, setting aside the time complexity, the most important measure of its performance. Again the situation varies widely depending on whether the number of available processors is bounded by, say, an integer P, or is unlimited. The design of efficient parallel algorithms involves choosing appropriate data structures, allocating processors and finally executing the algorithm. These three aspects together may be referred to as the computation organization. Some computation organizations which are frequently used in solving various problems on parallel computers are introduced as programming paradigms.

In particular, the definitions of bounded and unbounded parallelism are given in Section 3.2. The concepts of upper and lower bounds in relation to parallel algorithms are introduced in Section 3.3. Section 3.4 is concerned with the efficiency of parallel algorithms. In this section, formal definitions of cost and speedup of a parallel algorithm are also given. Programming paradigms for parallel computation are discussed in Section 3.5; finally, in Section 3.6, some techniques for improving the efficiency of parallel algorithms are described.

## 3.2 BOUNDED AND UNBOUNDED PARALLELISM

As for serial algorithms, the time complexity of a parallel algorithm is expressed as a function of n, the problem size. The time complexity is the most important measure of the performance of a parallel algorithm since the primary motivation for parallel computation is to achieve a speedup in the computation.

The *worst-case time complexity* (or simply *time complexity*) of a parallel algorithm to solve a problem $P_n$ of size n is a function t(n) which is the maximum time that elapses between the start of the algorithm's execution by one (or more) processor(s) and its termination by one or more processor(s), with any arbitrary input data.

Parallel algorithms are executed by a set of processors cooperatively and usually require interprocessor data transfer to complete execution successfully. Thus two different kinds of operations are involved. One is the computation (e.g., arithmetic or logical) performed locally by a processor; the other is the routing of data among processors. In a parallel algorithm an elementary step refers to the set of elementary operations which can be executed simultaneously by a set of processors — the time complexity of an elementary step is regarded as constant or O(1). The time complexity of a parallel algorithm is determined by counting both elementary steps and data routing steps remembering that the time required by each data routing step depends on the interconnection pattern among the processors. The term *depth* is often used in the literature to refer to the time complexity of a parallel algorithm (Shiloach and Vishkin 1982; Vishkin 1984).

The time complexity of a parallel algorithm depends on the type of computational model being used as well as on the number of processors available. Therefore, when giving the time complexity of a parallel algorithm it is important to give the maximum number of processors used by the algorithm as a function of the problem size n. This is referred to as the algorithm's *processor complexity*. It is also possible to express the time complexity as a function of the number of processors used but it is more common to express each of them separately as functions of the problem size. For example, a serial algorithm to find the maximum of a set with n elements has complexity O(n), since it requires (n − 1) comparisons. In contrast, a trivial parallel algorithm for the same problem has time and processor complexities O(log n) and O(n), respectively. By finding the maximum of every disjoint pair of elements simultaneously, the number of elements remaining to be compared can be reduced by half at each comparison step. Repeating this procedure guarantees that the largest element can be obtained after $\lceil \log n \rceil$ parallel steps. The maximum number of processors required is obviously that determined by the first comparison step, namely $\lfloor n/2 \rfloor$.

The synthesis and analysis of a parallel algorithm can be carried out under the assumption that the computational model consists of P processors only, where P > 1 is a fixed integer. This is referred to as *bounded parallelism*. In contrast, *unbounded parallelism* refers to the situation in which it is assumed that we have at our disposal an unlimited number of processors.

A given parallel algorithm implemented on a P-processor computation model is called *P-parallel*. If a P-parallel algorithm requires t(n) parallel steps for a problem of size n, then it is said to be P-computable in time t. Let us assume that a parallel algorithm A solves a problem of size n on P processors. If there exists a polynomial F such that for all n, $P \leq F(n)$, then the number of processors is said to be *polynomially bounded*; otherwise it is *polynomially unbounded*.

From a practical point of view algorithms for bounded parallelism are preferable. It is more realistic to assume that the number of processors available is limited, and is no more than the problem size. Although parallel algorithms for unbounded parallelism, in general, use a polynomially bounded number of processors (e.g., $O(n^2)$, $O(n^3)$, etc.) it may be that for very large problem sizes the processor requirement may become impractically large. However, algorithms for unbounded parallelism are of great theoretical interest, since they give limits for parallel computation and provide a deeper understanding of a problem's intrinsic complexity. Intuitively, this means that, even if we assume the existence of an infinite number of processors (i.e., the algorithm can use as many processors as it wants), and also that there are no communication and memory access restrictions, the computational time cannot be reduced below a certain limit. This is due to the fact that some intermediate results must be known before other parts of the computation can start. Unbounded parallel time complexity of a problem reflects this characteristic of a problem.

The number of processors on a real parallel computer is limited, and algorithms for unbounded parallelism only become practically useful if they can be transformed to P-parallel algorithms. There are two methods for carrying out such transformations. One is decomposition of the problem, and the other is decomposition of the algorithm. Consider a parallel algorithm A for a problem $P_n$ of size n that solves $P_n$ in time $t_1(n)$ using $p_1(n)$ processors. The object is to design a new algorithm B that solves $P_n$ in time $t_2(n)$ using $p_2(n)$ processors, where $p_2(n) < p_1(n)$. A problem is decomposed by splitting it into smaller subproblems of size m ($m < n$), each of which is then solved by the original algorithm using a smaller number of processors $p_2(m)$. When decomposing an algorithm, each of its steps is decomposed into substeps in such a way that each of them can be executed using a smaller number of processors. Some important results related to algorithm decomposition are given below.

As a consequence of the fact that a parallel algorithm that solves a given problem in $O(T)$ time with P processors yields a serial algorithm that solves the problem in time $O(TP)$ (see also Savage and Ja' Ja' 1981), we have the following lemma.

**Lemma 3.1:** Any parallel algorithm of time complexity $O(T)$ with P processors must have at most $O(TP)$ elementary operations.

Let us assume that an algorithm A that consists of e elementary operations can be performed in time T with a sufficiently large number of processors. Suppose that $e_i$ denotes the number of operations performed at step i ($i = 1, 2, \ldots T$), i.e., $\sum_{1 \leq i \leq T} e_i = e$. If we now use P processors then step i of algorithm A has $\lceil e_i/P \rceil$ steps in the transformed algorithm B when it performs the same computation. Every new step consists of at least P operations performed in parallel. Consequently, the transformed algorithm can perform the computation using P processors in time

$$\sum_{1 \leq i \leq T} \lceil e_i / P \rceil \leq \sum_{1 \leq i \leq T} ((e_i / P) + 1) \leq \lceil e / P \rceil + T$$

The above result is known as Brent's theorem (Brent 1974). From this the next theorem follows immediately.

**Theorem 3.1:** Any parallel algorithm of time complexity O(T) using a sufficiently large number of processors that consists of O(e) elementary operations can be implemented by P processors with a time complexity of $O(\lceil e/P \rceil + T)$.

A parallel algorithm is said to be *adaptive* or *self-reconfiguring* if for subsets of the processors available the algorithm can be executed and the product of time and the number of processors remains constant. That is, if the number of available processors decreases within a given range, the algorithm still works but the running time increases in such a manner that the product of time and the number of processors remains the same and vice-versa. The following lemma gives us a straightforward way to make algorithms adaptive when the number of processors available decreases.

**Lemma 3.2:** Any parallel algorithm A of time complexity O(T) with P processors can be implemented by $\lceil P/p \rceil$, $1 \le p \le P$ processors in time O(pT).

**Proof:** From Lemma 3.1 it follows that the number of elementary operations in A is at most O(TP). Therefore, using Theorem 3.1 we find that with $\lceil P/p \rceil$, $1 \le p \le P$ processors A can be implemented in time $O((TP/\lceil P/p \rceil) + T) = O(pT)$, $1 \le p \le P$.

## 3.3  UPPER AND LOWER BOUNDS

In the analysis of parallel algorithms, it often becomes necessary to examine quantities like the upper and lower bounds of time in which it is possible to solve a given problem by some algorithm selected from a given class of algorithms. The fastest known parallel algorithm for the computation of the solution of a given problem determines the upper bound of that computation. If someone invents a new parallel algorithm for a given problem which is faster than the previously fastest known parallel algorithm for the same problem, then we say that it has established a new upper bound for the computation of the solution of that problem. After obtaining this upper bound it is important to check whether it is possible to find a faster algorithm or whether the lower bound of the running time has been achieved. The lower bound determines the complexity of the problem, i.e., it gives the minimum amount of time required to solve the problem using an arbitrary parallel algorithm.

A problem $P_n$ of size n is said to be finite with respect to the class of algorithms C, if there exists an algorithm $c \in C$ which solves $P_n$ in a maximum time of $T_n$ such that $T_n < \infty$ for $n < \infty$; otherwise, $P_n$ is said to be an infinite problem with respect to C. We shall consider only finite problems.

As an illustration we now obtain a simple lower bound for solving a problem, with n inputs and a single output, that involves only binary operations. It is obvious that (n − 1) binary operations are necessary and may be sufficient to compute the output using a serial algorithm. We are interested to know how many of these operations may be performed in parallel. Let us consider the set B(P) of labeled binary trees defined as follows (Heller 1978):

  (i) the tree with a single node is in B(P) and is of depth 0;
 (ii) given a depth d tree in B(P), if we increase all levels by 1 and add both left-child and right-child to at most P leaves and label these newly added nodes by 0 then the new tree is in B(P) and has depth (d + 1);
(iii) all trees in B(P) are obtained using (i) and (ii).

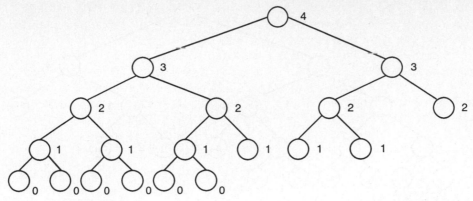

**Figure 3.1** A sample depth 4 tree with maximum number of leaves in B(3), i.e., d = 4, P = 3. This tree represents a parallel computation with 10 inputs (leaves) and one output (root). The labels beside the internal nodes denote the step in which the operation is performed.

Each tree in B(P) represents a computation process in which leaves represent operands and internal nodes represent binary associative operations. A depth d tree in B(P) corresponds to d parallel steps in the computation with P processors. Figure 3.1 shows a sample depth 4 tree with maximum number of leaves in B(3).

Let N(P, d) be the maximum number of leaves in a depth d tree in B(P), and, in addition, let t(P, n) be the minimum depth of any tree in B(P) with n leaves. We have by construction:

$N(P, 0) = 1,$
$N(P, d + 1) = N(P, d) + \min(P, N(P,d)),$
and $N(P, d - 1) < n \leq N(P, d)$ implies $t(P, n) = d.$

We can also express N(P, d) as $N(P, d) = 2^{\min(\lceil \log P \rceil, d)} + P \times \max(0, d - \lceil \log P \rceil)$, so $t(P, n) = \min(\lceil \log P \rceil, \lceil \log n \rceil) + \max(0, \lceil (n - 2^{\lceil \log P \rceil})/P \rceil).$

At least t(P, n) steps are required to compute one result from n inputs using P processors; hence the lower bound to such a problem is given by t(P, n). Let us consider an example in which the problem size is n = 12 and the number of processors available is P = 3. In this case the lower bound in the number of parallel steps is t(3, 12) = 2 + 3 = 5. The corresponding computation process is depicted in Figure 3.2 as one of the depth 5 trees in B(3).

A similar but more general lower bound on computation time was obtained by Munro and Paterson (1973). The theorem given below states their result.

**Theorem 3.2:** If for the computation of one number X at least x operations are required, then any parallel algorithm using P processors for the computation of X must contain at least t(P, x + 1) steps.

The proof of this theorem follows from the fact that the maximum number of operations that can be performed in d steps using P processors to compute one result is N(P, d) − 1, which is just the maximum number of internal nodes on a depth d tree in B(P). Now, let T be an integer such that N(P, (T − 1)) − 1 < x ≤ N(P, T) − 1, which implies that T = t(P, x + 1). X cannot be computed in fewer than T steps, although we cannot conclude that T steps are sufficient.

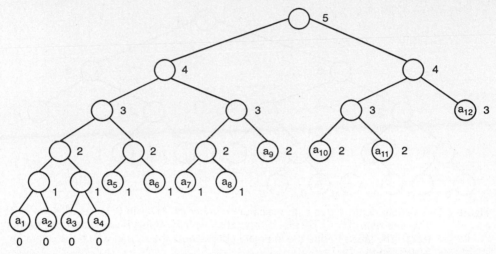

**Figure 3.2** Computation of $a_1$ op $a_2$ op . . . $a_{12}$ with 3 processors, where "op" is a binary associative operator. The node label corresponding to an internal node represents the step in which the operation is performed.

From Theorem 3.2 it follows that the lower bound to the computation of the product of two vectors of order n, for a P-parallel computation model with $\lceil \log P \rceil < \lceil \log n \rceil$, is $\lceil \log P \rceil + \lceil (2n - 2^{\lceil \log P \rceil})/P \rceil$ parallel steps. The lower bound for unbounded parallelism is $\lceil \log n \rceil + 1$ parallel steps.

## 3.4 COST, SPEEDUP, AND EFFICIENCY OF PARALLEL ALGORITHMS

Let T(A, n, P) denote the time required by a parallel algorithm A to solve a problem of size n using P processors. The *cost* of algorithm A denoted by C(A, n, P) is defined as the product of T(A, n, P) and P, i.e.,

$$C(A, n, P) = T(A, n, P) \times P.$$

We may omit the arguments A, n, and P when the context is clear. If the time complexity of a serial algorithm for a given problem is equal to or of the same order as its lower bound, the algorithm is said to be *optimal*. Clearly, it is the fastest possible serial algorithm for that particular problem; otherwise it is not the fastest possible algorithm and a faster algorithm may yet be invented. If the cost of a parallel algorithm is equal to or of the same order as the lower bound $T_L$ of the running time for the serial algorithm corresponding to the same problem, it is said to be *cost optimal*.

It follows directly from Lemma 3.2, by considering the case p = P, that any parallel algorithm of time complexity O(T) using P processors can be simulated on a serial computer and the time complexity of the transformed serial algorithm is given by O(TP), i.e., the cost of the parallel algorithm. If $T_L$ and $T \times P$ are of the same order, then the corresponding parallel algorithm cannot be improved so far as the cost is concerned. However, it may be possible to decrease the time complexity of the algorithm at the expense of employing more processors so that T × P remains constant. On the other hand, if the order of the cost of a parallel algorithm is more than the order of $T_L$, then that parallel algorithm is not cost optimal.

The most commonly used, and probably the most important, characteristic of a parallel algorithm for solving a given problem is *speedup*. It is a very good indicator of the success of a parallel algorithm. Let T(A, n, P) be the time required by a parallel algorithm A to solve a problem of size n using P processors, then the speedup S(A, n, P) is defined as

$$S(A, n, P) = \frac{\text{time required by the fastest known serial algorithm for the problem}}{T(A, n, P)}$$

Thus speedup measures the improvement in solution time using parallelism. It should be noted that, since speedup is a function of P, it is important to mention explicitly the number of processors used while indicating the speedup of a particular algorithm. For example, if the fastest known serial algorithm for a given problem runs in 24 seconds and a parallel algorithm for the same problem runs in 3 seconds when 16 processors are used, then the parallel algorithm is said to show a "speedup of 8 using 16 processors."

When designing parallel algorithms we aim for the speedup to be linear in P which implies that all processors are effectively exploited. More precisely, for problems of size n we desire an asymptotic speedup of the form $S(A, n, P) = kP - w(n, P)$, with $0 < k \leq 1$, $0 \leq w(n, P) = o(1)$ as $n \to \infty$; k should be independent of P and close to 1 (Heller 1978). The function w(n, P) can be interpreted as the loss incurred due to the application of parallelism in solving small problems. For large problems this factor is outweighed by the gain from parallelism. Ideally, we wish to achieve the maximum speedup of P when solving a problem using P processors. In reality, however, such a speedup cannot be achieved for all problems since the nature of the problem and the structure of the parallel computer are also involved. More precisely, the optimum performance cannot be achieved in all cases because every problem cannot be decomposed into P independent tasks such that each of these can be performed in time $T_s/P$ on a single processor where $T_s$ is the time required by a serial algorithm to solve the problem. In addition, the structure of the parallel computer imposes restrictions such that the desired running time cannot be attained.

The *efficiency* of a parallel algorithm is defined as the ratio of the speedup obtained to the total number of processors used by the algorithm. Thus, denoting the efficiency by E(A, n, P) with the usual meaning of the arguments A, n, and P, we have

$$E(A, n, P) = \frac{S(A, n, P)}{P}$$

$$= \frac{\text{time required by the fastest serial algorithm for the problem}}{C(A, n, P)}$$

where C(A, n, P) is the cost of the parallel algorithm.

The efficiency is an important measure of the performance of a parallel algorithm because it indicates how effectively the processors are used. Clearly, higher efficiency means better utilization of the processors and vice-versa. Values of E range between 0 and 1. For example, if a parallel algorithm exhibits a speedup of 8 using 16 processors, then it has an efficiency of 0.5 using 16 processors. For a cost optimal parallel algorithm, the efficiency is 1. The efficiency of a parallel algorithm cannot exceed 1.

# 3.5 PROGRAMMING PARADIGMS FOR PARALLEL COMPUTATION

There are several recognized paradigms used for the development of efficient serial algorithms. These include the divide-and-conquer method and the greedy and dynamic programming techniques (Aho et al. 1974; Brassard and Bratley 1988). These computational methods are not algorithms; rather they are the problem-solving strategies that are frequently used in developing efficient algorithms. The purpose of identifying paradigms is twofold. One is to have a scientific or mathematical insight that may enable us to solve apparently dissimilar problems by similar means; the other is that a set of accepted paradigms becomes the algorithm designer's or programmer's "tool kit."

Organizing a parallel algorithm to perform a computation may require a fairly large amount of interprocessor data transfer. In general, programming paradigms encapsulate information about useful patterns of data reference for serial computation. In the case of parallel computation the paradigms generally encapsulate information about useful communication patterns. Since an important problem in parallel computer architecture is the provision of efficient and effective communication among the processors, the paradigms also serve as a specification of which communication patterns are most useful. The paradigms introduced below may not be widely accepted but are used frequently for parallel computation:

- Binary tree paradigm
- Growing by doubling paradigm
- Spanning tree for graphs paradigm
- Systolic and other paradigms.

## 3.5.1  Binary Tree Paradigm

Consider the problem of computing the sum of N numbers $(n_1, n_2, \ldots, n_N)$, where N is a power of 2. Assuming that the data lies on the leaves of a binary tree, the computation can be performed in the following way.  N/2 processing elements (PEs) are employed to compute the sum of pairs of data items, e.g., $(n_1, n_2), (n_3, n_4), \ldots, (n_{N-1}, n_N)$. These can be performed in one computational step. Next, N/4 PEs perform the same task on N/4 pairs of data elements, and so on. It is clear that the computation proceeds from the leaves to the root of the tree and that the entire computation is terminated when the PE at the root performs its computation. This is illustrated in Figure 3.3. If the processing required at each step requires C units of time, then the entire computation takes $C \times \log N$ units of time with N/2 PEs. Thus, we say that this computation requires $O(\log N)$ time when $O(N)$ processors are employed.

In general, the binary tree paradigm can be applied to perform a computation on N data items $(n_1, n_2, \ldots, n_N)$, if the computation is such that it can be performed by combining the results of the same computation on data items $(n_1, n_2, \ldots, n_{N/2})$ and $(n_{(N/2)+1}, n_{(N/2)+2}, \ldots, n_N)$.

## 3.5.2  Growing by Doubling Paradigm

The binary tree method can be visualized in another way. At each step, a PE doubles the number of elements for which it has performed the required computation. Hence

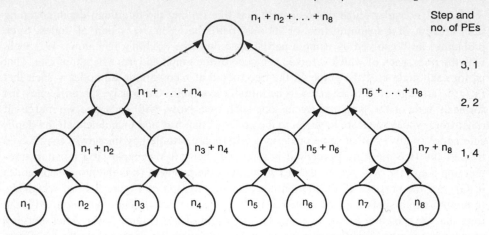

Step and
no. of PEs

3, 1

2, 2

1, 4

**Figure 3.3** This figure illustrates the binary tree paradigm of computing the sum of N = 8 numbers.

"growth" is achieved by doubling the number of data elements at each step. There are other ways, of course, in which this type of doubling technique can be used even when the problem has no associated binary tree structure. Some examples are now given.

Consider the *list-ranking* problem which is defined as follows. Given a linked list of N elements stored in an array A[1:N], compute for each element its rank. The rank of an element in a linked list is defined as its distance from the end of the list. Thus, the first element in the list has rank N and the last element in the list has rank 1. To solve this problem using the doubling technique, we assign a processor to each element. At the beginning each processor knows only the right neighbor of its element in the list. In the first step, each processor finds the neighbor of its neighbor. That is, after the first step each processor knows the element at distance 2 from its element. Let *next(i)* be the farthest element to the right of ith element in the list that is known to processor $p_i$ (say). Initially, next(i) is i's right neighbor with the exception of the last element in the list whose right neighbor is nil. In each step $p_i$ updates next(i) to next(next(i)) until the end of the list is reached. If at step k each processor knows the element at distance x from its element, then in one step each processor can find the element at distance 2x. Thus, the doubling process guarantees that each processor will reach the end of the list in at most $\lceil \log N \rceil$ steps and will know about its rank. The precise algorithm for this problem based on the above discussion is left as an exercise.

Another example is the problem of finding the tree-path between the root and every node in an arbitrary tree which is given in the form of "parent-of" relation; i.e., for each node i of the tree its parent or immediate predecessor, denoted by parent(i), is known. For the root node r, it is generally assumed that parent(r) = r. In this case the "parent-of" relation can be propagated in such a manner that, at the end of the first step, every node knows its parent (first ancestor) and parent-of-parent (second ancestor). At the end of the second step every node knows its first, second, third, and fourth ancestors. Thus the "growth" of the tree-path is by a factor of two at each step. Clearly, if the height of the tree is h then only $\lceil \log h \rceil$ steps are required to obtain the tree-path between every node and the root of the tree. The details of this technique are provided in Chapter 7.

Finally, consider graph theoretic problems like finding the minimum-depth spanning tree, breadth-first spanning tree, or shortest paths between every pair of nodes. Such problems can be solved by using a partial spanning tree doubling technique. We begin with the trees, each of which is rooted at a node of the graph and has a height of one. That is, for each node x of the graph G, the tree rooted at x containing all nodes y such that (x, y) is an edge of G is assumed to be initially available. Obviously, the adjacency list for each node of the graph represents one such tree. Now, with each tree we merge all other trees whose roots are identical to the nodes of that tree and then delete all the duplicate nodes (if any) so that some predefined criteria are satisfied by the newly constructed tree. If the tree-merging procedure is repeated then after at most $\lceil \log n \rceil$ such tree-merging steps, we will get the desired solution to the problem (n is the number of nodes in G). For the purpose of illustration consider the digraph of Figure 3.4a of which the minimum-depth spanning tree rooted at node 1 is to be determined. We begin with the trees that are rooted at a node of G and have a height of one (Figure 3.4b). After merging the tree in the way described above and without deleting the duplicate nodes we obtain the trees of height two or less as shown in Figure 3.4c. Now if the same node occurs more than once in a tree during the merging process we remove all duplicate nodes except the one whose distance from the root of the corresponding tree is minimum (this ensures that the trees constructed by this merging process preserve the minimum-depth property). Ties can be broken arbitrarily. The duplicate nodes which are to be deleted in the trees of Figure 3.4c are marked X. Since the digraph G has 6 nodes, three such tree-merging steps need to be carried out. The final minimum-depth spanning tree rooted at node 1 thus obtained is shown in Figure 3.4d. This technique will be used to design parallel algorithms for several graph theoretic problems in Chapters 7 and 8.

### 3.5.3  Spanning Tree for Graphs Paradigm

A large number of the parallel algorithms developed in the past few years are for the solution of graph theoretic problems. In serial computation, many graph theoretic problems are solved by first finding a depth-first spanning tree. The construction of a depth-first spanning tree for an arbitrary graph was suspected to be inherently serial for a long time. Many attempts have been made to design a fast (logarithmic time) parallel algorithm for this problem but without any success (see e.g., Eckstein and Alton 1977; Reghbati and Corneil 1978). Finally, it has been shown by Reif (1985) that depth-first search of graphs is P-complete which provides strong evidence that depth-first search of graphs cannot be achieved in deterministic logarithmic parallel time. Consequently, the approaches to the parallel solution of most graph theoretic problems are rather different from the corresponding serial algorithms which are based on the depth-first spanning trees of the graphs.

A common technique for constructing parallel solutions to graph theoretic problems whose serial algorithms are based on depth-first spanning trees is to make use of an arbitrary spanning tree (Tarjan and Vishkin 1984). It is possible to design a fast (logarithmic time) parallel algorithm for constructing an arbitrary spanning tree (Tarjan and Vishkin 1984), a breadth-first spanning tree (Dekel et al. 1981; Kim and Chwa 1986), and a minimum-depth spanning tree (Dekel et al. 1981; Chaudhuri 1988).

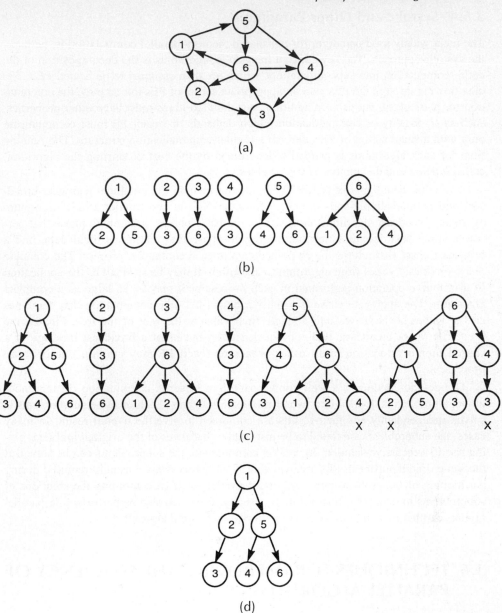

**Figure 3.4** (a) A digraph G with 6 nodes; (b) the trees, each of which is rooted at a node of G and has a height of one; (c) trees of height less than or equal to two, obtained after merging for the first time (nodes marked with X are the duplicates to be deleted); (d) the minimum-depth spanning tree of G rooted at node 1 is obtained after $\lceil \log 6 \rceil = 3$ such tree-merging steps.

### 3.5.4  Systolic and Other Paradigms

The most widely used paradigm for nonshared memory parallel computation is, perhaps, the systolic approach. The key concept in systolic algorithms is the decomposition of the entire computation into subcomputations which are then assigned to dedicated PEs. The data flowing through the PEs visit an appropriate subset of PEs to complete the computation for particular input data. In addition, systolic algorithms must have other properties, such as (i) locality of communication which demands that each PE must communicate only with a small subset of PEs, and (ii) a regular communication structure. The running time for such algorithms is generally determined by the cost of starting the algorithm, called *latency,* and the number of input values.

The other paradigms in parallel computation include the compute-aggregate-broadcast and parallel divide-and-conquer technique (Nelson and Snyder 1987). Compute-aggregate-broadcast algorithms consist of three basic phases: a compute phase that performs some basic computation, an aggregate phase that combines local data, and a broadcast phase that returns the combined data to each computing process. The compute phase obviously varies from algorithm to algorithm. It may be as small as the application of a primitive operation performed in each process or it may be as large as a complete algorithm. The aggregate phase is usually a binary-tree-like computation that combines all the values at the leaves into a single final value at the root of the tree. Finally, the broadcast phase broadcasts this combined data by means of a broadcast message or a shared memory location to all other processes (each PE may contain one or more processes).

Divide-and-conquer is a well-known paradigm in serial computation. In this technique, a problem is divided into two or more subproblems. Each of these subproblems is solved independently and their results are combined to give the overall result. In many cases, the subproblems are found to be just smaller instances of the original problem, giving rise to a recursive solution. In parallel computation, the subproblems can be solved at the same time if sufficient PEs are available. Some processing is usually required during partitioning of the problem into a set of subproblems and in combining the solutions of subproblems to obtain the final solution. Usually, these can also be performed in parallel giving a further reduction in the running time of the overall algorithm.

## 3.6  TECHNIQUES FOR IMPROVING THE EFFICIENCY OF PARALLEL ALGORITHMS

In executing any parallel algorithm there is always a trade-off between the computation time and the number of processors used (within some limits). In Section 3.2 we have seen in terms of Lemma 3.2 how to make algorithms adaptive when the number of available processors decreases. According to Lemma 3.2, while adapting a parallel algorithm the factor by which the number of available processors decreases appears as a multiplicative factor of the time complexity of the algorithm. Thus, the cost and hence the efficiency of the adapted algorithm remains the same as that of the original algorithm. However, in some cases, when the number of available processors decreases, the reallocation of the computation to the processors can be performed in such a way as to increase the efficiency of the new version of the algorithm. The increase in efficiency is achieved either by reducing the number of processors without increasing the time complexity or by reducing the time complexity without increasing the number of processors. Two such general techniques (Moitra and Iyengar 1987) are described below.

## 3.6.1  Reducing the Number of Processors

Consider the problem discussed in Section 3.5.1 of computing the sum of N numbers where N is a power of 2. A simple algorithm for this computation, based on the binary tree paradigm, takes $O(\log N)$ time with $N/2 \equiv O(N)$ processors. Therefore, its efficiency is $N/(N \times \log N) = 1/\log N$.

Let us assume that the number of processors avilable is $P \le N/2$. Again, think of the computation process in terms of a binary tree. Now, to compute the sum at the lowest level we require at most $\lceil N/2P \rceil$ time; the next higher level requires at most $\lceil N/4P \rceil$ time, and so on. Therefore, the time required to compute the sum T satisfies

$$T \;\le\; \lceil N/2P \rceil + \lceil N/4P \rceil + \ldots + \lceil N/2^{\lceil \log N \rceil} P \rceil$$

$$\le 1 + N/2P + 1 + N/4P + \ldots + 1 + N/2^{\lceil \log N \rceil} P$$

$$= \lceil \log N \rceil + N/P\,[\, 1/2 + 1/4 + \ldots + 1/2^{\lceil \log N \rceil}\,]$$

$$\le C \times \log N + D \times (N/P)$$

$$= O(\log N + (N/P))$$

where C and D are constants of proportionalities. Therefore, in this case, the adapted algorithm takes $O(\log N)$ time if $P = N/\log N$. The cost of this algorithm is $\log N \times (N/\log N) = N$ and the efficiency is 1. That is, we have reduced the number of processors without increasing the time complexity which implies an improvement in the cost and hence the efficiency of the adapted algorithm. This type of improvement can be made for a number of problems and may be regarded as a general technique.

## 3.6.2  Reducing the Time Complexity

The problem of finding the sum is considered again. This problem can be solved recursively by adding the sums of two smaller lists of numbers. This recursive structure was also the basis of the discussion above, where the recursion was fully unraveled. We now see how the time complexity can be reduced by partly unraveling the recursion without increasing the number of processors.

Let the recursion be unraveled until we are left with lists of size m whose sum has to be computed. We now employ one processor for each such list to obtain the sum in $O(m)$ time. After this step, we are left with only $N/m$ numbers whose sum can be computed in $O(\log N/m)$ time using the binary tree paradigm. Therefore, the time complexity of computing the complete sum can be expressed as $T = O(m + \log (N/m))$. To minimize the time complexity we require that $m = \log (N/m)$, i.e., $N = m \times 2^m$. Therefore, when $N = m \times 2^m$ we can compute the sum of N numbers in time $O(\log 2^m)$ with $2^m$ processors. The cost of this adapted algorithm is $2^m \times \log 2^m = 2^m \times m = N$ and hence the efficiency is 1. Thus, in this case, we have reduced the time complexity without increasing the number of processors required. This type of improvement can also be achieved for some other problems (see e.g., the sorting algorithm in Hirschberg 1978).

## 3.7 BIBLIOGRAPHIC NOTES

Several recent survey papers and books provide some discussion on various complexity-related issues for parallel algorithms. These include Heller (1978), Lakshmivarahan et al. (1984), Moitra and Iyengar (1987), Quinn and Deo (1984), Quinn (1987), and Akl (1989). There are some other measures of performances such as the chip area and the length of the wires connecting the processors in a given architecture. These are important when evaluating parallel algorithms for VLSI (Akl 1989). Area-time complexity measures have also received special attention for VLSI algorithms. They depend on two factors: chip area (A) and computation time (T). In particular, the complexity measure $AT^2$ is very popular in lower bound analysis of algorithms for VLSI. We have not addressed algorithms for VLSI in this book. However, the interested reader is referred to Kung (1988), and Ullman (1984).

Programming paradigms for parallel computation are included in a survey by Moitra and Iyengar (1987). The section "Techniques for improving the efficiency of parallel algorithms" owes much to their survey paper. The material presented in the section "Growing by doubling paradigm" is mostly based on the work due to Savage and Ja' Ja' (1981), Tsin and Chin (1984), Chaudhuri and Ghosh (1986), Ghosh and Bhattacharjee (1986), and Chaudhuri (1988). Programming paradigms for nonshared memory parallel computers can be found in Nelson and Snyder (1987).

## 3.8 EXERCISES

3.8.1   Applying Theorem 3.1, show that the addition of n numbers can be performed in O(log n) time using n/log n processors.

3.8.2   Make a list of some other problems for which a technique similar to that described in Section 3.6.1 can be employed to increase the efficiency of the corresponding straightforward parallel algorithms.

3.8.3   Given a list X containing $N = 2^k$ elements on which a linear order is defined. Assuming the elements in X are initially in random order, show that at least $\lceil \log N \rceil$ parallel time is required to sort X.

3.8.4   Determine how fast $x^n$ can be computed in parallel time.

3.8.5   Show that the set of values $x^2, x^3, \ldots, x^n$ can be computed in less than O(n) parallel time.

3.8.6   Develop an EREW PRAM algorithm for the list-ranking problem based on the ideas presented in Section 3.5.2.

3.8.7 Assume a set X containing $N = 2^k$ elements which are randomly ordered and let m(N) be the lower bound in parallel time to determine the largest element of X using N processors. Show that $m(N) \geq \log \log n - x$, where x is a constant (Valiant 1975).

3.8.8 Obtain the lower and upper bounds on the time required for cube network to simulate perfect shuffle and vice-versa (Siegel 1979).

3.8.9 Study Nicholas Pippenger's work defining a class of problems known as NC (Nick's Class) which are solvable in polylogarithmic time using polynomial number of processors (Pippenger 1979). Make a list of some problems which are in NC.

# 3.9 BIBLIOGRAPHY

Aho, A., Hopcroft, J., and Ullman, J. (1974). *The Design and Analysis of Computer Algorithms*. Addison-Wesley, Reading, Mass.

Akl, S. G. (1989). *The Design and Analysis of Parallel Algorithms*. Prentice Hall, Englewood Cliffs, NJ.

Brassard, G., and Bratley, P. (1988). *Algorithmics: Theory and Practice*. Prentice Hall, Englewood Cliffs, NJ.

Brent, R. P. (1974). The parallel evaluation of general arithmetic expressions. *J. ACM.* 21, 201-6.

Chaudhuri, P. (1988). Fast parallel graph searching with applications. *BIT* 28, 2-18.

Chaudhuri, P., and Ghosh, R. K. (1986). Parallel algorithms for analyzing activity networks. *BIT* 26, 418-29.

Dekel, E., Nassimi, D., and Sahni, S. (1981). Parallel matrix and graph algorithms, *SIAM J. Computing* 10, 657-75.

Eckstein, D. M., and Alton, D. A. (1977). Parallel graph processing using depth-first search. In *Proceedings of the Conference on Theoretical Computer Science,* Ontario.

Ghosh, R. K., and Bhattacharjee, G. P. (1986). Parallel algorithms for shortest paths. *IEE Proceedings* 133 Pt. E, 87-93.

Heller, D. (1978). A survey of parallel algorithms in numerical linear algebra. *SIAM Review* 20, 740-77.

Hirschberg, D. S. (1978). Fast parallel sorting algorithms. *Comm. ACM* 21, 657-61.

Kim, T., and Chwa, K. (1986). Parallel algorithms for a depth-first search and breadth-first search. *Intern. J. Computer Math.* 19, 39-54.

Kung, S. Y. (1988). *VLSI Array Processors*. Prentice Hall, Englewood Cliffs, NJ.

Lakshmivarahan, S., Dhall, S. K., and Miller, L. L. (1984). Parallel sorting algorithms. In *Advances in Computers*, vol. 23, M. Yovits, ed. Academic Press, NY, pp. 295-354.

Moitra, A., and Iyengar, S. S. (1987). Parallel algorithms for some computational problems. In *Advances in Computers*, vol. 26, M. Yovits, ed. Academic Press, NY, pp. 93-153.

Munro, I., and Paterson, M. (1973). Optimal algorithms for parallel polynomial evaluation. *J. Computer and System Sci.* 7, 189-98.

Nelson, P. A., and Snyder, L. (1987). Programming paradigms for nonshared memory parallel computers. In *The Characteristics of Parallel Algorithms*, L. H. Jamieson, D. B. Gannon, and R. J. Douglass, eds. MIT Press, pp. 3-20.

Pippenger, N. (1979). On simultaneous resource bounds. *Proceedings of the 20th Annual Symposium on Foundations of Computer Science*, IEEE Computer Society, Washington, DC, pp. 307-11.

Quinn, M. J. (1987). *Designing Efficient Algorithms for Parallel Computers*. McGraw-Hill, NY.

Quinn, M. J., and Deo, N. (1984). Parallel graph algorithms. *Computing Surveys* 16, 319-48.

Reghbati, E., and Corneil, D. G. (1978). Parallel computations in graph theory. *SIAM J. Computing* 2, 230-7.

Reif, J. H. (1985). Depth-first search is inherently sequential. *Inform. Process. Lett.* 20, 229-34.

Savage, C., and Ja' Ja', J. (1981). Fast, efficient parallel algorithms for some graph problems. *SIAM J. Computing* 10, 682-91.

Seigel, H. J. (1979). A model of SIMD machines and a comparison of various interconnection networks. *IEEE Transactions on Computers* C-28, 907-17.

Shiloach, Y., and Vishkin, U. (1982). An $O(n^2 \log n)$ parallel MAX_FLOW algorithm. *J. Algorithms* 3, 128-46.

Tarjan, R. E., and Vishkin, U. (1984) Finding biconnected components and computing tree functions in logarithmic parallel time. *Proceedings of the 25th Annual Symposium on Foundations of Computer Science*, IEEE Computer Society, Washington, DC, 12-20.

Tsin, Y. H., and Chin, F. Y. (1984). Efficient parallel algorithms for a class of graph theoretic problems. *SIAM J. Computing* 13, 580-99.

Ullman, J. (1984). *Computational Aspects of VLSI*. Computer Science Press, Rockville, Md.

Valiant, L. G. (1975). Parallelism in comparison problems. *SIAM J. Computing* 4, 348-55.

Vishkin, U. (1984). An optimal parallel connectivity algorithm. *Discrete App. Math.* 9, 197-207.

# CHAPTER 4

# Merging and Sorting

## 4.1 INTRODUCTION

Comparison problems such as merging and sorting are of fundamental importance in computer science, and much effort has been devoted to finding efficient algorithms for these problems within both serial and parallel computational models. Many algorithms use merging or sorting as an intermediate step so that the processing of information at a later stage can be performed efficiently. In this chapter, we consider the problems of merging and sorting in the context of parallel processing.

*Merging*: Given two lists $X = \{x_1, x_2, \ldots, x_m\}$ and $Y = \{y_1, y_2, \ldots, y_n\}$ whose elements are sorted in nondecreasing order, it is required to form a third sorted list $Z = \{z_1, z_2, \ldots, z_{m+n}\}$, such that each $z_i$ in Z belongs either to X or Y and each $x_i$ and each $y_i$ appears exactly once in Z.

*Sorting*: Given a list $X = \{x_1, x_2, \ldots, x_n\}$ of n elements which are in random order, it is required to arrange them in nondecreasing order. In other words, find a sequence of distinct indices $1 \leq i1, i2, \ldots, in \leq n$, such that the elements in X can be arranged to form a new list $X' = \{x_{i1}, x_{i2}, \ldots, x_{in}\}$ in which $x_{ij} \leq x_{ij+1}$ for $j = 1, 2, \ldots, n - 1$.

Merging and sorting have been extensively studied within the serial model of computation and there are efficient algorithms for them, the complexities of which match with their respective lower bounds. For merging the following serial algorithm takes $O(n)$ time in the worst case when $m = n$.

### *Algorithm* SERIAL_MERGE

Input: Two sorted lists $X = \{x_1, x_2, \ldots, x_m\}$ and $Y = \{y_1, y_2, \ldots, y_n\}$.

Output: A sorted list $Z = \{z_1, z_2, \ldots, z_{m+n}\}$ containing all the keys from X and Y in non-decreasing order.

$i := 1; j := 1; k := 1;$
*while* $i \le m$ AND $j \le n$ *do*
    *if* $x_i \le y_j$
    *then* $z_k := x_i; i := i + 1$
    *else* $z_k := y_j; j := j + 1$
    *fi*
    $k := k + 1$
*od*
*if* $i > m$
*then* copy $y_j, \ldots, y_n$ to $z_k, \ldots, z_{m+n}$
*else* copy $x_i, \ldots, x_m$ to $z_k, \ldots, z_{m+n}$
*fi*

Thus $O(n)$ is the upper bound for merging two sorted lists of length n. On the other hand, since each element of the two sorted lists must be examined at least once, no merging algorithm can exist that takes fewer than a constant multiple of n time units in the worst case. That is, the lower bound for merging is $\Omega(n)$. Since the time complexity of algorithm SERIAL_MERGE is of the same order of the lower bound of the problem, this algorithm is optimal.

For sorting by comparisons, the lower bound is $\Omega(n \log n)$, i.e., asymptotically a constant multiple of n log n operations are required to sort n elements in the worst case. In other words, no serial algorithm can sort n items in fewer than a constant multiple of n log n time units in the worst case (see Aho et al. 1974). The upper bound for the sorting problem is $O(n \log n)$ which implies that there is at least one sorting algorithm with time complexity $O(n \log n)$. Mergesort and Heapsort are two such algorithms (Aho et al. 1974; Goodman and Hedetniemi 1977). Obviously, these sorting algorithms are optimal.

The problems of merging and sorting are closely related to each other in the sense that the problem of merging is defined on sorted lists. Alternatively, several efficient sorting algorithms (both serial and parallel) are based on efficient merging techniques. Because of their close relationship, these two problems are included in the same chapter. In the section on merging, we begin by presenting Batcher's odd-even merging network in Section 4.2. In Sections 4.3, 4.4 and 4.5, merging algorithms on CREW PRAM and EREW PRAM models are described. The study of merging is concluded in Section 4.6 by presenting an algorithm implemented on a linear array of processors The problem of sorting using various parallel models of computation is considered in Sections 4.7 through 4.12. More precisely, in Sections 4.7 and 4.8 we present Batcher's parallel sorting network and Bitonic sorting network. Parallel sorting algorithms on different PRAM models are discussed in Section 4.9. Section 4.10 is devoted to discussing a sorting algorithm on a linear array of processors. Sorting on mesh connected and perfect shuffle computers are presented in Sections 4.11 and 4.12, respectively.

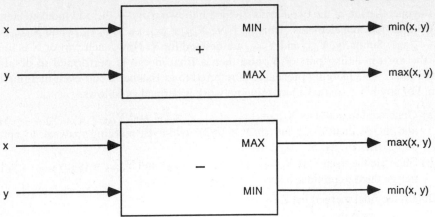

**Figure 4.1** Comparator unit ( + : low-to-high; − : high-to-low).

## 4.2 BATCHER'S ODD-EVEN MERGING NETWORK

In this section we consider a special-purpose network consisting of a collection of processing elements (PEs) for merging two sorted lists. Each PE is basically a two-input comparator unit as shown in Figure 4.1. It receives two numbers at its inputs and delivers the minimum of the two on one of its output lines labeled MIN, and the maximum of the two on the other output line MAX.

Such a comparator unit is used as the building block in the development of the merging network. The merge algorithm presented here is based on the well-known work of Batcher (1968). Let $X \{x_1 \leq x_2 \leq \ldots \leq x_n\}$ and $Y \{y_1 \leq y_2 \leq \ldots \leq y_n\}$ be two lists to be merged, and let $Z \{z_1 \leq z_2 \leq \ldots \leq z_{2n}\}$ be the final merged list. We assume for simplicity that the lists to be merged are of equal length n and $n = 2^k$, $k \geq 0$. When $k = 0$, the network is a single comparator unit. When $k = 1$, two lists $X = \{x_1, x_2\}$ and $Y = \{y_1, y_2\}$ can easily be merged using a $(2 \times 2)$ merging network with three comparator units as shown in Figure 4.2.

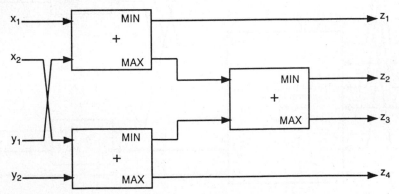

**Figure 4.2** The $(2 \times 2)$ merging network for merging two sorted lists $X = \{x_1, x_2\}$ and $Y = \{y_1, y_2\}$.

In general, each of the two lists is divided into two parts — the odd indexed elements and the even indexed elements. Thus we have $X_{odd} = \{x_1, x_3, \ldots, x_{n-1}\}$ and $X_{even} = \{x_2, x_4, \ldots, x_n\}$. Similarly, $Y_{odd}$ and $Y_{even}$ are defined for Y. Now, each part of X is merged with the corresponding part of Y, and then a final merge is performed to obtain the desired list Z. This merging procedure is referred to as Batcher's odd-even merging algorithm. For any $k \geq 1$, an $(n \times n)$ merging network is defined as follows:

1. (a) Generate the odd lists $X_{odd} = \{x_1, x_3, \ldots, x_{n-1}\}$ and $Y_{odd} = \{y_1, y_3, \ldots, y_{n-1}\}$, and merge them using an $((n/2) \times (n/2))$ odd-even merging network to obtain a sorted list $\{d_1, d_2, \ldots, d_n\}$.

   (b) Generate the even lists $X_{even} = \{x_2, x_4, \ldots, x_n\}$ and $Y_{even} = \{y_2, y_4, \ldots, y_n\}$ and merge them to produce a sorted list $\{v_1, v_2, \ldots, v_n\}$.

2. Obtain the final merged list Z from

$$z_1 = d_1$$
$$z_{2i} = \min\{d_{i+1}, v_i\}$$
$$z_{2i+1} = \max\{d_{i+1}, v_i\}$$
$$z_{2n} = v_n$$

for $i = 1, 2, \ldots, n - 1$.

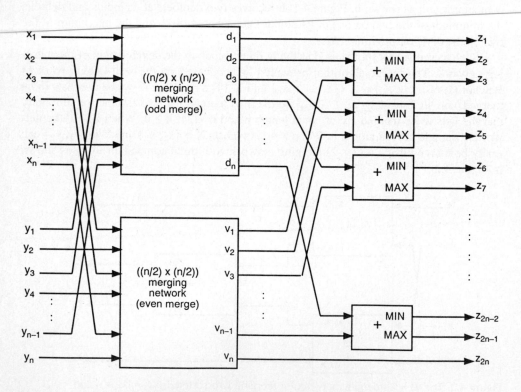

**Figure 4.3** The network for odd-even merging of two sorted lists of length n each.

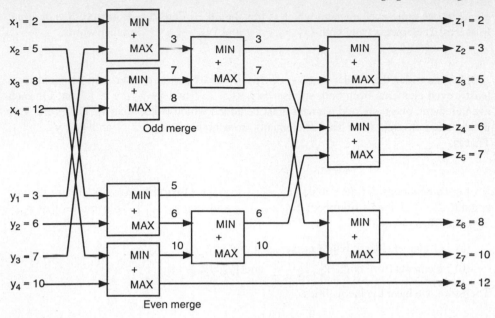

**Figure 4.4** An example of (4 × 4) odd-even merging network.

The merging of the odd lists ($X_{odd}$ and $Y_{odd}$) and the even lists ($X_{even}$ and $Y_{even}$) are performed in parallel. Each of these (($n/2$) × ($n/2$)) merging networks is obtained by applying the same rule recursively. Figure 4.3 illustrates the general network for recursive merge. A specific example for merging two sorted lists, each of length four, is shown in Figure 4.4.

The special-purpose merging network described here is very attractive because of its simplicity and because it seems to be practicable since the comparator units can be easily produced in large scale and can be well laid out on integrated circuit (IC) chips. However, there are three main limitations on the applicability of such networks. One is that these networks are designed for a specific number of inputs. The others are that the network structure is highly irregular and the length of the wires connecting the comparator units varies with n. Moreover, for very large n the number of comparator units needed becomes so high that the merging network turns out to be infeasible.

### Correctness of Odd-Even Merging

The following theorem establishes the correctness of odd-even merging.

**Theorem 4.1:** The odd-even merging technique correctly merges two sorted lists of length n into a single list of length 2n.

**Proof:** Following the notation used in this section, consider the sublist $\{d_1, d_2, \ldots, d_{i+1}\}$. Now, $d_{i+1}$ is greater than or equal to at least $i + 1$ odd elements from both sublists $\{x_1, x_3, \ldots \}$ and $\{y_1, y_3, \ldots \}$. With the exception of $x_1$ and $y_1$ there is, for each odd element, one more even element which is less than $d_{i+1}$. Thus $d_{i+1}$ is greater than or equal to at least 2i elements from both $\{x_1, x_2, \dots\}$ and $\{y_1, y_2, \dots\}$. In other words,

$$d_{i+1} \geq z_{2i}.$$

Now consider the sublist $\{v_1, v_2, \dots, v_i\}$. Clearly, $v_i$ is greater than or equal to at least i even elements from both sublists $\{x_2, x_4, \dots\}$ and $\{y_2, y_4, \dots\}$. But, for each even element, one more odd element must be added which is less than $v_i$. Therefore, $v_i$ is greater than or equal to at least 2i elements from both $\{x_1, x_2, \dots\}$ and $\{y_1, y_2, \dots\}$. That is,

$$v_i \geq z_{2i}.$$

Let us now consider the sublist $\{z_1, z_2, \dots z_{2i+1}\}$. Obviously, $z_{2i+1}$ is greater than or equal to 2i + 1 elements from both $\{x_1, x_2, \dots\}$ and $\{y_1, y_2, \dots\}$. This implies that $z_{2i+1}$ is greater than or equal to

(a) i+1 elements from both $\{x_1, x_3, \dots\}$ and $\{y_1, y_3, \dots\}$,

(b) i elements from both $\{x_2, x_4, \dots\}$ and $\{y_1, y_2, \dots\}$.

Therefore, we have the inequalities

$$z_{2i+1} \geq d_{i+1},$$
and
$$z_{2i+1} \geq v_i.$$

Since, $z_{2i} \leq z_{2i+1}$, the above four inequalities imply that

$$z_{2i} = \min\{d_{i+1}, v_i\},$$
and
$$z_{2i+1} = \max\{d_{i+1}, v_i\}$$

for i = 1, 2, ..., n − 1. Also, we have assigned $z_1$ the value $d_1$ which is the smallest value of the odd merge and $z_{2n}$ the value $v_n$ which is the largest value of the even merge. Therefore, the theorem follows.

### Complexity of Odd-Even Merging

Let T(n, n) be the time required to merge two sorted lists of length n ($=2^k$) using the merging network of Figure 4.3. We assume that each comparator unit takes constant (i.e., O(1)) time for reading inputs, performing comparison and producing outputs. Clearly, T(n, n) is the number of comparator units along the longest path through the network. The recurrence relation for T(n, n) can be written as

$$T(n, n) = \begin{cases} 1, & \text{if } k = 0 \\ T(n/2, n/2) + 1, & \text{if } k \geq 1. \end{cases}$$

The solution of these equations is

$$T(n, n) = \log n + 1 = O(\log n).$$

The number of processors used (i.e., the processor complexity) is simply the number of comparisons necessary to merge the lists. Let P(n, n) be the number of comparisons (and thus the number of comparator units) required to merge two sorted lists of length n ($=2^k$) each. By inspection of Figure 4.3, the recurrence relation for P(n, n) can be expressed as

$$P(n, n) = \begin{cases} 1, & \text{if } k = 0 \\ 2P(n/2, n/2) + (n - 1), & \text{if } k \geq 1. \end{cases}$$

Therefore, the total number of comparator units used is

$$P(n, n) = n \log n + 1 = O(n \log n).$$

The cost C(n, n) of odd-even merging is given by

$$C(n, n) = T(n, n) \times P(n, n) = O(n \log^2 n).$$

It is clear that the odd-even merging algorithm is significantly faster than the fastest known serial algorithm for this problem. However, the cost of this algorithm is far from optimal.

## 4.3 MERGING ON THE CREW PRAM MODEL

This section deals with the problem of merging using the CREW PRAM model. We begin with a simple parallel algorithm for the case when both the lists to be merged are of equal length n (say), and the number of processors available in the CREW PRAM is also n.

*Algorithm* **MERGE1_CREW**

Input: Two sorted lists $X = \{x_1, x_2, \ldots, x_n\}$ and $Y = \{y_1, y_2, \ldots, y_n\}$.

Output: A sorted list $Z = \{z_1, z_2, \ldots, z_{2n}\}$ resulting from the merging of X and Y.

*for* i = 1 *to* n *dopar*
    find the smallest $y_j$ such that $x_i < y_j$;
    *if* $y_j$ exists
    *then* $z_{i+j-1} := x_i$
    *else* $z_{n+i} := x_i$
    *fi*
    find the smallest $x_j$ such that $y_i < x_j$;
    *if* $x_j$ exists
    *then* $z_{i+j-1} := y_i$
    *else* $z_{n+i} := y_i$
    *fi*
*odpar*

All n processors execute the four steps of the loop of the algorithm MERGE1_CREW in parallel. In order to find the smallest $y_j$ such that $x_i < y_j$, in the second step, we can use the binary search algorithm. Thus this step can be implemented in time O(log n) with a single processor for each i. This is also the time complexity for the third step. Each of the two remaining steps takes O(1) time to perform the required assignment. Therefore, the overall time complexity of this algorithm, using n processors, is O(log n).

Although algorithm MERGE1_CREW is simple in structure and easy to understand, it works only when the two sorted lists to be merged are of equal length. It is also assumed that no equality occurs between an element of X and an element of Y. However, if this happens, then the algorithm can be used by assuming X's element as smaller than Y's element. Moreover, the algorithm is not cost optimal since its cost is O(n log n). We now present a parallel merging algorithm which is much more general than algorithm MERGE1_CREW. In particular, this algorithm merges two sorted lists of lengths m and n (say), respectively, where $m \leq n$. The algorithm is adaptive or self-reconfiguring in nature. That is, the algorithm can modify its behavior and works for a wide range in the number of available processors ($P \leq m$). The algorithm is also shown to be cost optimal to within a constant multiplicative factor. First, we give an informal description of the algorithm.

Assume that we are given two sorted lists $X = \{x_1, x_2, \ldots, x_m\}$ and $Y = \{y_1, y_2, \ldots, y_n\}$, where $m \leq n$, from which the final merged list $Z = \{z_1, z_2, \ldots, z_{m+n}\}$ is to be formed. The algorithm consists of two phases. The first phase preprocesses the input lists in order to facilitate the efficient merging process of the second phase.

The first phase begins by partitioning both input lists X and Y into P intervals of approximately the same size. This is done by selecting $P - 1$ distinct elements from X (Y) to form a sublist $X_s$ ($Y_s$) so that each element of $X_s$ ($Y_s$) is the first element of each partition. This partitioning can be done very easily and later will be shown explicitly. Finally, in this phase the sublists $X_s$ and $Y_s$ are merged into a list L of length $2P - 2$. While merging $X_s$ and $Y_s$ to produce L, we store, with each element in L, the list from which it originated (either X or Y) and its position (index) in that list.

The second phase accepts as inputs L, X and Y. In this phase each processor merges two sublists of X and Y, serially, and inserts them into the final list Z. Now each processor p, $2 < p \leq P$, checks the origin of the $(2P - 2)$th element in L in order to obtain its starting point for merging. If its starting point belongs to X (Y) then processor p finds the smallest element in Y (X) that is greater than this element. Processor p is responsible for merging the sublists of X and Y, which begin with these two elements. The starting point for processor 1 is $x_1$ and $y_1$. After determining the starting point for each processor, the final step of this phase is to perform serial merging of the assigned sublists and place their elements in the appropriate positions in the final list Z. Clearly, each processor p, $2 \leq p \leq P - 1$ merges and inserts into Z all of the elements that fall between the $(2P - 2)$th element and the 2Pth element of L. Processor 1 merges the elements of X and Y which are smaller than the second element of L and processor P merges the elements of X and Y that are greater than the last element of L.

Let us now consider a specific example to illustrate how this merging method works. Suppose we need to merge the following two sorted lists of lengths 8 and 11, respectively.

$$X = \{5, 8, 9, 12, 16, 17, 19, 22\}$$

$$Y = \{1, 3, 7, 10, 11, 14, 18, 21, 24, 25, 28\}$$

Let us assume that the number of processors available is $P = 3$. In the first step of phase 1, X and Y are partitioned into three sublists by picking up two distinct elements from each of the lists X and Y, respectively. Thus, we obtain

$X_s = \{9, 17\}$, and $Y_s = \{10, 21\}$.

Phase 1 is completed by merging $X_s$ and $Y_s$ as discussed, producing the list L as follows:

$$L = \{(9, 1, X), (10, 1, Y), (17, 2, X), (21, 2, Y)\}.$$

In phase 2, each processor first computes its starting point for merging its pair of sublists and then produces the merged sublists as follows:

Processor 1: starts from $x_1 = 5$, $y_1 = 1$ and merges the elements of X and Y less than the second element of L, i.e., 10.

Processor 2: starts from $x_4 = 12$, $y_4 = 10$ and merges the elements of X and Y less than the fourth element of L, i.e., 21.

Processor 3: starts from $x_8 = 22$, $y_8 = 21$ and merges all of the remaining elements of both X and Y.

Thus, the merged sublist produced by processor 1 is $\{1, 3, 5, 7, 8, 9\}$; by processor 2 is $\{10, 11, 12, 14, 16, 17, 18, 19\}$; and by processor 3 is $\{21, 22, 24, 25, 28\}$. The final merged list Z becomes

$$Z = \{1, 3, 5, 7, 8, 9, 10, 11, 12, 14, 16, 17, 18, 19, 21, 22, 24, 25, 28\}.$$

A detailed description of the CREW merging algorithm based on the discussion above is given below.

### *Algorithm* MERGE2_CREW

Input: Two sorted lists $X = \{x_1, x_2, \ldots, x_m\}$ and $Y = \{y_1, y_2, \ldots, y_n\}$, where $m \leq n$.

Output: A sorted list $Z = \{z_1, z_2, \ldots, z_{m+n}\}$ obtained by merging X and Y.

*for* i = 1 *to* P − 1 *dopar*
/* Each processor i finds $x_{is}$ and $y_{is}$ from the lists X and Y, respectively to form the sublists $X_s = \{x_{1s}, x_{2s}, \ldots, x_{(P-1)s}\}$ and $Y_s = \{y_{1s}, y_{2s}, \ldots, y_{(P-1)s}\}$ */
    $x_{is} := x_{i\lceil m/P \rceil}$;
    $y_{is} := y_{i\lceil n/P \rceil}$
*odpar*
*for* i = 1 *to* P − 1 *dopar*
/* This step constructs the list L of length 2P − 2. L is produced as a (2P − 2) × 3 array, where for each k ($1 \leq k \leq 2P - 2$), L(k, 1) contains the value of the kth element in the merging of $X_s$ and $Y_s$; L(k, 2) contains the index of its original position in $X_s$ or $Y_s$; and L(k, 3) records which of X or Y is the source of the value */
    find the smallest j such that $x_{is} < y_{js}$;
    *if* $y_{js}$ exists
    *then do*
            L(i + j − 1, 1) := $x_{is}$;
            L(i + j − 1, 2) := i;
            L(i + j − 1, 3) := X
        *od*

```
        else  do
                L(i + P - 1, 1) := x_is;
                L(i + P - 1, 2) := i;
                L(i + P - 1, 3) := X
            od
    fi
    find the smallest j such that y_is < x_js;
    if x_js exists
    then do
                L(i + j - 1, 1) := y_is;
                L(i + j - 1, 2) := i;
                L(i + j - 1, 3) := Y
            od
    else  do
                L(i + P - 1, 1) := y_is;
                L(i + P - 1, 2) := i;
                L(i + P - 1, 3) := Y
            od
    fi
odpar
for i = 1 to P dopar
```

/* Each processor i finds its starting points $BX(i)$ and $BY(i)$ for merging two sublists of X and Y, i.e., processor i will be responsible for merging the sublists beginning with $x_{BX(i)}$ and $y_{BX(i)}$ in X and Y, respectively */

```
    if i = 1
    then do
                BX(1) := 1;
                BY(1) := 1
            od
    else  if L(2i - 2, 3) = X
            then do
                    find the smallest j such that L(2i - 2, 1) < y_j;
                    BX(i) := L(2i - 2, 2) ⌈m/P⌉;
                    BY(i) := j
                od
            else  do
                    find the smallest j such that L(2i - 2, 1) < x_j;
                    BX(i) := j;
                    BY(i) := L(2i - 2, 2)⌈n/P⌉
                od
            fi
    fi
odpar
```

*for* i = 1 *to* P *dopar*

/∗ Each processor merges two sublists of X and Y and inserts the result in Z serially ∗/

    *if* i < P

        *then*  merge the sublist of X beginning at $x_{BX(i)}$ and the sublist of Y beginning at $y_{BY(i)}$ until an element greater than or equal to L(2i, 1) is reached in each of X and Y and insert the result in Z beginning at position BX(i) + BY(i) − 1

        *else*  merge the sublist of X beginning at $x_{BX(P)}$ and the sublist of Y beginning at $y_{BY(P)}$ until no element is left in either of X or Y and insert the result in Z beginning at position BX(P) + BY(P) − 1

    *fi*

*odpar*

### Complexity of Algorithm MERGE2_CREW

The first parallel for-loop requires constant time to select P − 1 distinct elements by P − 1 processors. The second parallel for-loop is also executed simultaneously by P − 1 processors. The body of this for-loop consists of two identical blocks. Each of the tasks specified consists of searching a sorted list of length P − 1 and finally executing an if-statement. For searching a sorted list of length P − 1 by a single processor, we can use the binary search algorithm which requires only O(log P) time. The if-statement performs a fixed number of assignments in both of the cases and thus takes a constant time. Thus, the second for-loop requires O(log P) time using P − 1 processors. The third parallel for-loop also consists of searching a sorted list of length at most n and performing a fixed number of assignments on each processor. Clearly, this for-loop can be implemented using the binary search algorithm in O(log n) time with P − 1 processors. The final parallel for-loop performs a serial merge of two sublists of X and Y. Now, the list L contains 2P − 2 elements which partition the final merged list Z into 2P − 1 sublists whose maximum possible size is ($\lceil m/P \rceil + \lceil n/P \rceil$). In this step, each processor produces two such sublists of Z, with the exception of processor P which produces one such sublist. Thus, the time complexity of this for-loop is O($\lceil m/P \rceil + \lceil n/P \rceil$) = O(n/P).

Hence, the overall time complexity of algorithm MERGE2_CREW denoted by T(m, n) is O((n/P) + log n) with P(1 ≤ P ≤ n) processors. The cost of the algorithm is given by

$$C(m, n) = T(m, n) \times P = O(n + P \log n)$$

which is clearly optimal for P ≤ n/log n.

## 4.4 ADAPTATION OF CREW PRAM MERGING ALGORITHM ON EREW PRAM

In algorithms MERGE1_CREW and MERGE2_CREW, concurrent read is performed each time the search algorithm is invoked. These algorithms can be adapted for use on an EREW PRAM with the same number of processors if the concurrent read operation can be efficiently simulated on an EREW PRAM. A trivial way of simulating the concurrent

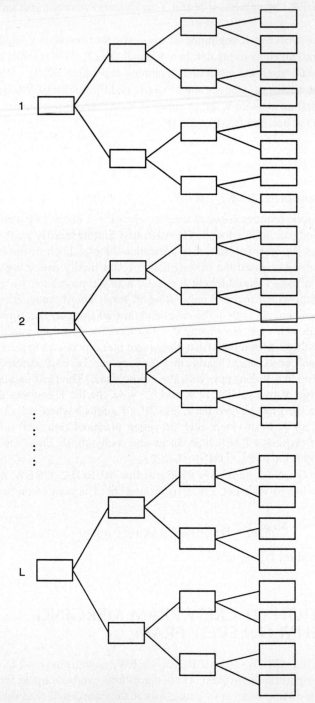

**Figure 4.5** Organization of the common memory for concurrent access to memory cells 1 to L. Each box represents a unique memory cell.

read operation is to allow the processors to read from the desired memory location one after another in some order. In this case, the simulation of each concurrent read operation will take time proportional to k, if k processors are involved in reading the content of a memory location simultaneously. Therefore, in the worst case, the adaptation of an algorithm working on a P processor CREW PRAM on a P processor EREW PRAM may increase the time complexity of the algorithm by a factor of P. Clearly, this is not an acceptable method of adapting CREW PRAM algorithms on the EREW PRAM model. In this section, we first consider the problem of simulation of simultaneous memory address access in EREW PRAM, in general. If such a simulation technique is available, any parallel algorithm on CRCW PRAM or CREW PRAM can be adapted on an EREW PRAM. The time complexity of the adapted algorithm will be increased by a factor equal to the time required to simulate the simultaneous memory address access. Also, some additional memory space will be required for this purpose. In the following two sections we will show how to perform this simulation efficiently. We assume that during concurrent write, the value in the processor with lowest index is written into the memory address. This essentially implements the other variation of concurrent write in which all of the processors attempt to write the same value simultaneously to the same memory address.

## 4.4.1 A Simple Method for Simulating Concurrent Memory Access on EREW PRAM

Let us first consider the simulation of concurrent read operations on an EREW PRAM. The method described here, based on the idea of Eckstein (1979), is straightforward but space inefficient.

Assume that the maximum number of memory cells (locations) in the common memory is L and that the number of processors is P ($P = 2^k$ for $k \geq 1$). In order to simulate concurrent read on EREW PRAM we need an additional $2L(P - 1)$ memory cells. The basic idea is to organize the memory cells in the form of binary trees, each rooted at a cell of the L locations. The number of leaves in each binary tree is P. Such a memory organization for $P = 8$ is shown in Figure 4.5. Let us now concentrate on a single memory address (location) — memory cell 1 (say) — and see how simultaneous access to this location by an arbitrary subset of processors can be handled. If during the read operation a processor $p_i$, $1 \leq i \leq P$, wants to read the content of memory location 1, then it places a request at the memory location corresponding to the ith leaf of the binary tree rooted at location 1. This is depicted in Figure 4.6 assuming that processors with indices i = 1, 2, 3, 6, 7 attempt to read the content of memory location 1 simultaneously.

The simulation algorithm consists of two phases: one is the forward phase and the other is the backward phase. In the forward phase, the read request is transmitted up to the locations representing the left-child and the right-child of 1 (Figure 4.7). Then the backward phase is initiated. At the beginning of this phase, two processors in turn read the content of location 1 (say, v) and write into the left-child and right-child positions of 1, provided that both of these originally contained read requests — otherwise one processor just ignores it. In the next step four processors, each pair in turn, read the content of their corresponding parent location and write it in the appropriate locations at level 2. Next, eight processors perform this task at level 3, and so on until level log P is reached. At this stage the content of location 1 is available to all the processors which requested

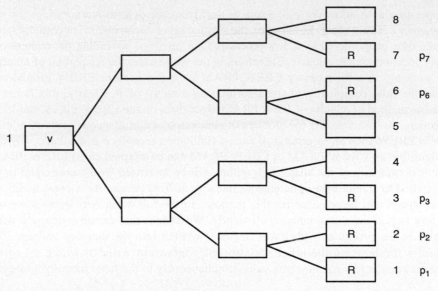

**Figure 4.6** Processors $p_1$, $p_2$, $p_3$, $p_6$, and $p_7$ attempt to read the value stored at memory location 1 simultaneously. Each has placed a request by storing R at the corresponding leaf location of the binary tree rooted at location 1.

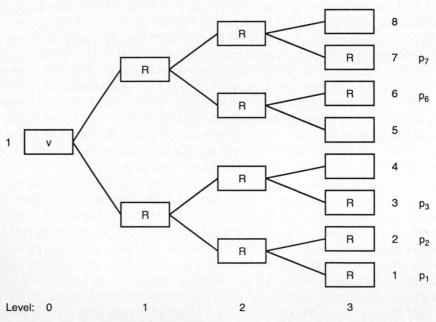

**Figure 4.7** Propagation of the read request up to the left-child and right-child of location 1.

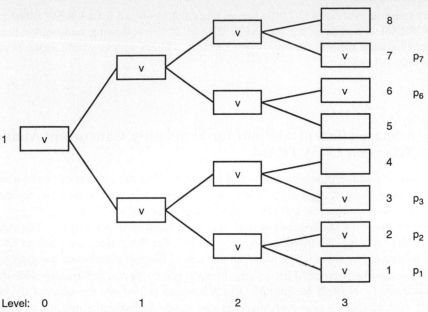

Level:  0          1          2          3

**Figure 4.8** Contents of different memory locations at the end of the simulation process corresponding to the concurrent read operation.

this value. For the specific example with eight processors, Figure 4.8 shows the memory contents at the end of the simulation process. Algorithmic descriptions of the forward and backward phases of the simulation of the concurrent read operation are straightforward and are omitted.

It is obvious that both the forward and backward phases require $O(\log P)$ time with P processors. Hence the overall time complexity of the simulation of concurrent read on an EREW PRAM is also $O(\log P)$.

In order to simulate a concurrent write operation, a processor $p_i$, $1 \leq i \leq P$, intending to write to location 1 (say) copies the value to be written into the location corresponding to the ith leaf in the binary tree rooted at 1. If, at each step of this process, both the left-child and the right-child corresponding to a location want to transmit a value to their parent location then only the content of the left-child is transmitted and that of the right-child is ignored. If a right-child location wants to transmit some value to its parent location and the left-child does not, then the value of the right-child is transmitted to the parent location. If this process is continued, then after $\log P$ steps the lowest numbered processor's value is written into the designated location. The other standard rule for concurrent write, i.e., that all the processors trying to write to the same memory location simultaneously must wish to write the same value, is clearly simulated by this method, because in this case, it is immaterial whose value gets written to that location. Thus the concurrent write operation can also be simulated in $O(\log P)$ time on a P processor EREW PRAM.

Although the simulation methods described above are very simple and fast, they require $O(LP)$ space to simulate concurrent memory address access with memory size L on a P processor EREW PRAM. Thus, using this kind of simulation, we can achieve memory space utilization of $O(1/P)$ when an algorithm designed for a CREW PRAM or a CRCW PRAM is translated for an EREW PRAM. In the following section, we present another simulation method for concurrent memory address access whose space requirement is only $O(L + P)$.

## 4.4.2  A Space-efficient Method for Simulating Concurrent Memory Access on EREW PRAM

Let us assume that the processor numbered i wants to read the content of (write a value to) the memory location $m_i$, $1 \leq i \leq P$. If a processor does not want to read (write) during a particular read (write) cycle it is provided with a nonexistent location.

The simulation of the concurrent read operation consists of three steps. The first of the three steps requires the use of a sorting algorithm. For this purpose, we use an EREW PRAM sorting algorithm which is based on the idea of Batcher's odd-even merging.

Assume that the two sorted lists, each of length n/2, to be merged are available in the common memory. Now, if we employ $O(n)$ processors to perform the tasks of the comparators then Batcher's odd-even merging can easily be implemented on an EREW PRAM in $O(\log n)$ time with $O(n)$ processors. With this as the basis we can sort n ($=2^x$ for $x \geq 0$) elements on an EREW PRAM as follows:

For $i = 0, 2, \ldots, x - 1$ do the following:

merge, in parallel, all of the $2^{x-i-1}$ pairs of ordered lists each of length $2^i$ using odd-even merge on EREW PRAM.

Clearly, in the worst case, this sorting process will take $O(\log^2 n)$ time using $O(n)$ processors.

An informal description of the simulation algorithm for the concurrent read operation is as follows:

Step 1.   Sort the pairs $(m_1, 1), (m_2, 2), \ldots, (m_P, P)$ into lexicographic order. In this order $(m_a, a) < (m_b, b)$ if and only if $m_a < m_b$ or $m_a = m_b$ and $a < b$. Let the sorted list be denoted as $(m_{j1}, j1), (m_{j2}, j2), \ldots, (m_{jP}, jP)$.

Step 2.   Processor 1 copies the content of $m_{j1}$ into $X(1, 1)$ and sets $X(1, 2)$ to TRUE. Processor i $(2 \leq i \leq P)$ copies the contents of $m_{ji}$ into $X(i, 1)$ and sets $X(i, 2)$ to TRUE, if $m_{ji-1} \neq m_{ji}$.

In this step we assume the availability of an auxiliary $P \times 3$ array denoted by X. For each i $(1 \leq i \leq P)$, $X(i, 1)$ contains the content of the location $m_{ji}$ when the algorithm terminates. $X(i, 2)$ contains either TRUE or FALSE — $X(i, 2)$ is "TRUE" if the content of $m_{ji}$ is already written in $X(i, 1)$ and "FALSE" otherwise. When the algorithm terminates $X(i, 3)$ contains the content of location $m_i$.

At the end of Step 2 the situation is as follows. For every ji $(i = 1, 2, \ldots, P)$ such that processor ji has the smallest index among these processors which want to read from location $m_{ji}$, the correct value is copied in $X(ji, 1)$. The next task is to broadcast this value to the other $X(ji, 1)$'s. This is done in Step 3.

Step 3.　　*for* i = 1 *to* P *dopar*

$r_i := 0;$

wait until X(i, 2) = TRUE;

*while* $i + 2^{r_i} \le$ P AND X($i + 2^{r_i}$, 2) = FALSE *do*

X($i + 2^{r_i}$, 2) := TRUE;

X($i + 2^{r_i}$, 1) := X(i, 1);

$r_{i+2^{r_i}} := r_i + 1;$

$r_i := r_i + 1$

*od*

X(ji, 3) := X(i, 1);

Read X(i, 3)

*odpar*

In this step, the processor i ($1 \le i \le$ P), immediately upon finding that X(i, 2) has been set to TRUE copies the content of X(i, 1) into X(r, 1) for an appropriate r > i such that $a_{jr} = a_{ji}$. Clearly, in the first cycle r = i +1 and, in the kth cycle, $r = i + 2^{k-1}$. When a processor i joins this updating process, it starts with an $r_i$ that depends on the current cycle.

The time complexity of this concurrent read simulation is dominated by the complexity of the sorting algorithm required in Step 1. If for sorting we use an adaptation of Batcher's odd-even merging algorithm on an EREW PRAM, then Step 1 can be implemented in $O(\log^2 P)$ time. Obviously, Step 2 requires a constant time. The while-loop of Step 3 is executed at most $\lceil \log P \rceil$ times and each execution of the loop takes constant time. Hence, Step 3 requires $O(\log P)$ time. The overall complexity of this concurrent read simulation algorithm on an EREW PRAM is thus $O(\log^2 P)$.

The space requirement for this algorithm is proportional to the number of processors P. Thus, to simulate concurrent read on a P processor EREW PRAM $O(L + P)$ space is required to make L shared memory addresses available.

In order to simulate a concurrent write operation we need only two steps. These are:

Step 1. Identical to Step 1 of the procedure for simulation of the concurrent read operation.

Step 2. Processor 1 writes in $m_{j1}$ the value that processor j1 intended to write there. Processor i ($2 \le i \le$ P) writes in $m_{ji}$ the value that processor ji intended to write there, provided that $m_{ji-1} \ne m_{ji}$.

Clearly, the lowest indexed processor's value is written into the common memory address. The time complexity of this algorithm is determined by the complexity of Step 1, since Step 2 requires a constant time. Thus, simulation of concurrent write on an EREW PRAM requires $O(\log^2 P)$ time. The time complexity of the sorting algorithm on an EREW PRAM dominates complexities of the simulation of both concurrent read and concurrent write operations.

## 4.4.3  Complexity of Merging on EREW PRAM

We shall now analyze the complexity of the merging algorithms developed for the CREW PRAM model, namely, algorithms MERGE1_CREW and MERGE2_CREW when adapted to work on the EREW PRAM model. In order to adapt these algorithms we only need an efficient algorithm to simulate the concurrent read operation on an EREW PRAM. We have already discussed two such simulation algorithms. One of these takes $O(\log P)$ time and $O(LP)$ space to simulate concurrent read on a P processor EREW PRAM to make available L memory addresses for concurrent access. The other algorithm takes $O(\log^2 P)$ time but only $O(L + P)$ space for the same purpose. Thus we have two ways to adapt the CREW PRAM merging algorithms on an EREW PRAM.

First, consider the algorithm MERGE1_CREW which merges two sorted lists, each of length n, to produce a sorted list of length 2n. This algorithm takes $O(\log n)$ time with n processors. In this algorithm concurrent read is required to search both the lists using the binary search algorithm by several processors simultaneously. Now, every read operation (by a single processor or multiple processors) can be simulated in either (i) $O(\log n)$ time using $O(n^2)$ space, or (ii) $O(\log^2 n)$ time using $O(n)$ space. Let us denote the time complexity of the adapted algorithm using the first (second) method to simulate concurrent read as $T_1^{EREW}(MERGE1)$ $(T_2^{EREW}(MERGE1))$.

Thus, we get

$$T_1^{EREW}(MERGE1) = O(\log^2 n) \text{ with n processors using } O(n^2) \text{ space;}$$

and    $$T_2^{EREW}(MERGE1) = O(\log^3 n) \text{ with n processors using } O(n) \text{ space.}$$

Using a similar notation, we find the cost of each of these adapted algorithms to be:

$$C_1^{EREW}(MERGE1) = O(n \log^2 n);$$

and    $$C_2^{EREW}(MERGE1) = O(n \log^3 n).$$

Thus, both of these adapted algorithms are far from being cost optimal.

Now consider the algorithm MERGE2_CREW which merges two sorted lists of lengths m and n, respectively, to produce a sorted list of length m + n. This algorithm has time complexity of $O((n/P) + \log n)$ with P $(P \leq n)$ processors on a CREW PRAM. Using similar notation to that above, we find the complexities of the adapted algorithms based on MERGE2_CREW on an EREW PRAM to be:

$$T_1^{EREW}(MERGE2) = O((n/P) \log P + \log n \log P) \text{ with P } (P \leq n)$$
$$\text{processors using } O(nP) \text{ space;}$$

and    $$T_2^{EREW}(MERGE2) = O((n/P) \log^2 P + \log n \log^2 P) \text{ with P } (P \leq n)$$
$$\text{processors using } O(n) \text{ space.}$$

The costs of these algorithms are given by

$$C_1^{EREW}(MERGE2) = O(n \log P + P \log n \log P);$$

and    $$C_2^{EREW}(MERGE2) = O(n \log^2 P + P \log n \log^2 P).$$

Again, these adapted algorithms are not cost optimal. It is clear that, in order to reduce the additional space requirements of the adapted algorithms by a factor of P $(P \leq n)$, we increased the execution time, and hence the cost of each of the algorithms, by a factor of log P. A cost optimal merging algorithm that works on an EREW PRAM and uses only $O(n)$ space is presented next.

# 4.5 AN EFFICIENT MERGING ALGORITHM ON EREW PRAM

The parallel merging algorithm presented in this section for an EREW PRAM is adaptive (self-reconfiguring) and cost optimal. We have seen earlier that a straightforward adaptation of a cost optimal CREW PRAM algorithm achieved simply by simulating the concurrent read operation on an EREW PRAM, cannot produce a cost optimal EREW merge algorithm. This suggests that a different approach is required to design an efficient parallel merge algorithm, particularly for an EREW PRAM. The algorithm presented here is based on the work of Akl and Santoro (1987).

The basis for this algorithm is a serial algorithm that finds the median of two sorted lists. More precisely, given two sorted lists $X = \{x_1, x_2, \ldots, x_m\}$ and $Y = \{y_1, y_2, \ldots, y_n\}$, and let $Z$ be the sorted list of length $m + n$ obtained by merging $X$ and $Y$. We need to find the lower median, i.e., the $\lceil (m + n)/2 \rceil$th element of $Z$. We show that it is possible using a serial algorithm with time complexity $O(\log(\min\{m, n\}))$ to find a pair of values $(x_r, y_s)$ satisfying the following two properties:

(P1) One element of the pair $(x_r, y_s)$ is the lower median of $Z$. That is, either $x_r$ or $y_s$ is greater than precisely $\lceil (m + n)/2 \rceil - 1$ elements and less than precisely $\lfloor (m + n)/2 \rfloor$ elements of $Z$.

(P2) If $x_r$ ($y_s$) is the lower median, then $y_s$ ($x_r$) is either the largest element in $Y$ ($X$) less than or equal to $x_r$ ($y_s$), or the smallest element in $Y$ ($X$) greater than or equal to $x_r$ ($y_s$).

It can be seen that $x_r$ is the median of $Z$ if one of the following conditions is satisfied:

(a) $x_r > y_s$ and $r + s - 1 = \lceil (m + n)/2 \rceil - 1$,

(b) $x_r < y_s$ and $(m + n) - (r + s - 1) = \lfloor (m + n)/2 \rfloor$;

and $y_s$ is the median of $Z$ otherwise.

We refer to $(x_r, y_s)$ as the median pair of $Z$, and $r$ and $s$ as the indices of the median pair. The most important feature of the median pair-finding algorithm is that it finds the median pair (one of which is the median of $Z$) without merging $X$ and $Y$. The algorithm consists of a sequence of stages. At the end of each stage some elements which are no longer of interest as far as the next stage is concerned are deleted from consideration from both $X$ and $Y$. Let us assume that $x$ and $y$ are the medians of the elements of $X$ and $Y$ still under consideration at the beginning of a stage. Also let $r_x$ and $r_y$ be the numbers of the remaining elements to be examined in $X$ and $Y$, respectively. Now each stage proceeds as follows: $x$ and $y$ are compared; if $y \geq x$ ($x \geq y$), then all elements in $X$ ($Y$) preceding and including $x$ ($y$), and all elements in $Y$ ($X$) that follow $y$ ($x$), are removed from consideration. This process is repeated until one element remains to be considered in at least one of the two lists. Then the median pair is determined from a finite set of element pairs. The details of the median pair-finding algorithm are given below.

## *Algorithm* SERIAL_MEDIAN_PAIR

Input: Two sorted lists, $X = \{x_1, x_2, \ldots, x_m\}$ and $Y = \{y_1, y_2, \ldots, y_n\}$.

Output: The median pair $(x_r, y_s)$.

LX := 1; LY := 1; HX := m; HY := n;
$r_x$ := m; $r_y$ := n; u := $\lceil m/2 \rceil$; v := $\lceil n/2 \rceil$;
*while* $r_x$ > 1 AND $r_y$ > 1 *do*
    *if* $x_u \geq y_v$
    *then do*
            $r_x$ := u – LX + 1;
            $r_y$ := HY – v;
            HX := u;
            LY := v + 1
        *od*
    *else  do*
            $r_x$ := HX – u;
            $r_y$ := v – LY + 1;
            LX := u + 1;
            HY := v
        *od*
    *fi*
    u := LX + $\lceil (HX - LX - 1)/2 \rceil$;
    v := LY + $\lceil (HY - LY - 1)/2 \rceil$
*od*
U := $\{x_{u-1}, x_u, x_{u+1}\}$;
V := $\{y_{v-1}, y_v, y_{v+1}\}$;
find the pair $(x_r, y_s) \in U \times V$ satisfying properties P1 and P2;
*if* one such pair exists
*then* return the pair $(x_r, y_s)$
*else* return the pair for which the sum of the two elements is minimum
*fi*

It can be seen that with the exception of the while-loop, all the remaining steps require constant time. The body of the while-loop is executed no more than log(min {m, n}) times and on each occasion requires a constant time. Thus, the overall time complexity of algorithm SERIAL_MEDIAN_PAIR is O(log (min{m, n})).

Using algorithm SERIAL_MEDIAN_PAIR as a building block we can develop an algorithm to merge two sorted lists X = $\{x_1, x_2, \ldots, x_m\}$ and Y= $\{y_1, y_2, \ldots, y_n\}$, to produce the sorted list Z = $\{z_1, z_2, \ldots, z_{m+n}\}$ on an EREW PRAM. We present below an informal description of this algorithm. It has two major steps.

Step 1:  Partition, in parallel, each of X and Y using P ($1 \leq P \leq m + n$) processors, into P (possibly empty) sublists $\{X_1, X_2, \ldots, X_P\}$ and $\{Y_1, Y_2, \ldots, Y_P\}$ in such a way that the following conditions hold:

(i) $|X_i| + |Y_i| = (m + n)/P$, $1 \leq i \leq P$, and

(ii) all elements in the merged list $X_i.Y_i$ ( we denote by $X_i.Y_j$ the list formed by merging the lists $X_i$ and $Y_j$) are less than those elements in the merged list $X_{i+1}.Y_{i+1}$, for $1 \leq i \leq P$.

Step 2:  Merge serially each pair of sublists $X_i$ and $Y_i$ using processor $p_i$, $1 \leq i \leq P$.

We shall now see how Step 1 can be efficiently implemented using the median pair-finding algorithm. Let $X_{ij}$ denote the sublist $(x_i, x_{i+1}, \ldots, x_j)$, if $i \leq j$; otherwise $X_{ij}$ is empty. $Y_{ij}$ is defined similarly. The implementation of Step 1 consists of log P stages as described below.

Stage 1: Processor $p_1$ finds the indices x and y of the median pair of $X_{1m} \cdot Y_{1n}$, and communicates the values (x + 1, m, y + 1, n) to processor $p_2$.

Stage k ($2 \leq k \leq \log P$): Processor $p_i$ ($1 \leq i \leq 2^{k-1}$), which has received the 4-tuple (a, b, c, d) in the previous stage, finds the indices e and f of the median pair of $X_{ab} \cdot Y_{cd}$. It then communicates the values (a, e, c, f) to processor $p_{2i-1}$ and the values (e + 1, b, f + 1, d) to processor $p_{2i}$.

This implementation of Step 1 of the EREW merging algorithm indicates that, during each stage, the processors work on mutually disjoint sublists to determine the new position. Thus the processors do not need to engage in concurrent read operations.

Step 2 of the EREW merging algorithm can be implemented in a straightforward manner. Assume that (a, b, c, d) are the values communicated to processor $p_i$ at the last stage of Step 1. Then $X_i = X_{ab}$ and $Y_i = Y_{cd}$ and the result of merging $X_i$ and $Y_i$ is placed in locations ((i − 1)(m + n)/P) + 1 to min{i(m + n)/P, (m + n)} of Z.

**Complexity Analysis**

In order to analyze the time complexity of the EREW merging algorithm discussed above, consider Step 1 first. Each processor involved in the computation at stage k of Step 1 has to find the median pair of $(m + n)/2^{k-1}$ elements. Thus each of the log P stages of Step 1 can be performed in time log $((m + n)/2^{k-1})$ + C, where C is a constant representing the time required for communicating the result to two other processors through the shared memory. Since there are log P stages, the overall time complexity of Step 1 is O(log P log (m + n)).

Step 2 of the algorithm requires each processor to merge at most (m + n)/P elements. This step can be performed using a linear merging algorithm and thus requires O((m + n)/P) time. Therefore, the overall time complexity of the EREW merging algorithm is O((m + n)/P + log P log (m + n)). If we assume m ≤ n, then this time complexity can be expressed as

$$T^{EREW}(\text{MERGE}) = O(n/P + \log P \log n).$$

The cost of this EREW merging algorithm is given by

$$C^{EREW}(\text{MERGE}) = O(n + P \log P \log n),$$

which is optimal for $P \leq n/\log^2 n$.

# 4.6 MERGING ON LINEAR ARRAY OF PROCESSORS

In this section, we present a parallel merging algorithm for an SIMD machine in which processors are interconnected in a one-dimensional array. We assume that there are 2n processors connected in a one-dimensional array and that they contain two sorted lists each of length n. One sorted list is stored in the first n processors and the other in the remaining n processors. The merging algorithm rearranges these elements in such a manner that the kth-smallest element is placed in the kth processor. The algorithm presented here is due to Thompson and Kung (1977). It is an implementation of Batcher's odd-even merging algorithm on a one-dimensional array of processors.

The algorithm uses shuffle and unshuffle operations on a linearly connected array. For a linear array of processors numbered 0 through n − 1, an unshuffle operation on the elements stored in them is equivalent to moving the elements stored in the odd-indexed processors to the right half of the array and the even-indexed processors to the left half. An example illustrating this operation is given in Figure 4.9a for an eight-processor linear array.

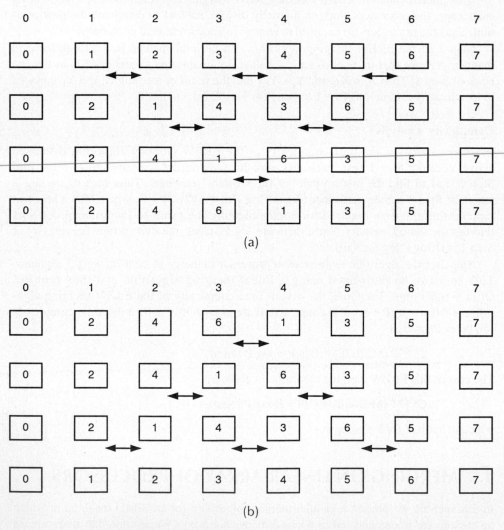

(a)

(b)

**Figure 4.9** (a) Unshuffle; and (b) shuffle operations on a linear array of eight processors.

The inverse pattern of interchanges is shown in Figure 4.9b which illustrates the shuffle operation on this eight-processor linear array. Both the unshuffle and shuffle operations can be implemented on a linear array of 2n processors in n − 1 interchanges or 2(n − 1) routing steps. An informal description of the algorithm is given below.

*Algorithm* **MERGE_LINEAR_ARRAY**

Input: Two sorted lists each of size n stored in a linearly connected array of 2n processors. One list is stored in the first n processors and the other list is stored in the other n processors.

Output: A merged list of the inputs in which the kth smallest element is placed in the kth processor.

*for* i = 1 *to* (n − 1) *do*
    *for* j = (n − i − 1) *downto* 0 *dopar*
        $p_{i+2j}$ and $p_{i+2j+1}$ interchange their contents
    *odpar*
*od*
merge the odd- and even-numbered terms;
*for* i = (n − 1) *downto* 1 *do*
    *for* j = 0 *to* (n − i − 1) *dopar*
        $p_{i+2j}$ and $p_{i+2j+1}$ interchange their contents
    *odpar*
*od*
*for* i = 0 *to* (n − 2) *dopar*
    $p_{2i+1}$ compares its element with that of $p_{2i+2}$, keeps the smaller of these, and routes
        the other number to $p_{2i+2}$
*odpar*

Figure 4.10 illustrates the execution of the algorithm when merging the lists X = {20, 22, 25, 30} and Y = {12, 18, 26, 28}.

**Complexity Analysis**

The first for-loop of algorithm MERGE_LINEAR_ARRAY performs the unshuffle operation and, as already mentioned, requires (n − 1) interchanges or 2(n − 1) routing steps. The merging of the odd- and even-numbered terms can be done recursively in parallel. If T(n, n) is the time required for merging two sorted lists each of length n, then this parallel recursive step can be implemented in time T(n/2, n/2) (i.e., the number of comparison steps). Similarly, if R(2n) is the number of routing steps needed by the algorithm, then this step requires R(n) routings. The second for-loop performs the shuffle operation and the number of routing steps required is the same as that for the unshuffle operation (the first for- loop). Finally, in the third for-loop each parallel step requires one comparison and two routing steps.

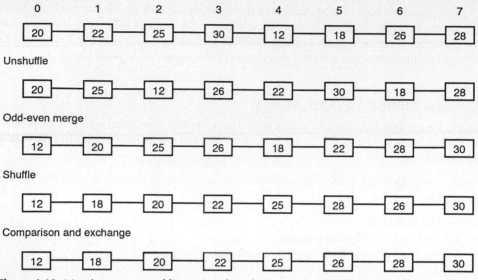

**Figure 4.10**  Merging two sorted lists using algorithm MERGE_LINEAR_ARRAY.

Thus, the number of comparisons required by algorithm MERGE_LINEAR_ARRAY is given by

$$T(n, n) = \begin{cases} 1, & \text{if } n = 1 \\ T(n/2, n/2) + 1, & \text{if } n > 1 \end{cases}$$

from which it follows that $T(n, n) = \log n + 1$.

Likewise, the number of routing steps can be expressed as

$$R(2n) = \begin{cases} 2, & \text{if } n = 1 \\ R(n) + (4n - 2), & \text{if } n > 1 \end{cases}$$

from which it follows that $R(2n) = 8n - 2 \log n - 6$.

## 4.7  BATCHER'S PARALLEL SORTING NETWORK

Batcher's odd-even merging network is used as the basis for the construction of a parallel sorting network. Let $X = \{x_1, x_2, \ldots, x_n\}$ be a list of $n = 2^k$, $k \geq 0$, arbitrary numbers to be sorted. The idea is initially to use $n/2$ comparator units to create $n/2$ sorted lists of length 2. At the second stage, $n/4$ ($2 \times 2$) merging networks are used to merge each pair of sorted lists of length 2 to form sorted lists of length 4. This process continues until two sorted lists of length $n/2$ are merged by using one $((n/2) \times (n/2))$ merging network to form the required sorted list of length $n$. The collection of the odd-even merging networks employed in this manner forms what is referred to as the odd-even sorting network. More precisely, Batcher's odd-even sorting algorithm may be presented as follows :

*Algorithm* **ODD_EVEN_SORT**

Input: An arbitrary list of n numbers.

Output: The input list sorted into nondecreasing order.

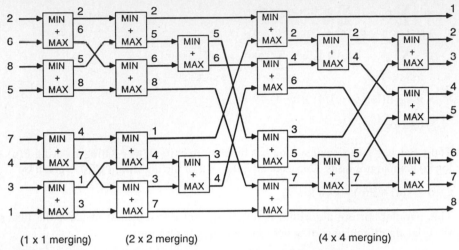

**Figure 4.11** Odd-even sorting network to sort a list of eight numbers.

*for* i = 0 *to* k − 1 *do*
   *for* all of $2^{k-i-1}$ pairs of sorted lists *dopar*
       merge two sorted lists of length $2^i$ to form a sorted list of length
         $2^{i+1}$ using Batcher's odd-even merging algorithm
  *odpar*
*od*

The odd-even sorting network for sorting a list X = {2, 6, 8, 5, 7, 4, 3, 1} is illustrated in Figure 4.11.

**Complexity Analysis**

Let T(n) be the time required to sort an arbitrary list of n numbers using P(n) comparator units on Batcher's odd-even sorting network. Then, T(n) can be expressed as follows:

$$T(n) = \sum_{0 \le i \le k-1} T(2^i, 2^i),$$

where $T(2^i, 2^i)$ is the time required to merge two sorted lists of length $2^i$ using an odd-even merging network. But we have already seen that T(n, n) = log n + 1. Therefore,

$$T(n) = \sum_{0 \le i \le k-1} (i + 1)$$

$$= \log n(\log n + 1)/2$$

$$= O(\log^2 n).$$

Now, to obtain the processor complexity, we observe that, at stage i we need, to merge $2^{k-i-1}$ pairs of sorted lists each of length $2^i$, a total of $p_i = 2^{k-i-1}P(2^i, 2^i)$ comparator units where $P(2^i, 2^i)$ is the number of comparator units required to merge two sorted lists each of length $2^i$ using the odd-even merging network. Thus, we can express P(n) as

$$P_n = \sum_{0 \le i \le k-1} P_i = \sum_{0 \le i \le k-1} 2^{k-i-1} P(2^i, 2^i)$$

$$= \sum_{0 \le i \le k-1} 2^{k-i-1}(i2^i + 1) = \sum_{0 \le i \le k-1} i2^{k-1} + \sum_{0 \le i \le k-1} 2^{k-i-1}$$

$$= n \log n(\log n - 1)/4 + (n - 1)$$

$$= O(n \log^2 n).$$

Thus, Batcher's odd-even sorting has time complexity $T(n) = O(\log^2 n)$ using $P(n) = O(n \log^2 n)$ comparator units. Consequently, the cost of the algorithm $C(n)$ is given by

$$C(n) = T(n) \times P(n) = O(n \log^4 n).$$

This parallel sorting algorithm is obviously not cost optimal because the fastest known serial algorithm for sorting has time complexity $O(n \log n)$.

## 4.8 BITONIC SORTING NETWORK

In this section, we present another network sorting scheme known as the *bitonic sort* (Batcher 1968). Bitonic sorting networks are based on the idea of merging pairs of sublists or subsequences having the bitonic property defined as follows:

A sequence (or list) $\{x_1, x_2, \ldots, x_{2n}\}$ is said to be bitonic if either (i) there exists an index $j$, $1 \le j \le 2n$, such that $x_1 \le x_2 \le \ldots \le x_j \ge x_{j+1} \ge x_{j+2} \ge \ldots \ge x_{2n}$, or (ii) there exists a cyclic shift of indices for which condition (i) is satisfied.

Let $\{x_1, x_2, \ldots, x_{2n}\}$ be a given bitonic sequence of size (or order) $2n$, where $n = 2^k$ for some integer $k \ge 0$. Although the algorithm does not require that the length of the ascending portion of the sequence be equal to the length of its descending portion, we assume here, for convenience, that the lengths of the two portions are equal. Thus, we have $x_1 \le x_2 \le \ldots \le x_n$ and $x_{n+1} \ge x_{n+2} \ge \ldots \ge x_{2n}$. Now, consider the following two sequences constructed from the given bitonic sequence:

$$\min(x_1, x_{n+1}), \min(x_2, x_{n+2}), \ldots, \min(x_n, x_{2n})$$

and       $\max(x_1, x_{n+1}), \max(x_2, x_{n+2}), \ldots, \max(x_n, x_{2n})$.

Both of these sequences of order $n$ are bitonic. In addition, each element in the first sequence is smaller than every element in the second sequence, i.e., $\max\{\min(x_i, x_{n+i}) \mid i = 1, 2, \ldots, n\} \le \min\{\max(x_i, x_{n+i}) \mid i = 1, 2, \ldots, n\}$.

These properties suggest that we can sort a bitonic sequence $\{x_1, x_2, \ldots, x_{2n}\}$ into a sorted sequence by constructing a sorting network as shown below:

 (i) A single bitonic sequence of order $2n$ is transformed into two bitonic sequences of lengths $n$ in a single compare and exchange step using $n$ comparator units.

(ii) Since each of these two subsequences is bitonic we can sort each of them recursively using a sorting network to sort bitonic sequences of order $n$. Clearly, the $n$ smallest elements of the complete sorted sequence of length $2n$ will be produced by one of these sorting networks and the $n$ largest elements by the other.

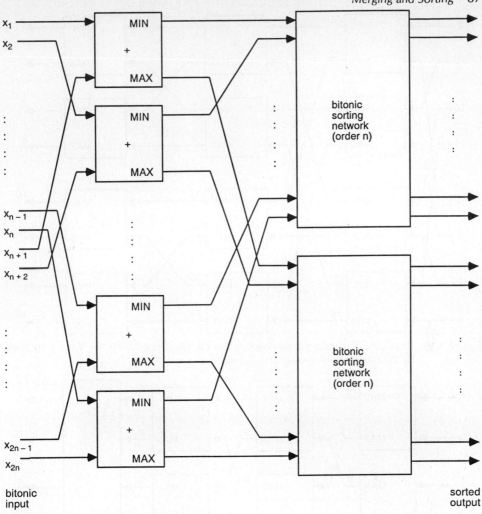

**Figure 4.12** Bitonic sorting network of order 2n.

A general bitonic sorting network is shown in Figure 4.12. A specific network for sorting a bitonic sequence of order 8 is given in Figure 4.13.

If an input sequence to be sorted $X = \{x_1, x_2, \ldots, x_n\}$, $n = 2^k$ for some integer $k \geq 0$, is not bitonic, then bitonic subsequences of $X$ are sorted and combined to form larger bitonic subsequences. This process is continued until a bitonic sequence of length $n$ is obtained. This sequence is then sorted to complete the process. In order to produce the intermediate bitonic subsequences bitonic sorting networks of appropriate order are used. A network for sorting an arbitrary sequence (not bitonic) of order 8 is shown in Figure 4.14. It can be seen that, in the first part of the network, which produces the intermediate bitonic subsequences, both "positive" (+) and "negative" (−) types of comparator units are required.

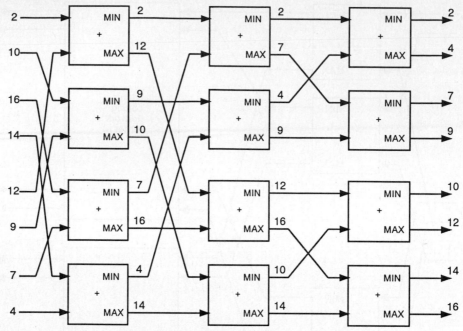

**Figure 4.13** This figure illustrates the sorting of a bitonic sequence {2, 10, 16, 14, 12, 9, 7, 4} by the bitonic sorting network of order 8.

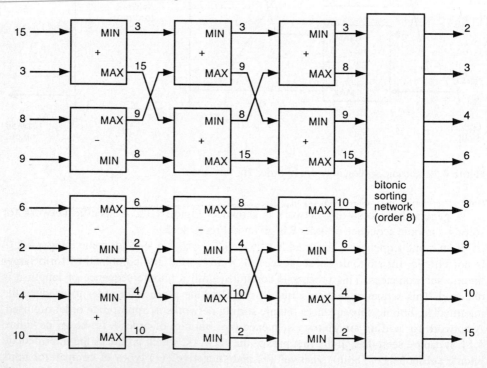

**Figure 4.14** Bitonic sorting network for sorting an arbitrary sequence of order 8.

**Complexity Analysis**

Let us first analyze the time and processor complexities of the network for sorting a bitonic sequence of order $2n$ where $n = 2^k$, $k \geq 0$. From Figure 4.12, we see that the time complexity of this algorithm, denoted by $T(2n)$, can be expressed as follows :

$$T(2n) = \begin{array}{ll} 1, & \text{if } k = 0 \\ T(n) + 1, & \text{if } k \geq 1. \end{array}$$

The solution of these equations is $T(2n) = \log n + 1$. Thus, $T(2n) = O(\log n)$. Similarly, following Figure 4.12, we can express the total number of comparator units required by the network as

$$P(2n) = \begin{array}{ll} 1, & \text{if } k = 0 \\ 2P(n) + n, & \text{if } k \geq 1. \end{array}$$

From which it can be verified that $P(2n) = n \log n + n$, i.e., $P(2n) = O(n \log n)$.

If an input sequence $\{x_1, x_2, \ldots, x_n\}$, $n = 2^k$, $k \geq 0$, is not bitonic, then, as has been discussed above, we have to use bitonic sorting networks of appropriate order to create the bitonic subsequences stage by stage. At the ith stage, $i = 0, 1, \ldots, k - 1$, $2^{k-i-1}$ bitonic sorting networks of order $2^{i+1}$ are needed. The total time for this sorting scheme is expressed as:

$$T(n) = \sum_{0 \leq i \leq k-1} T(2^{i+1}) = \sum_{0 \leq i \leq k-1} (i + 1)$$

$$= \log n(\log n + 1)/2$$

$$= O(\log^2 n).$$

We can express the total number of comparator units needed as

$$P(n) = \sum_{0 \leq i \leq k-1} 2^{k-i-1} P(2^{i+1}) = \sum_{0 \leq i \leq k-1} 2^{k-i-1}(i2^i + 2^i)$$

$$= n \log n(\log n + 1)/4$$

$$= O(n \log^2 n).$$

The cost of this sorting network is $O(n \log^4 n)$, which is clearly not optimal.

# 4.9 SORTING ON PRAM MODELS

In this section sorting algorithms on synchronous shared-memory models — i.e., PRAM models — are considered. All three types of PRAM, namely, the CRCW PRAM, the CREW PRAM, and the EREW PRAM models, are considered as models of computation for developing the algorithms.

## 4.9.1 Sorting on CRCW PRAM

The CRCW PRAM is the most unrestricted and strongest PRAM model. When two or more processors attempt to write concurrently into the same memory location it is assumed that each intends to write either 0 or 1 into that location. Now, the question arises as to what value the memory location will assume after such a concurrent write operation. Here, we assume that the sum of all the values (0's and 1's), which the processors intend to write, will actually be written into that location. This is, of course, a very strong conflict resolution rule for a CRCW PRAM. However, using this rule, it is shown that a parallel sorting algorithm can be designed which requires constant time to sort any number of elements on an unbounded CRCW PRAM. More precisely, a list of n elements can be sorted in $O(1)$ time using $O(n^2)$ processors. This algorithm uses ideas of Kucera (1982) for finding the maximum or minimum of n elements on a CRCW PRAM. In the sorting algorithm, each element is compared in parallel with all other elements (including itself) to find its position in the final sorted list. It is assumed that if two elements are equal then the element occurring first in the unsorted list is considered to be the smaller of the two. The details of the algorithm are given below.

*Algorithm* **SORT_CRCW**

Input: An arbitrary list of n elements $X = \{x_1, x_2, \ldots, x_n\}$.

Output: The sorted input list where the elements are in nondecreasing order.

*for* i = 1 *to* n *dopar*
   *for* j = 1 *to* n *dopar*
      *if* $x_i > x_j$
        *then* processor $p_{ij}$ stores 1 in location $m_i$
      *else* processor $p_{ij}$ stores 0 in location $m_i$
      *fi*
   *odpar*
*odpar*
*for* j = 1 *to* n *dopar*
   processor $p_{1j}$ copies $x_j$ into location $m_{i+1}$ of X
*odpar*

As an illustration, the sorting of a list containing eight numbers is shown in Figure 4.15.

### Complexity Analysis

In algorithm SORT_CRCW, the first nested for-loop requires $n^2$ processors to compute $m_i$, i = 1, 2, \ldots, n in $O(1)$ time. The second for-loop requires n processors to produce the final sorted list in $O(1)$ time. Thus, the overall time complexity of this CRCW PRAM sorting algorithm is $O(1)$ using $n^2$ processors. The cost of the algorithm is $O(n^2)$ which is not optimal.

This sorting algorithm has not much practical value since in addition to requiring $n^2$ processors it assumes simultaneous memory access during both read and write operations. However, its importance is to show that, by assuming a very strong conflict resolution rule, it is possible to sort an arbitrary list in constant time, irrespective of the size of the list.

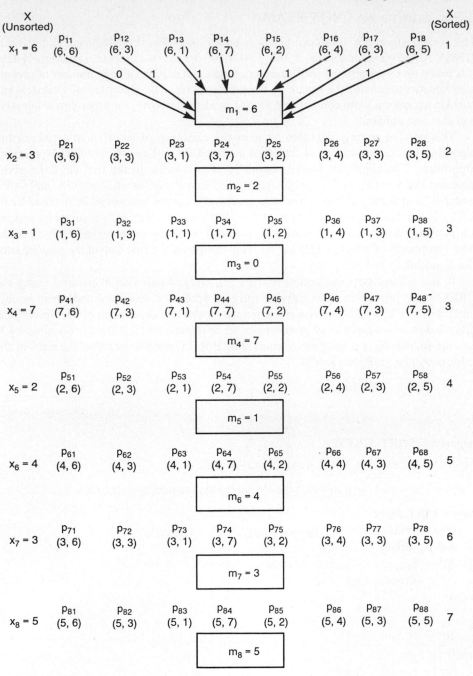

**Figure 4.15** Sorting eight numbers using the CRCW PRAM model. The labels on the arrowheads indicate the values which the different processors attempt to write to location $m_1$ simultaneously. The value assumed by location $m_i$, $1 \le i \le 8$, after the comparison step is also shown.

## 4.9.2  Sorting on CREW PRAM

The sorting algorithm developed below is based on the work of Shiloach and Vishkin (1981). Although the algorithm SORT_CRCW of the previous section is extremely fast, it is based on a very strong conflict resolution rule and requires a large number of processors which varies with the square of the problem size. The algorithm of Shiloach and Vishkin assumes a write conflict-free PRAM model. Moreover, the algorithm is adaptive and also cost optimal.

This parallel sorting algorithm assumes the existence of an efficient serial sorting algorithm to sort the sublists of the given unsorted list and an efficient CREW merging algorithm. The algorithm consists basically of two steps. In the first step, the given unsorted list $X = \{x_1, x_2, \ldots, x_n\}$ is partitioned into P sublists of sizes $\lfloor n/P \rfloor$ and $\lceil n/P \rceil$, where P ($\leq$ n) is the number of available processors. Let the processors be denoted by $p_i$, $1 \leq i \leq P$ and the P sublists of X by $X_i$, $1 \leq i \leq P$. Now, each sublist $X_i$ is sorted by processor $p_i$ using an efficient serial sorting algorithm. For this purpose, we use Quicksort, the time complexity of which is O(N log N). This completes the first step of the parallel sorting algorithm.

In the second step, the sorted sublists are merged pairwise in parallel using the CREW merge algorithm. This pairwise merging process is continued until there is only one list of size n. This is the required sorted list. A detailed description of the algorithm is given below. For simplicity of presentation, let us assume that n is exactly divisible by P, i.e., the sublists $X_i$, $1 \leq i \leq P$ are of equal size. If this is not the case then the sizes of the sublists will be $\lfloor n/P \rfloor$ and $\lceil n/P \rceil$.

*Algorithm* **SORT_CREW**

Input: An arbitrary list $X = \{x_1, x_2, \ldots, x_n\}$ of n elements.

Output: The sorted input in which the elements are in nondecreasing order.

*for* i = 1 *to* P *dopar*
  read the sublist $X_i = \{x_{(i-1)n/P +1}, x_{(i-1)n/P +2}, \ldots, x_{i(n/P)}\}$;
  sort $X_i$ serially;
  $X_i^1 := X_i$;
  $p_i^1 := \{$Processor $p_i\}$
*odpar*

s := 1;
t := P;
*while* t > 1 *do*
  *for* j = 1 *to* $\lfloor t/2 \rfloor$ *dopar*
    $p_j^{s+1} := p^s_{2j-1} \cup p^s_{2j}$;
    merge the sorted sublists $X^s_{2j-1}$ and $X^s_{2j}$ into $X_j^{s+1}$ using the
      set $p_j^{s+1}$ of processors
  *odpar*

*if* t is odd
*then do*

$$p^{s+1}_{\lceil t/2 \rceil} := p_t^{s};$$
$$X^{s+1}_{\lceil t/2 \rceil} := X_t^{s}$$

    *od*
*fi*
  s := s + 1;
  t := $\lceil t/2 \rceil$
*od*

**Complexity Analysis**

The algorithm SORT_CREW has a for-loop and a while-loop. The for-loop is executed in parallel by all P processors. Each processor $p_i$ is required to sort the sublist $X_i$, $1 \leq i \leq P$, serially. For this purpose we use Quicksort and, since the size of each $X_i$, $1 \leq i \leq P$, is n/P, this for-loop requires time $O((n/P) \log (n/P))$.

The while-loop is executed $\lceil \log P \rceil$ times. It is clear that for each merge operation the ratio between the number of elements and the number of processors involved is bounded by $\lceil n/P \rceil$. Therefore, the time complexity of each iteration of this while-loop is $O((n/P) + \log n)$ if algorithm MERGE2_CREW is used for the merging step. Since the while-loop is executed $\lceil \log P \rceil$ times, the overall time complexity of the while-loop is $O(\log P ((n/P) + \log n))$. Considering both the for-loop and the while-loop, the time complexity of algorithm SORT_CREW is given by

$$T(n) = O((n/P) \log (n/P) + \log P ((n/P) + \log n))$$
$$= O((n/P) \log n + \log P \log n)$$

using $P \leq n$ processors.

The cost of this algorithm is

$$C(n) = P \times T(n) = O(n \log n + P \log P \log n).$$

Thus, the algorithm SORT_CREW is cost optimal for $P \leq n/\log n$.

## 4.9.3  Adaptation of CREW PRAM Sorting Algorithm on EREW PRAM

We have seen in Section 4.4, when adapting CREW PRAM merging algorithms on EREW PRAM, that both the concurrent read and concurrent write operations can be simulated on an EREW PRAM in two different ways. The first method requires $O(\log P)$ time but uses $O(nP)$ space if concurrent access to a common memory of size n is desired. The second method is space efficient but requires more time. In particular, this method requires $O(\log^2 P)$ time and uses $O(n + P)$ space.

Thus, to adapt algorithm SORT_CREW on an EREW PRAM, we can use either of these two simulation methods to resolve the read conflict in SORT_CREW. It may be noted that the concurrent read operation is needed by the merging algorithm used in the while-loop of algorithm SORT_CREW. Therefore, the time complexity of algorithm

SORT_CREW when adapted to an EREW PRAM using the first simulation method to resolve the read conflict becomes

$$T_1(n) = O(((n/P) \log n + \log P \log n) \log P)$$

$$= O(((n/P) + \log P) \log n \log P)$$

with $P \leq n$ processors using $O(nP)$ space.

Similarly, using the second simulation method, the time complexity of the adapted sorting algorithm on an EREW PRAM is

$$T_2(n) = O(((n/P) + \log P) \log n \log^2 P)$$

with $P \leq n$ processors using $O(n + P)$ space. Clearly, in both the cases the adapted algorithms are not cost optimal.

# 4.10  SORTING ON LINEAR ARRAY OF PROCESSORS

The sorting algorithm developed in this section assumes that the underlying machine is an SIMD computer in which the processors are interconnected in a one-dimensional array. There are n processors $p_1, p_2, \ldots, p_n$, where n is the size of the list to be sorted. Each processor can communicate only with its two neighbors except for processors $p_1$ and $p_n$. For $p_1$ there is no left-neighbor and for $p_n$ there is no right-neighbor. Initially, each processor $p_i$ holds one element $x_i$, $1 \leq i \leq n$, of the unsorted input list $X = \{x_1, x_2, \ldots, x_n\}$. It is required to distribute the elements of X among the processors so that processor $p_i$ holds the ith smallest element of X, for $1 \leq i \leq n$.

The algorithm works as follows. Each processor compares its value with the value of one of its neighbors. If the values are not in order then it exchanges them. The same processor then compares its current value with that of its other neighbor and again exchanges values if they are out of order. This compare and exchange process is continued until all the values are in the correct order. The steps in the algorithm are divided into *odd* and *even* steps. In the odd steps, the odd-numbered processors compare their values with those of their right neighbors. In the even steps, the even-numbered processors compare their values with those of their right neighbors. All the processors are synchronized in such a manner that a comparison always takes place between processors in correct positions. If there is no corresponding neighbor for a processor (this happens for the first and last processors in the array), it remains idle during that step. The processors involved during the odd and even comparison and exchange steps are shown in Figure 4.16. The algorithm is usually referred to as *odd-even transposition* sort.

A detailed description of the algorithm is given below. It is assumed that at any time during the execution of the algorithm, $c_i$ denotes the element of the input list X which is stored in processor $p_i$, $1 \leq i \leq n$. The odd and even steps are repeatedly performed. After $\lceil n/2 \rceil$ applications, no further exchange can take place. Thus, after $\lceil n/2 \rceil$ iterations of its outer loop the algorithm terminates and processor $p_i$ holds the ith smallest element.

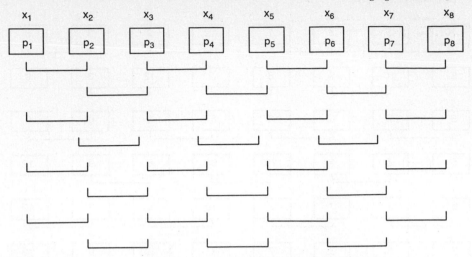

**Figure 4.16** This figure illustrates the processors involved during the odd and even steps of the odd-even transposition sort.

*Algorithm* **SORT_ODD_EVEN**

Input: An arbitrary list $X = \{x_1, x_2, \ldots, x_n\}$ distributed so that $x_i$ is in $p_i$, $1 \leq i \leq n$.

Output: The sorted input list with $p_i$ holding the ith smallest element.

*for* j = 1 *to* $\lceil n/2 \rceil$ *do*
   *for* i = 1, 3, ..., $2 \lceil n/2 \rceil - 1$ *dopar*
      *if* $c_i > c_{i+1}$
      *then* exchange $c_i$ and $c_{i+1}$
      *fi*
   *odpar*
   *for* i = 2, 4, ..., $2 \lfloor (n-1)/2 \rfloor$ *dopar*
      *if* $c_i > c_{i+1}$
      *then* exchange $c_i$ and $c_{i+1}$
      *fi*
   *odpar*
*od*

Figure 4.17 illustrates the operation of algorithm SORT_ODD_EVEN when applied to the list $X = \{10, 5, 8, 7, 12, 2, 3, 9\}$.

## Complexity and Correctness of Algorithm SORT_ODD_EVEN

Each of the two inner for-loops of algorithm SORT_ODD_EVEN requires constant time to perform one comparison and one exchange operation. Therefore, the body of the outer for-loop is performed in constant parallel time by the processors involved. Since the outer for-loop is executed $\lceil n/2 \rceil$ times, the parallel running time of algorithm SORT_ODD_EVEN is $O(n)$. In this analysis we have assumed that the elements $x_i$ are

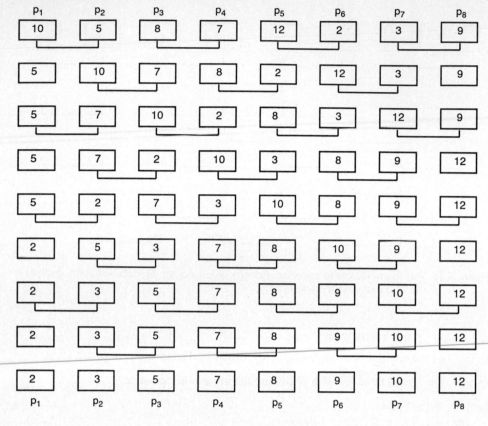

**Figure 4.17** Odd-even transposition sort of a list of eight elements X = {10, 5, 8, 7, 12, 2, 3, 9}.

initially loaded into $p_i$ simultaneously, and also after sorting, all processors output their corresponding $c_i$ simultaneously, for $1 \leq i \leq n$.

The time complexity of this sorting algorithm is optimal for a one-dimensional array. No algorithm can do better than algorithm SORT_ODD_EVEN on a linear array. This can be observed by considering the worst case, in which the largest element $x_m$ (say) of X is initially in $p_1$. Clearly $x_m$ has to be moved n − 1 times before it arrives in its final position in $p_n$. The cost of the algorithm is $O(n^2)$. Hence it is not cost optimal.

Although the idea on which algorithm SORT_ODD_EVEN is based is very simple, its proof of correctness is not obvious. Its correctness is established by the following theorem.

**Theorem 4.2:** Algorithm SORT_ODD_EVEN correctly sorts a list of n elements after at most n odd and even steps.

**Proof** (Outline): The proof is by induction on the number of elements or processors n. It is easy to verify that, in the base cases i = 1, 2 or 3, the theorem is true.

We now assume that algorithm SORT_ODD_EVEN sorts any list of q elements in at most q steps. Now consider the case where we have q + 1 elements. Let us consider

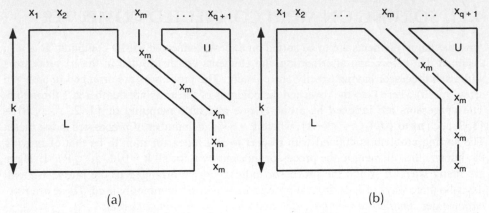

**Figure 4.18** The sort diagram showing the movements of the largest element $x_m$ of X through the processors: (a) for even m; (b) for odd m.

the diagram representing the operations carried out by the algorithm on the list $X = \{x_1, x_2, \ldots, x_{q+1}\}$. Let us concentrate our attention on the movement of the largest element of X, which we assume to be $x_m$. If m is even then $x_m$ will move as shown in Figure 4.18a. If m is odd then the corresponding movements of $x_m$ are as shown in Figure 4.18b. In each case the diagram represents the sorting of q + 1 elements, in k steps (say).

The path taken by $x_m$ divides each sort diagram into two parts L and U. Consider the new diagram which results from deleting the path of $x_m$ and merging L and U. This is illustrated in Figure 4.19. By merging L and U, as shown in Figure 4.19b, we get, from the second row downwards, a complete sort diagram of q elements. Since, by the induction hypothesis q elements are correctly sorted in at most q steps, we have that k − 1 = q and hence k = q + 1. Therefore, the theorem follows.

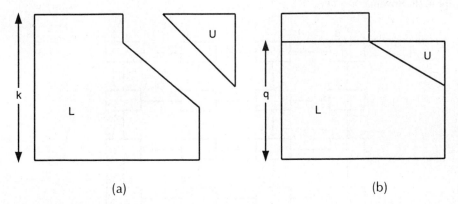

**Figure 4.19** (a) Sort diagram after deleting the path of $x_m$; (b) Sort diagram after merging L and U from (a).

# 4.11  SORTING ON MESH CONNECTED COMPUTER

Assume that $n^2$ elements are to be sorted on a mesh connected SIMD computer. It is also assumed that before and after sorting, the elements are distributed in the $n^2$ processors with each processor having exactly one element. The processors are arranged in an $n \times n$ array (mesh) where both the rows and the columns of the array are numbered 1 through n. The processors are indexed by a one-to-one and onto mapping of $\{1, 2, \ldots, n\} \times \{1, 2, \ldots, n\}$ to $\{0, 1, \ldots, P - 1\}$, where $P = n^2$ is the number of processors in the mesh. The sorting problem is defined with respect to any index function to be that of moving the kth smallest element to the processor indexed by k for all $k = 0, 1, \ldots, P - 1$. There are many ways in which the processor indices can be arranged in the array. We will describe three ways of indexing the processors which are commonly used. These are *row-major* order, *shuffled row-major* order, and *snake-like row-major* order.

**(i) Row-major order:** In this indexing scheme processor $p_k$ is placed in row i and column j of the array such that $k = (i - 1)n + j - 1$ for $0 \leq k \leq P - 1$, and $1 \leq i, j \leq n$. Figure 4.20 illustrates this indexing for n = 4 (i.e., P = 16).

**(ii) Shuffled row-major order:** This indexing scheme is illustrated in Figure 4.21 for n = 4. Shuffled row-major order is obtained by perfectly shuffling the bits of the binary

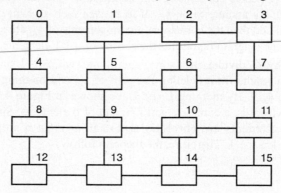

**Figure 4.20**  Row-major order.

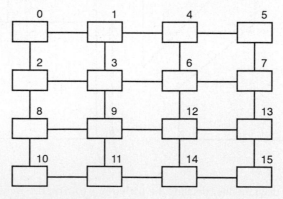

**Figure 4.21**  Shuffled row-major order.

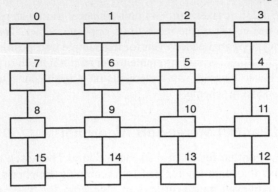

**Figure 4.22** Snake-like row-major order.

representations of the row-major order indices. Thus, after shuffling we obtain the mapping $0 \to 0, 1 \to 1, 2 \to 4, 3 \to 5, 4 \to 2, 5 \to 3, 6 \to 6, 7 \to 7, 8 \to 8, 9 \to 9, 10 \to 12, 11 \to 13, 12 \to 10, 13 \to 11, 14 \to 14, 15 \to 15$. For example, a binary number $x_1x_2x_3x_4x_5x_6x_7x_8$, where each $x_i$, $1 \le i \le 8$ is either 0 or 1, after shuffling becomes $x_1x_5x_2x_6x_3x_7x_4x_8$.

**(iii) Snake-like row-major order:** This indexing is obtained by reversing the indices of the even-numbered rows in the row-major order. Thus, processor $p_k$ is placed in row i and column j of the processor array such that, for odd i, $k = (i - 1)n + j - 1$ and for even i, $k = (i - 1)n + n - j$, where $0 \le k \le P - 1$ and $1 \le i, j \le n$. Figure 4.22 illustrates snake-like row-major order for $n = 4$.

## 4.11.1 Lower Bound for Sorting on a Mesh

For any indexing scheme there may be situations in which two elements x and y (say) initially loaded at the diagonally opposite corners of the mesh have to be swapped during

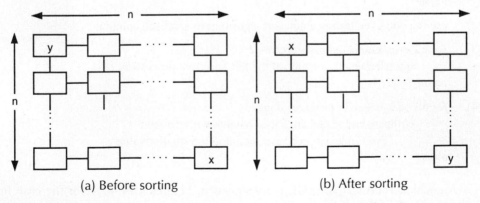

(a) Before sorting    (b) After sorting

**Figure 4.23** This figure illustrates the situation which gives a lower bound on the time complexity of sorting on a mesh.

sorting (see Figure 4.23). It takes $2(n - 1)$ unit-distance routing steps to transfer each of the elements from one corner of the mesh to its opposite corner. Thus, at least $4(n - 1)$ unit-distance routing steps are needed even for this simple transposition. This immediately implies that no algorithm can sort $n^2$ elements on an $n \times n$ mesh in time less than $O(n)$. Thus $\Omega(\sqrt{n})$ is the lower bound to sort n elements on a mesh connected SIMD computer, irrespective of the indexing scheme.

## 4.11.2  Hybrid Parallel Merge-Sort Algorithm

A two-way merge algorithm for an $(n \times 2)$ mesh due to Thompson and Kung (1977) is presented here. The algorithm is obtained by combining Batcher's odd-even merging algorithm and the odd-even transposition sort algorithm for linear arrays. Assume we have a two-dimensional array of mesh connected processors with n rows and two columns. The processors are assumed to be indexed in snake-like row-major order. We have two sorted lists each of size n stored in each of the two columns. In the degenerate case, when $n = 1$, a single comparison-interchange step is sufficient to sort the two unit subarrays. The following algorithm merges two sorted lists each of size $n \geq 2$.

*Algorithm* **HYBRID_MERGE**

Input: Two sorted lists each of size n stored in the two columns of the mesh with each processor holding one element.

Output: The merged list stored in snake-like row-major order with each processor holding one element.

(1)    *for* all odd-numbered rows *dopar*
                move the contents of the processor
                        on the right to the left processor
        *odpar*
        *for* all even-numbered rows *dopar*
                move the contents of the processor
                        on the left to the right processor
        *odpar*

(2)    use the odd-even transposition sort algorithm to sort each column;

(3)    *for* all even-numbered rows *dopar*
                interchange the contents of the left and right processors
        *odpar*

(4)    *for* all odd-indexed processors *dopar*
                compare and interchange the contents with the next
                        even-indexed processor retaining the smaller value
        *odpar*

    Algorithm HYBRID_MERGE is illustrated in Figures 4.24–4.28 for the case in which $n = 4$. If the initial lists in the two columns are not sorted then each of them can easily be sorted using the odd-even transposition sort algorithm.

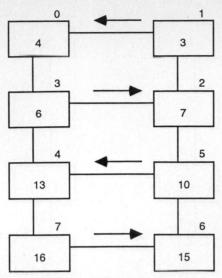

**Figure 4.24** Step 1 of algorithm HYBRID_MERGE. Move all odds to left and all evens to right as shown by arrows.

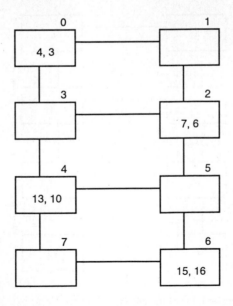

**Figure 4.25** Step 2 of algorithm HYBRID_MERGE. Odd-even transposition sort.

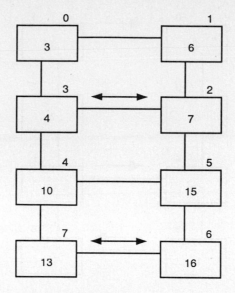

**Figure 4.26** Step 3 of algorithm HYBRID_MERGE. Interchange the elements on even rows as shown by the double-headed arrows.

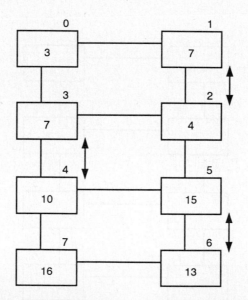

**Figure 4.27** Step 4 of algorithm HYBRID_MERGE. Compare and exchange, if out of order, every odd and the next even as shown by the double-headed arrows.

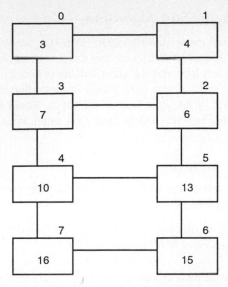

**Figure 4.28** The output produced by algorithm HYBRID_MERGE for the input lists shown in Figure 4.24.

**Complexity Analysis**

Let us denote the time required for a unit-distance routing step (i.e., the movement of one element from a processor to one of its neighbors) by $t_r$, and the time required for a comparison step by $t_c$. Concurrent data movement is allowed if all the movements are in the same direction. In addition, any number (up to P) of comparisons can be made concurrently. Thus a comparison-interchange step of two elements in adjacent processors requires time $2t_r + t_c$ (route left, compare, route right).

Now we can calculate the number of routing and comparison steps required by the different steps of algorithm HYBRID_MERGE. Steps 1 and 3 each require two routings. Step 2 requires 2n routings and n comparisons. Finally, Step 4 requires two routings and one comparison operation. Therefore, to merge two columns of size n, algorithm HYBRID_MERGE requires (2n + 6) routings and (n + 1) comparisons. Let $T(n, 2)$ denote the time needed by this algorithm. Then, we have

$$T(n, 2) = (2n + 6) \, t_r + (n + 1) \, t_c.$$

If two unsorted lists, each of length n, are initially loaded into the two columns of the mesh then we first apply the odd-even transposition sort algorithm in parallel to the elements of the two columns and then use algorithm HYBRID_MERGE. This step takes O(n) routing steps. Thus, the complexity of algorithm HYBRID_MERGE is O(n) to sort 2n elements on an (n × 2) mesh.

### 4.11.3  Two-way Merge-Sort Algorithm

In this section, we will first generalize algorithm HYBRID_MERGE to an (n × k) mesh, where n > 2 and k > 2. For this, let us assume that the (n × k) mesh is logically partitioned into two parts, with the left half and the right half each consisting of nk/2 processors. Consider two sorted lists each of size nk/2 sorted in snake-like row-major order, one in the left half and the other in the right half of the mesh. These two sorted lists can be merged using the following two-way merge algorithm which is an extension of algorithm HYBRID_MERGE.

*Algorithm* **TWO_WAY_MERGE**

Input: Two sorted lists, each of size nk/2, stored in snake-like row-major order in the left and right half of an (n × k) mesh.

Output: The merged list of nk elements stored in snake-like row-major order in the (n × k) mesh with each processor holding one element.

(1)    *for* all even-numbered rows *dopar*
        interchange the contents of the processors so that
            columns contain either all evens or all odds only
    *odpar*

(2)    *for* all rows *dopar*
        unshuffle the contents of the processors
    *odpar*

(3)    merge the two sorted lists of size nk/4 on each half of the array;

(4)    *for* all rows *dopar*
        shuffle the contents of the processors
    *odpar*

(5)    interchange on even-numbered rows as in Step (1);

(6)    *for* all odd-indexed processors *dopar*
        compare and interchange the element with the next
            even-indexed processor and retain the minimum
    *odpar*

The execution of the algorithm is illustrated in Figures 4.29–4.35. The merging algorithm can be applied repeatedly in order to sort $n^2$ elements on an (n × n) mesh if n = k. The details are discussed on page 107 in the Complexity Analysis of algorithm TWO_WAY_MERGE.

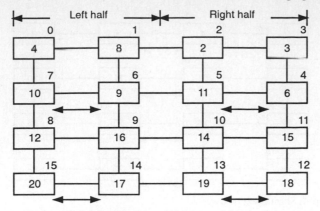

**Figure 4.29** Step 1 of algorithm TWO_WAY_MERGE. Interchange on even rows as indicated by the double-headed arrows. The two initial sorted lists are {4, 8, 9, 10, 12, 16, 17, 20} and {2, 3, 6, 11, 14, 15, 18, 19}.

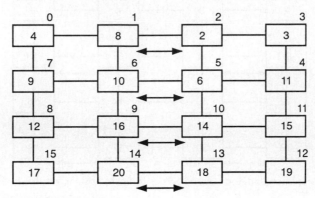

**Figure 4.30** Step 2: Unshuffle each row.

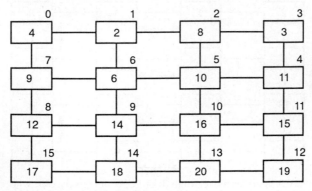

**Figure 4.31** Step 3: Merge on each half of the mesh.

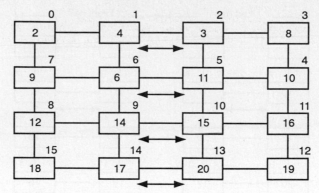

**Figure 4.32** Step 4: Shuffle each row.

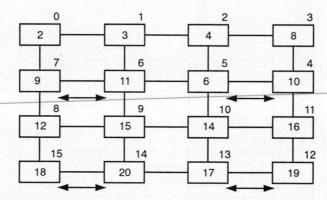

**Figure 4.33** Step 5: Interchange on even rows as indicated by the double-headed arrows.

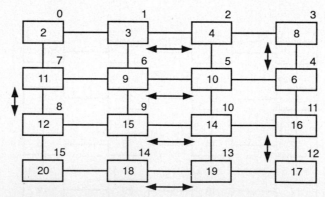

**Figure 4.34** Step 6: Compare and exchange (if out of order) every odd with the next even as shown by the double-headed arrows.

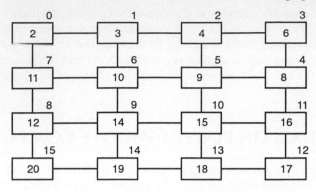

**Figure 4.35** The sorted list produced by algorithm TWO_WAY_MERGE.

**Complexity Analysis**

It can be seen that each of Steps 1 and 5 requires two routings. Steps 2 and 4 require
$(k - 2)$ routings each to perform the unshuffle and shuffle operations, respectively. Step 3
is a recursive call of the algorithm. The recursion continues until the individual merge
problems are reduced to the merging of two adjacent columns. Thus, if $T(n, k)$ denotes
the total time required to merge two sorted lists, each of size $nk/2$, using this algorithm,
then Step 3 requires a total time of $T(n, k/2)$. Finally, Step 6 requires only one comparison and four routings. Thus, we have

$$T(n, k) = T(n, k/2) + (2k + 4)\, t_r + t_c$$

and    $T(n, 2) = (2n + 6)\, t_r + (n + 1)\, t_c$  (from algorithm HYBRID_MERGE).

By repeated substitution, we get the following time bound

$$T(n, k) \le (2n + 4k + 4 \log k)\, t_r + (n + \log k)\, t_c.$$

For an $(n \times n)$ mesh the time bound becomes

$$\begin{aligned} T(n, n) &= (6n + 4 \log n)\, t_r + (n + \log n)\, t_c \\ &= O(n). \end{aligned}$$

Algorithm TWO_WAY_MERGE can be used to sort $n^2$ elements on an $(n \times n)$ mesh
as follows. First sort each column in parallel by using the odd-even transposition sort
algorithm. This takes $O(n)$ routings and comparisons. Next, merge in parallel pairs of
sorted columns (it is assumed that $n = 2^x$ for some $x \ge 2$) using algorithm
HYBRID_MERGE. Then merge, in parallel, the sorted lists of size $2n$ contained in the
rectangular array of size $(n \times 2)$ using algorithm TWO_WAY_MERGE. Continue this
process to merge sorted lists of increasing sizes $4n, 8n, 16n, \ldots, n^2/2$ to obtain, finally,
the sorted list of size $n^2$. Because algorithm TWO_WAY_MERGE has time complexity
$O(n)$ and since there are $\log n$ levels of such parallel mergings to be performed, the overall time complexity for sorting $n^2$ elements in an $(n \times n)$ mesh using algorithm
TWO_WAY_MERGE is $O(n \log n)$.

Clearly, this algorithm, based on algorithm TWO_WAY_MERGE, is not optimal. There are two reasons for this poor performance. First, the comparisons between elements are extremely local in the sense that no comparisons are made between elements initially in the different halves of the array until the very end, when each half has been sorted. Second, the recursive subproblems which are generated are decreasing in size in only one dimension.

## 4.12  SORTING ON PERFECT SHUFFLE COMPUTER

An efficient algorithm for sorting a list containing n elements on the perfect shuffle SIMD model is presented in this section. The number of steps required by this algorithm is $O(\log^2 n)$ when n/2 comparison-exchange operations can take place simultaneously. This algorithm, due to Stone (1971), is an adaptation of Batcher's bitonic sorting algorithm (Batcher 1968) on the perfect shuffle model.

A complete sorter for eight elements constructed from bitonic sorters is shown in Figure 4.36. The figure shows a definite pattern of "positive" and "negative" comparators in the network. It can also be seen from the labels on the comparators that the indices of every pair of elements entering a comparator differ by a single bit in their binary representations. This suggests that, instead of using n/2 comparators, at each step of the sorting network we can use n/2 processors and a shuffle network to perform the Batcher's bitonic sort. Each of these n/2 processors operates as a comparator module and is capable of performing the functions of both "positive" and "negative" comparators. An important part of the algorithm is determining whether a comparator module should act as a "positive" comparator or a "negative" comparator when comparing a particular pair of elements. For this purpose, we use a mask vector, denoted by MASK, whose kth component determines

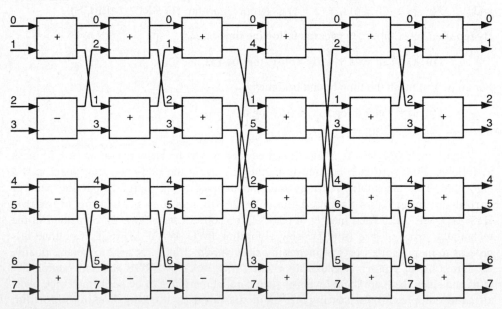

**Figure 4.36**  A sorting network for eight elements based on Batcher's bitonic sorter.

the behavior of processor k. A value of 0 indicates that a "positive" comparator is needed and a value of 1 indicates that a "negative" comparator is needed.

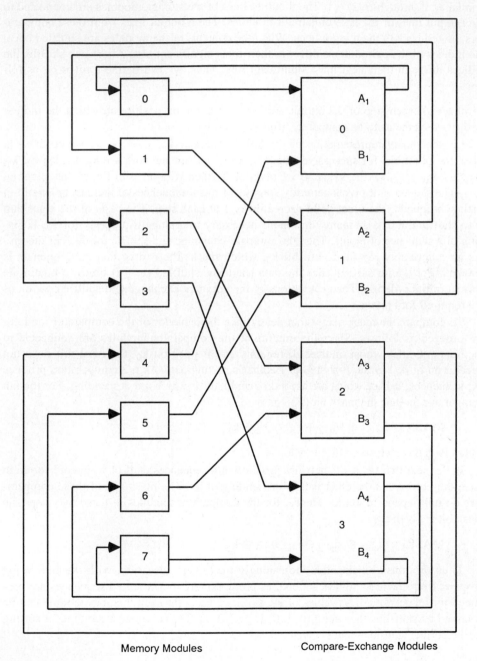

Memory Modules                    Compare-Exchange Modules

**Figure 4.37** The structure of a parallel computer for sorting using the perfect shuffle interconnection.

In the perfect shuffle model of Figure 4.37 each processor is connected to a pair of storage modules. We have n storage or memory modules numbered 0 through n − 1 which contain the list of n elements to be sorted and n/2 comparator modules (processors) numbered 0 through (n/2) − 1. The n output lines of the storage modules are connected to the n input lines of the n/2 comparator modules. The n output lines from these comparators are fed back to the n input lines. When the contents of the modules are shuffled once, the indices of the paired items differ in their most significant bits. After each shuffle, the indices differ in their next most significant bits. Thus, we can define a *pivot bit* as follows.

*Pivot bit*: At each step of the bitonic sort algorithm, the bit position in which the indices of the two elements to be compared differ is called the pivot bit.

Let the binary representation of the index $k$ be $k_{m-1}k_{m-2} \ldots k_1k_0$, where $2^m = n$. Then the pivot bits for successive stages of a bitonic sort network are $k_0$; $k_1, k_0$; $k_2, k_1, k_0$; $\ldots$; $k_{m-1}, k_{m-2}, \ldots, k_1, k_0$. If we pivot on $k_s$, then after one shuffle, we can pivot on $k_{s-1}$. The sequence of pivots naturally consists of m subsequences of increasing length. In each subsequence the pivot point decreases by 1 at each step. The basis of the algorithm is to shuffle the data as many times as is necessary to arrange it properly for the beginning of a sequence of pivots. Then the compare-exchange and shuffle for each of the pivots are alternately repeated until bit $k_0$, which marks the end of that subsequence, is reached. For the ith subsequence the data has to be shuffled (m − i) times to obtain the correct initial ordering. Then i iterations of the compare-exchange and shuffle operations are required for i pivots.

To compare the mask vector that determines the behavior of the comparator modules we proceed as follows. Since the outputs of the comparator modules are connected to memory modules whose indices differ only in bit position $k_0$, the mask bit does not depend on bit $k_0$. In the first step of Batcher's sorting network n/2 comparators produce n/2 sequences, half of which are ascending and half of which are descending. For the kth comparator module the mask bit is given by

$$\text{MASK}_k = k_{m-1} \oplus k_{m-2} \oplus \ldots \oplus k_2 \oplus k_1$$

where $\oplus$ is the exclusive-OR operation.

In the next two steps, the network produces n/4 sequences, half of which are sorted in ascending order and the other half in descending order. The mask bits of these comparators do not depend on bit $k_1$. Hence, for the comparator modules in these two steps the mask bit is given by

$$\text{MASK}_k = k_{m-1} \oplus k_{m-2} \oplus \ldots \oplus k_3 \oplus k_2.$$

Thus the mask bit depends increasingly on fewer index bits, with the bits being dropped from the least significant end, as progressively longer sorted sequences are produced in the network. The values of $k_1, k_2, \ldots, k_{m-1}$ for each memory module can be obtained by shuffling the vector $(0, 1, 0, 1, \ldots, 0, 1)$. The complete algorithm for sorting on the perfect shuffle model is given below.

### *Algorithm* PS_SORT

Input: An arbitrary list L containing n elements, each of which is stored in a separate memory module.

Output: The sorted list is available in the n memory modules; the kth module holds the kth smallest element of L.

```
V := vector(0, 1, 0, 1, . . . , 0, 1);
MASK := V;
for i = 1 to m do
    MASK := MASK ⊕ V;
    shuffle(MASK)
od
compare-exchange(L);
for i = 1 to m - 1 do
    shuffle(V);
    MASK := MASK ⊕ V;
    for j = 1 to m - 1 - i do
        shuffle(L)
    od
    for j = m - i to m do
        shuffle(L);
        compare-exchange(L)
    od
od
```

When the *compare-exchange(L)* instruction is executed, each processor adopts the function of either a "positive" comparator or a "negative" comparator depending on the value of the corresponding mask bit.

### Complexity of Algorithm PS_SORT

Algorithm PS_SORT requires $m(m + 1)/2$ compare-exchange steps, $m(m - 1)$ shuffle steps of the vector L, and $2m - 1$ shuffle steps of the vectors MASK and V. Since $m = \log n$, the time complexity $T(n)$ of algorithm PS_SORT is $O(\log^2 n)$. The processor complexity $P(n)$ is $O(n)$ because $n/2$ comparators are used. Therefore, the cost of the algorithm is given by

$$C(n) = T(n) \times P(n) = O(n \log^2 n).$$

## 4.13 BIBLIOGRAPHIC NOTES

Special-purpose networks, namely, odd-even and bitonic merging networks were introduced by Batcher (1968). Implementations of odd-even and bitonic merging algorithms on one- and two-dimensional mesh connected computers appeared in Kumar and Hirschberg (1983), Nassimi and Sahni (1979), and Thompson and Kung (1977). Merging networks are also discussed in the books by Akl (1985, 1989). Two in-depth surveys on sorting which also include a description of these special-purpose merging networks are by Bitton et al. (1984) and Lakshmivarahan et al. (1984).

Gavril (1975) and Valiant (1975) are early works on merging algorithms for synchronous parallel computational models. Gavril (1975) presented an algorithm for merging two sorted lists of lengths m and n (where m ≤ n) using P parallel processors working synchronously. The time complexity of Gavril's algorithm is O((m/P) log (n/m)), where only comparisons are considered. On a similar model to that used by Gavril, Valiant (1975) presented a parallel merging algorithm whose time complexity is O(log log n) for P = ⌈√(mn)⌉. Valiant also considered only comparisons when analyzing the time complexity. The disadvantage of his algorithm is that there is no apparent way to overcome the allocation problem (i.e., to allocate P processors to P tasks in constant time). Using the comparison model of Gavril and Valiant, Borodin and Hopcroft (1985) have shown that Ω(log log n) is the lower bound on the computing time to merge two lists of length n. The parallel merging algorithm on the CREW PRAM model, presented in Section 4.3, is based on the work of Shiloach and Vishkin (1981). Kruskal (1983) presented a merging algorithm on the same model as that used by Shiloach and Vishkin. This algorithm has been shown to be optimal to within a constant factor when merging two lists of equal size (independent of the number of processors). As a special case Kruskal's algorithm merges two sorted lists, each of length n using n processors, in 1.893 log log n + 4 comparison steps.

The two different methods presented in Sections 4.4.1 and 4.4.2 for simulating the concurrent memory address access on the EREW PRAM model are based on the work of Eckstein (1979) and Vishkin (1983), respectively. The optimal merging algorithm on the EREW PRAM presented in this chapter is based on the work of Akl and Santoro (1987). In a recent paper, Hagerup and Rub (1989) describe an optimal algorithm that can merge two sorted lists of total length n in time O((n/P) + log P) using P ≤ n/2 processors. A similar EREW PRAM merging algorithm is also reported in Anderson et al. (1989).

The sorting problem has been the object of extensive study in the context of parallel processing for the past twenty years. The book by Akl (1985) contains a wealth of information about parallel sorting algorithms. Other survey papers on parallel sorting include Bitton et al. (1984) and Lakshmivarahan et al. (1984).

Sorting networks for the odd-even merge-sort and the bitonic sort were first proposed by Batcher (1968). Lee et al. (1981), Miranker et al. (1983), Tseng and Lee (1984), and Winslow and Chow (1983) present various other sorting networks. Some other parallel sorting algorithms based on bitonic merge appeared in Baudet and Stevenson (1978), Flanders (1982), Kumar and Hirschberg (1983), Nassimi and Sahni (1979, 1982), Perl (1983), and Schwartz (1980). Wong and Ito (1984) presented a re-circulating systolic sorting array and two sorting algorithms. These algorithms are amenable to VLSI implementation. The sorting time and the number of comparators are both O(n) for sorting n elements. Leighton (1985) has described the theoretically fastest possible network, based on the ideas in Ajtai et al. (1983), for sorting n elements in O(log n) time with O(n) processors. This algorithm is cost optimal. However, the constant of proportionality which is absorbed within the "big oh" notation is very large, making it impractical for use with less than $10^{100}$ elements. Siegel (1985) analyzed the sorting of n k-bit numbers in a minimum storage network and established new $AT^2$ lower bounds for a VLSI sorting model. Reif and Valiant (1987) presented a randomized algorithm that sorts n elements in parallel on a natural fixed-connection graph having n nodes and constant valence in O(log n) time.

Several authors have addressed the sorting problem on the PRAM model. Hirschberg (1978) proposed a sorting algorithm on the CREW PRAM model that takes O(k log n) time with $n^{1+(1/k)}$ processors, where k is an arbitrary integer. Preparata (1978) described a parallel algorithm on the CREW PRAM model that sorts n elements in time O(log n) with n log n processors. Kruskal (1983) improved the results of both Hirschberg and Preparata and showed that his algorithm sorts n elements in 1.893 log n log log n/log log log n (plus lower order terms) comparison steps and works on the CREW PRAM model. The CRCW PRAM sorting algorithm presented in this chapter follows the ideas in Kucera (1982). The CREW PRAM sorting algorithm of Section 4.9.2 is based on the work of Shiloach and Vishkin (1981). An optimal parallel sorting algorithm on the EREW PRAM model has been developed by Akl and Santoro (1987). This algorithm runs in $O((\log^2 P + n/P) \log n)$ time with $1 \le P \le n$ processors. Cole (1988) presents a parallel implementation of merge-sort on a CREW PRAM that uses n processors and O(log n) time. He has also shown that it is possible to have a more complex version of the algorithm for the EREW PRAM model which has the same resource bounds, i.e., O(log n) time with n processors. However, the constant of proportionality in the running time in the latter is large compared with that of the former. Recently, Hagerup and Rub (1989) presented another optimal parallel sorting algorithm that takes $O(\log^2 n)$ time on the EREW PRAM model using O(n/log n) processors. Another recent paper by Levcopoulos and Petersson (1989) addresses a different variant of the sorting problem. They propose an optimal parallel algorithm for sorting presorted sequences. The measure of presortedness they used is *Rem*, i.e., the smallest number of elements whose removal leaves a sorted sequence. This algorithm sorts a sequence X of length n, with *Rem*(X) = r, in O(log n) time using O((n + r log n)/log n) processors on the EREW PRAM model.

Odd-even transposition sort has been discussed by Habermann (1972), Knuth (1973), and Kung (1980). Other implementations of the odd-even transposition sort appear in Chen et al. (1978a, 1978b), Kumar and Hirschberg (1983), and Lee et al. (1981). The odd-even transposition sort presented in this chapter is based on the work of Habermann (1972); it is also described in Lakshmivarahan et al. (1984). The proof of correctness of this algorithm, given in Section 4.10, follows Goodman and Hedetniemi (1977).

The two-dimensional mesh connected computer is used as the model of computation for sorting in Thompson and Kung (1977), Nassimi and Sahni (1979), and Kumar and Hirschberg (1983). Thompson and Kung discussed the row-major, shuffled row-major and snake-like row-major processor indexing schemes on the two-dimensional mesh and also provided the lower bound for sorting on a mesh. Parallel sorting algorithm on the perfect shuffle computer is presented in Stone (1971). A sorting algorithm for the perfect shuffle model which sorts a list of length n using $n^{1+(1/k)}$ processors, $1 \le k \le \log n$, in O(k log n) time is described in Nassimi and Sahni (1982). This algorithm assumes that each processor is connected to three other processors (corresponding to exchange, shuffle, and unshuffle connections, respectively). Other references to parallel sorting algorithms on a variety of interconnection-network SIMD computers include Bentley and Brown (1980), Horowitz and Zorat (1983), Orenstein et al. (1983), and Nassimi and Sahni (1982).

Muller and Preparata (1975) proposed a parallel algorithm for enumeration sort. Other references on parallel enumeration sort include Hsiao and Snyder (1983), Leighton (1981), and Nath et al. (1983). Asynchronous sorting on multiprocessors and parallel external sorting algorithms have been extensively treated by Akl (1985).

## 4.14  EXERCISES

4.14.1   Draw the odd-even merging network to merge the lists X = {2, 6, 8, 12} and Y = {3, 4, 6, 10}.

4.14.2   Consider the odd-even merging network corresponding to Exercise 4.14.1. If you attach an identification tag to each of the two 6s in X and Y respectively, to keep track of the flow of these numbers in the network, then you will see the element $y_3 = 6$ occur above the element $x_2 = 6$ in the final merged list. Thus the relative order of equal elements in two lists is not preserved in odd-even merging. This is referred to as the *instability* of the odd-even merging. Show that a simple modification at Step 2 of the algorithm given in Section 4.2 can induce *stability* into this merging scheme.

4.14.3   In the odd-even merging network of Section 4.2, it is assumed that the two input lists are of equal length. How can you modify the network to merge two lists of unequal length?

4.14.4   Show the detailed steps involved in obtaining the solutions to the recurrence relations for T(n, n) and P(n, n) of Section 4.2.

4.14.5   Describe how an O(n) processor EREW PRAM can be used to implement the tasks of the comparators of Batcher's odd-even merging network in O(log n) time.

4.14.6   Show that any merging network that can merge 1 element with n elements to produce a sorted list of length (n + 1) must have at least $\lceil \log (n + 1) \rceil$ steps.

4.14.7   Show that a slight modification of algorithm MERGE2_CREW of Section 4.3 solves the merging problem when m < P ≤ n without any change in its complexity.

4.14.8   Develop a CREW PRAM algorithm for merging two sorted lists of lengths m and n, respectively, where m ≤ n, using P ≥ n processors (Shiloach and Vishkin 1981).

4.14.9   Show how the following list of 8 elements, which are in random order, can be sorted using a bitonic sorting network of order 8: {12, 3, 6, 8, 4, 2, 1, 8}.

4.14.10  A sorting algorithm is said to be *stable* if it preserves the relative order of identical elements. From your answer to Exercise 4.14.9, you can see that the bitonic sorting is not stable. How can you develop a stable version of a bitonic sorter?

4.14.11  The bitonic sorting network of Section 4.8 assumes the number of inputs to be a power of 2. Describe how a bitonic sorter can be constructed when the number of inputs is not a power of 2.

4.14.12 Study Muller and Preparata's sorting scheme which, unlike Batcher's scheme, requires only O(log n) time. Show that this sorting scheme is stable. What is the major difficulty in implementing the Muller-Preparata algorithm as a sorting network (Muller and Preparata 1975)?

4.14.13 Develop an efficient CREW PRAM sorting algorithm to sort an arbitrary list of n elements using P processors, where $P \geq n$ (Shiloach and Vishkin 1981).

4.14.14 Develop a parallel version of the "bucket sort" algorithm to sort an arbitrary list X of length n. Show that it can be implemented on an n processor CREW PRAM model in O(log n) time using O(kn) space, where the largest number in X is $k - 1$.

4.14.15 Show that an identical time and processor bounds of Exercise 4.14.14 can also be achieved even if the read conflicts are not permitted.

4.14.16 Outline the possible ways to exploit parallelism in "Quicksort."

4.14.17 Describe an O(log n) time algorithm to sort by enumeration an arbitrary list of length n on an $n^{3/2}$ processor CREW PRAM.

4.14.18 Develop a parallel algorithm for sorting a list of $n = 2^k$ elements on a cube connected SIMD computer having n processors. Analyze the time complexity of your algorithm.

# 4.15 BIBLIOGRAPHY

Aho, A., Hopcroft, J., and Ullman, J. (1974). *The Design and Analysis of Computer Algorithms.* Addison-Wesley, Reading, Mass.

Ajtai, M., Komlos, J., and Szemeredi, E. (1983). An O(n log n) sorting network. *Proceedings of the 15th Annual ACM Symposium on Theory of Computing,* ACM, NY, pp. 1-9.

Akl, S. G. (1985). *Parallel Sorting Algorithms.* Academic Press, Orlando, Fla.

Akl, S. G. (1989). *The Design and Analysis of Parallel Algorithms.* Prentice Hall, Englewood Cliffs, NJ.

Akl, S. G., and Santoro, N. (1987). Optimal parallel merging and sorting without memory conflicts. *IEEE Transactions on Computers* C-36, 1367-9.

Anderson, R. J., Mayr, E. W., and Warmuth, M. K. (1989). Parallel approximation algorithms for bin packing. *Inform. and Comput.* 82, 262-77.

Batcher, K. E. (1968). Sorting networks and their applications. *Proceedings of the AFIPS 1968 Spring Joint Computer Conference,* New Jersey, AFIPS Press, NJ, pp. 307-14.

Baudet, G., and Stevenson, D. (1978). Optimal sorting algorithms for parallel computers. *IEEE Transactions on Computers* C-27, 84-7.

Bentley, J L., and Brown, D. J. (1980). A general class of recurrence tradeoffs. *Proceedings of the 21st Annual Symposium on Foundations of Computer Science,* IEEE Computer Society, Washington, DC, pp. 217-28.

Bitton, D., DeWitt, D. J., Hsiao, D. K., and Menon, J. (1984). A taxonomy of parallel sorting. *Computing Surveys* 13, 287-318.

Borodin, A., and Hopcroft, J. (1985). Routing, merging and sorting on parallel models of computation. *J. Computer and System Sci.* 30, 130-45.

Chen, T. C., Eswaran, K. P., Lum, V. Y., and Tung, C. (1978a). Simplified odd-even sort using multiple shift-register loops. *Intern. J. Computer and Information Sci.* 7, 295-314.

Chen, T. C., Lum, V. Y., and Tung, C. (1978b). The rebound sorter: an efficient sort engine for large files. *Proceedings of the 4th International Conference on Very Large Data Bases,* Berlin, Germany, pp. 312-8.

Cole, R. (1988). Parallel merge sort. *SIAM J. Computing* 17, 770-85.

Eckstein, D. M. (1979). *Simultaneous memory access.* Tech. Rep. # 79-6, Dept. of Computer Science, Iowa State University, Ames, Iowa.

Flanders, P. M. (1982). A unified approach to a class of data movements on an array processor. *IEEE Transactions on Computers* C-31, 809-19.

Gavril, F. (1975). Merging with parallel processors. *Comm. ACM.* 18, 588-91.

Goodman, S. E., and Hedetniemi, S. T. (1977). *Introduction to the Design and Analysis of Algorithms.* McGraw-Hill, NY.

Habermann, A. N. (1972). *Parallel neighbour sort.* Computer Science Rep., Carnegie-Mellon University, Pittsburgh, Pa.

Hagerup, T., and Rub, C. (1989). Optimal merging and sorting on the EREW PRAM. *Inform. Process. Lett.* 33, 181-5.

Hirschberg, D. S. (1978). Fast parallel sorting algorithms. *Comm. ACM.* 21, 657-61.

Horowitz, H., and Zorat, A. (1983). Divide-and-Conquer for parallel processing. *IEEE Transactions on Computers* C-32, 582-5.

Hsiao, C. C., and Snyder, L. (1983). Omni-sort: a versatile data processing operation for VLSI. *Proceedings of the 1983 International Conference on Parallel Processing,* IEEE Computer Society, Washington, DC, pp. 222-5.

Knuth, D. E. (1973). *The Art of Computer Programming vol. 3: Sorting and Searching*, Addison-Wesley, Reading, Mass.

Kruskal, C. P. (1983). Searching, merging, and sorting in parallel computation. *IEEE Transactions on Computers* C-32, 942-6.

Kucera, L. (1982). Parallel computation and conflicts in memory access. *Inform. Process. Lett.* 14, 93-6.

Kumar, M., and Hirschberg, D. S. (1983). An efficient implementation of Batcher's odd-even merge algorithm and its applications in parallel sorting schemes. *IEEE Transactions on Computers* C-32, 254-64.

Kung, H. T. (1980). The structure of parallel algorithms. In *Advances in Computers*, vol. 19, M. Yovits, ed. Academic Press, NY, pp. 65-112.

Lakshmivarahan, S., Dhall, S. K., and Miller, L. L. (1984). Parallel sorting algorithms. In *Advances in Computers*, vol. 23, M. Yovits, ed. Academic Press, NY, pp. 295-354.

Lee, D. T., Chang, H., and Wong, C. K. (1981). An on-chip compare/steer bubble sorter. *IEEE Transactions on Computers* C-30, 396-405.

Leighton, T. (1981). New lower bound techniques for VLSI. *Proceedings of the 22nd Annual Symposium on Foundations of Computer Science,* IEEE Computer Society, Washington, DC, pp. 1-12.

Leighton, T. (1985). Tight bounds on the complexity of parallel sorting. *IEEE Transactions on Computers* C-34, 344-54.

Levcopoulos, C., and Petersson, O. (1989). A note on adaptive parallel sorting. *Inform. Process. Lett.* 33, 187-91.

Miranker, G., Tang, L., and Wong, C. K. (1983). A "zero-time" VLSI sorter. *IBM J. Research and Development* 27, 140-8.

Muller, D. E., and Preparata, F. P. (1975). Bounds to complexities of networks for sorting and for switching. *J. ACM.* 22, 195-201.

Nassimi, D., and Sahni, S. (1979). Bitonic sort on a mesh-connected parallel computer. *IEEE Transactions on Computers* C-28, 2-7.

Nassimi, D., and Sahni, S. (1982). Parallel permutation and sorting algorithms and a new generalized connection network. *J. ACM.* 29, 642-67.

Nath, D., Maheshwari, S. N., and Bhatt, P. C. P. (1983). Efficient VLSI networks for parallel processing based on orthogonal trees. *IEEE Transactions on Computers* C-32, 569-81.

Orenstein, J. A., Merrett, T. H., and Devroye, L. (1983). Linear sorting with O(log n) processors. *BIT* 23, 170-80.

Perl, Y. (1983). *Bitonic and odd-even networks are more than merging.* Tech. Rep., Rutgers University, New Brunswick, NJ.

Preparata, F. P. (1978). New parallel-sorting schemes. *IEEE Transactions on Computers* C-27, 669-73.

Preparata, F. P., and Vuillemin, J. (1981). The cube-connected cycles: a versatile network for parallel computation. *Comm. ACM* 24, 300-9.

Reif, J. H., and Valiant, L. G. (1987). A logarithmic time sort for linear size networks. *J. ACM.* 34, 60-76.

Schwartz, J. T. (1980). Ultracomputers. *ACM Transactions on Programming Languages and Systems* 2, 355-61.

Stone, H. S. (1971). Parallel processing with the perfect shuffle. *IEEE Transactions on Computers* C-20, 153-61.

Shiloach, Y., and Vishkin, U. (1981). Finding the maximum, merging, and sorting in a parallel computation model. *J. Algorithms* 2, 88-102.

Siegel, A. R. (1985). Minimum storage sorting networks. *IEEE Transactions on Computers* C-34, 396-405.

Thompson, C. D., and Kung, H. T. (1977). Sorting on a mesh-connected parallel computer. *Comm. ACM* 20, 263-71.

Tseng, S. S., and Lee, R. C. T. (1984). A new parallel sorting algorithm based upon min-mid-max operations. *BIT* 24, 187-95.

Valiant, L. G. (1975). Parallelism in comparison problems. *SIAM J. Computing* 4, 348-55.

Vishkin, U. (1983). Implementation of simultaneous memory address access in models that forbid it. *J. Algorithms* 4, 45-50.

Winslow, L. E., and Chow, Y. -C. (1983). The analysis and design of some new sorting machines. *IEEE Transactions on Computers* C-32, 677-83.

Wong, F. S., and Ito, M. R. (1984). Parallel sorting on a re-circulating systolic sorter. *Computer Journal* 27, 260-9.

# CHAPTER
# 5

# Selection and Searching

## 5.1 INTRODUCTION

In this chapter, we deal with two basic problems concerned with finite lists of elements in the context of parallel processing. These are the problems of *selection* and *searching*. As for merging and sorting, algorithms for the solutions of these two problems are of fundamental importance and are intrinsic to a great many computational tasks. The selection and searching problems are stated below.

*Selection*: Given a list $X = \{x_1, x_2, \ldots, x_n\}$ of n elements whose elements are in random order and an integer k satisfying $1 \le k \le n$, find the kth-smallest element in X.

*Searching*: Given a list $X = \{x_1, x_2, \ldots, x_n\}$ whose elements are either in random order or are sorted and an element x, find an index i such that $x_i = x$ for some $x_i$ in X.

The problem of selection is also called *order statistics*. Two special cases of the general selection problem are the problems of finding the maximum (i.e., k = n) and minimum (i.e., k = 1) elements of the list X. Finding the maximum (or minimum) element of a list X of n elements is straightforward in a serial computing environment. If we know the maximum (minimum) of n − 1 elements of X, then it remains only to compare this element to the nth element to find the maximum (minimum) of the list X. Finding the maximum (minimum) of a single element of X is trivial. Maximum (minimum) finding takes one comparison per element, starting with the second element. Hence the number of comparisons is n − 1, i.e., this process requires O(n) time. This is clearly optimal since, to obtain the maximum (minimum) of n elements which are in random order, every element must be examined once. If in the general selection problem of finding the kth-smallest element of X, k is very close

118

to 1 or n, then the desired element can be obtained by employing the algorithm for finding the minimum (or maximum) element k times. This approach requires O(kn) time. However, a linear (i.e., O(n) time) serial algorithm exists that finds the kth-smallest element of a list for any value of k. Obviously, this is an optimal algorithm. In many applications of order statistics we need to find the *median*, i.e., the (n/2)th-smallest element. For this problem the general selection algorithm is employed. Thus both upper and lower bounds for the selection problem are $\Omega(n)$.

Applications of searching are widespread and involve a variety of operations. Often we need to retrieve some particular piece or pieces of information from a large amount of previously stored information. Normally we think of information as divided into *records* with each record having a *key*. Search algorithms operate on keys and the goal of a search is to access information within the record for processing. Records are organized in the form of a table (or list) of finite size. In a serial computing environment, the problem of searching for an element (key) x in a list X is solved by scanning the list X and comparing each of its elements with x until an element $x_i$ of X is found such that $x_i = x$ or the list X is exhausted. The corresponding algorithm obviously requires O(n) time in the worst case and it is clearly optimal since each element of X has to be examined once. Therefore, in the case of searching for an element in a random list both the upper and lower bounds are $\Omega(n)$. If the list is sorted, then we use the binary search technique to search X for an element x. Binary search never requires more than (log n + 1) comparisons for either successful or unsuccessful search. The binary search algorithm is also optimal, since log n bits are required to distinguish one among n elements.

In Sections 5.2 through 5.5 of this chapter the two different forms of the selection problems are considered. More specifically, we begin by presenting the maximum finding algorithms for CRCW PRAM, EREW PRAM and a tree machine. The general selection problem is considered in Section 5.3 and a cost optimal parallel algorithm on EREW PRAM is described. In Section 5.4 we present an improved parallel selection algorithm for the EREW PRAM model. The selection problem is studied on a tree machine in Section 5.5. The problem of parallel searching is considered using different computational models in Sections 5.6 through 5.9. In particular, the complexity of parallel search on the CREW PRAM model is discussed in Section 5.6. Parallel searching algorithms for both unsorted and sorted lists on PRAM models are discussed in Section 5.7. A searching algorithm on a mesh connected computer is presented in Section 5.8. Finally, Section 5.9 deals with the searching problem on tree machines.

## 5.2  PARALLEL ALGORITHMS FOR FINDING THE MAXIMUM

A variant of the general selection problem is that of finding the maximum (or minimum) of a list of elements. The problem of finding the maximum (minimum) among n distinct elements is frequently encountered as an intermediate step in solving many other problems. In this section, we develop algorithms for the solution of this problem on different parallel computational models. Since finding the minimum is logically equivalent to finding the maximum, we will only discuss the problem of finding the maximum of a list.

## 5.2.1  Maximum Finding on CRCW PRAM

In this section, we will first show that, on a CRCW PRAM with $n(n - 1)/2$ processors, it is possible to find the maximum of a list of n elements in constant time. Finally, we will show how to increase the efficiency of the maximum finding algorithm on the CRCW PRAM model. The equality resolution rule is followed in case of write conflicts, i.e., two or more processors are allowed to write to the same shared memory location at the same time only if they write the same value.

Let us assume that we want to find the maximum of list $X = \{x_1, x_2, \ldots, x_n\}$ containing n numbers and that $n(n - 1)/2$ processors are available. Each processor is labeled as $p_{ij}$, i, j = 1, 2, . . . , n. The algorithm is as follows:

*Algorithm* **CRCW_MAXIMUM**

Input: A list $X = \{x_1, x_2, \ldots, x_n\}$ containing n numbers.

Output: The maximum element of X stored in location M.

*for* i = 1 *to* n *dopar*
    $p_{i1}$ sets the value of $m_i$ to 0
*odpar*

*for* i = 1 *to* n *dopar*
    *for* j = 1 *to* n *dopar*
        *if* $x_i > x_j$
        *then* $p_{ij}$ sets the value of $m_j$ to 1
        *fi*
        *if* $m_i = 0$ AND i < j
        *then* $p_{ij}$ sets the value of $m_j$ to 1
        *fi*
    *odpar*
*odpar*

*for* i = 1 to n *dopar*
    *if* $m_i = 0$
    *then* $p_{i1}$ sets the value of M to $x_i$
    *fi*
*odpar*

After execution of the first if-statement in the second, nested, parallel for-loop we have $m_i = 0$ if and only if $x_i = \max\{x_1, x_2, \ldots, x_n\}$; after the execution of the following if-statement we have $m_i = 0$ if and only if $x_i = \max\{x_1, x_2, \ldots, x_n\}$ and $i \leq j$ for all j such that $x_j = \max\{x_1, x_2, \ldots, x_n\}$. Thus, after this step there is a unique i such that $m_i = 0$ and no conflict can occur. Clearly the time complexity of all of the parallel for-loops is $O(1)$. Hence, the overall time complexity of algorithm CRCW_MAXIMUM is $O(1)$ with $n(n - 1)/2$ processors. The cost of this algorithm is $O(n^2)$ and it is thus far from being cost optimal, since a serial algorithm requires $O(n)$ time for this problem. The efficiency of algorithm CRCW_MAXIMUM is $1/n$, which is very poor. Below, we describe a method, based on the work of Shiloach and Vishkin (1981), that increases the efficiency of the maximum finding algorithm.

We partition the input into groups so that enough processors can be allocated to each group in order to find the maximum of that group by algorithm CRCW_MAXIMUM. As the computation progresses the number of candidates for the maximum is reduced. This implies that the number of processors available per candidate increases, and so the group size can be increased. If the group size is s, then $s(s - 1)/2$ processors are needed to find the maximum of that group in $O(1)$ time. Let us assume that $n = 2^k$ processors are available. At the first stage the size of each group is 2 and the maximum of each group can be found by one comparison. At the second stage, we still have n processors but the number of candidates has been reduced to $n/2$. We can make the size of each group 4 and have $n/8$ groups. Thus we can allocate 8 processors per group which is sufficient for a group of size 4. At the third stage, we have $n/8$ remaining candidates. If we select the group size as s, then we have $n/8s$ groups and $8s$ processors per group. To apply algorithm CRCW_MAXIMUM to each group, we must have $s(s - 1)/2 \leq 8s$, i.e., $s \leq 17$. Therefore, at the third stage we can, for convenience, use a group size of 16. Similarly, at the fourth stage we find the group size $s \leq 257$, and so a group size of 256 can be used. Thus, we find that the size of the group can be squared at each stage. This implies that after log log n stages the maximum of the list X will be found.

From the above discussion we know that it is possible to find the maximum of a list of n numbers in $O(\log \log n)$ time with n processors on a CRCW PRAM. Although this algorithm is slower than algorithm CRCW_MAXIMUM, its cost, $O(n \log \log n)$, is close to the time complexity of the corresponding serial algorithm. Also the efficiency of this algorithm $O(1/\log \log n)$ is much better than the efficiency of algorithm CRCW_MAXIMUM.

## 5.2.2 Maximum Finding on EREW PRAM

The maximum finding problem on the EREW PRAM model is considered here. We show that a simple algorithm can be constructed to find the maximum of a list of n numbers in $O(\log n)$ time on an EREW PRAM model. We assume that each processor $p_i$, $1 \leq i \leq n$, holds an element $x_i$ of X in its local memory. The algorithm is as follows:

*Algorithm* **EREW_MAXIMUM**

Input: Each processor $p_i$, $1 \leq i \leq n$, contains an element $x_i$ of the list $X = \{x_1, x_2, \ldots, x_n\}$.

Output: The element contained in processor $p_1$ is the largest of the $x_i$'s.

*for* $j = 1$ *to* $\lceil \log n \rceil - 1$ *do*
   *for* $i = 1$ *to* n in steps of $2^{j+1}$ *dopar*
      $p_i$ obtains $x_{i+2^j}$ through shared memory;
      *if* $x_{i+2^j} \geq x_i$
      *then* $x_i := x_{i+2^j}$
      *fi*
   *odpar*
*od*

The parallel for-loop can be executed in $O(1)$ time. Since the inner for-loop is repeated $\lceil \log n \rceil$ times, algorithm EREW_MAXIMUM requires $O(\log n)$ time with n processors.

If we assume that the list X is initially stored in the shared memory, then it can easily be verified that the maximum of X can be obtained in $O(\log n)$ time with $\lfloor n/2 \rfloor$ processors on the EREW PRAM. The cost of this algorithm is $O(n \log n)$, which is obviously not optimal.

Although algorithm EREW_MAXIMUM is not cost optimal, we can improve its cost by reducing the number of processors without increasing the time complexity, as follows. Let us assume that n/log n processors are available. We first partition the input list X into n/log n sublists, with about log n elements in each sublist. Now, each processor can find the maximum of each of these sublists in about log n time using the serial maximum finding algorithm. In the second phase we have n/log n elements, of which the maximum is to be obtained using n/log n processors. This will take (log n − log log n) time. Thus, the overall time complexity of this algorithm is O(log n) using n/log n processors. In fact, this result is a direct consequence of Brent's theorem of Section 3.2. The cost of this algorithm is O(n) and so it is optimal.

## 5.2.3  Maximum Finding on a Tree Machine

Consider an SIMD computer in which the processors are interconnected in a binary tree. Such an architecture is also referred to as a tree connected computer and has already been introduced in Chapter 2. It is assumed that the time taken by a datum to propagate between any two adjacent levels of the tree is constant.

Assume that we are required to find the maximum of a list X of n distinct elements on a tree machine with n leaves. Each nonleaf processor can store two elements and find their maximum. The basic idea on which the algorithm is based is very simple. Initially, the n elements are loaded in the leaf processors, each processor holding one element. Now each nonleaf processor determines the maximum of the two elements held by its children and routes it to its parent. After (log n + 1) steps the maximum of the list X is returned by the root processor. The algorithm is now given.

*Algorithm*  **TREE_MAXIMUM**

Input: A list X = {$x_1, x_2, \ldots, x_n$} of n elements.

Output: The maximum of X returned in the root processor.

*for* log n iterations *do*
    *for* all nonleaf processors *dopar*
        *if* the processor is the root and nonempty
        *then* return this element as the maximum of X
        *else if* the processor is empty
            *then do*
                acquire the contents of its two children;
                *if* the children are nonempty
                *then* keep the maximum of the two elements
                *fi*
            *od*
        *fi*
      *fi*
    *odpar*
*od*

Clearly this algorithm takes O(log n) time to find the maximum of n elements. The number of processors used is 2n − 1, i.e., O(n). Obviously this algorithm is not cost optimal.

# 5.3 SELECTION OF THE kth-SMALLEST ELEMENT ON EREW PRAM

The general selection problem is considered in this section and we develop an adaptive parallel algorithm for the solution of the problem on the EREW PRAM model. The algorithm is adaptive in the sense that it takes $O(n^h)$ time with $n^{1-h}$ processors, where h $(0 < h < 1)$ depends on the number of available processors. The algorithm described here is based on the ideas presented in Akl (1984). It is assumed that each processor is capable of executing an optimal serial selection algorithm. Also it is assumed that two parallel algorithms on the EREW PRAM model are available — one is required to read into all of the processors an element from a shared memory location; the other is used to compute all sums of the form $s_1 + s_2 + \ldots + s_i$, $1 \le i \le N$, where each processor $p_i$ holds the element $s_i$ in its local memory. These three basic algorithms are described first. Then the parallel selection algorithm based on them is presented.

## 5.3.1 An Optimal Serial Selection Algorithm

The serial selection algorithm given below is recursive in nature and uses the divide-and-conquer technique (see also Aho et al. 1974).

*Algorithm* SERIAL_SELECTION

Input: A list X containing n elements. Also a small integer constant c $(\ge 5)$.

Output: The kth-smallest element of X in location x.

*if* $|X| < c$
*then do*
      sort X;
       x := kth element of X
    *od*
*else* partition X into $|X|/c$ sublists
*fi*
sort each sublist and find its median;
find the median m of the $|X|/c$ medians;
obtain three sublists $X_1$, $X_2$, and $X_3$ from the elements of X as follows:
    $X_1 = \{x_i \in X \mid x_i < m\}$, $X_2 = \{x_i \in X \mid x_i = m\}$, and $X_3 = \{x_i \in X \mid x_i > m\}$;
*if* $|X_1| \ge k$
*then* find the kth-smallest element of $X_1$
*else if* $|X_1| + |X_2| \ge k$
    *then* x := m
    *else* find the $(k - |X_1| - |X_2|)$th-smallest element of $X_3$
    *fi*
*fi*

    To find the complexity T(n) of algorithm SERIAL_SELECTION, we observe that the first if-statement requires O(n) time. Sorting each of the $|X|/c$ sublists of size c takes constant time. Hence, considering all $|X|/c$ sublists, this step also takes O(n) time. The next step which finds m is a recursive call to algorithm SERIAL_SELECTION with $|X|/c$ elements. This step requires time $T(n/c)$. The sublists $X_1, X_2,$ and $X_3$ can be constructed by scanning each element of X once. Thus $O(n)$ time is required to implement this step. To calculate the complexity of the last if-statement observe that, since m is the median of $|X|/c$ elements, there are $|X|/2c$ elements greater than or equal to m. Again, each of these $|X|/c$ elements is itself a median of a list of c elements; hence each of these lists has $c/2$ elements greater than or equal to the corresponding median. Therefore, $|X|/4$ elements of X must be greater than or equal to m and so $|X_1| \leq 3|X|/4$. Similarly it can be shown that $|X_3| \leq 3|X|/4$. Since this step consists of a recursive call to algorithm SERIAL_SELECTION for a list with a maximum possible number of elements of $3|X|/4$, it takes time $T(3n/4)$. Thus the overall time complexity of algorithm SERIAL_SELECTION is given by

$$T(n) = O(n) + T(n/c) + T(3n/4).$$

If we select c so that $(n/c) + (3n/4) < n$, then the two recursive calls of algorithm SERIAL_SELECTION are performed on smaller and smaller instances of the original problem. Thus, for $c \geq 5$ the time complexity of algorithm SERIAL_SELECTION becomes $T(n) = O(n)$, which is optimal in view of the $\Omega(n)$ lower bound for this problem.

### 5.3.2  Simultaneous Reading of an Element from a Shared Memory Location by all Processors

In order to read an element from a shared memory location simultaneously by all of the N processors on an EREW PRAM a simple broadcasting mechanism can be used. Let s be a shared memory location holding an element x which all of the processors want to read simultaneously. The following algorithm implements such a read operation on the EREW PRAM model.

*Algorithm* **PARALLEL_BCAST**

Input: An element x in shared memory to be broadcast to N processors $p_1, p_2, \ldots, p_N$ using a shared memory array $M[1 : N]$ which is initially empty.

Output: Each of N processors holds x.

$p_1$ copies x into its local memory and then writes it into $M[1]$;
*for* $i = 0$ *to* $\lceil \log n \rceil - 1$ *do*
    *for* $j = 2^i + 1$ *to* $2^{i+1}$ *do*
        $p_j$ copies $M[j - 2^i]$ into its local memory and then writes it into $M[j]$
    *od*
*od*

It is clear that this algorithm requires $O(\log N)$ time.

### 5.3.3  Computing all Sums in Parallel

Here we develop two algorithms for computing sums on the EREW PRAM Model. One is for computing the sum of N elements $s_1, s_2, \ldots, s_N$; the other is for computing all sums of the form $s_1 + s_2 + \ldots + s_i, 1 \leq i \leq N$. The second summation problem is also known as the *prefix sums* problem. For both these algorithms let us assume that N processors $p_1, p_2, \ldots, p_N$ are available in the EREW PRAM model. We use balanced binary trees for the computation of both sums and partial sums.

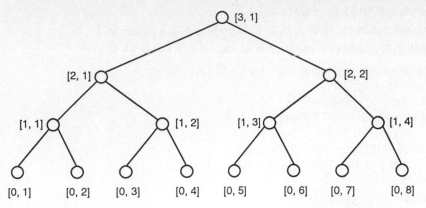

**Figure 5.1** The ps-tree with eight leaves.

To compute the sum of N elements we assume the existence of a balanced binary tree T with N leaves. The nodes of the tree are denoted by [h, j], where h is its height in the tree and j its position within the other nodes at the same height. Such a tree is referred to as the *partial sums tree*, or *ps-tree* and is shown in Figure 5.1. The height of all the leaf nodes is 0. Thus, node [0, j] represents leaf j and corresponds to the element $s_j$. Let us associate an element S[h, j] with each node [h, j] of the tree. For each internal node S[h, j] represents the sum of all the elements in the leaves of the complete subtree rooted at node [h, j]. The algorithm is given below.

*Algorithm* **PARALLEL_SUM**
Input: A list of N elements $s_1, s_2, \ldots, s_N$ where N is a power of 2.
Output: S[log N, 1] holds the desired sum.

*for* j = 1 *to* N *dopar*
    S[0, j]:= $s_j$
*odpar*
*for* h = 1 *to* log N *do*
    *for* j = 1 *to* $2^{(\log N) - h}$ *dopar*
        S[h, j] := S[h − 1, 2j − 1] + S[h − 1, 2j]
    *odpar*
*od*

It is easy to verify that the required sum S[log N, 1] will be available at the root after O(log N) time. We assumed initially that the EREW PRAM consists of N processors. Now, if we apply Brent's theorem (see Section 3.2) then we get an alternative implementation that uses P = N/log N processors and runs in O($\lceil$N/P$\rceil$ + log N) time, i.e., O(log N) time.

The algorithm above can be extended to solve the partial sums problem as follows. First, execute the summation algorithm given above. Then an additional parallel level-by-level traversal of the tree from the root to the leaves which roughly amounts to reversing the operation of the summation algorithm completes the job. Let us associate another element P[h, j] with each node [h, j]. At the termination of the algorithm P[0, j] holds the value $s_1 + s_2 + \ldots + s_j$, $1 \leq j \leq N$. The algorithm is as follows.

*Algorithm* **PARTIAL_SUMS**

Input: A list of N numbers $s_1, s_2, \ldots, s_N$ where N is a power of 2.

Output: P[0, j] holds the partial sum $s_1 + s_2 + \ldots + s_j$, $1 \leq j \leq N$.

Compute all S[h, j] using algorithm PARALLEL_SUM;
P[log N, 1] := 0;
*for* h = log N − 1 *downto* 0 *do*
    *for* j = 1 *to* $2^{(\log N) - h}$ *dopar*
        *if* j is odd
        *then* P[h, j] := P[h + 1, (j + 1)/2]
        *else* P[h, j] := P[h + 1, j/2] + S[h, j − 1]
        *fi*
    *odpar*
*od*
*for* j = 1 *to* N *dopar*
    P[0, j] := P[0, j] + S[0, j]
*odpar*

It is easy to verify that algorithm PARTIAL_SUMS takes O(log N) time with N processors on an EREW PRAM. Once again we can apply Brent's theorem and find that algorithm PARTIAL_SUMS can be implemented in time O(N/P + log N) using P processors on an EREW PRAM.

## 5.3.4 The Parallel Selection Algorithm

The parallel selection algorithm we present here is a parallel implementation of algorithm SERIAL_SELECTION which was described in Section 5.3.1. As before, we assume that the EREW PRAM consists of N processors $p_1, p_2, \ldots, p_N$. A list containing n elements is given of which the kth-smallest element is to be determined. It is assumed that the number n is broadcast to all the processors and that each processor has computed h from the relation $N = n^{1-h}$, $0 < h < 1$. A vector A, of length N, in the shared memory, is used whose ith position is A(i). In addition, we assume the availability of algorithms SERIAL_SELECTION, PARALLEL_BCAST, and PARTIAL_SUMS on all processors. The parallel selection algorithm is now given.

*Algorithm* **EREW_SELECTION**

Input: A list $X = \{x_1, x_2, \ldots, x_n\}$ and an integer k $(1 \leq k \leq n)$.

Output: The kth-smallest element of X in location x.

*for* i = 1 *to* N *dopar*
    read a distinct sublist $X_i = \{x_{(i-1)n^h+1}, x_{(i-1)n^h+2}, \ldots, x_{in^h}\}$ of X;
    obtain the median $m_i$ of $X_i$, i.e., the $\lceil |X_i|/2 \rceil$th element of $X_i$
           using algorithm SERIAL_SELECTION;
    A(i) := $m_i$
*odpar*

obtain the median m of A;

broadcast m to all the processors using algorithm PARALLEL_BCAST;

*for* i = 1 *to* N *dopar*

 partition $X_i$ into three sublists $X_{i1}$, $X_{i2}$, and $X_{i3}$ with elements

     smaller than, equal to, and greater than m, respectively;

 merge $X_{i1}$, $X_{i2}$, and $X_{i3}$ to form $X_1$, $X_2$, and $X_3$, respectively

*odpar*

*if* $|X_1| \geq k$

*then* find, in parallel, the kth-smallest element of $X_1$

*else if* $|X_1| + |X_2| \geq k$

 *then* x := m

 *else* find, in parallel, the $(k - |X_1| - |X_2|)$th-smallest element of $X_3$

 *fi*

*fi*

### Complexity Analysis

The first for-loop of algorithm EREW_SELECTION is executed by all the processors in $O(n^h)$ time. In the next step the median m of the N elements in vector A is obtained by a recursive call to algorithm EREW_SELECTION. Therefore, if T(n) is the overall time complexity of algorithm EREW_SELECTION then this step requires time $T(N) = T(n^{1-h})$. Broadcasting m to all of the processors takes $O(\log n^{1-h}) \equiv O(\log n)$ time. The first step of the second for-loop takes $O(n^h)$ time to construct, in parallel, $X_{i1}$, $X_{i2}$, and $X_{i3}$, for $1 \leq i \leq N$. The second step of this loop merges $X_{i1}$, $X_{i2}$, and $X_{i3}$, $1 \leq i \leq N$, to form $X_1$, $X_2$, and $X_3$, respectively. Consider the case of $X_{i1}$, $1 \leq i \leq N$, as an example to show how this merging process can be implemented. Using algorithm PARTIAL_SUMS, for each i $(1 \leq i \leq n^{1-h})$, the sums $s_{i1} = |X_{11}| + |X_{21}| + \ldots |X_{i1}|$ are first computed. This step requires $O(\log n^{1-h}) \equiv O(\log n)$ time. Then each processor $p_i$ copies $X_{i1}$ into $X_1$ beginning at location $s_{(i-1)1} + 1$ where it is assumed that $s_{01} = 0$. This step obviously requires $O(n^h)$ time. The final if-statement involves two recursive calls to algorithm EREW_SELECTION. By a similar line of reasoning to that used for the last if-statement of algorithm SERIAL_SELECTION (see Section 5.3.1), we find that $|X_1| \leq 3n/4$, and $|X_3| \leq 3n/4$ which implies that this statement also requires time T(3n/4). Thus, the overall time complexity of algorithm EREW_SELECTION is

$$T(n) = O(n^h) + T(n^{1-h}) + T(3n/4).$$

From this equation, we find the time complexity of algorithm EREW_SELECTION to be $T(n) = O(n^h)$, for n > 4, using $P(n) = n^{1-h}$ processors. Thus, the cost of the algorithm is given by

$$C(n) = T(n) \times P(n) = O(n),$$

which is optimal.

## 5.4 ANOTHER PARALLEL SELECTION ALGORITHM ON EREW PRAM

The parallel selection algorithm due to Akl (1984), described in the previous section, runs in $O(n/P)$ time using $P \leq n^{1-h}$ processors, where $0 < h < 1$. In this section, we present another selection algorithm on the EREW PRAM model, based on the work of Vishkin (1987). This algorithm requires $O((n/P) + \log^2 n \log \log n)$ time using $P \leq n/(\log^2 n \log \log n)$ processors. The steps in this algorithm are as follows: (a) reduce the original selection problem of size $n$ into a smaller instance, of size $n_1$ (say), of the selection problem such that $n_1 \leq n/\log^2 n$. This reduction is performed by applying an optimal but slow selection algorithm; (b) apply a parallel sorting algorithm to the reduced selection problem. The sorting algorithm is used as a nonoptimal but fast selection algorithm. Thus, we are essentially composing an efficient parallel algorithm from two existing algorithms for the same problem. Onc is optimal but slow and the other is fast but nonoptimal. The second is faster but the total number of operations it requires is larger. The new algorithm has as its first phase the first algorithm and switches to the second algorithm at the right time. The new algorithm is faster than the first algorithm but its total number of operations is less than that of the second algorithm. A more formal description of the algorithm is as follows.

### *Algorithm* ANOTHER_EREW_SELECTION

Input: A list $X = \{x_1, x_2, \ldots, x_n\}$ and an integer k $(1 \leq k \leq n)$. It is assumed that $P = n/(\log^2 n \log \log n)$ processors are available.

Output: The kth-smallest element of X.

m := n; r := k;
broadcast m and r to all the processors using algorithm PARALLEL_BCAST;
Y := X;
*while* m > P *do*
   *for* i = 1 *to* P *dopar*
       read a distinct sublist $Y_i = \{y_{(i-1)m/P + 1}, y_{(i-1)m/P + 2}, \ldots, y_{im/P}\}$ of Y;
       obtain the median $m_i$ of $Y_i$ using algorithm SERIAL_SELECTION;
       A(i) := $m_i$
   *odpar*
   sort the P medians A(i), $1 \leq i \leq P$;
   obtain the median m of A;
   broadcast m to all the processors using algorithm PARALLEL_BCAST;
   record in $n_1$, $n_2$, and $n_3$ the number of elements smaller than,
         equal to, and greater than m, respectively;
   broadcast $n_1$, $n_2$, and $n_3$ to all processors;
   *if* $n_1 < r \leq n_1 + n_2$
   *then* output m and terminate the algorithm
   *else if* $r \leq n_1$
      *then* Y := "all elements smaller than m"; m := $n_1$
      *else* Y := "all elements greater than m"; m := $n_3$; r := r − $(n_1 + n_2)$
      *fi*
   *fi*
*od*
sort the elements of array Y and output the rth element

## Complexity Analysis

In the initialization part of the algorithm m and r are broadcast to all P ( = $n/(\log^2 n \log \log n)$) processors. This requires $O(\log P) \equiv O(\log n)$ time. List X can be copied into list Y in $O(n/P) = O(\log^2 n \log \log n)$ time.

To compute $n_1$, $n_2$, and $n_3$ we use algorithm PARALLEL_SUM. Consider the computation of $n_1$. The computation of each of $n_2$ and $n_3$ is similar. We enter 1 in the corresponding leaf of the ps-tree for each element smaller than m, 0 otherwise (see Section 5.3.3). Algorithm PARALLEL_SUM is then used. Thus, the computation of the values of $n_1$, $n_2$, and $n_3$ takes time $O((m/P) + \log n)$.

Assignment into list Y in the final if-statement of the while-loop is required in two cases. Consider this assignment in the case $r \leq n_1$. As before, we enter 1 in the corresponding leaf of the ps-tree for each element smaller than m, 0 otherwise. Algorithm PARTIAL_SUMS is then applied. The partial sum at each element smaller than m is its serial number among elements smaller than m in the "old" list Y and its entry number in the "new" list Y. The assignment to Y in the case $r > n_1 + n_2$ is similar. Thus, whichever assignment is made can be performed in $O((m/P) + \log m)$ time.

Let us now consider an iteration of the while-loop for a list of length m for some $m \leq n$. Clearly, the parallel for-statement takes $O(m/P)$ time to find P medians, using algorithm SERIAL_SELECTION. In order to sort P medians, we use the EREW PRAM implementation of Batcher's sorting network discussed in Section 4.4. Since this sorting algorithm takes $O(\log^2 n)$ time with $O(n)$ processors to sort n numbers, the computation of the median m of P medians by sorting requires $O(\log^2 P) \equiv O(\log^2 n)$ time with P (= $n/\log^2 n \log \log n$) processors. Broadcasting m to all the processors takes $O(\log P) \equiv O(\log n)$ time. We have already seen that computing $n_1$, $n_2$, and $n_3$, and then broadcasting their values to all of the processors can be implemented in $O((m/P) + \log m)$ time. The if-statement also takes $O((m/P) + \log m)$ time. Following the same line of reasoning as for analyzing algorithm SERIAL_SELECTION, we find that $n_1 \leq 3m/4$, and $n_3 \leq 3m/4$. Let $m_j$ be the length of the list Y at the beginning of the jth iteration of the while-loop. From the above discussion, we find that $m_j \leq (3/4)^{j-1}n$. The body of the while-loop is repeatedly executed until $m_j \leq P$ (= $n/(\log^2 n \log \log n)$). Thus, the number of times this loop is executed is $O(\log \log n)$. Hence, the total time required by the while-loop is

$$\leq \sum_{1 \leq j \leq O(\log \log n)} O((3/4)^{j-1}n / P + \log^2 n)$$

$$= O((n / P) + \log^2 n \log \log n)$$

which is $O(\log^2 n \log \log n)$ since $P = n/(\log^2 n \log \log n)$.

Finally, to sort the elements of the updated list Y (with $|Y| \leq P$), and return its rth element requires $O(\log^2 P) \equiv O(\log^2 n)$ time. This is the kth-smallest element of X. Therefore, the overall complexity of algorithm ANOTHER_EREW_SELECTION is $O(\log^2 n \log \log n)$ with $n/(\log^2 n \log \log n)$ processors. We can use Brent's theorem (Section 3.2) to implement this algorithm using a smaller number of processors and obtain $O(n/P)$ time algorithm with $P \leq n/(\log^2 n \log \log n)$ processors. Alternatively, algorithm ANOTHER_EREW_SELECTION takes $O((n/P) + \log^2 n \log \log n)$ time using P processors. Clearly, the cost of this parallel selection algorithm is $O(n)$ and is optimal.

# 5.5  SELECTION ON A TREE MACHINE

In this section a parallel algorithm for selecting the kth-smallest integer from among n given unsorted m-bit positive integers is developed. The computational model used is an SIMD computer in which the processors are interconnected in the form of a binary tree as described in Section 2.2. The algorithm presented here is based on the work of Cooper and Akl (1986). We assume that there are 2n − 1 processors organized in the form of a binary tree with n leaf processors, where n is a power of 2. The leaf processors are designated as $p_1, p_2, \ldots, p_n$. Each of the leaf processors can hold an m-bit integer, send the ith bit of this integer ($1 \leq i \leq m$) to its parent, and can terminate or switch itself off. Each of the n − 2 internal node processors can route an integer or an instruction (encoded suitably), and can add two integers. The root processor can store and update four values, route instructions to its descendants, and compare and add two integers.

Let us assume that the given list X consists of n m-bit integers and we are required to find the kth-smallest integer, where $1 \leq k \leq n$. Now, if we can find the sublist S consisting of the |S| largest integers of X then either (a) the kth-smallest integer is included in S and in this case we can ignore all of the integers in X − S, or (b) the kth-smallest integer is not in S and in this case we can ignore all the integers in S. This process can be continued until we are left with the kth-smallest integer. The kth-smallest integer may be duplicated, in which case any one will be selected by the algorithm. To find the integers of the sublist S we consider the most significant bit of the integers in X. For example, if the binary representation of the jth integer in X is $a_j(m)a_j(m-1) \ldots a_j(1)$ then all the integers with $a_j(m) = 1$, $1 \leq j \leq n$, belong, in the first round, to S. In the second round the integers with $a_j(m-1) = 1$, $1 \leq j \leq n$ belong to S, and so on. By considering successive bits and by removing a portion of the original list in each round, we will be left with the required kth-smallest integer. The algorithm is given below.

### *Algorithm* TREE_SELECTION

Input: A list X of n m-bit positive integers each stored in a leaf processor of the tree machine. The root processor contains the values of n and k ($1 \leq k \leq n$) in locations R and x, respectively.

Output: The kth-smallest integer of X returned in the root processor.

i := m;
terminated := FALSE;
*while* not terminated *do*
    each leaf processor sends the value of ith bit to its parent;
    each parent processor adds the two values it receives and
        sends the result to its parent;
    SUM := sum obtained at root;
    *if* R − x − SUM ≥ 0
    *then do*
        R := R − SUM;
        route, through the internal nodes, the instruction
            "if ith bit = 1 then terminate" to all the leaves
    *od*

*else if* R − x − SUM = −1 AND SUM = 1

    **then** route, through the internal nodes, the instruction "if ith bit = 1 then send
            value to root" to all the leaves

    **else do**

        x := x − (R − SUM);

        R := SUM;

        route, through the internal nodes, the instruction "if ith bit = 0
            then switch off" to all the leaves

    **od**

    *fi*

*fi*

i := i − 1;

*if* R = 1

*then do*

    route, through the internal nodes, the instruction "send the value remaining
        in one leaf to the root" to all the leaves;

    terminated := TRUE

    **od**

*fi*

*if* i = 0 AND not terminated

*then do*

    route, through the internal nodes, the instruction "send value from any leaf
        to the root" to all the leaves;

    terminated := TRUE

    **od**

  *fi*

**od**

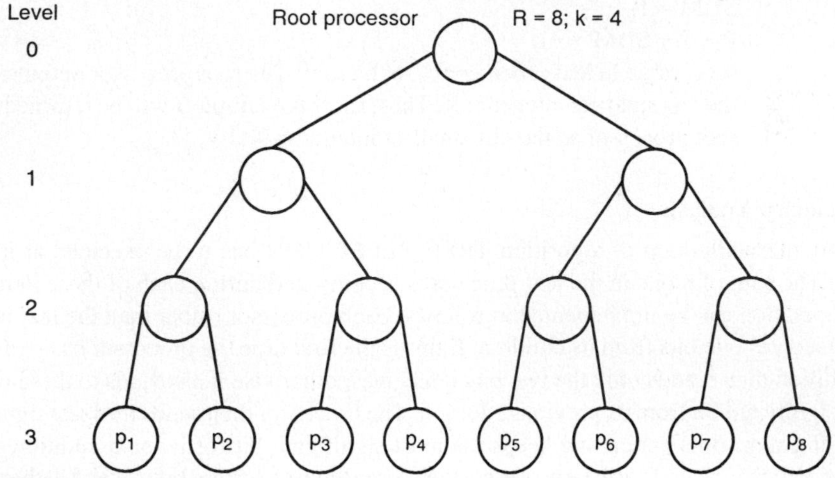

**Figure 5.2** Tree machine for selection. Initially each leaf processors holds one integer of the list.

Consider the following example which illustrates the application of algorithm TREE_SELECTION. Suppose we want to find the 4th-smallest integer in X = {8, 12, 2, 14, 3, 6, 7, 15}. We need a tree machine with n = 8 leaf processors where each leaf holds one integer from the list X (Figure 5.2, on previous page).

Start:

| Leaf processor: | $p_1$ | $p_2$ | $p_3$ | $p_4$ | $p_5$ | $p_6$ | $p_7$ | $p_8$ |
|---|---|---|---|---|---|---|---|---|
| Content: | 1000 | 1100 | 0010 | 1110 | 0011 | 0110 | 0111 | 1111 |
| Root: | R = 8; x = 4. | | | | | | | |

The action of the algorithm is described by giving the effect of each execution of its loop

1st iteration:

SUM = 4;
R − x − SUM = 0;
switch off leaf processors $p_1$, $p_2$, $p_4$, and $p_8$;
R = 4; x = 4.

2nd iteration:

SUM = 2;
R − x − SUM = −2;
switch off leaf processors $p_3$, and $p_5$;
R = 2; x = 2.

3rd iteration:

SUM = 2;
R − x − SUM = −2;
R = 2; x = 2.

4th iteration:

SUM = 1;
R − x − SUM = −1;
send value in leaf processor $p_7$ to the root. The root processor outputs this as the 4th-smallest integer in X. Thus, for this example 7 will be returned by the root processor as the 4th-smallest integer in X.

## Complexity Analysis

Clearly, the while-loop of algorithm TREE_SELECTION has to be executed at most m times. The sum of n bits in the leaf processors is computed during each of these iterations. This operation can be implemented as follows. Each processor (other than the leaf processors) receives two bits from its children. If this is the first time the processor has performed an addition then it adds only the two bits it receives; otherwise it also adds to these bits the most significant bit from its previous addition. The processor then sends the least significant bit of the sum to its parent and keeps the most significant bit for its next addition. These operations are repeated until the processor's children have no further bits to send. It then sends its last bit to its parent. Thus the log n bits of the sum at the root processor can be obtained in bit-serial manner in O(log n) time. When the root processor sends an instruction to the leaf processors through its descendants the transmission takes O(log n) time. Thus each of the required m iterations takes O(log n) time and hence the overall time complexity of algorithm TREE_SELECTION becomes O(m log n).

Since the number of processors used is 2n − 1, the cost of algorithm TREE_SELECTION is O(mn log n). This algorithm is not cost optimal because, in order to select the kth-smallest integer of n m-bit positive integers, the best-known serial algorithm has complexity O(mn) (see Blum et al. 1972).

Although the cost of algorithm TREE_SELECTION differs from its serial counterpart by a factor of log n, the discussion below shows how the parallel algorithm can be extended to produce the optimal cost of O(mn). Assume that the tree machine consists of N leaf processors, where N is a power of 2 and that N log N ≤ n. We assign n/N integers of the list X to each leaf processor. The extended parallel algorithm differs from algorithm TREE_SELECTION only in that each leaf processor performs the addition of n/N bits of its integers serially and, during the removal of integers from further consideration, it scans all n/N integers serially. In the extended algorithm a leaf processor switches itself off if all the n/N integers it initially contained are removed from consideration.

Thus, each of the m iterations consists of the following actions:

(a) O(n/N) steps are required within the leaf processors to find the sum of n/N bits;

(b) O(log N) steps are required to move information up and down the tree;

(c) O(n/N) steps are required to remove rejected elements within each leaf processor.

Therefore, the time per iteration is O(n/N) and the overall time complexity of the extended parallel selection algorithm is O(mn/N). Since 2N − 1 processors are used, the cost of the algorithm is O(mn). This cost is optimal in view of the $\Omega(mn)$ bit operations required to read the input serially.


# 5.6 COMPLEXITY OF PARALLEL SEARCH ON THE CREW PRAM MODEL

In this section, we obtain a bound on the number of comparison steps required for searching on the CREW PRAM model. This bound gives a limit for the best possible running time for searching on this model. Since CREW PRAM is a relatively strong model of parallel computation (in the sense that it has practically no communication restriction and it also allows read-conflict) the bound obtained on this model provides a useful lower bound on the time complexity of parallel search. The result presented here was first reported by Kruskal (1983).

**Theorem 5.1:** Let $T_s(n, P)$ be the number of comparison steps required by P processors to search for a key in a sorted list of n elements on the CREW PRAM model. Assume also that $n = (P + 1)^k − 1$, where k is an integer. Then,

$$T_s(n, P) = \lceil \log (n + 1)/\log (P + 1) \rceil.$$

**Proof:** We use induction to show that in k comparison steps, we can search a sorted list consisting of $(P + 1)^k − 1$ elements.

The basis k = 1 is simple. In this case n = P and $T_s(P, P) = 1$, i.e., one comparison step is required to search for the key.

Now, as the induction hypothesis, assume that the formula is true for all $i \le k - 1$. We show that under this assumption the result must hold for $i = k$. To search a list containing $(P + 1)^k - 1$ elements, we can compare the element being searched to the elements in the list indexed by $j.(P + 1)^{k-1}$, for $j = 1, 2, \ldots, P$. This comparison step can be performed, in parallel, in one step with P processors. After this step either the element has been found or it lies in one of the $P + 1$ unexamined sequences. Thus, in the next step, the problem is reduced to searching a list consisting of $(P + 1)^{k-1} - 1$ elements. By the induction hypothesis, $k - 1$ comparison steps are sufficient to search a list consisting of $(P + 1)^{k-1} - 1$ elements. Thus, the theorem is proved. In general, in order to search a list of n elements in k comparison steps, we must have

$$(P + 1)^k - 1 \ge n$$
$$k = \lceil \log (n + 1)/\log (P + 1) \rceil.$$

To prove that the bound is tight we have to show that the number of parallel steps required by any search algorithm is at least k as specified above. We have seen that, during the first step, any algorithm can examine P elements using P processors. Therefore, there must be some segment of unexamined elements with length at least

$$\lceil (n - P)/(P + 1) \rceil \ge (n - P)/(P + 1) = \{(n + 1)/(P + 1)\} - 1.$$

After the kth step, there must be one or more segments of unexamined elements with length at least $\{(n + 1)/(P + 1)^k\} - 1$. Thus, the number of parallel steps required by any algorithm is at least the minimum k such that

$$\{(n + 1)/(P + 1)^k\} - 1 \le 0$$
$$k = \lceil \log (n + 1)/\log (P + 1) \rceil.$$

Thus we have seen that $T_s(n, P) = \lceil \log (n + 1)/\log (P + 1) \rceil$ is the best possible running time for searching a list of length n on the CREW PRAM model with P processors. Since the list is already sorted the serial binary search can be used which takes $O(\log n)$ time to search for a key. Thus, in such a case the maximum possible speedup achieved by any parallel search algorithm is $O(\log P)$. That is, the maximum speedup achievable for the searching problem through parallelization is only logarithmic in the number of processors. Although this result has been obtained for the CREW PRAM model, the same can be extended to any other model of parallel computation. The reason is that, since the CREW PRAM requires as many as $\lceil \log (n + 1)/\log (P + 1) \rceil$ parallel steps in the worst case, any other (more) realistic model will require *at least* $\lceil \log (n + 1)/\log (P + 1) \rceil$ parallel steps in the worst case.

## 5.7  SEARCHING ON PRAM MODELS

From Kruskal's theorem (Theorem 5.1), we have seen that the speedup obtained by parallel search on any model of parallel computation with P processors is no more than a factor of log P. In this section, we consider the searching problem on shared memory SIMD models for both unsorted and sorted lists. From the performances of these algorithms it would seem that it is not suitable to search a *single* element in a parallel environment since the serial algorithm for searching a sorted list has logarithmic complexity.

## 5.7.1 Searching an Unsorted List

We first present a general algorithm for searching an unsorted list on the shared memory SIMD model with P processors and then examine its time complexity under different memory access restrictions. It is assumed that the length of the list to be searched is n $(1 < P \leq n)$, where the elements are not necessarily distinct. The algorithm is as follows.

*Algorithm* **PRAM_SEARCH**

Input: A list X= $\{x_1, x_2, \ldots, x_n\}$ and an element s.

Output: If the search is successful then the algorithm returns in location m the smallest index of an occurrence of the element s in X; otherwise it returns the value 0.

```
m := 0;
for i = 1 to P dopar
    read s
odpar
for i = 1 to P dopar
    read the sublist X_i = {x_(i-1)(n/P) + 1, x_(i-1)(n/P) + 2, ... , x_i(n/P)};
    search X_i serially and return the index m_i if the search
                is successful otherwise return a value 0
odpar
if only one m_i is nonzero
then m := m_i
else if m_s is the smallest of all nonzero m_i's
    then m := m_s
    fi
fi
```

**Complexity Analysis**

If we assume that the computational model is EREW PRAM then the implementation of the first parallel for-loop requires $O(\log P)$ time using the standard broadcast mechanism. The second parallel for-loop obviously requires $O(n/P)$ time to execute on each processor a serial search algorithm on a sublist of length n/P. Finally, to output m, we require a further $O(\log P)$ time. The overall complexity of algorithm PRAM_SEARCH on the EREW PRAM model is thus

$$T_{EREW}(SEARCH) = O(\log P) + O(n/P).$$

On the CREW PRAM model, the first parallel for-loop can be implemented in $O(1)$ time while the complexity of other statements remain unchanged. Therefore, in this case also we have

$$T_{CREW}(SEARCH) = O(\log P) + O(n/P).$$

Clearly, both of these implementations of algorithm PRAM_SEARCH are not cost optimal.

We will now consider the implementation of algorithm PRAM_SEARCH on the strongest variant of the PRAM — namely, the CRCW PRAM. In this case, the first and the second parallel for-loops require $O(1)$ and $O(n/P)$ times, respectively, as for the CREW PRAM model. Finally, the if-statement can be implemented in $O(1)$ time if the write conflict resolution rule used is that the lowest indexed processor's value is written into the shared memory location. Thus, the time complexity of algorithm PRAM_SEARCH on CRCW PRAM is

$$T_{CRCW}(SEARCH) = O(n/P).$$

The cost of the algorithm in this case is $O(n)$, which is optimal.

## 5.7.2  Searching a Sorted List

The problem of searching a sorted list is now considered. It is shown that, although searching a sorted list on the EREW PRAM is no better than serial search, searching on the CREW PRAM achieves the best possible running time when all of the elements in the list are distinct. However, on the CRCW PRAM model the best possible time bound can be achieved even if the elements in the list are not distinct.

Consider first the case of a P-processor EREW PRAM model. Assume that we have a list $X = \{x_1, x_2, \ldots, x_n\}$ whose elements are sorted in nondecreasing order. The structure of the algorithm in this case is exactly the same as that of algorithm PRAM_SEARCH with the exception that now searching the P sublists (within the second parallel for-loop) is performed using the binary search algorithm. Thus, the overall time complexity of searching a sorted list of length n on the EREW PRAM with P processors is $O(\log P) + O(\log (n/P)) \equiv O(\log n)$. This is no better than that of the binary search algorithm on a single processor. Thus, searching a sorted list on the EREW PRAM is not to be recommended.

We now consider the CREW PRAM as the model of computation and assume that all of the elements of the list $X = \{x_1, x_2, \ldots, x_n\}$ are distinct. We will see that, without this assumption, the CREW PRAM searching algorithm will perform no better than the serial binary search algorithm. The algorithm presented is based on the ideas used in the proof of Theorem 5.1. The algorithm works as follows. During each iteration of the algorithm we partition the current list into $(P + 1)$ sublists of equal length. P processors are then employed to compare, in parallel, the element being searched for (s) with the P elements at the boundary of these sublists. As in Theorem 5.1, let us assume that $n = (P + 1)^k - 1$. Then, at the first step each processor $p_i$ compares s with $x_j$, where $j = i(P + 1)^{k-1}$, for $i = 1, 2, \ldots, P$. If $x_j < s$ then $x_j$ and all elements preceding $x_j$ in the list are removed from consideration; otherwise if $x_j > s$ then $x_j$ and all elements following $x_j$ are removed from consideration. At the next step only a sublist of length $(P + 1)^{k-1} - 1$ has to be searched and a similar procedure is followed. This process continues either until s is found in the list or the list is exhausted without success. A more formal description of the algorithm is now given.

*Algorithm* **SEARCH_SORTED_LIST**

Input: A sorted list $X = \{x_1, x_2, \ldots, x_n\}$ of distinct elements and an element s.

Output: The algorithm returns the index of the position of s within X in location m if the search is successful; otherwise it returns the value 0.

m := 0;
k := $\lceil \log (n + 1)/\log (P + 1) \rceil$;

*while* ((the list is not exhausted) AND m = 0) *do*

   *for* i = 1 *to* P *dopar*

      *if* $x_{i(P+1)^{k-1}} = s$

      *then* m := index of element $x_{i(P+1)^{k-1}}$ in the initial list X

      *else if* $x_{i(P+1)^{k-1}} < s$

          *then* remove $x_{i(P+1)^{k-1}}$ and all the elements preceding it

          *else* remove $x_{i(P+1)^{k-1}}$ and all the elements following it

          *fi*

      *fi*

      k := k − 1

   *odpar*

*od*

To illustrate the execution of algorithm SEARCH_SORTED_LIST, consider the following examples. Suppose that the given list to be searched is

$$X = \{2, 3, 5, 8, 12, 14, 16, 17, 18, 20, 25, 28, 30, 35, 40\}.$$

A number of successful and unsuccessful searches are shown below assuming that the CREW PRAM has P = 3 processors.

(a) Suppose that s = 16. During the first execution of the while-loop of the algorithm $p_1$, $p_2$, and $p_3$ compare 16 with $x_4$, $x_8$, and $x_{12}$ respectively. After removal of all elements from X which cannot be equal to s, we are left with the sublist $X_1 = \{12, 14, 16\}$. This is shown in Figure 5.3a.

During the second iteration of the while-loop $p_1$, $p_2$, and $p_3$, compare 16 with $x_1$, $x_2$, and $x_3$ of the sublist $X_1$, respectively (Figure 5.3b). Processor $p_3$ finds a match and returns the index, 7, of element with value 16 in the initial list.

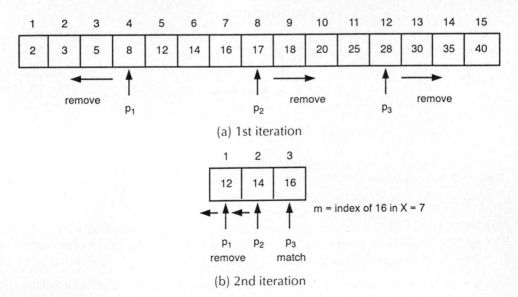

(a) 1st iteration

(b) 2nd iteration

**Figure 5.3** Searching X for s = 16 using algorithm SEARCH_SORTED_LIST.

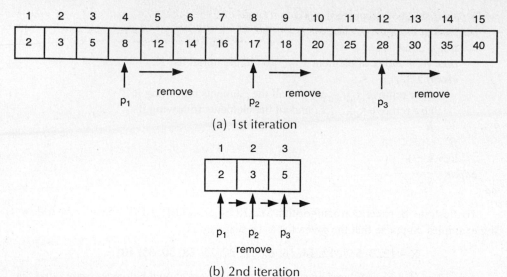

(a) 1st iteration

(b) 2nd iteration

**Figure 5.4** Searching X for s = 1. The search is unsuccessful.

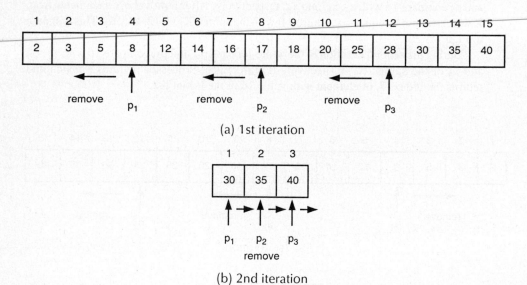

(a) 1st iteration

(b) 2nd iteration

**Figure 5.5** Searching X for s = 42. The search is unsuccessful.

(b)  s = 28. During the first iteration of the while-loop $p_1, p_2$, and $p_3$, compare 28 with $x_4, x_8$, and $x_{12}$, respectively. Processor $p_3$ finds a match and returns the index, 12, of the value 28 in X. The algorithm then terminates.

(c)  s = 1. At the end of the first iteration of the while-loop we are left with the sublist $X_1 = \{2, 3, 5\}$.

During the second iteration of the while-loop $p_1$, $p_2$, and $p_3$, compare 1 with $x_1$, $x_2$, and $x_3$ of the sublist $X_1$, respectively, without success. Since at the end of the second iteration the list X is exhausted, the algorithm halts without succeeding and it returns m = 0. This is illustrated in Figure 5.4.

(d)  s = 42. At the end of the first iteration of the while-loop the sublist which remains to be searched is $X_1$ = {30, 35, 40}.

During the second iteration of the while-loop $p_1$, $p_2$, and $p_3$, compare 42 with $x_1$, $x_2$, and $x_3$ of the sublist $X_1$, respectively, without success. The search is completed without success and m = 0 is returned. This is illustrated in Figure 5.5.

### Complexity Analysis

The time complexity of algorithm SEARCH_SORTED_LIST follows from Theorem 5.1. The algorithm shows that there can be at most $\lceil \log (n + 1)/\log (P + 1) \rceil$ iterations of the body of the parallel for-loop. It can be verified that the statements in the parallel for-loop can be implemented in constant time. Therefore, the overall time complexity of algorithm SEARCH_SORTED_LIST is $O(\log (n + 1)/\log (P + 1))$.

Although the cost of this parallel algorithm $C(n) = O(P \log (n + 1)/\log (P + 1))$ is not optimal, the algorithm achieves the best possible running time for the search problem.

Algorithm SEARCH_SORTED_LIST is based on the assumption that all the elements of the list X are distinct. If we remove this constraint, then more than one processor will succeed in finding an element of X equal to s. As a result the algorithm suffers from write-conflict, since more than one processor will attempt to assign a value to the variable m at the same time. To resolve this conflict we may use the standard broadcasting mechanism. However, in this case the time complexity of algorithm SEARCH_SORTED_LIST increases to $O(\log n)$, which is the same as that of serial binary search. Thus algorithm SEARCH_SORTED_LIST is useful *only* when all of the elements are distinct. However, if we use the CRCW PRAM model then the write-conflict which arises in this algorithm can be resolved in constant time using an appropriate conflict resolution rule. Therefore, algorithm SEARCH_SORTED_LIST shows the same performance on the CRCW PRAM model even when the elements of the list are not distinct.

## 5.8  SEARCHING ON MESH CONNECTED COMPUTER

A two-dimensional mesh consisting of n processors is considered as the computational model for the searching problem. We assume that each processor stores one element of the list to be searched. Processors are identified by a pair of integers i, j = 1, 2, . . . , $\sqrt{n}$. Processor $p_{1,1}$ is used for input and output, as shown in Figure 5.6.

We assume that the list to be searched is represented by X = $\{x_{i,j} | i, j = 1, 2, . . . , \sqrt{n}\}$. The algorithm we describe here returns either "TRUE" or "FALSE" depending on whether the search is successful or not. We also discuss how the index of an element with value s (say) in X can also be obtained. In case of the multiple occurrences of s we can easily modify the algorithm to return as output the index of the lowest indexed processor holding s. In presenting the algorithm we use two well-defined basic steps as explained on page 140.

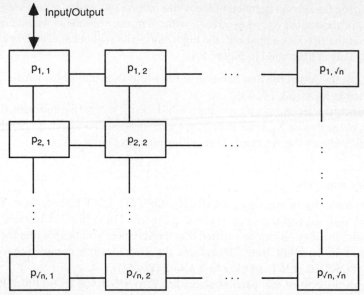

**Figure 5.6** A two-dimensional mesh connected computer for searching. Each processor stores an element of the list to be searched.

### Compare and Distribute

In this step s is sent to all of the n processors of the mesh and the processors perform a comparison operation. More precisely, when processor $p_{1,1}$ receives s it compares it with $x_{1,1}$. If $x_{1,1} = s$, $p_{1,1}$ sets $r_{1,1}$ (the result of comparison) to "TRUE"; otherwise $r_{1,1}$ is set to "FALSE." Processor $p_{1,1}$ retains $r_{1,1}$ and transmits s to $p_{1,2}$. When it receives s, $p_{1,2}$ sets $r_{1,2}$ either to "TRUE" or "FALSE" depending on whether $x_{1,2} = s$ or not. Then, the two row neighbors $p_{1,1}$ and $p_{1,2}$ simultaneously send s to processors $p_{2,1}$ and $p_{2,2}$, respectively. In the next stage $r_{2,1}$ and $r_{2,2}$ are computed and then the two column neighbors $p_{1,2}$ and $p_{2,2}$ send s to $p_{1,3}$ and $p_{2,3}$, respectively, at the same time. This process continues until s has reached all the processors. The following algorithm can be used to perform this step.

*Algorithm* **COMPARE_AND_DISTRIBUTE**

Input: The list $X = \{x_{i,j} \mid i, j = 1, 2, \ldots, \sqrt{n}\}$ stored in a mesh so that the processor $p_{i,j}$ stores the element $x_{i,j}$, for $i, j = 1, 2, \ldots, \sqrt{n}$; the element s is available in processor $p_{1,1}$.

Output: In processor $p_{i,j}$ the variable $r_{i,j}$ = TRUE if s is stored in $p_{i,j}$; otherwise $r_{i,j}$ = FALSE, for all $i, j = 1, 2, \ldots, \sqrt{n}$.

*if* $s = x_{1,1}$ *then* $r_{1,1} :=$ TRUE *else* $r_{1,1} :=$ FALSE *fi*
*for* i = 1 *to* $\sqrt{n} - 1$ *do*
    *for* j = 1 *to* i *dopar*
        *if* $s = x_{j,i+1}$
        *then* $r_{j,i+1} :=$ TRUE
        *else* $r_{j,i+1} :=$ FALSE
        *fi*
        $p_{j,i}$ sends s to $p_{j,i+1}$
    *odpar*

*for* j = 1 *to* i + 1 *dopar*
   *if* s = $x_{i+1,\,j}$
   *then* $r_{i+1,\,j}$ := TRUE
   *else* $r_{i+1,\,j}$ := FALSE
   *fi*
   $P_{i,\,j}$ sends s to $P_{i+1,\,j}$
*odpar*
*od*

The bodies of both of the parallel for-loops of algorithm COMPARE_AND_DISTRIBUTE require constant time. Since the body of the outermost for-loop which is repeated $\sqrt{n} - 1$ times consists of these two parallel for-loops, the overall complexity of this algorithm is $O(\sqrt{n})$. The execution of algorithm COMPARE_AND_DISTRIBUTE is illustrated in Figure 5.7 using an example.

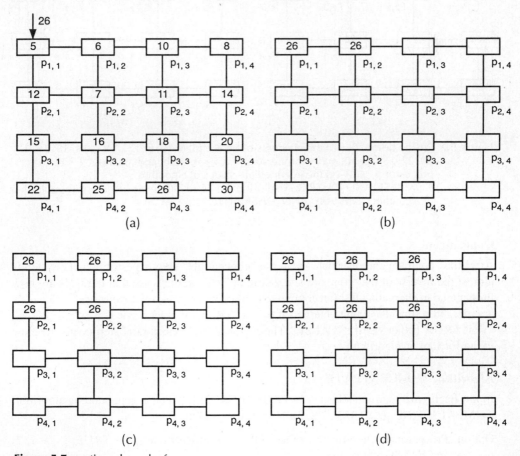

**Figure 5.7** continued overleaf.

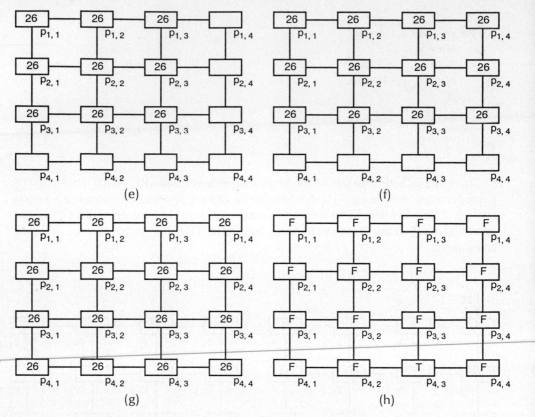

**Figure 5.7** (a) The distribution of the elements of list X = {5, 6, 10, 8, 12, 7, 11, 14, 15, 16, 18, 20, 22, 25, 26, 30} on the processors of a 4 × 4 mesh, and the input s = 26 to processor $p_{1,1}$; (b)–(g) the intermediate stages of algorithm COMPARE_AND_DISTRIBUTE distributing 26 to different processors; (h) output of algorithm COMPARE_AND_DISTRIBUTE.

## Concentrate

After the "compare and distribute" step the "concentrate" step is performed. This step is almost the inverse of the "compare and distribute" step in the sense that the $r_{i,j}$'s are now propagated in alternating fashion column to column and row to row towards $p_{1,1}$. The $r_{i,j}$'s are merged so that the output obtained at $p_{1,1}$ is "TRUE" if at least one $r_{i,j}$, i, j = 1, 2, . . . , $\sqrt{n}$ is "TRUE"; otherwise it is "FALSE". The details of the "concentrate" step are given below in the form of an algorithm.

## Algorithm  CONCENTRATE

Input: Each processor $p_{i,j}$ holds $r_{i,j}$ (= TRUE or FALSE), which is generated by algorithm COMPARE_AND_DISTRIBUTE, for i, j = 1, 2, . . . , $\sqrt{n}$.

Output: Processor $p_{1,1}$ returns the value "TRUE" if at least one $r_{i,j}$ = TRUE, i, j = 1, 2, . . . , $\sqrt{n}$ and FALSE otherwise.

*for* i = √n *downto* 2 *do*

    *for* j = 1 *to* i *dopar*

        $p_{j,i}$ sends $r_{j,i}$ to $p_{j,i-1}$;

        *if* ($r_{j,i-1}$ = TRUE OR $r_{j,i}$ = TRUE)

        *then* $r_{j,i-1}$ := TRUE

        *else* $r_{j,i-1}$ := FALSE

        *fi*

    *odpar*

    *for* j = 1 *to* i − 1 *dopar*

        $p_{i,j}$ sends $r_{i,j}$ to $p_{i-1,j}$;

        *if* ($r_{i-1,j}$ = TRUE OR $r_{i,j}$ = TRUE)

        *then* $r_{i-1,j}$ := TRUE

        *else* $r_{i-1,j}$ := FALSE

        *fi*

    *odpar*

*od*

In algorithm CONCENTRATE the body of the outermost for-loop is repeated √n − 1 times. Each of the two inner parallel for-loops takes constant time. Therefore, the overall time complexity of algorithm CONCENTRATE is also O(√n). Figure 5.8 illustrates the execution of algorithm CONCENTRATE using an example.

An algorithm for searching on the mesh connected computer, based on algorithms COMPARE_AND_DISTRIBUTE and CONCENTRATE, is straightforward and is given on page 145.

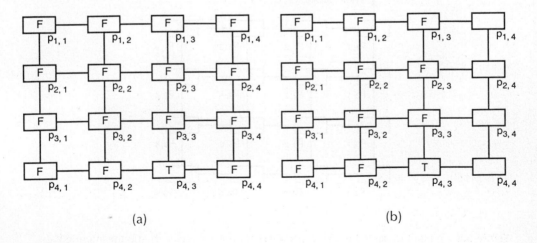

(a)                                              (b)

**Figure 5.8** continued overleaf.

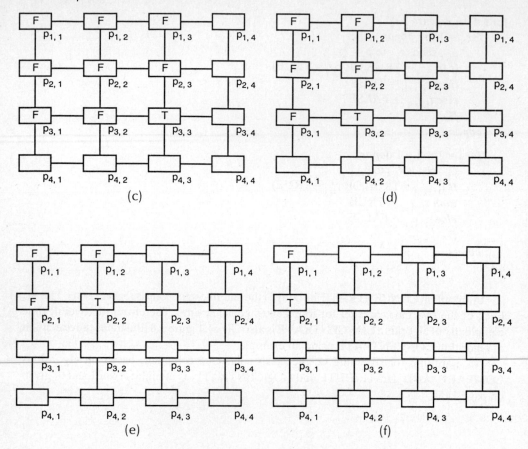

(c)    (d)

(e)    (f)

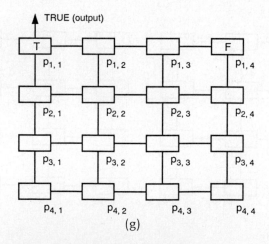

(g)

**Figure 5.8** (a) Input to algorithm CONCENTRATE for a 4 × 4 mesh; (b)–(g) the intermediate stages and output of algorithm CONCENTRATE.

## *Algorithm* MESH_CONNECTED_SEARCH

Input: The list $X = \{x_{i,j} \mid i, j = 1, 2, \ldots, \sqrt{n}\}$ stored into the mesh, processor $p_{i,j}$ having the element $x_{i,j}$; the element s to be searched for is in processor $p_{1,1}$.

Output: Processor $p_{1,1}$ returns either "search successful" if the element s is in X, otherwise $p_{1,1}$ returns "search unsuccessful".

$p_{1,1}$ reads s;
s is distributed to all the processors of the mesh and compared with
     every element of X using algorithm COMPARE_AND_DISTRIBUTE;
results of the comparison performed by algorithm
     COMPARE_AND_DISTRIBUTE are propagated and merged
     from column to column and row to row until $p_{1,1}$ is reached
     using algorithm CONCENTRATE;
*if* $r_{1,1}$ = TRUE
*then* $p_{1,1}$ returns "search successful"
*else* $p_{1,1}$ returns "search unsuccessful"
*fi*

### Complexity Analysis

The two main steps of algorithm MESH_CONNECTED_SEARCH are implemented using algorithms COMPARE_AND_DISTRIBUTE and CONCENTRATE. We have shown previously that each of these algorithms requires $O(\sqrt{n})$ time. Now, reading s and returning the result of the search by processor $p_{1,1}$ takes constant time. Thus, the overall complexity of searching on the mesh connected computer is $O(\sqrt{n})$.

Figures 5.7 and 5.8 together illustrate the execution of algorithm MESH_ CONNECTED_SEARCH for list X = {5, 6, 10, 8, 12, 7, 11, 14, 15, 16, 18, 20, 22, 25, 26, 30} and s = 26.

The output of algorithm MESH_CONNECTED_SEARCH only conveys whether or not s is in X. It may be desirable to have, in addition, the index of the occurrence of s in X. Assuming that all the elements in X are distinct, we can first modify algorithm COMPARE_AND_DISTRIBUTE so that if the processor $p_{i,j}$ finds a match it sets $r_{i,j}$, $i, j \in \{1, 2, \ldots, \sqrt{n}\}$ to its index, otherwise it sets $r_{i,j}$ to $\emptyset$. Next we modify algorithm CONCENTRATE so that the index of s in X is propagated towards and finally stored in processor $p_{1,1}$.

If we assume that the elements of X are not necessarily distinct, then we have to modify only algorithm CONCENTRATE. Now, when each processor receives the index of a successful match from one of its row or column neighbors it checks whether it holds s itself. If it does then it ignores the index received from its neighbor and sends its own index during the next step; otherwise it sends the index received from its neighbor. This process results in processor $p_{1,1}$ holding the index of the lowest indexed processor holding s. It may be noted that these modifications to algorithms COMPARE_AND_DISTRIBUTE and CONCENTRATE do not affect the time complexity of algorithm MESH_CONNECTED_SEARCH which remains as $O(\sqrt{n})$.

# 5.9 SEARCHING ON TREE MACHINES

In this section we consider the problem of searching on (i) an SIMD computer in which the processors are interconnected to form a binary tree; and (ii) the TSC (tree-structured computer) introduced by Bentley and Kung (1979) as a systolic machine. These computational models were introduced in Chapter 2.

## 5.9.1 Searching on a Binary Tree

Assume that we want to search for an element s in a list $X = \{x_1, x_2, \ldots, x_n\}$ of n elements on a tree machine which has n leaf processors. Let us denote the leaf processors by $p_1$, $p_2$, $\ldots, p_n$. The n elements of X are initially loaded in the leaf processors, one element per leaf. The element s is supplied as input to the root processor. On completion of the search algorithm the root processor outputs the result of the search. This may be "yes" (successful search) or "no" (unsuccessful search), or may be the index of s in X. The idea on which the algorithm is based is simple. The root processor reads s and then routes it through the intermediate processors to all of the leaf processors. Each leaf processor then compares its element to s. This comparison step is performed in parallel. The results of these comparisons are appropriately merged and propagated to the root processor. Finally, the root processor returns the output. A detailed description of the algorithm is given below.

*Algorithm* **TREE_SEARCH**

Input: The list $X = \{x_1, x_2, \ldots, x_n\}$ such that $x_i$ is available at the leaf processor $p_i$, $1 \leq i \leq$ n, and the element s.

Output: The root processor returns the index of s in X. If s occurs more than once then the index of the lowest indexed element is returned.

the root processor reads s and sets index := $\emptyset$;
*for* log n iterations *do*
    *for* all processors other than the root *dopar*
        *if* the processor is empty
        *then* acquire the contents of its parent
        *fi*
    *odpar*
*od*
*for* all leaf processors *dopar*
    *if* s is the element stored in this processor
    *then* index := index of the processor
    *else* index := $\infty$
    *fi*
*odpar*

*for* log n iterations *do*
    *for* all nonleaf processors *dopar*
        *if* the processor is the root
        *then if* index $\neq \emptyset$
            *then if* index $\neq \infty$
                *then* return "index"
                *else* return "search unsuccessful"
                *fi*
            *else do*
                acquire the values of "index" from the two children;
                *if* both the index values are not $\emptyset$
                *then* index := minimum of the two indices
                *fi*
            *od*
        *fi*
        *else do*
            *if* index = $\emptyset$
            *then* acquire the values of "index" of two children
            *fi*
            *if* both the index values are not $\emptyset$
            *then* index := minimum of the two indices
            *fi*
        *od*
        *fi*
    *odpar*
*od*

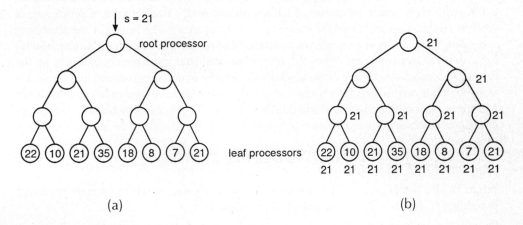

(a)                                            (b)

**Figure 5.9** continued overleaf.

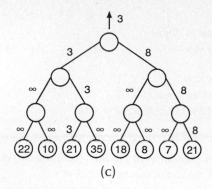

(c)

**Figure 5.9** (a) The list X = {22, 10, 21, 35, 18, 8, 7, 21} is stored in the leaf processors and s = 21 is the input to the root; (b) the value 21 is routed through the intermediate processors to the leaf processors; (c) the results of comparisons at the leaf processors are merged and propagated towards the root.

It is clear that all three parallel for-loops take constant time. Since each of the first and last parallel for-loops is repeated log n times, the overall complexity of algorithm TREE_SEARCH is O(log n). The number of processors used is O(n). Thus the cost of the algorithm is O(n log n). It may be noted that this algorithm does not require all of the elements of X to be distinct. Algorithm TREE_SEARCH is illustrated using an example in Figure 5.9. An important property of the tree machine is that searching for k elements can be pipelined to perform in O(log n) + O(k) time.

## 5.9.2  Searching on a TSC

In this section we consider a variant of the tree machine used above. The machine model assumed here is Bentley and Kung's TSC. It is assumed that the list X = {$x_1, x_2, \ldots, x_n$} of elements are stored on the square processors, one per square processor. Figure 5.10 shows a TSC with eight square processors. Such a mirrored-binary tree network of processors is used in conjunction with a driver computer (see Chapter 2). The basis for the searching algorithm for a TSC is also simple and similar to that for the tree machine. The element s is input to the driver computer. When the algorithm terminates the output is available on the driver. A detailed description of the algorithm using the notation introduced in Section 2.4 is given below. In this algorithm we have specified the processes to be executed at the driver computer, square processors, and triangle processors. The processes to be executed on the circle processors are omitted because their task is simply to broadcast the data they receive to the next level.

*Algorithm* TSC_SEARCH

Input: The list X = {$x_1, x_2, \ldots, x_n$} stored on the square processors with the square processor $p_i$ holding $x_i$, for i = 1, 2, . . . , n, and s is on the driver.

Output: The driver returns the index of the lowest indexed element with value s, if there is one; otherwise the driver returns "search unsuccessful."

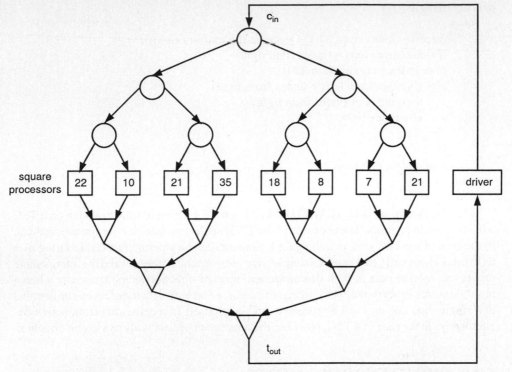

**Figure 5.10** A TSC with eight square processors in which the list X = {22, 10, 21, 35, 18, 8, 7, 21} is stored.

*process* driver (d) *is*
 read s;
 index := ∅;
 send s to topmost circle;
 *loop*
   receive index;
   *if* index ≠ ∞
   *then* return index; exit loop
   *else* return "search unsuccessful"; exit loop
   *fi*
 *end*
*process* square (p) *is*
 *loop*
   receive s;
   *if* s matches with the element stored in this processor
   *then* index := index of the processor
   *else* index := ∞
   *fi*
   send index; exit loop
 *end*

*process* triangle (t) *is*
    **loop**
           (receive (index from left)) // (receive (index from right));
           *if* (index from left) < (index from right)
           *then* index := (index from left)
           *else if* (index from left) > (index from right)
               *then* index := (index from right)
               *else* index := $\infty$
               *fi*
        *fi*
        send index; exit loop
    **end**

Clearly, algorithm TSC_SEARCH takes $2 \log n + 2 = O(\log n)$ time to search on a TSC with n square processors. The operation of the TSC and the tree machine are almost identical. In the case of the TSC also, searching for k elements can be pipelined and takes $O(\log n) + O(k)$ time. However, in the case of a simple binary tree machine, the root and the intermediate processors receive data in both downward and upward directions simultaneously when a multiple search is pipelined. Thus, we have to assume that both data transfers can be handled in a single time unit and that a processor can switch itself to receive data from both sides alternately. In the case of a TSC, however, the movement of data is always in one direction.

## 5.10 BIBLIOGRAPHIC NOTES

The problem of finding the maximum (minimum), which is a special case of the general selection problem, has been thoroughly studied in parallel processing environments. Early work on this problem can be found in Valiant (1975). The maximum finding algorithms for CRCW PRAM presented in Section 5.2.1 are based on the ideas in Kucera (1982), and Shiloach and Vishkin (1981). Algorithms similar to EREW_MAXIMUM presented in Section 5.2.2 can be found in Akl (1986) and Chaudhuri (1990). The maximum (minimum) finding problem on different variants of the tree machine has been discussed in Akl (1985), Ottman et al. (1982), and Song (1980). They considered this problem in connection with sorting, and suggested repeatedly extracting the minimum as the basis for a parallel sorting algorithm on a tree machine. The problem of finding the maximum on an array processor with a global bus has been addressed in Bokhari (1984). Bokhari considered two types of interconnection patterns — the eighth nearest neighbor connections and fourth nearest neighbor connections. It is shown that the time required to find the maximum in both cases is $O(n^{2/3})$, assuming that the propagation speed of the global bus is constant and independent of the array size. In the case where the propagation speed is logarithmic in the number of processors, this time complexity becomes $O((n^2 \log n)^{1/3})$.

The serial selection algorithm presented in Section 5.3.1 is based on the work of Blum et al. (1972). Similar algorithms can be found in many texts on serial algorithms including Aho et al. (1974), Brassard and Bratley (1988), and Manber (1989). Algorithm PARALLEL_BCAST is based on the algorithm presented in Akl (1986). The algorithms for finding the sum and all partial sums (prefix sums) in Section 5.3.3 are based on the ideas presented in Vishkin (1987). Other references on parallel prefix computations include Kruskal et al. (1985), Ladner and Fisher (1980), and Reif (1984).

The EREW parallel selection algorithm of Section 5.3.4 is based on the work of Akl (1984). The other EREW parallel selection algorithm presented in Section 5.4 is adapted from Vishkin (1987). Vishkin used an EREW PRAM adaptation of the sorting algorithm due to Ajtai et al. (1983) which requires O(log n) time to sort n elements using O(n) processors. As a result Vishkin's parallel selection algorithm takes O(log n log log n) time with n/(log n log log n) processors. In fact, we can also use the EREW sorting algorithm due to Cole (1988) which requires O(log n) time and O(n) processors to sort n elements. Using this, the time complexity of algorithm ANOTHER_EREW_SELECTION becomes O(log n log log n) with n/(log n log log n) processors. It may be noted that the time estimates for the algorithms due to Ajtai et al. (1983) and Cole (1988) both involve large constants. The parallel selection algorithm on a tree machine described in Section 5.5 is based on the work due to Cooper and Akl (1986).

The selection problem has also been studied on other parallel computational models. Cole and Yap (1985) considered the "comparison model" first introduced by Valiant (1975), for designing a parallel selection algorithm. Their algorithm finds the median of a set of n elements deterministically in O((log log n)$^2$) time using O(n) processors. Stout (1983) presented a parallel selection algorithm that runs on a mesh connected computer with broadcasting capability. Greenberg and Manber (1987) proposed a probabilistic pipeline algorithm for this problem that works on a tree machine. In a recent paper, Sen (1990) has given an approximate median finding algorithm that works on the CRCW PRAM model and runs in constant time using a linear number of processors. A variant of the selection problem is to find the s smallest elements in any order from a set of n elements (s ≤ n). This problem has been considered by Wah and Chen (1984) and they proposed a special-purpose selection network. Their selection network has O($\lceil \log n \rceil \times \lceil \log s \rceil$) time complexity.

Searching on sets or lists is another important problem which has been studied extensively in the context of parallel processing. Kruskal (1983) obtained an important result related to the complexity of parallel search on CREW PRAM. Algorithm SEARCH_SORTED_LIST is adapted from Kruskal (1983). Snir (1985) also investigated the complexity of parallel search of a sorted table of length n on the PRAM model with P processors. He has shown that Ω(log n – log P) steps are required in the case of EREW PRAM, whereas O(log n/log P) steps are sufficient in the case of CREW PRAM. Baer et al. (1983) considered several multiprocessor organizations and compared their performances for parallel search assuming that the main sources of overhead are memory interference and interprocessor synchronization.

Searching algorithms on a mesh connected computer are given in the text by Akl (1989), and in Schmeck and Schroder (1985). The searching problem has been investigated extensively on a variety of tree machines and references to such work include Atallah and Kosaraju (1985), Bentley (1980), Bentley and Kung (1979), Bonuccelli et al. (1983), Leiserson (1983), Ottman et al. (1982), Somani and Agarwal (1984), and Song (1980).

Parallel balancing and manipulation of binary search trees were investigated by Wong and Chang (1974), Chang (1974), and Kung and Lehman (1980). A systolic algorithm for implementing search trees on MIMD machines has been proposed by Carey and Thompson (1984). Ramamoorthy et al. (1978) presented a searching machine based on associative memory. Rudolph and Schlosser (1984), and Weller and Davidson (1975) described a "parallel pipelined" computer and studied the solution of the searching problem on that model.

## 5.11 EXERCISES

5.11.1   Develop an O(log log n) time algorithm for finding the maximum of n numbers on an n-processor CRCW PRAM model based on the ideas presented in Section 5.2.1.

5.11.2   Illustrate the working of algorithm EREW_SELECTION of Section 5.3 for selecting the tenth smallest element of the following list assuming that the EREW PRAM consists of four processors:

$X = \{16, 30, 19, 22, 27, 10, 32, 14, 26, 9, 21, 8, 14, 18, 34, 25\}$

5.11.3   Incorporate the modifications suggested at the end of Section 5.5 to algorithm TREE_SELECTION in order to explicitly obtain an optimal algorithm.

5.11.4   Show that on Valiant's comparison model (Valiant 1975), in which only the comparisons are counted to determine the time complexity ignoring the time spent in communications, the kth-smallest element in a list of n elements can be obtained in $O((\log \log n)^2)$ parallel time with O(n) processors (Cole and Yap 1985).

5.11.5   Study Bokhari's work on finding the maximum on an array processor with a global bus (Bokhari 1984).

5.11.6   Design an algorithm for finding the kth-smallest element of a list of n elements on a linear array of n processors assuming that each processor holds one element.

5.11.7   The *range search problem* for a table of size n is defined as follows: Given n + 1 distinct elements $x_1, x_2, \ldots, x_n$, s such that $x_1 < x_2 < \ldots < x_n$, find the index i such that $x_i < s < x_{i+1}$ (it is assumed that $x_0 = -\infty$ and $x_{n+1} = \infty$).

Prove that the range-searching problem of size n can be solved on a P-processor CREW PRAM in time $O(\log (n + 1)/\log (P + 1))$ (Snir 1985).

5.11.8   Show that $\Omega(\log n)$ is a lower bound in computing time to search a sorted list of n elements on an n-processor EREW PRAM model.

5.11.9   Develop an algorithm to solve by comparisons the general range-searching problem on a P-processor CREW PRAM model, where P < n (Snir 1985).

5.11.10  Consider an SIMD computer where the processors are connected in the form of a linear array. Moreover, there is a global bus to which each of the processors are connected. Only one processor at a time can broadcast a datum to all other processors through this global bus. It is assumed that for the broadcast operation

O(1) time is required. Assuming that each processor has a copy of the list X of n distinct elements, develop an algorithm for searching X for an element s on this parallel model of computation. Analyze the complexity of your algorithm.

5.11.11 Study the "Dictionary Machine" proposed by Ottman et al. Explain how each of *search, insert, delete,* and *extract-min* operations can be performed in this machine on an arbitrary list. Discuss its suitability for VLSI implementation (Ottman et al. 1982).

# 5.12 BIBLIOGRAPHY

Aho, A., Hopcroft, J., and Ullman, J. (1974). *The Design and Analysis of Computer Algorithms.* Addison-Wesley, Reading, Mass.

Ajtai, M., Komlos, J., and Szemeredi, E. (1983). Sorting in c log n parallel steps. *Combinatorica* 3, 1-19.

Atallah, M. J., and Kosaraju, S. R. (1985). A generalized dictionary machine for VLSI. *IEEE Transactions on Computers* C-34, 151-5.

Akl, S. G. (1984). An optimal algorithm for parallel selection. *Inform. Process. Lett.* 19, 47-50.

Akl, S. G. (1985). *Parallel Sorting Algorithms.* Academic Press, Orlando, Fla.

Akl, S. G. (1986). An adaptive and cost-optimal parallel algorithm for minimum spanning trees. *Computing* 36, 271-7.

Akl, S. G. (1989). *The Design and Analysis of Parallel Algorithms.* Prentice Hall, Englewood Cliffs, NJ.

Baer, J. L., Du, H. -C., and Ladner, R. E. (1983). Binary search in a multiprocessing environment. *IEEE Transactions on Computers* C-32, 667-77.

Bentley, J. L. (1980). A parallel algorithm for constructing minimum spanning trees. *J. Algorithms* 1, 51-9.

Bentley, J. L., and Kung, H. T. (1979). *Two papers on a tree-structured parallel computer.* Tech. Rep. CMU-CS-79-142, Dept. of Computer Science, Carnegie-Mellon University, Pittsburgh, Pa.

Blum, M., Floyd, R. W., Pratt, V., Rivest, R. L., and Tarjan, R. E. (1972). Time bounds for selection. *J. Computer and System Sci.* 7, 448-61.

Bokhari, S. H. (1984). Finding maximum on an array processor with a global bus. *IEEE Transactions on Computers* C-33, 133-9.

Bonuccelli, M. A., Lodi, E., Lucio, F., Maestrini, P., and Pagli, L. (1983). A VLSI tree machine for relational databases. *Proceedings of the 10th Annual ACM International Symposium on Computer Architecture,* ACM, NY, pp. 67-73.

Brassard, G., and Bratley, P. (1988). *Algorithmics: Theory & Practice.* Prentice Hall, Englewood Cliffs, NJ.

Carey, M. J., and Thompson, C. D. (1984). An efficient implementation of search trees on $\lceil \log n + 1 \rceil$ processors. *IEEE Transactions on Computers* C-33, 1038-41.

Chang, S. -K. (1974). Parallel balancing of binary search trees. *IEEE Transactions on Computers* C-23, 441-5.

Chaudhuri, P. (1990). An adaptive parallel algorithm for analyzing activity networks. *Operations Research Lett.* 9, 31-4.

Cole, R. (1988). Parallel merge sort. *SIAM J. Computing* 17, 770-85.

Cole, R., and Yap, C. K. (1985). A parallel median algorithm. *Inform. Process. Lett.* 20, 137-9.

Cooper, J., and Akl, S. G. (1986). Efficient selection on a binary tree. *Inform. Process. Lett.* 23, 123-6.

Greenberg, A. G., and Manber, U. (1987). A probabilistic pipeline algorithm for k selection on the tree machine. *IEEE Transactions on Computers* C-36, 261-8.

Kruskal, C. P. (1983). Searching, merging, and sorting in parallel computation. *IEEE Transactions on Computers* C-32, 359-62.

Kruskal, C. P., Rudolph, L., and Snir, M. (1985). The power of parallel prefix. *IEEE Transactions on Computers* C-34, 965-8.

Kucera, L. (1982). Parallel computation and conflicts in memory access. *Inform. Process. Lett.* 14, 93-6.

Kung, H. T., and Lehman, P. L. (1980). Concurrent manipulation of binary search trees. *ACM Transactions on Database Systems* 5, 354-82.

Ladner, R. E., and Fischer, M. J. (1980). Parallel prefix computation. *J. ACM* 27, 831-8.

Leiserson, C. E. (1983). *Area-Efficient VLSI Computation.* MIT Press, Mass.

Manber, U. (1989). *Introduction to Algorithms: A Creative Approach.* Addison-Wesley, Reading, Mass.

Ottman, T. A., Rosenberg, A. L., and Stockmeyer, L. J. (1982). A dictionary machine (for VLSI). *IEEE Transactions on Computers* C-31, 892-7.

Ramamoorthy, C. V., Turner, J. L., and Wah, B. W. (1978). A design of a fast cellular associative memory for ordered retrieval. *IEEE Transactions on Computers* C-27, 800-15.

Reif, J. H. (1984). Probabilistic parallel prefix computation. *Proceedings of the 1984 International Conference on Parallel Processing,* IEEE Computer Society, Washington, DC, pp. 291-8.

Rudolph, D., and Schlosser, K. -H. (1984). Optimal searching algorithms for parallel pipelined computers. In *Parallel Computing* 83, M. Feilmeier, J. Joubert, and U. Schendel, eds., North-Holland, Amsterdam.

Schmeck, H., and Schroder, H. (1985). Dictionary machines for different models of VLSI. *IEEE Transactions on Computers* C-34, 151-5.

Sen, S. (1990). Finding an approximate median with high probability in constant parallel time. *Inform. Process. Lett.* 34, 77-80.

Shiloach, Y., and Vishkin, U. (1981). Finding the maximum, merging, and sorting in a parallel computation model. *J. Algorithms* 2, 88-102.

Snir, M. (1985). On parallel searching. *SIAM J. Computing* 14, 688-708.

Somani, A. K., and Agarwal, V. K. (1984). An efficient VLSI dictionary machine. *Proceedings of the 11th Annual ACM International Symposium on Computer Architecture,* ACM, NY, pp. 142-50.

Song, S. W. (1980). A highly concurrent tree machine for database applications. *Proceedings of the 1980 International Conference on Parallel Processing,* IEEE Computer Society, Washington, DC, pp. 259-68.

Stout, Q. F. (1983). Mesh-connected computers with broadcasting. *IEEE Transactions on Computers* C-32, 826-30.

Valiant, L. G. (1975). Parallelism in comparison problems. *SIAM J. Computing.* 4, 348-55.

Vishkin, U. (1987). An optimal parallel algorithm for selection. *Advances in Computing Research* 4, 79-86.

Wah, B. W., and Chen, K. -L. (1984). A partitioning approach to the design of selection networks. *IEEE Transactions on Computers* C-33, 261-8.

Weller, D. L., and Davidson, E. S. (1975). Optimal searching algorithms for parallel-pipelined computers. In *Parallel Processing*, G. Goos, and J. Hartmanis, eds., Springer-Verlag, NY, pp. 291-305.

Wong, C. K., and Chang, S. -K. (1974). Parallel generation of binary search trees. *IEEE Transactions on Computers* C-23, 268-71.

# 6

# Matrix
# Computations

## 6.1 INTRODUCTION

Matrix computations are of fundamental importance in scientific computations. One of the most important matrix computations is matrix multiplication. A large portion of this chapter is devoted to the study of general and Boolean matrix multiplication algorithms in the context of parallel processing. We also consider some other useful matrix computations such as matrix transposition, matrix-vector multiplication, and the convolution problem in the rest of this chapter.

Matrix multiplication algorithms have wide application as components of other algorithms for the solution of many numerical and non-numerical problems. The importance of parallel Boolean matrix multiplication algorithms lies mainly in the fact that many graph theoretic problems can be formulated in terms of Boolean matrix multiplication.

The product of a $(p \times q)$ matrix A and a $(q \times r)$ matrix B is a $(p \times r)$ matrix C whose elements are defined by

$$C[i, j] = \sum_{0 \le k \le q-1} A[i, k] \times B[k, j]$$

for $0 \le i \le p - 1$ and $0 \le j \le r - 1$.

If A and B are Boolean matrices then their product C, which is also a Boolean matrix, is defined by

$$C[i, j] = \bigvee_{0 \le k \le q-1} A[i, k] \wedge B[k, j]$$

for $0 \leq i \leq p - 1$ and $0 \leq j \leq r - 1$, where "$\vee$" stands for the inclusive-OR operation and "$\wedge$" for the bitwise AND operation.

In serial computation, the lower bound to the complexity of matrix multiplication for two $n \times n$ matrices is known to be $\Omega(n^2)$, because there are $n^2$ elements in the resulting matrix and $O(n^2)$ time is required simply to output this matrix. The obvious serial multiplication algorithms, for both general and Boolean matrices, take $O(n^3)$ time if all the matrices are of size $n \times n$. Strassen (1969) showed that two $n \times n$ general matrices can be multiplied in $O(n^{2.81})$ arithmetic operations. This result was quite surprising when it first appeared, since it had previously been thought that $O(n^3)$ arithmetic operations were necessary. The problem of matrix multiplication has been studied intensively and, although the best possible algorithm for this problem has still not been found, methods slightly better than that due to Strassen have been discovered. It should be noted that Strassen's general matrix multiplication algorithm cannot be applied directly to Boolean matrix multiplication. However, there is a serial Boolean matrix multiplication algorithm that takes $O(n^{2.81})$ time (see Aho et al. 1974). A more practical and popular serial algorithm for Boolean matrix multiplication is due to Arlazarov et al. (1970). This is often called the Four Russians' algorithm. The complexity of this algorithm is $O(n^3/\log n)$.

This chapter is organized as follows. Algorithms for general matrix multiplication on PRAM, mesh connected, cube connected, and perfect shuffle models are considered in Section 2. In Section 3, Boolean matrix multiplication algorithms on both unbounded and bounded parallel computational models are investigated. Finally, in Section 4, we develop parallel algorithms for some other important matrix operations including matrix transposition, matrix-vector multiplication, and the convolution problem.

# 6.2 GENERAL MATRIX MULTIPLICATION

The parallel algorithms for general matrix multiplication presented in this section are all obtained by straightforward parallelization of the $O(n^3)$ time serial algorithm. Obviously, the cost of each of these parallel algorithms cannot be lower than $O(n^3)$.

## 6.2.1 Matrix Multiplication on PRAM Models

We present a general algorithm for multiplying two matrices each of size $n \times n$ on the shared memory SIMD model and then analyze its complexity under different memory access restrictions. Although we are assuming for simplicity that the matrices to be multiplied are $n \times n$, we can, without loss of generality, take the sizes of A, B, and C to be $p \times n$, $n \times q$, and $p \times q$, respectively. The results obtained in this section will still be valid if $p \leq n$ and $q \leq n$, since in that case each of $p$ and $q$ can simply be replaced by $n$ in the complexity results. The following is an informal description of the algorithm.

*Algorithm* **PRAM_MATRIX_MULT**

Input: Two $n \times n$ matrices A and B.
Output: The matrix $C = A \times B$.

*for* i = 0 *to* n − 1 *dopar*
   *for* j = 0 *to* n − 1 *dopar*
      C[i, j] := 0;
      *for* k = 0 *to* n − 1 *do*
         C[i, j] := C[i, j] + A[i, k] × B[k, j]
     *od*
   *odpar*
*odpar*

## Complexity Analysis

If we assume that the computational model is EREW PRAM, then simultaneous reading of every element of A and B by n processors can be implemented in O(log n) time using algorithm PARALLEL_BCAST from Section 5.3.2. There are two statements in the nested parallel for-loops of algorithm PRAM_MATRIX_MULT. One initializes all of the elements of matrix C to zero and the other computes the elements of C using cumulative products. A cumulative product is a multiply-add operation of the form c + a × b. The initialization of C requires O(1) time using $n^2$ processors. The cumulative multiplication can be implemented very easily, in parallel, by first computing all products of the form A[i, k] × B[k, j] for k = 0, 1, . . . , n − 1 in O(1) time with n processors. The addition of these n products, to give a single element of C, can be implemented on an EREW PRAM in O(log n) time with O(n) processors using algorithm PARALLEL_SUM (Section 5.3.3). Clearly, the complete process of finding all the elements of C requires O(log n) time when $O(n^3)$ processors are available. Thus, the overall time complexity of algorithm PRAM_MATRIX_MULT on the EREW PRAM model is O(log n) using $O(n^3)$ processors.

On the CREW PRAM model, the implementation of algorithm PRAM_MATRIX_MULT is a little simpler, since reading every element of A and B concurrently can be accomplished by n processors in O(1) time because of the relatively stronger nature of the computational model which allows read conflict. However, the computation of the sum of n products, as required to obtain each element of C, still takes O(log n) time using O(n) processors. Thus the overall time complexity of algorithm PRAM_MATRIX_MULT on the CREW PRAM model remains O(log n) with $O(n^3)$ processors.

Clearly, the implementations of algorithm PRAM_MATRIX_MULT on both EREW and CREW PRAMs take O(log n) time with $O(n^3)$ processors and so its cost in both the cases is given by $O(n^3 \log n)$ which exceeds the time complexity of the trivial serial matrix multiplication algorithm by a factor of log n.

We now consider the implementation of algorithm PRAM_MATRIX_MULT on the strongest variant of the PRAM, namely, CRCW PRAM. In this case, the write conflicts are assumed to be resolved in the following manner. When a number of processors attempt to write to the same shared memory location, the sum of all the values to be written is stored in the location. The implication of this write conflict resolution rule is that the cumulative product in the second statement of the body of the nested parallel for-loops can be implemented in constant time with n processors. Therefore, the time complexity of the CRCW PRAM matrix multiplication algorithm is O(1) using $O(n^3)$ processors. The cost of algorithm PRAM_MATRIX_MULT on the CRCW PRAM model is thus $O(n^3)$, which matches with the time complexity of the straightforward serial matrix multiplication algorithm.

## 6.2.2  Matrix Multiplication on Mesh

Assume that two n × n matrices A and B are to be multiplied on a mesh connected SIMD computer with $n^2$ processors. The processors are arranged in an n × n array (mesh) where the rows and columns of the mesh are numbered 0 through n − 1. In this section, we study matrix multiplication on two different variants of the two-dimensional mesh connected computer. One has wraparound connections and the other has not. First, we present an important lower bound result for matrix multiplication on mesh given by Gentleman (1978).

### 6.2.2.1  *Lower Bound for Matrix Multiplication on Mesh*

Given a processor interconnection pattern, we define a function b(x) to be the maximum number of processors at which data, originally available on a single processor, can be made available in less than or x data movement steps. For example, if the processors are connected in the form of a two-dimensional mesh, such as in ILLIAC-IV, then $\beta(x) = 2x^2 + 2x + 1$.

Assume that (A1) each element of the matrices to be multiplied is represented only once within the computational model; and (A2) no two elements of the same matrix are stored within the same processor. These assumptions are quite reasonable since assumption A1, in general, holds not only initially but for matrices computed at intermediate stages. In addition, assumption A2 is necessary to exploit the full parallelism available for componentwise operations such as matrix addition or multiplication by a scalar.

**Theorem 6.1:** Under assumptions A1 and A2 above, and without using any broadcast facility, the multiplication of two n × n matrices A and B to obtain the n × n matrix C requires at least d data movement steps, where $\beta(2d) \geq n^2$.

**Proof** (Gentleman 1978): Let us consider any element C[i, j] of the product matrix C. Since C[i, j] = A[i, 0] × B[0, j] + A[i, 1] × B[1, j] + . . . + A[i, n − 1] × B[n − 1, j], there must be a path between the processor where each A[i, k], k = 0, 1, . . . , n − 1 is originally stored and the processor where C[i, j] is finally stored. Along these paths A[i, k], k = 0, 1, . . . , n − 1 or quantities computed from them can be moved. Similarly, there must be a path between each processor holding B[k, j], k = 0, 1, . . . , n − 1 and the processor that finally stores C[i, j]. Let the length of the longest such path be denoted by d. Thus, computing C[i, j], i, j = 0, 1, . . . , n − 1, and hence C, requires at least d data movement steps.

Observe that the paths just considered define a set of paths of length at most 2d from any element B[p, q] to every element A[i, j], i, j = 0, 1, . . . , n − 1. This is true because there is a path of length at most d from the processor holding B[p, q] to the processor where C[i, q] will be stored, and there is also a path of length at most d from the processor holding A[i, j] to the processor where C[i, q] will be stored. Hence, there is a path of length at most 2d from any element B[p, q] to every element A[i, j], i, j = 0, 1, . . . , n − 1. Likewise, there is a path of length at most 2d between every element B[i, j] and an element A[p, q].

Since each of the $n^2$ elements A[i, j], i, j = 0, 1, . . . , n − 1 are stored in a different processor and there are paths of length at most 2d to all of them from the processor storing B[p, q], we have from the definition of β that $\beta(2d) \geq n^2$. Therefore, the theorem follows.

As a corollary of the above theorem we find that in the case of a mesh connected computer

$$\beta(2d) = 2(2d)^2 + 2(2d) + 1 \geq n^2$$
or,   $$8d^2 + 4d + 1 \geq n^2$$
or,   $$d^2 + (d/2) + (1/8) \geq n^2/8$$

or,         $(d + (1/4))^2 \geq (n^2/8) - (1/16)$
or,         $(d + (1/4))^2 \geq (1/4)((n^2/2) - (1/4))$
or,         $d \geq (1/2) \sqrt{((n^2/2) - (1/4))} - (1/4).$

Therefore, the lower bound to the number of data movement steps for matrix multiplication on a mesh connected computer is $\Omega(n)$.

### 6.2.2.2  *Matrix Multiplication on a Mesh with Wraparound Connections*

The mesh connected computer with wraparound connections considered here as the computational model is shown in Figure 6.1. Assume that the matrices to be multiplied are of size $n \times n$ and that the number of processors in the mesh is $n^2$ (i.e., $n \times n$ mesh). $p_{ij}$ is the processor at row i and column j, and it is connected to the four processors $p_{(i-1)j}$, $p_{i(j+1)}$, $p_{(i+1)j}$, and $p_{i(j-1)}$ if they exist. In addition, it is assumed that the boundaries of the mesh are wrapped around so that each $p_{i(n-1)}$ is connected to $p_{i0}$ and each $p_{(n-1)i}$ is connected to $p_{0i}$, for i = 0, 1, . . . , n − 1. These wraparound connections indicate that all additions and subtractions of indices are performed modulo n.

We assume that A[i, j] and B[i, j] are initially available on the processor $p_{ij}$ and that after the computation is complete C[i, j] will be stored on processor $p_{ij}$, for i, j = 0, 1, . . . , n − 1. We use the straightforward serial matrix multiplication algorithm and parallelize it to work on the mesh connected computer described above. To obtain the product matrix, $n^3$ multiplications are required. If we wish to compute all of the products in O(n) time, i.e., in n steps with $n^2$ processors, then each of the processors must contribute towards the result by multiplying two elements at every step. Now the problem is to move the data so that, at every step, the right elements will be available on the right processors. For example, consider the element C[0, 0] which results from taking the inner product of the first row of A with the first

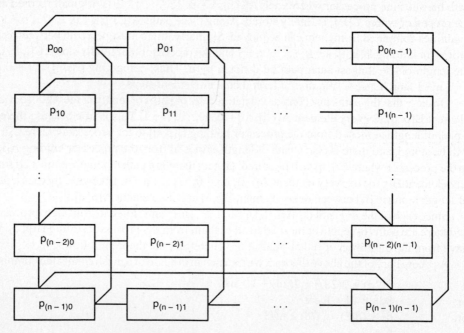

**Figure 6.1** A two-dimensional mesh with wraparound connections for $n^2$ processors.

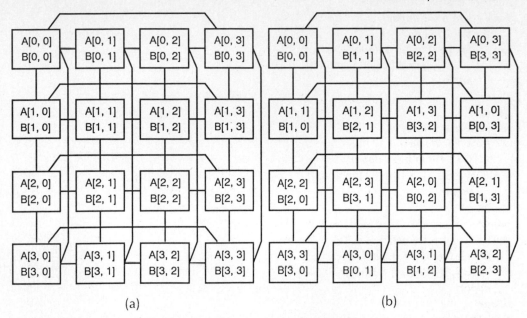

| A[0, 0] | A[0, 1] | A[0, 2] | A[0, 3] |
| B[0, 0] | B[0, 1] | B[0, 2] | B[0, 3] |

**Figure 6.2** (a) The initial data placement (input to the algorithm); (b) the data rearrangement before the multiplications of the matrix elements start.

column of B. We want to compute $C[0, 0]$ on processor $p_{00}$ in $O(n)$ time. This can be done by shifting both the first row of A to the left and the first column of B upwards one step at a time. At the first step, $p_{00}$ has $A[0, 0]$ and $B[0, 0]$, and it computes their product; in the second step $p_{00}$ receives $A[0, 1]$ and $B[1, 0]$ from its right and lower neighbors, respectively, and adds their product to the partial result, and so on. Clearly, the value of $C[0, 0]$ will be available after n steps. The movements of data through the whole mesh must be such that, not only does $p_{00}$ acquire the required elements at every step, but also that every other processor does. Unfortunately, we cannot achieve this sort of data movement and hence sharing of data starting with the obvious data distribution in which each $p_{ij}$ stores $A[i, j]$ and $B[i, j]$. It is necessary to rearrange the data appropriately before the computation begins so that at every step of the computation data can be moved in such a way that each processor will have two elements whose product it requires. The data rearrangement is crucial and it is done in such a way that the processor $p_{ij}$ holds $A[i, (i + j) \bmod n]$ and $B[(i + j) \bmod n, j]$. This can be achieved by shifting the ith row of A i steps to the left and the jth column of B j steps upwards and repeating this for all rows and columns of A and B, respectively. This initial rearrangement of data is illustrated in Figure 6.2. The algorithm is as follows.

### *Algorithm* **MESH_MATRIX_MULT1**

Input: The elements $A[i, j]$ and $B[i, j]$ of the matrices A and B to be multiplied are available on processor $p_{ij}$, $0 \le i, j \le n - 1$.

Output: The element $C[i, j]$ of the product matrix C is available on processor $p_{ij}$, $0 \le i, j \le n - 1$.

```
for i = 1 to n - 1 dopar
    for s = 1 to i do
        for j = 0 to n - 1 dopar
            A[i, j] := A[i, (j + 1) mod n]
        odpar
    od
odpar
for j = 1 to n - 1 dopar
    for t = 1 to j do
        for i = 0 to n - 1 dopar
            B[i, j] := B[(i + 1) mod n, j]
        odpar
    od
odpar
for i = 0 to n - 1 dopar
    for j = 0 to n - 1 dopar
        C[i, j] := A[i, j] × B[i, j]
    odpar
odpar
for k = 1 to n - 1 do
    for i = 0 to n - 1 dopar
        for j = 0 to n - 1 dopar
            A[i, j] := A[i, (j + 1) mod n];
            B[i, j] := B[(i + 1) mod n, j];
            C[i, j] := C[i, j] + A[i, j] × B[i, j]
        odpar
    odpar
od
```

## Complexity Analysis

It is clear that the initial row shifts achieved by the first parallel for-loop takes no more than $O(n)$ time. In fact, we can implement this row-shifting step in $n/2$ parallel steps by shifting an element towards the right when the number of shifts is greater than $n/2$. Similarly, the second parallel for-statement which shifts the columns takes $O(n)$ time. We have not yet started the arithmetic operations. These are performed by the third and fourth for-loops. The third for-loop obviously requires $O(1)$ parallel time. Finally, the fourth for-loop requires $O(n)$ time since the body of this for-loop which consists of two nested parallel for-loops can be implemented in $O(1)$ time. Therefore, the overall time complexity of algorithm MESH_MATRIX_MULT1 is $O(n)$ on a mesh with $n^2$ processors. Clearly, this algorithm is optimal in view of the $\Omega(n)$ lower bound in the computation time for matrix multiplication on a two-dimensional mesh. The cost of the algorithm is $O(n^3)$ which is the same as that for the straightforward serial matrix multiplication algorithm.

### 6.2.2.3  Matrix Multiplication on a Mesh without Wraparound Connections

In this section, we discuss a matrix multiplication algorithm on a two-dimensional mesh connected computer without wraparound connections. In this model every processor is connected to its four neighbors except for the processors at the boundaries which are connected either to their two (in the case of the processors at the corners of the mesh) or their three (processors at the boundaries other than the four corners) neighbors. The algorithm we present here assumes that the elements of A and B are delivered into the boundary processors in the first column and the first row of the mesh, respectively. The elements of the matrices are delivered in such a way that row i of A lags one time unit behind row i − 1, for $1 \leq i \leq$ n − 1. Similarly, column j of B lags one time unit behind column j − 1, for $1 \leq j \leq n - 1$. This is shown in Figure 6.3a for the case of two 2 × 2 matrices. Each processor $p_{ij}$ upon receiving A[i, k] and B[k, j], for $0 \leq k \leq n - 1$, multiplies them and adds the result to the partial result C[i, j] (C[i, j] is initialized to 0 at the beginning). Finally, $p_{ij}$ transmits A[i, k] to $p_{i(j+1)}$ if j < n − 1 and B[k, j] to $p_{(i+1)j}$ if i < n − 1. This process is repeated until the product matrix C = A × B becomes available as the output. The parallel algorithm based on the above idea is presented below.

### *Algorithm* MESH_MATRIX_MULT2

Input: The elements A[i, j] and B[i, j], i, j = 0, 1, . . . , n − 1, of A and B are delivered to the processors in the leftmost column (j = 0) and the topmost row (i = 0), respectively.

Output: The matrix C = A × B is stored so that its elements C[i, j] are available on processor $p_{ij}$, i, j = 0, 1, . . . , n − 1.

*for* i = 0 *to* n − 1 *dopar*
    *for* j = 0 *to* n − 1 *dopar*
        C[i, j] := 0
    *odpar*
*odpar*
*for* i = 0 *to* n − 1 *dopar*
    *for* j = 0 *to* n − 1 *dopar*
        *while* ($p_{ij}$ receives A[i, k] and B[k, j], k ∈ {0, 1, . . . , n − 1}) *do*
            C[i, j] := C[i, j] + A[i, k] × B[k, j]
            *if* i < n − 1
            *then* send B[k, j] to $p_{(i+1)j}$
            *fi*
            *if* j < n − 1
            *then* send A[i, k] to $p_{i(j+1)}$
            *fi*
        *od*
    *odpar*
*odpar*

The execution of algorithm MESH_MATRIX_MULT2 is illustrated using an example in Figure 6.3.

### Complexity Analysis

It can be easily verified that algorithm MESH_MATRIX_MULT2 terminates when the processor $p_{(n-1)(n-1)}$ completes the computation of C[n − 1, n − 1] by executing C[n − 1, n − 1] := C[n − 1, n − 1] + A[n − 1, 0] × B[0, n − 1]. The processors $p_{(n-1)0}$ and $p_{0(n-1)}$ receive inputs n units of time after $p_{00}$ receives input and begins execution of the algorithm. Again,

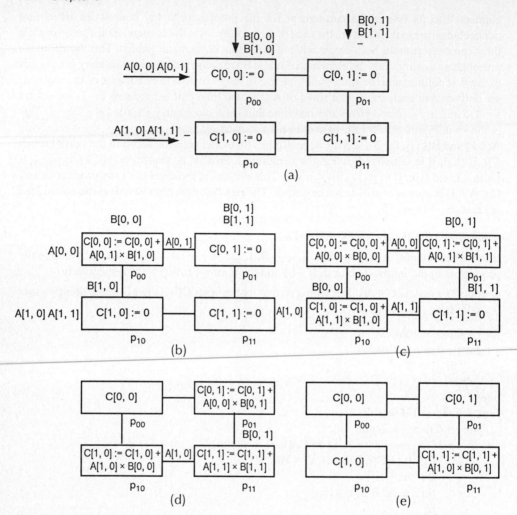

**Figure 6.3** Multiplication of two 2 × 2 matrices A and B on a mesh having four processors using algorithm MESH_MATRIX_MULT2. The steps of the algorithm are shown in figures (a)-(e).

another $2(n-1)$ units of time is required by the elements $A[n-1, 0]$ and $B[0, n-1]$ to reach processor $p_{(n-1)(n-1)}$ through processors $p_{(n-1)0}$ and $p_{0(n-1)}$, respectively. Thus, the total time required by $p_{(n-1)(n-1)}$ to receive its last pair of required elements is $3n-2$. Thus the algorithm terminates after $3n-1$ units of time. That is, algorithm MESH_MATRIX_MULT2 has time complexity $O(n)$ on a mesh with $n^2$ processors. The cost of the algorithm is $O(n^3)$ which is the same as the time complexity of the simple matrix multiplication algorithm. It may be noted that if the matrices A, B, and C have sizes $p \times n$, $n \times q$ and $p \times q$, respectively, then we need pq processors and the running time of algorithm MESH_MATRIX_MULT2 becomes $p + n + q - 1$, i.e., $O(n)$, if both p, q ≤ n.

## 6.2.3 Matrix Multiplication on Cube

We have seen that the cost of parallel matrix multiplication on both CRCW PRAM and on a mesh connected computer is $O(n^3)$ as expected, since these algorithms are obtained by parallelizing the corresponding $O(n^3)$ time serial algorithm. The CRCW PRAM algorithm takes only $O(1)$ time but assumes a strong write conflict resolution rule which is somewhat unrealistic. In contrast, the parallel algorithm for the mesh runs in $O(n)$ time and is thus considerably slower. In this section, we consider a cube connected SIMD computer as the computational model and design a fast parallel matrix multiplication algorithm. Once again, for simplicity of presentation, we assume that all of the matrices are of size n × n. The algorithm we present is faster than that for the mesh; it takes $O(\log n)$ time on a cube with $n^3$ processors.

Let us assume that $N = 2^k$ and let $i_{k-1} i_{k-2} \cdots i_0$ be the binary representation of i for $0 \le i \le n - 1$. Let $i^{(b)}$ be the integer whose binary representation is $i_{k-1} i_{k-2} \cdots i_{b+1} i'_b i_{b-1} \cdots i_0$, where $i'_b$ is the complement of $i_b$, for $b = 0, 1, \ldots, k - 1$. In the cube model the ith processor is connected to the $i^{(b)}$th processor, for $b = 0, 1, \ldots, k - 1$. Clearly, each processor requires $k = \log N$ connections. Let us assume a cube connected computer with $N = n^3 = 2^{3q}$ processors. These processors may be considered as being arranged in an n × n × n array pattern. Assuming that the processors are indexed in row-major order, processor $p_{ijk}$ in position (i, j, k) of this array has index $in^2 + jn + k$, for $0 \le i, j, k \le n - 1$. Thus, if $y = y_{3q-1} y_{3q-2} \cdots y_0$ is the binary representation of the processor position (i, j, k) then $i = y_{3q-1} y_{3q-2} \cdots y_{2q}$, $j = y_{2q-1} y_{2q-2} \cdots y_q$, and $k = y_{q-1} y_{q-2} \cdots y_0$. Let us assume that every processor $p_y$ in position (i, j, k) in the array has three registers (or memory locations) represented by A(y), B(y), and C(y) or A(i, j, k), B(i, j, k), and C(i, j, k), respectively. Note that the elements of the matrices A, B, and C are represented by A[i, j], B[i, j], and C[i, j], for $0 \le i, j, k \le n - 1$. The initial distribution of the matrices is given by

$$A(0, j, k) = A[j, k]$$
$$B(0, j, k) = B[j, k]$$

for $0 \le j, k \le n - 1$. The desired final distribution is given by

$$C(0, j, k) = C[j, k]$$

for $0 \le j, k \le n - 1$, where

$$C[j, k] = \sum_{0 \le s \le n-1} A[j, s] \times B[s, k].$$

Like the parallel matrix multiplication algorithms above, we compute the product matrix C on the cube by directly adapting the corresponding serial algorithm. The parallel algorithm consists of three distinct phases. In the first phase, elements of A and B are distributed over the $n^3$ processors so that we have $A(s, j, k) = A[j, s]$ and $B(s, j, k) = B[s, k]$. The second phase consists of computing the products $C(s, j, k) = A(s, j, k) \times B(s, j, k) = A[j, s] \times B[s, k]$. Finally, the sums $C(0, j, k) + C(1, j, k) + \ldots + C(n - 1, j, k)$ are computed. A detailed description of the algorithm is given below in which we denote by $\{N \mid y_s = z\}$ the set of integers y, $0 \le y \le N - 1$, whose binary representation is $y_{3q-1} y_{3q-2} \cdots y_{s+1} z y_{s-1} \cdots y_0$. In this algorithm all processor references are made using processor indices, e.g., the index of processor $p_{ijk}$ is $in^2 + jn + k$. We use "←" to denote an assignment requiring data movement between processors which are directly connected. The statement of the form $A(y^{(s)}) \leftarrow B(y)$ will be used to represent a data route where data from register B of the processors with index y is routed to the register A of the corresponding processors with bit s equal to $1 - y_s$. To denote an assignment involving only local variables ":=" is used as usual.

### *Algorithm* CUBE_MATRIX_MULT

Input: The elements A[j, k], and B[j, k] of the matrices A and B, respectively, are stored on processors $p_{0jk}$, for $0 \le j$, $k \le n - 1$. That is, $A(0, j, k) = A[j, k]$ and $B(0, j, k) = B[j, k]$, for all $0 \le j, k \le n - 1$.

Output: The elements C[j, k] of the product matrix C are stored on processor $p_{0jk}$, for $0 \le j$, $k \le n - 1$.

*for* s = 3q - 1 *downto* 2q *do*
    *for* all $y \in \{N \mid y_s = 0\}$ *dopar*
        $A(y^{(s)}) \leftarrow A(y)$;
        $B(y^{(s)}) \leftarrow B(y)$
    *odpar*
*od*
*for* s = q - 1 *downto* 0 *do*
    *for* all $y \in \{N \mid y_s = y_{2q+s}\}$ *dopar*
        $A(y^{(s)}) \leftarrow A(y)$
    *odpar*
*od*
*for* s = 2q - 1 *downto* q *do*
    *for* all $y \in \{N \mid y_s = y_{q+s}\}$ *dopar*
        $B(y^{(s)}) \leftarrow B(y)$
    *odpar*
*od*
*for* y = 0 *to* N - 1 *dopar*
    $C(y) := A(y) \times B(y)$
*odpar*
*for* s = 2q *to* 3q - 1 *do*
    *for* y = 0 *to* N - 1 *dopar*
        $C(y) \leftarrow C(y) + C(y^{(s)})$
    *odpar*
*od*

    The first for-loop copies the data initially in processor $p_{0jk}$, to the processors $p_{ijk}$, $1 \le i \le n - 1$. At the end of the execution of this for-loop, we have

$$A(i, j, k) = A[j, k]$$
$$B(i, j, k) = B[j, k]$$

for $0 \le i \le n - 1$. The second for-loop replicates A(i, j, i) over A(i, j, k), $0 \le k \le n - 1$. Since A(i, j, i) = A[j, i] this replication results in A(i, j, k) = A[j, i], $0 \le k \le n - 1$. Similarly, the third for-loop replicates B(i, i, k) = B[i, k] over B(i, j, k), $0 \le j \le n - 1$.

    The fourth for-loop computes, in parallel, the product C(i, j, k) = A(i, j, k) × B(i, j, k) = A[j, i] × B[i, k] in processor $p_{ijk}$, for $0 \le i, j, k \le n - 1$. Finally, the last for-loop computes the sums

$$C(0, j, k) = \sum_{0 \le i \le n-1} C(i, j, k)$$

We thus obtain the elements $C[j, k] = C(0, j, k)$, $0 \le j, k \le n - 1$, of the product matrix C at each processor $p_{0jk}$. The execution of the algorithm is illustrated in Figure 6.4.

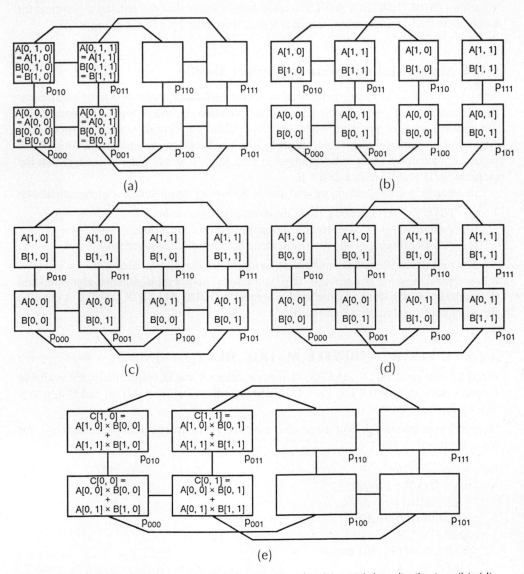

**Figure 6.4** Multiplication of two $2 \times 2$ matrices on a cube. (a) Initial data distribution; (b)–(d) data distribution at the end of the execution of first, second, and third for-loops, respectively; (e) the elements of the product matrix C as computed by the last for-loop.

**Complexity Analysis**

The time complexity of algorithm CUBE_MATRIX_MULT can be obtained by analyzing the complexities of the five for-loops. The first for-loop requires 2q unit-distance routings whereas each of the second, third, and fifth for-loops requires q unit-distance routings. The fourth for-loop clearly takes constant, i.e., $O(1)$ time to perform $n^3$ products, in parallel, with $n^3$ processors. Thus, the overall complexity of algorithm CUBE_MATRIX_MULT is $5q \equiv O(\log n)$. Since $n^3$ processors are used, the cost of this algorithm is $O(n^3 \log n)$. Thus, algorithm CUBE_MATRIX_MULT is considerably faster than the parallel algorithms for mesh connected computers but its cost is higher than these by a factor of $\log n$.

## 6.2.4  Matrix Multiplication on Perfect Shuffle

The perfect shuffle computer introduced in Section 2.2.1.4 is considered to be a computational model for designing a parallel matrix multiplication algorithm. We use the same three-dimensional view of processors and the same initial configuration as used for a cube connected computer above. More precisely, we use the same row-major indexing of the processors assuming them to be arranged in an $n \times n \times n$ array. We also assume that the matrices A, B, and C are of size $n \times n$.

In describing the algorithm, we will use the following unit-distance routing statements:

(a)  $A(y^{(0)}) \leftarrow A(y)$, routing along the exchange connections;
(b)  $A(\text{shuffle}(y)) \leftarrow A(y)$, routing along the shuffle connection;
(c)  $A(\text{unshuffle}(y)) \leftarrow A(y)$, routing along the unshuffle connection.

The perfect shuffle matrix multiplication algorithm can also be obtained by a straight-forward parallelization of the simple $O(n^3)$ time serial matrix multiplication algorithm and its basic steps are the same as those used in algorithm CUBE_MATRIX_MULT. A detailed description of the algorithm follows.

*Algorithm* **PERFECT_SHUFFLE_MATRIX_MULT**

Input: The elements A[j, k], and B[j, k] of the matrices A and B, respectively, are available on processors $p_{0jk}$, for $0 \leq j, k \leq n - 1$. In other words, $A(0, j, k) = A[j, k]$ and $B(0, j, k) = B[j, k]$, for $0 \leq j, k \leq n - 1$.

Output: The elements C[j, k] of the product matrix C are returned on the processors $p_{0jk}$, for $0 \leq j, k \leq n - 1$.

*for* s = 0 *to* q - 1 *do*
    *for* y = 0 *to* N - 1 *dopar*
        A(shuffle(y)) ← A(y);
        B(shuffle(y)) ← B(y)
    *odpar*
    *for* all z ∈ {N | $y_0$ = 0} *dopar*
        A($z^{(0)}$) ← A(z);
        B($z^{(0)}$) ← B(z)
    *odpar*
*od*

*for* s = 0 *to* q − 1 *do*
   *for* y = 0 *to* N − 1 *dopar*
      A(shuffle(y)) ← A(y)
   *odpar*
*od*
*for* y = 0 *to* N − 1 *dopar*
   C(y) := A(y) × B(y)
*odpar*
*for* s = 0 *to* q − 1 *do*
   *for* y = 0 *to* N − 1 *dopar*
      C(shuffle(y)) ← C(y)
   *odpar*
   *for* all z ∈ {N | $y_0$ = 0} *dopar*
      C(z) ← C(z) + C($z^{(0)}$)
   *odpar*
*od*
*for* s = 0 *to* q − 1 *do*
   *for* y = 0 *to* N − 1 *dopar*
      C(shuffle(y)) ← C(y)
   *odpar*
   *for* z ∈ {N | $y_0$ = $y_q$ = 1} *dopar*
      C($z^{(0)}$) ← C(z)
   *odpar*
*od*
*for* s = 0 *to* q − 1 *do*
   *for* y = 0 *to* N − 1 *dopar*
      C(unshuffle(y)) ← C(y)
   *odpar*
*od*

The execution of algorithm PERFECT_SHUFFLE_MATRIX_MULT is illustrated using two 2 × 2 matrices in Figure 6.5. The first for-loop copies the data initially in processor $p_{0jk}$ to the processors $p_{ijk}$, $1 \le i \le n - 1$. Thus, after the execution of this step we have A(i, j, k) = A[i, j] and B(i, j, k) = B[i, j], for $0 \le i \le n - 1$. At the end of the second for-loop, we have A(i, j, k) = A[k, i] and B(i, j, k) = B[i, j]. The third for-loop computes the product C(i, j, k) = A(i, j, k) × B(i, j, k) = A[k, i] × B[i, j] in processor $p_{ijk}$, for $0 \le i \le n - 1$. All of these product terms are then transmitted appropriately through the shuffle and exchange links and combined to obtain the elements C[i, j], for $0 \le i, j \le n - 1$. In particular, at the end of the fourth for-loop we obtain the elements of the product matrix C as C(j, k, i) = C[k, j], for $0 \le i \le n - 1$. At the end of the fifth for-loop, we have C(k, j, 0) = C[k, j]. Finally, on termination of the algorithm we have C(0, k, j) = C[k, j] on each processor $p_{0kj}$, for $0 \le k, j \le n - 1$.

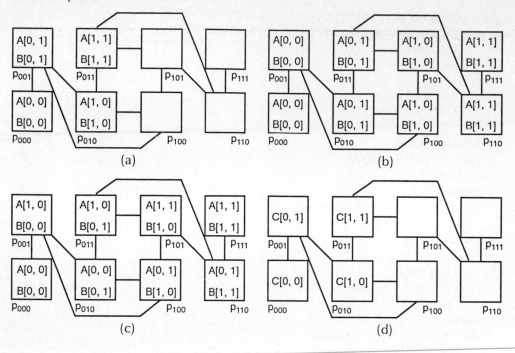

**Figure 6.5** Multiplication of two 2 × 2 matrices on a perfect shuffle computer with eight processors. (a) Initial data distribution; (b)–(c) data distribution at the end of the execution of first and second for-loops, respectively; (d) the product matrix C obtained using the algorithm.

**Complexity Analysis**

Analysis of algorithm PERFECT_SHUFFLE_MATRIX_MULT is straightforward. A total of 10q unit-distance routing steps are required. Since all other computations take constant time, the overall time complexity of the algorithm is $O(q) = O(\log n)$. Therefore, its time complexity is the same as that for the cube connected computer solution to the same problem. The cost of the algorithm is $O(n^3 \log n)$, which exceeds the time complexity of the simple serial matrix multiplication algorithm by a factor of $\log n$.

## 6.3 BOOLEAN MATRIX MULTIPLICATION

The problem of Boolean matrix multiplication is studied in this section using both unbounded and bounded PRAM models as well as a mesh connected computer. The PRAMs we consider include both CREW and CRCW models. For simplicity we assume that the Boolean matrices A and B to be multiplied are each of size n × n and produce a Boolean product matrix C of size n × n. We take three different approaches in designing parallel Boolean matrix multiplication algorithms. The first approach is to parallelize the straightforward $O(n^3)$ time serial algorithm for this problem. The second approach is to design parallel algorithms based on the fact that only nonzero elements of A can be used to determine the elements of C, provided that all the elements of C are initialized to zero. The third approach is to parallelize the famous Four Russians' serial Boolean matrix multiplication algorithm.

## 6.3.1  Boolean Matrix Multiplication on Unbounded PRAM Models

For Boolean matrix multiplication on the EREW PRAM and CREW PRAM models we use an algorithm similar to algorithm PRAM_MATRIX_MULT (see Section 6.2.1). We need only to replace the addition and multiplication operations by inclusive-OR and AND operations, respectively. An analysis similar to that of Section 6.2.1 shows that both EREW and CREW Boolean matrix multiplication algorithms require $O(\log n)$ time when $O(n^3)$ processors are employed.

Consider now an unbounded CRCW PRAM model for the multiplication of two Boolean matrices. We assume that every processor involved in the concurrent write operation must attempt to write the same value; otherwise the algorithm is considered to be incorrect. Thus, we have to ensure that the converse will never happen during any concurrent write operation. Clearly, on this model it does not matter which processor's value is written into the shared memory location. The algorithm presented below is a straightforward parallelization of the simple $O(n^3)$ serial Boolean matrix multiplication algorithm.

*Algorithm* **CRCW_BOOL_MATRIX_MULT**

Input: Two n × n Boolean matrices A and B.

Output: The Boolean matrix C = A × B.

*for* i = 0 *to* n − 1 *dopar*
   *for* j = 0 *to* n − 1 *dopar*
      C[i, j] := 0
   *odpar*
*odpar*
*for* i = 0 *to* n − 1 *dopar*
   *for* j = 0 *to* n − 1 *dopar*
      *for* k = 0 *to* n − 1 *dopar*
         *if* A[i, k] ∧ B[k, j] = 1
         *then* C[i, j] := 1
         *fi*
      *odpar*
   *odpar*
*odpar*

**Complexity Analysis**

It is clear that the first parallel for-loop takes $O(1)$ time using $n^2$ processors while the second can be implemented in $O(1)$ time if $n^3$ processors are available. Therefore, the overall time complexity of algorithm CRCW_BOOL_MATRIX_MULT is $O(1)$ with $O(n^3)$ processors. The cost of the algorithm is $O(n^3)$ which is identical to that of the corresponding straightforward serial algorithm.

## 6.3.2  Boolean Matrix Multiplication on Bounded PRAM Models

Two efficient matrix multiplication algorithms for multiplying two n × n Boolean matrices on a P-processor CREW PRAM model, where P ≤ n, are proposed in this section. The straightforward way to adapt the algorithm of Section 6.3.1 on a P-processor CREW PRAM is by using Lemma 3.2.3. However, the cost of the CREW Boolean matrix multiplication algorithm obtained in this manner is still $O(n^3 \log n)$, which not only far exceeds the $\Omega(n^2)$ lower bound in computing time for the serial Boolean matrix multiplication but also exceeds the time complexity of the simple serial algorithm for this problem by a factor of log n. Our object is to design a parallel Boolean matrix multiplication algorithm on a P-processor CREW PRAM whose cost is at most $O(n^3)$.

Without loss of generality, we assume that n is exactly divisible by P. Our first algorithm is based on the observation that, as the matrices A and B are multiplied, each nonzero element A[i, j], $0 \le i, j \le n - 1$ of A is required to be logically-ANDed with all n elements of the jth row of B. It is unnecessary to consider those elements of A which are 0, provided that each element of the product matrix is initialized to 0.

To implement the above idea in the algorithm, let the ith row of A be represented as a set

$$A[i, *] = \{(i, j) \mid (0 \le j \le n - 1) \land A[i, j] = 1\}$$

for $0 \le i \le n - 1$. The matrix A can be considered to be equivalent to

$$A_L = \bigcup_{0 \le i \le n-1} A[i, *].$$

Thus, for each row i of A, we store in consecutive locations the indices (i, j), $0 \le i, j \le n - 1$, of its nonzero elements, as shown in Figure 6.6. Let us assume that $A_L$ consists of e elements, i.e., $|A_L| = e$. In order to construct $A_L$, we use one processor in each of the first P rows of A. The processor which is employed by row x (say), $0 \le x \le P - 1$, can construct A[x, *] in O(n) time simply by scanning, serially, each element of row x. Thus, in O(n) time, the first P rows of matrix A can be compressed to give A[0, *], A[1, *], . . . , A[P − 1, *]. Since there are n rows in A, we can, by repeating this procedure $\lceil n/P \rceil$ times, construct $A_L$ in $O(n^2/P)$ time. Once the list $A_L$ has been constructed the computation of C is straightforward. It is described in the following algorithm.

$$
\begin{bmatrix}
0 & 1 & 0 & 0 & 1 & 1 & 0 & 0 \\
0 & 0 & 0 & 0 & 0 & 0 & 0 & 0 \\
1 & 0 & 1 & 1 & 1 & 0 & 0 & 0 \\
1 & 1 & 0 & 0 & 0 & 0 & 0 & 0 \\
0 & 0 & 0 & 0 & 0 & 0 & 0 & 1 \\
1 & 0 & 0 & 0 & 0 & 0 & 0 & 1 \\
0 & 1 & 1 & 0 & 1 & 0 & 0 & 0 \\
1 & 0 & 0 & 1 & 0 & 0 & 1 & 0
\end{bmatrix}
$$

$A_L = \{(0, 1), (0, 4), (0, 5), (2, 0), (2, 2), (2, 3),$
$(2, 4), (3, 0), (3, 1), (4, 7), (5, 0), (5, 7),$
$(6, 1), (6, 2), (6, 4), (7, 0), (7, 3), (7, 6)\}$

(a)                                        (b)

**Figure 6.6**  (a) An arbitrary 8 × 8 Boolean matrix; (b) the list $A_L$ corresponding to matrix A.

*Algorithm* **CREW_BOOL_MATRIX_MULT1**

Input: Two Boolean matrices A and B, each of size n × n.

Output: The matrix C = A × B of size n × n.

*for* q = 0 *to* P − 1 *dopar*
   *for* i = q(n/P) *to* (q + 1)(n/P) − 1 *do*
      *for* j = 0 *to* n − 1 *do*
         C[i, j] := 0
      *od*
   *od*
*odpar*
construct $A_L$ from A;
*for* q = 0 *to* P − 1 *dopar*
   *for* j = q(n/P) *to* (q + 1)(n/P) − 1 *do*
      *for* each (i, v) ∈ $A_L$ *do*
         *if* B[v, j] = 1
         *then* C[i, j] := 1
         *fi*
      *od*
   *od*
*odpar*

The analysis of algorithm CREW_BOOL_MATRIX_MULT1 is straightforward. The first parallel for-loop which initializes the elements of matrix C to 0 can be executed in $O(n^2/P)$ time with $P \leq n$ processors. Construction of the list $A_L$ from A also requires $O(n^2/P)$ time with $P \leq n$ processors, as has been explained. Finally, the last parallel for-loop takes $O(ne/P)$, $P \leq n$, time, since $|A_L| = e$. Combining the complexities of each of these steps, we have the following theorem.

**Theorem 6.2:** On a P-processor CREW PRAM model, C = A × B can be computed by algorithm CREW_BOOL_MATRIX_MULT1 in $O(\max((n^2/P), (ne/P)))$ time for $P \leq n$, where $e = |A_L|$.

Observe that, in the worst case, where every element of A is 1 we have $e = |A_L| = n^2$ making the time complexity of algorithm CREW_BOOL_MATRIX_MULT1 $O(n^3/P)$, for $P \leq n$. Thus, the cost of the algorithm in the worst case is $O(n^3)$, which is better than that of the simple unbounded CREW PRAM algorithm and is exactly the same as that of the unbounded CRCW PRAM algorithm for this problem. On the other hand, if the number of nonzero elements in A is $O(n)$, i.e., $e = |A_L| = O(n)$, then the time complexity of algorithm CREW_BOOL_MATRIX_MULT1 becomes $O(n^2/P)$, for $P \leq n$. In this case, its cost, $O(n^2)$, coincides with the lower bound in computing time for the serial Boolean matrix multiplication. In many applications we encounter, Boolean matrices to be multiplied are sufficiently sparse, i.e., $e \ll n^2$. Thus, the parallel algorithm presented above is very efficient in many practical situations.

The underlying idea of our second Boolean matrix multiplication algorithm on the bounded CREW PRAM model is the identification of chains of 1's in each row of A. Each row of A is now defined by a set of triples

$$A_t[i, *] = \{(i, r, m) \mid (r \le j \le m) \wedge A(i, j) = 1\}$$

for $0 \le i, j, r, m \le n - 1$. Thus, A can be represented by a set of triples

$$A_I = \bigcup_{0 \le i \le n-1} A_t[i, *].$$

Thus, for each row i of matrix A, we store only the triples $(i, r, m)$, which indicates that the consecutive elements $A[i, r]$, $A[i, r + 1]$, ..., $A[i, m]$ of row i of A are each 1. Assume that $A_I$ has f elements, i.e., $|A_I| = f$. Using a technique similar to that for the construction of $A_L$ in the last algorithm, we can generate $A_I$ in $O(n^2/P)$ time by scanning P rows simultaneously using $P \le n$ processors, where for each row, $O(n)$ time is required to construct $A[i, *]$, $0 \le i \le n - 1$. B is transformed into another matrix $B_R$, each element $B_R[i, j]$, $0 \le i, j \le n - 1$, of which has two attributes. The first of these, denoted by $VAL(i, j)$, is the magnitude — either 0 or 1; the second is a positive integer, denoted by $NEXT(i, j)$ which is the smallest integer s such that $i < s$ and $VAL(s, j) = 1$. If there is no such s then $NEXT(i, j)$ is set to n. The transformation of A and B into $A_I$ and $B_R$, respectively, is illustrated in Figure 6.7. $B_R$ can also be constructed in $O(n^2/P)$ time using $P \le n$ processors. In this case the elements of B must be scanned cloumnwise in reverse order starting at the $(n - 1)$th row. The following algorithm shows how $A_I$ and $B_R$ are used to produce another efficient Boolean matrix multiplication algorithm which, in general, is superior to algorithm CREW_BOOL_MATRIX_MULT1.

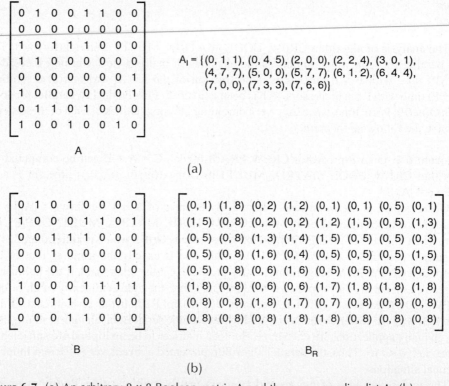

$A_I = \{(0, 1, 1), (0, 4, 5), (2, 0, 0), (2, 2, 4), (3, 0, 1),$
$(4, 7, 7), (5, 0, 0), (5, 7, 7), (6, 1, 2), (6, 4, 4),$
$(7, 0, 0), (7, 3, 3), (7, 6, 6)\}$

A

(a)

B

$B_R$

(b)

**Figure 6.7**  (a) An arbitrary 8 × 8 Boolean matrix A and the corresponding list $A_I$; (b) an arbitrary 8 × 8 Boolean matrix B and the matrix $B_R$ each of whose 64 elements is a pair $(VAL(i, j), NEXT(i, j))$, $0 \le i, j \le 7$.

*Algorithm* **CREW_BOOL_MATRIX_MULT2**

Input: Two n × n Boolean matrices A and B.

Output: The n × n Boolean matrix C = A × B.

*for* q = 0 *to* P − 1 *dopar*
   *for* i = q(n/P) *to* (q + 1)(n/P) − 1 *do*
      *for* j = 0 *to* n − 1 *do*
         C[i, j] := 0
      *od*
   *od*
*odpar*
construct $A_I$ from A;
construct $B_R$ from B;
*for* q = 0 *to* P − 1 *dopar*
   *for* j = q(n/P) *to* (q + 1)(n/P) − 1 *do*
      *for* each (i, r, m) ∈ $A_I$ *do*
         *if* VAL(r, j) = 1
         *then* C[i, j] : = 1
         *else if* NEXT(r, j) ≤ m
            *then* C[i, j] := 1
            *fi*
         *fi*
      *od*
   *od*
*odpar*

It is clear that the first parallel for-loop requires $O(n^2/P)$ time, $P \leq n$. Construction of $A_I$ and $B_R$ from matrices A and B, respectively, takes $O(n^2/P)$ time, $P \leq n$, as described earlier. Finally, the last parallel for-loop requires $O(nf/P)$ time with $P \leq n$ processors, where $f = |A_I|$. Thus, the overall time complexity of this algorithm is $O(\max((n^2/P), (nf/P)))$, for $P \leq n$. Hence, we can state the following theorem.

**Theorem 6.3:** Algorithm CREW_BOOL_MATRIX_MULT2 computes the product of two n × n Boolean matrices A and B in $O(\max((n^2/P), (nf/P)))$ time with $P \leq n$ processors, where $f = |A_I|$.

The worst case situation is when matrix A has alternate 1's and 0's in each row. In this case, we have $f = |A_I| = n\lceil n/2 \rceil$ and the time complexity of algorithm CREW_BOOL_ MATRIX_MULT2 becomes $O(n^3/2P) \equiv O(n^3/P)$. On the other hand, if $f = O(n)$ then the above complexity reduces to only $O(n^2/P)$ and the algorithm shows optimal behavior. Moreover, when comparing the performance of algorithm CREW_BOOL_MATRIX_MULT2 with that of algorithm CREW_BOOL_MATRIX_MULT1, observe that $f \leq e$ and so the second algorithm is to be preferred in most cases. It is also interesting to note that the worst case for algorithm CREW_BOOL_MATRIX_MULT1 — the case in which A consists entirely of 1's giving $e = n^2$ — is the best case for algorithm CREW_BOOL_MATRIX_ MULT2, since in this case $f = n$. However, the reverse is not true.

### 6.3.3  Boolean Matrix Multiplication on Mesh

In this section Boolean matrix multiplication is considered on a two-dimensional mesh connected computer having n processors (i.e., a $\sqrt{n} \times \sqrt{n}$ mesh). The parallel algorithm is obtained by suitably parallelizing the Four Russians' algorithm for serial Boolean matrix multiplication. We begin with an informal description of the Four Russians' algorithm.

#### 6.3.3.1  *The Four Russians' Boolean Matrix Multiplication Algorithm*

The serial Boolean matrix multiplication algorithm described here was first proposed by Arlazarov et al. (1970). It has also been explained in detail by Aho et al. (1974).

Assume that A and B represent two n × n Boolean matrices and we want to compute C = A × B. For convenience of presentation, assume that log n divides n evenly. First, the matrices A and B are partitioned into n × log n and log n × n submatrices, respectively. Denote these submatrices by $A_0, A_1, \ldots, A_{(n/\log n)-1}$, and $B_0, B_1, \ldots, B_{(n/\log n)-1}$, respectively, as shown in Figure 6.8. The product A × B is then given by

$$C = A \times B = \bigvee_{0 \le i \le (n/\log n)-1} C_i$$

where $C_i = A_i \times B_i$. There are n/log n such $C_i$ and each $C_i$ is itself an n × n Boolean matrix. Thus, the time to construct C from n/log n $C_i$'s is $O(n^3/\log n)$. Now the obvious way of computing $C_i = A_i \times B_i$ takes $O(n^2 \log n)$ time, since $A_i$ is a matrix of size n × log n and $B_i$ is a matrix of size log n × n. Thus, to compute all $C_i$, for $0 \le i \le (n/\log n) - 1$, we need $O(n^3)$ time. Clearly, in that case there is no improvement in the time complexity using this partitioning approach. The clever part of the Four Russians' algorithm is that the product $C_i$ is computed, not by actual multiplication of $A_i$ and $B_i$, but by using a "table lookup" method. This method requires only $O(n^2)$ time to compute each $C_i$.

The jth row of $C_i$, denoted by $C_i[j, *]$, is the vector sum of a subset of the set of rows of $B_i$. This subset depends on the jth row of $A_i$, i.e., $A_i[j, *]$. For example, if columns 0, 2, and 5 of $A_i[j, *]$ are 1's and all other columns of $A_i[j, *]$ are 0's, then $C_i[j, *] = B[0, *] \vee$

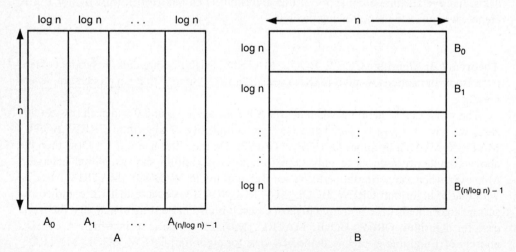

**Figure 6.8** The Boolean matrices A and B are each partitioned into n/log n submatrices.

$B[2, *] \lor B[5, *]$. Since there are log n elements in each row of $A_i$, there can be at most $2^{\log n} = n$ distinct rows among all the $A_i$'s. Thus only n possible sums (bitwise OR operations) of rows of $B_i$ are required to be formed. All possible sums of rows of $B_i$ can be precomputed, and the results can be stored in a table. Since this table depends on $B_i$, log n such tables must be constructed. Let us denote these tables by $T_i$, for $0 \leq i \leq (n/\log n) - 1$. The jth row of $C_i$ can be found simply by using $A_i[j, *]$ to index the table $T_i$ and obtain the desired $C_i[j, *]$.

The table $T_i$ of row sums of $B_i$ can be computed in $O(n^2)$ time as explained below. Note that any subset of rows of $B_i$ is either empty, a single row, or the union of two smaller subsets. Thus by choosing the correct order, each row sum can be obtained by adding one row of $B_i$ to a previously computed row sum. The complete process obviously requires $O(n^2)$ time.

Once $T_i$, $0 \leq i \leq (n/\log n) - 1$ is constructed, $C_i$ can be computed in $O(n^2)$ time. Let the table index be denoted by $IND(A_i[j, *])$ which is the integer represented by the reverse of vector $A_i[j, *]$ of 0's and 1's. This can be computed in $O(\log n)$ time from $A_i[j, *]$. Then the jth row of $C_i$ is formed in $O(n)$ time by selecting row $IND(A_i[j, *])$ of $T_i$ and copying it into $C_i$. Since $C_i$ consists of n rows, $O(n^2)$ time is required to construct $C_i$. The number of $C_i$'s is $n/\log n$ and so $O(n^3/\log n)$ time is required to obtain all $C_i$, $0 \leq i \leq (n/\log n) - 1$. Once all the $C_i$'s are available the rest of computing the product matrix C is simple and takes another $O(n^3/\log n)$ time. Thus, the time complexity of the Four Russians' serial Boolean matrix multiplication algorithm is $O(n^3/\log n)$.

### 6.3.3.2 The Four Russians' Algorithm on Mesh

We now consider a parallel implementation of the Four Russians' algorithm on a two-dimensional n processor mesh connected computer. We assume wraparound connections similar to that of the ILLIAC network (Chapter 2). For convenience, the interconnection pattern for such a computer is shown in Figure 6.9.

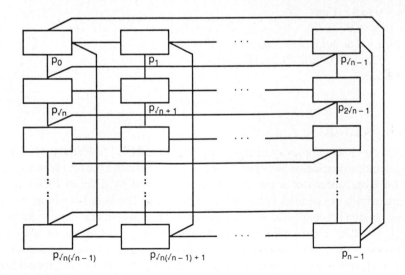

**Figure 6.9** The $\sqrt{n} \times \sqrt{n}$ mesh connected computer with wraparound connections similar to that of the ILLIAC network.

Given an n processor mesh connected computer, one decomposition of the Four Russians' Boolean matrix multiplication algorithm is achieved by assigning to $p_j$ ($0 \leq j \leq n - 1$) the task of computing column j of each table matrix $T_i$, $0 \leq i \leq (n/\log n) - 1$. This can be performed in a straightforward manner in $O(n)$ time if each $p_j$ is initialized with the jth column of B, i.e., $B[*, j]$. In addition, $p_j$ can compute $IND(A_i[j, *])$ in $O(\log n)$ time, if it is assumed that $p_j$ also contains the jth row of A. Each $p_j$ now computes a column of $C_i$ as $C_i[k, j] = T_i[IND(A_i[k, *]), j]$, $0 \leq k \leq n - 1$. To do this $p_j$ must obtain $IND(A_i[k, *])$ which has been computed by $p_k$. A detailed description of the algorithm is given below.

### Algorithm MESH_BOOL_MATRIX_MULT

Input: Two n × n Boolean matrices A and B such that each processor $p_j$ contains $A[j, *]$ and $B[*, j]$, $0 \leq j \leq n - 1$.

Output: Column j of the product matrix, i.e., $C[*, j]$ is stored in processor $p_j$, $0 \leq j \leq n - 1$.

*for* i = 0 *to* (n/log n) − 1 *do*
    *for* j = 0 *to* n − 1 *dopar*
        compute $T_i[*, j]$;
        IX[j] := $IND(A_i[j, *])$
    *odpar*
    *for* s = 0 *to* n − 1 *do*
        *for* j = 0 *to* n − 1 *dopar*
            $C_i[(j + s) \bmod n, j] := T_i[IX[j], j]$;
            IX[j] ← IX[(j + 1) mod n]
        *odpar*
    *od*
*od*
*for* j = 0 *to* n − 1 *dopar*
    *for* r = 0 *to* n − 1 *do*
        C[r, j] := 0;
        *for* i = 0 *to* (n/log n) − 1 *do*
            $C[r, j] := C[r, j] + C_i[r, j]$
        *od*
    *od*
*odpar*

### Complexity Analysis

To analyze the time complexity of algorithm MESH_BOOL_ MATRIX_MULT, observe that the algorithm consists of two main for-loops. Now, consider the first for-loop. The body of this for-loop consists of a parallel for-loop followed by a serial for-loop. The two statements within the parallel for-loop take $O(n)$ time. The serial for-loop, which again contains a parallel for-loop, also takes $O(n)$ time if it is assumed that moving an index from $p_{(j+1) \bmod n}$ to $p_j$ takes constant time. Thus the overall time complexity of the body of the first main for-loop is $O(n)$. This loop is repeated n/log n times and hence it takes $O(n^2/\log n)$ time. The body of the second main for-loop requires $O(n/\log n)$ time and since it is repeated n times, the time required to implement this for-loop is also $O(n^2/\log n)$. Thus, the overall time complexity of algorithm MESH_BOOL_MATRIX_MULT is $O(n^2/\log n)$ using n processors. The cost of the algorithm is $O(n^3/\log n)$ which is identical to the time complexity of the Four Russians' algorithm.

Observe that in the above algorithm, we were required to move data from processor $P_{(j+1) \bmod n}$ to processor $p_j$ and, for this purpose, we used the wraparound connections. The same algorithm can also be implemented within the same time and processor bounds if we assume the interconnection pattern to be a ring.

# 6.4 OTHER MATRIX COMPUTATIONS

In addition to the parallel matrix multiplication algorithms for both general and Boolean matrices, discussed in the previous sections, there are parallel algorithms for other common matrix computations such as matrix transposition, matrix-vector multiplication, matrix inversion, computing the determinant, etc. In this section we discuss only the problems of matrix transposition, matrix-vector multiplication and convolution. Appropriate references for other operations are provided in the Bibliographic Notes section.

## 6.4.1 Matrix Transposition

One of the simplest matrix computations is matrix transposition. The transpose of an $n \times n$ matrix A denoted by $A^T$ is obtained simply by interchanging rows and columns. An $n \times n$ matrix A and its transpose $A^T$ are shown in Figure 6.10.

The transpose of an $n \times n$ matrix can easily be obtained in $O(n^2)$ time on a serial model of computation. It may be noted that the trivial serial algorithm for this problem is optimal, since the lower bound for this problem is known to be $\Omega(n^2)$ (this amount of time is required simply to output $n^2$ elements of the transpose matrix). In this section, we study the transposition problem on three different parallel computational models, namely, EREW PRAM, mesh, and perfect shuffle.

### 6.4.1.1 Transposition on EREW PRAM

The algorithm for transposition of an $n \times n$ matrix on the EREW PRAM model is obtained simply by parallelizing the serial algorithm.

We assume that the matrix A is stored in the shared memory in locations $A[i, j]$, $0 \le i, j \le n - 1$, and that the transposition matrix $A^T$ becomes available in locations $A^T[i, j]$, $0 \le i, j \le n - 1$. Let us also assume that we have $n^2$ processors, denoted by $p_{ij}$, for $0 \le i, j \le n - 1$. Although $n(n-1)/2$ processors could be used to implement this algorithm, choosing $n^2$ allows a clearer presentation without affecting the processor complexity which is $O(n^2)$ in both cases.

$$
A = \begin{bmatrix}
A[0, 0] & A[0, 1] & \ldots & A[0, n-1] \\
A[1, 0] & A[1, 1] & \ldots & A[1, n-1] \\
\vdots & & & \\
A[n-1, 0] & A[n-1, 1] & \ldots & A[n-1, n-1]
\end{bmatrix}
\quad
A^T = \begin{bmatrix}
A[0, 0] & A[1, 0] & \ldots & A[n-1, 0] \\
A[0, 1] & A[1, 1] & \ldots & A[n-1, 1] \\
\vdots & & & \\
A[0, n-1] & A[1, n-1] & \ldots & A[n-1, n-1]
\end{bmatrix}
$$

**Figure 6.10** The $n \times n$ matrix A and its transpose $A^T$. The elements of $A^T$ are given by $A^T[i, j] = A[j, i]$, for $0 \le i, j \le n - 1$.

*Algorithm* **EREW_TRANSPOSITION**

Input: An n × n matrix A.

Output: The n × n matrix $A^T$.

*for* i = 0 to n − 1 *dopar*
    $A^T[i, i] := A[i, i]$
*odpar*

*for* i = 1 to n − 1 *dopar*
    *for* j = 0 to i − 1 *dopar*
        $A^T[i, j] := A[j, i]$;
        $A^T[j, i] := A[i, j]$
    *odpar*
*odpar*

The complexity analysis of this algorithm is simple. Each of the two parallel for-loops takes constant time. The first loop uses O(n) processors while the other requires $O(n^2)$ processors. Thus, algorithm EREW_TRANSPOSITION runs in O(1) time using $O(n^2)$ processors. The cost of the algorithm is $O(n^2)$ which is optimal since it is the same as for the time complexity of the optimal serial algorithm for this problem.

### 6.4.1.2  Transposition on Mesh

Each element A[i, j] of an n × n matrix can be mapped onto a unique processor $p_{ij}$, $0 \le i$, $j \le n - 1$, of a two-dimensional mesh connected computer with $n^2$ processors. If A is available in this way, computation of $A^T$ is straightforward. We need to move all the elements (except those in the diagonal) stored in the $p_{ij}$'s in such a manner that, at the end of this process, processor $p_{ij}$ contains A[j, i], for $0 \le i, j \le n - 1$. It can be seen from Figure 6.11 that the longest path through which an element has to move is from processor $p_{0(n-1)}$ to processor $p_{(n-1)0}$. The length of this path is $2(n - 1)$. Hence, on this model, the transposition of an n × n matrix cannot be performed in time less than $2(n - 1)$. Thus, the lower bound on the execution time of a matrix transposition algorithm on a two-dimensional mesh connected computer is $\Omega(n)$.

The straightforward algorithm for matrix transposition on a mesh has time complexity O(n). In this respect, this algorithm is the best possible on a mesh. The idea on which the algorithm is based is simple. The processors which lie below the diagonal, i.e., $p_{ij}$, $0 \le i$, $j \le n - 1$ such that i > j, transfer their contents A[i, j], $0 \le i, j \le n - 1$ and i > j, to processors $p_{ji}$. Similarly, all of the processors which lie above the diagonal, i.e., $p_{ij}$, $0 \le i, j \le n - 1$ and j > i, transfer their contents A[i, j], $0 \le i, j \le n - 1$ and j > i, to $p_{ji}$. These two-way transfers are performed in parallel by means of the bidirectional links between adjacent processors. Clearly, the process of data movement comes to an end after $2(n - 1)$ units of time. Thus, the overall complexity of this algorithm is O(n) using $n^2$ processors. The algorithmic description of matrix transposition on a mesh is straightforward and is omitted. The cost of the algorithm is $O(n^3)$ which is obviously not optimal since the corresponding serial algorithm for this problem takes only $O(n^2)$ time.

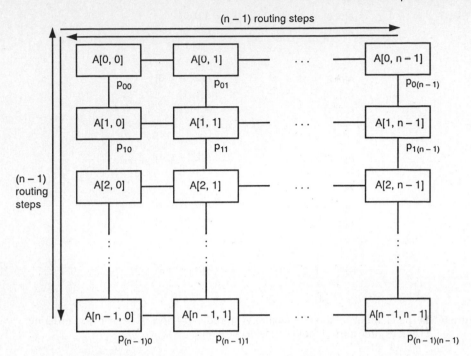

**Figure 6.11** This figure shows the path for data movement between processor $p_{0(n-1)}$ and $p_{(n-1)0}$.

### 6.4.1.3  Transposition on Perfect Shuffle

It has been shown that the transposition of an $n \times n$ matrix can be obtained in $O(1)$ time on the EREW PRAM whereas it takes $O(n)$ time on the mesh connected computer, both using $O(n^2)$ processors. In this section, we study the transposition problem on the perfect shuffle computer and show that it requires $O(\log n)$ time with $n^2$ processors. This algorithm is obviously slower than the EREW PRAM algorithm but it is much faster than the corresponding mesh algorithm.

Assume that the elements of the $n \times n$ matrix A, where $n = 2^m$ and m is a positive integer, are stored in a table in row-major order. In other words, the elements of A are stored in lexicographic order by index with the row index as major key (see Figure 6.12a). Clearly, the element A[i, j] is displaced from A[0, 0] by an amount given by $i2^m + j$. In order to obtain the transpose $A^T$, we have to store A in column-major order. That is, the elements of A are to be stored in lexicographic order by index with the column index as the major key. This implies that, after transposition, A[i, j] is displaced from A[0, 0] by an amount given by $j2^m + i$ (see Figure 6.12b).

Now we show that, for each element A[i, j] of A, $0 \leq i, j \leq n - 1$, the indices of its position in the transpose matrix $A^T$ can be obtained by performing m shuffles on the indices of a vector consisting of 2m bits in which the leftmost m-bits represent i, and the rightmost m-bits j, respectively. For the purpose of illustration, consider the binary shift register with 2m-bits shown in Figure 6.13a. The m most significant bits hold the binary representation of i and the m least significant bits hold the binary representation of j. In other words, the shift register

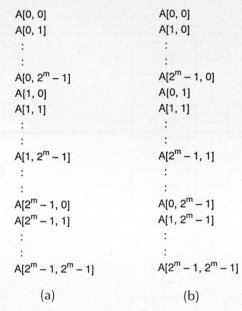

(a)                                          (b)

**Figure 6.12**  The elements of the n × n matrix A stored in (a) normal (row-major) ordering; and (b) transposed (column-major) ordering.

holds the binary representation of $i2^m + j$ which is just the displacement of $A[i, j]$ relative to $A[0, 0]$ (see Figure 6.12). We have seen earlier that the action of shuffle on the indices of a vector is the same as a cyclic shift of the binary representation of the indices. Thus, after m shuffles, the index whose representation is that shown in Figure 6.13a is changed to the index whose representation is given in Figure 6.13b. Alternatively, we can say that the element that

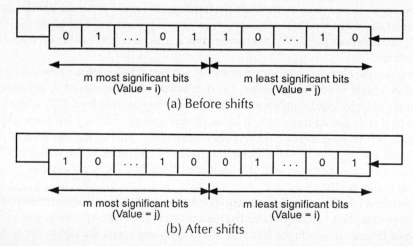

(a) Before shifts

(b) After shifts

**Figure 6.13**  The effect of m shuffles on a 2m-bit vector is shown using a shift register and giving m cyclic left-shifts to its content. The effect is to transform the index $i2^m + j$ to $j2^m + i$.

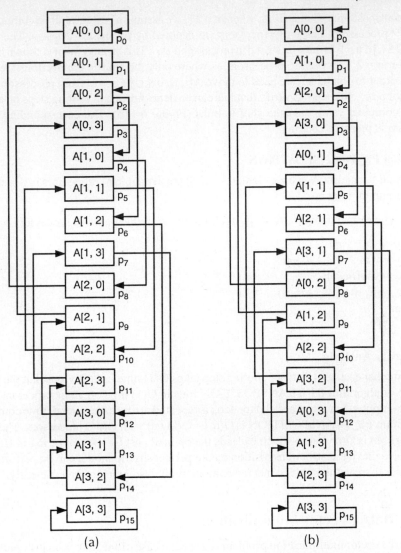

(a)                                      (b)

**Figure 6.14**  (a) The elements of a 4 × 4 matrix A loaded on a 16 processor perfect shuffle computer in which only the shuffle connections are shown; (b) the transpose $A^T$ of the 4 × 4 matrix A shown in (a).

is displaced from A[0, 0] by $i2^m + j$ before the shuffles is displaced from A[0, 0] by $j2^m + i$ after the shuffles. That is, A[i, j] is moved into the position occupied by A[j, i]. If this is performed for all $0 \le i, j \le n - 1$, then we have the transpose of A (see Figure 6.12b). Thus, given an element A[i, j], $0 \le i, j \le n - 1$, we can obtain its position in the transposed matrix $A^T$ by shuffling m-times the indices of a 2m-bit vector representing i, j. This fact is exploited in the design of a parallel algorithm for matrix transposition on the perfect shuffle model.

To transpose an $n \times n$ matrix A, where $n = 2^m$, we assume a perfect shuffle computer with $n^2 = 2^{2m}$ processors. These $n^2$ processors are denoted by $p_0, p_1, \ldots, p_{2^{2m}-1}$. The element $A[i, j], 0 \leq i, j \leq n - 1$, is initially stored in processor $p_{i2^m+j}$. This arrangement is shown in Figure 6.14a for $m = 2$, i.e., with 16 processors — where only the shuffle connections are shown. Now in order to obtain $A^T$, we need to move $A[i, j], 0 \leq i, j \leq n - 1$, from processor $p_{i2^m+j}$ to processor $p_{j2^m+i}$. It is easy to verify that this can be done through m routing steps on a perfect shuffle computer using only the shuffle links (Figure 6.14b). The corresponding parallel algorithm is presented below.

## *Algorithm* PS_TRANSPOSITION

Input: An $n \times n$ matrix A, whose elements $A[i, j]$ are available in processors $p_{i2^m+j}$, for $0 \leq i$, $j \leq n - 1$ and $m = \log n$.

Output: The elements of $A^T$, $A^T[i, j], 0 \leq i, j \leq n - 1$, are available in processors $p_{i2^m+j}$.

*for* $x = 0$ *to* $m - 1$ *do*
    *for* $y = 0$ *to* $2^{2m} - 1$ *dopar*
        $z := \text{shuffle}(y);$
        $p_z(A[i, j]) \leftarrow p_y(A[i, j])$
    *odpar*
*od*

## Complexity Analysis

Assuming that each unit distance routing step takes $O(1)$ time, it is obvious that the parallel for-loop of algorithm PS_TRANSPOSITION runs in $O(1)$ time on an $n^2$ processor perfect shuffle computer. Since this parallel for-loop is repeated m times, the overall time complexity of algorithm PS_TRANSPOSITION is $O(m) = O(\log n)$ with $O(n^2)$ processors. The cost of the algorithm is $O(n^2 \log n)$ which exceeds the optimal cost by a factor of $\log n$. However, we observe that the matrix transposition on the perfect shuffle model can be performed not only faster than on the mesh connected computer, but also much more efficiently.

## 6.4.2 Matrix-Vector Multiplication

The matrix-vector multiplication problem is a special case of the matrix-matrix multiplication. The problem is to find the product $X = A \times V$ of an $m \times n$ matrix A with a column vector V of length n to produce a column vector X of length m. We develop parallel algorithms for this problem on CREW PRAM and on a linear array of processors in the following sections.

### 6.4.2.1 Matrix-Vector Multiplication on CREW PRAM

Matrix-vector multiplication on the CREW PRAM model is simple and an algorithm is given below.

## *Algorithm* CREW_MV_MULT

Input: The $m \times n$ matrix A, and the $n \times 1$ column vector V.

Output: The $m \times 1$ column vector X.

*for* i = 0 *to* m − 1 *dopar*
    *for* j = 0 *to* n − 1 *dopar*
        C[i, j] := A[i, j] × V[j]
    *odpar*
*odpar*
*for* i = 0 *to* m − 1 *dopar*

$$X[i] := \sum_{0 \le j \le n-1} C[i, j]$$

*odpar*

## Complexity Analysis

It is clear that mn multiplications, performed by the first parallel for-loop, take $O(1)$ time with mn processors. The second parallel for-loop can be implemented in $O(\log n)$ time using $O(mn)$ processors to perform the m summations, of n elements each. Therefore, the overall time complexity of algorithm CREW_MV_MULT is $O(\log n)$ with $O(n^2)$ processors, assuming $m \le n$. The cost of the algorithm is $O(n^2 \log n)$, which is a factor of $\log n$ more than that of the straightforward serial algorithm. Note that the trivial $O(n^2)$ time serial algorithm for this problem is optimal, since $\Omega(n^2)$ steps are required to read the matrix A serially.

Although the straightforward implementation of algorithm CREW_MV_MULT discussed above is not cost optimal, we have an alternative implementation which follows from Brent's theorem (see Section 3.2) that takes $O(\log n)$ time using only $O(n^2/\log n)$ processors. This algorithm has cost $O(n^2)$ and is optimal. The implementation is as follows. The $O(n^2)$ multiplications required within the first for-loop are performed by applying $n^2/\log n$ processors $\log n$ times. Finally, each of the m summations in the second parallel for-loop is performed in $O(\log n)$ time using $n/\log n$ processors (applying Brent's theorem as shown in Section 5.3.3). Therefore, the overall time complexity of the matrix-vector multiplication algorithm on the CREW PRAM model becomes $O(\log n)$ with $O(n^2/\log n)$ processors.

### 6.4.2.2 *Matrix-Vector Multiplication on Linear Array of Processors*

In this section, the computational model used to develop a parallel matrix-vector multiplication algorithm is a linear array of n processors. Each processor $p_i$, $0 \le i \le n-1$, is responsible for adding to the partial product the term involving V[i]. It is assumed that V[i] resides in processor $p_i$, $0 \le i \le n-1$. The data movements and the actions of each processor, for the case in which m = n = 5, are illustrated in Figures 6.15a and 6.15b, respectively. The partial results are accumulated as they move from left to right through the processors. Eventually the rightmost processor outputs

$$X[i] = \sum_{0 \le j \le n-1} A[i, j] \times V[j]$$

for $0 \le i \le m - 1$. The X[i]'s are initially 0. In the first step, X[0] = 0 and A[0, 0] are fed to the processor $p_0$, and all other inputs move one step closer. Processor $p_0$ computes X[0] + A[0, 0] × V[0], and sends the result to its right. In the second step, $p_1$ receives X[0] = A[0, 0] × V[0] from the left, together with A[0,1] from below; it computes X[0] + A[0,1] × V[1], and sends the result to its right, and so on. In general, at each step, processor $p_i$ receives a partial result, say, x from the left and the appropriate element of the matrix from below.

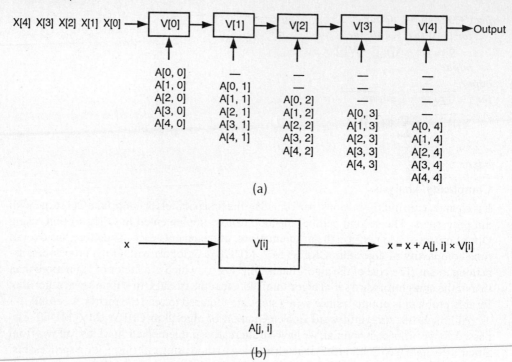

**Figure 6.15** (a) Matrix-vector multiplication using a linear array of processors; (b) the function of an individual processor.

Processor $p_i$ then computes $x + A[j, i] \times V[i]$ and passes it to its right neighbor. In this way, when x leaves the array as output from the rightmost processor, it has the required value. This process is repeated until all the X[i]'s, $0 \le i \le m - 1$ are obtained from the rightmost processor. The following algorithm is based on the above discussion.

*Algorithm* **ARRAY_MV_MULT**

Input: Processor $p_i$ holds V[i], $0 \le i \le n - 1$, in its local memory. The elements X[i] (initially all 0) are fed to $p_0$ from the left, serially, one in each time interval. A column of A is fed to each processor, one element in each time interval, such that column j lags one time unit behind column j − 1, $1 \le j \le n - 1$.

Output: The elements X[i], $0 \le i \le m - 1$, of the vector X are output from processor $p_{n-1}$, one element in each time interval.

*for* i = 0 *to* n − 1 *dopar*
    *while* $p_i$ receives x from left and A[j, i] from below *do*
        x := x + A[j, i] × V[i]
        *if* i < n − 1
        *then* send x to $p_{i+1}$
        *else* output x as an element of X
        *fi*
    *od*
*odpar*

**Complexity Analysis**

The last multiply-add operation of algorithm ARRAY_MV_MULT is performed in processor $p_{n-1}$ when it calculates $x + A[m - 1, n - 1] \times V[n - 1]$. Now $A[m - 1, n - 1]$ takes $m + n - 1$ steps to reach $p_{n-1}$ and so after the algorithm begins execution, it takes $m + n$ steps to output the last element, i.e., $X[m - 1]$. Therefore, algorithm ARRAY_MV_MULT runs in $O(n)$ time (assuming $m \leq n$) on a linear array containing $O(n)$ processors. The cost of the algorithm is $O(n^2)$ which is identical to the time complexity of the simple serial algorithm. Since $\Omega(n^2)$ is also the lower bound in computing time for this problem on a serial model of computation, algorithm ARRAY_MV_MULT is cost optimal.

## 6.4.3  Convolution

The convolution problem is much more demanding than the matrix-vector multiplication problem. In matrix-vector multiplication every element of the matrix is used once only and the corresponding parallel algorithm is simple. If the same matrix elements are used several times, then the policy for data movements and as a result the corresponding algorithm, becomes much more complicated. In solving the convolution problem, we need to use the same matrix element several times. The convolution problem is defined formally as follows. Given two sequences of real numbers $A = A_0, A_1, \ldots, A_{n-1}$ and $W = W_0, W_1, \ldots, W_{k-1}$, where $k < n$, compute $B_0, B_1, \ldots, B_{n-k}$, which satisfy $B_i = W_0 \times A_i + W_1 \times A_{i+1} + \ldots + W_{k-1} \times A_{i+k-1}$. The vector B is called the convolution of A and W. The convolution problem can be reduced to the matrix-vector multiplication problem shown below.

$$
\begin{bmatrix}
A_0 & A_1 & A_2 & \cdots & A_{k-1} \\
A_1 & A_2 & A_3 & \cdots & A_k \\
\vdots & \vdots & \vdots & & \vdots \\
\vdots & \vdots & \vdots & & \vdots \\
A_{n-k} & A_{n-k+1} & A_{n-k+2} & \cdots & A_{n-1}
\end{bmatrix}
\times
\begin{bmatrix}
W_0 \\
W_1 \\
\vdots \\
\vdots \\
W_{k-1}
\end{bmatrix}
=
\begin{bmatrix}
B_0 \\
B_1 \\
\vdots \\
\vdots \\
B_{n-k}
\end{bmatrix}
$$

In the following sections, we develop parallel algorithms for the convolution problem on CREW PRAM and a linear array of processors.

### 6.4.3.1  Convolution on CREW PRAM

The parallel algorithm for convolution of two sequences of lengths n and k, respectively, works on a CREW PRAM with $(n - k)(k - 1)$ processors. The algorithm is self-explanatory and is given below.

**Algorithm  CREW_CONVOLUTION**

Input: Two sequences $A = A_0, A_1, \ldots, A_{n-1}$ and $W = W_0, W_1, \ldots, W_{k-1}$ of real numbers with $k < n$.

Output: The sequence $B = B_0, B_1, \ldots, B_{n-k}$ such that $B_i = W_0 \times A_i + W_1 \times A_{i+1} + \ldots + W_{k-1} \times A_{i+k-1}$.

*for* i = 0 *to* n − k *dopar*
  *for* j = 0 *to* k − 1 *dopar*
    M[i, j] := $A_{i+j}$
  *odpar*
*odpar*

*for* i = 0 *to* n − k *dopar*
  *for* j = 0 *to* k − 1 *dopar*
    C[i, j] := M[i, j] × $W_j$
  *odpar*
*odpar*

*for* i = 0 *to* n − k *dopar*

  $B_i := \sum_{0 \le j \le k-1} C[i, j]$

*odpar*

## Complexity Analysis

The first nested parallel for-loop constructs a matrix M, from the sequence A, whose elements are as follows:

$$
M = \begin{bmatrix}
A_0 & A_1 & A_2 & \cdots & A_{k-1} \\
A_1 & A_2 & A_3 & \cdots & A_k \\
\vdots & \vdots & \vdots & & \vdots \\
\vdots & \vdots & \vdots & & \vdots \\
A_{n-k} & A_{n-k+1} & A_{n-k+2} & \cdots & A_{n-1}
\end{bmatrix}
$$

This step obviously takes O(1) time when (n − k)(k − 1) processors are available. The second nested parallel for-loop also runs in O(1) time with (n − k)(k − 1) processors to compute (n − k)(k − 1) products. Finally, the last parallel for-loop, which computes (n − k) summations each having k elements, can be implemented in O(log k) time using (n − k)(k − 1)/2 processors. Thus, the overall time complexity of algorithm CREW_ CONVOLUTION is O(log k) using O(nk) processors. Since k < n, this complexity result can be expressed as O(log n) time with O($n^2$) processors.

### 6.4.3.2  Convolution on Linear Array of Processors

Using the same computational model as for matrix-vector multiplication in Section 6.4.2.2, we can solve the convolution problem in a similar manner. The input matrix A[i, j], 0 ≤ i, j ≤ n − 1, of the matrix-vector multiplication is replaced with the matrix

$$
M = \begin{bmatrix}
A_0 & A_1 & A_2 & \cdots & A_{k-1} \\
A_1 & A_2 & A_3 & \cdots & A_k \\
: & : & : & & : \\
: & : & : & & : \\
A_{n-k} & A_{n-k+1} & A_{n-k+2} & \cdots & A_{n-1}
\end{bmatrix}
$$

In the local memory of each processor $p_i$, we store $W_i$, for $0 \le i \le k - 1$. This is shown in Figure 6.16 in which each processor receives two inputs and sends one output. The output sequence $B = B_0, B_1, \ldots, B_{n-k}$ is produced by the rightmost processor $p_{k-1}$. The input from the left to $p_0$ is the sequence $B_0, B_1, \ldots, B_{n-k}$, with values initialized to all 0. The time complexity of parallel convolution on a k processor linear array is $O(n + k) \equiv O(n)$, since $k < n$.

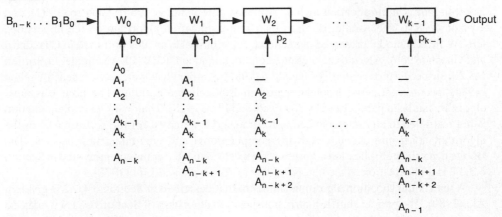

**Figure 6.16** Convolution using linear array of processors.

# 6.5 BIBLIOGRAPHIC NOTES

Matrix multiplication is one of the most important matrix computations and has wide application in scientific computing. The problem has been studied intensively for both serial and parallel computational models. Efficient serial matrix multiplication algorithms that take less than $O(n^3)$ multiplications are discussed in Aho et al. (1974), Manber (1989), Strassen (1969, 1986), and Wilf (1986). Parallel matrix multiplication algorithms on PRAM models similar to that described in Section 6.2.1 are also treated in Horowitz and Zorat (1983), and Stone (1980). A parallelization of Strassen's algorithm which has time complexity $O(\log n)$ when $O(n^{2.81}/\log n)$ processors are used appears in Chandra (1976). The lower bound result on mesh matrix multiplication presented in Section 6.2.2.1 is due to Gentleman (1978). Matrix multiplication algorithms on a mesh connected computer are described by Akl (1989), Dekel et al. (1981), Flynn and Kosaraju (1976), Preparata and Vuillemin (1980), and Ullman (1984). In particular, the algorithm on mesh with wraparound connections presented in Section 6.2.2.2 is based on the algorithm of Cannon (1969), which is also described in Dekel et al. (1981), and Manber (1989). An algorithm, similar to that presented in Section 6.2.2.3, is also given in Akl (1989). Ramakrishnan and Varman (1984) have designed an optimal matrix multiplication algorithm for a linear array of processors. Algorithms for matrix multiplication on cube connected and perfect shuffle computers are given in Dekel et al. (1981); the algorithms in Sections 6.2.3 and 6.2.4 are based mainly on their work. Performance analysis and experimental results for matrix multiplication on a hypercube are given in Fox et al. (1987), and Fox et al. (1988). A matrix multiplication algorithm for a tightly coupled multiprocessor model is presented in Quinn (1987). Some references for matrix multiplication on other interconnection networks including VLSI systems are Cheng and Sahni (1987), Horowitz (1979), Horowitz and Zorat (1983), Hwang and Cheng (1982), Kung and Leiserson (1978), and Varman et al. (1984).

Boolean matrix multiplication has applications in many parallel graph algorithms. However, not many parallel algorithms have appeared in the literature for this problem. In the serial model, the most popular Boolean matrix multiplication algorithm is due to Arlazrov et al. (1970), commonly known as the Four Russians' algorithm. Other references for serial Boolean matrix multiplication include Atkinson and Santoro (1988), Santoro (1981), and Vyskoc (1984). The parallel Boolean matrix multiplication algorithm on the unbounded CRCW PRAM model presented in Section 6.3.1 is based on an idea proposed in Chaudhuri and Ghosh (1986). Algorithms presented on the bounded CREW PRAM model in Section 6.3.2 are based on those given by Chaudhuri (1987). Similar ideas were earlier used in Vyskoc (1984) to construct serial Boolean matrix multiplication algorithm. The Four Russians' algorithm has been parallelized by Agerwala and Lint (1978). Their parallel implementation is not restricted to any interconnection scheme and the analysis of the performance of the algorithm takes into account both the computational and communication aspects. The Boolean matrix multiplication algorithm on a mesh connected computer presented in Section 6.3.3.2 is an adaptation of the algorithm due to Agerwala and Lint (1978).

A matrix transposition algorithm similar to that described in Section 6.4.1.2 is given in Akl (1989). The perfect shuffle matrix transposition algorithm of Section 6.4.1.3 is adapted from Stone (1971). Matrix-vector multiplication and convolution on linear array of processors, as described in Sections 6.4.2.2 and 6.4.3.2, are also treated in Akl (1989) and Manber (1989). Other references to parallel matrix-vector multiplication algorithms include Kung (1979), Mead and Conway (1980), and Nath et al. (1983).

Matrix inversion has been investigated in Pease (1967) in the context of parallel processing. Parallel algorithms to compute the determinant and characteristic polynomial of matrices are presented in Borodin et al. (1982). Their algorithms run in $O(\log^2 n)$ time using a polynomially bounded number of processors. Geist et al. (1987) reviewed the characteristics of parallel architectures which most strongly affect the design and performance of parallel algorithms for various matrix computations.

# 6.6  EXERCISES

6.6.1    Design an $O(\log n)$ time matrix multiplication algorithm on the CREW PRAM model with $O(n^3/\log n)$ processors.

6.6.2    Illustrate the functions $\beta(1)$ and $\beta(2)$ with reference to a two-dimensional mesh connected computer.

6.6.3 Show that for the two-dimensional mesh connected computer $\beta(x) = 2x^2 + 2x + 1$.

6.6.4 Show that two ($n \times n$) matrices can be multiplied in $O(n)$ time on a cube connected computer with $n^2$ processors (Dekel et al. 1981).

6.6.5 Design a matrix multiplication algorithm on a cube connected computer with $n^2m$ processors, where $1 \leq m \leq n$. Analyze the complexity of this algorithm (Dekel et al. 1981).

6.6.6 Design a perfect shuffle matrix multiplication algorithm that runs in $O((n/m) + \log n)$, $1 \leq m \leq n$, using $n^2m$ processors (Dekel et al. 1981).

6.6.7 Develop a matrix multiplication algorithm for an MIMD computer.

6.6.8 Describe how the Four Russians' Boolean matrix multiplication can be implemented on an n-processor SIMD computer in which the processors are connected in the form of a ring.

6.6.9 Parallelize the Four Russians' algorithm on an EREW PRAM. Analyze the complexity of your algorithm. Will there be any improvement in the complexity if it is implemented on CREW or CRCW PRAM models?

6.6.10 Show that it is possible to develop a parallel algorithm based on the Four Russians' algorithm to multiply two ($n \times n$) Boolean matrices in $O(\log n)$ time when $O(n^3/\log n \log \log n)$ processors are available (Agerwala and Lint 1978).

6.6.11 Design a parallel algorithm to obtain the inverse of an ($n \times n$) matrix.

6.6.12 Develop completely an algorithm to obtain the transpose of an ($n \times n$) matrix on a two-dimensional mesh connected computer with $n^2$ processors.

6.6.13 Show how to use a systolic array to obtain the transpose of an ($n \times n$) matrix.

6.6.14 What will be the time complexity of algorithm CREW_MV_MULT of Section 6.4.2 if implemented on each of the EREW and CRCW PRAM models?

6.6.15 Discuss how algorithm CREW_CONVOLUTION of Section 6.4.3 can be implemented on an EREW PRAM. What will be its time complexity? Will there be any improvement in time complexity if CRCW PRAM model is used?

## 6.7 BIBLIOGRAPHY

Agerwala, T., and Lint, B. (1978). Communication in parallel algorithms for Boolean matrix multiplication. *Proceedings of the 1978 International Conference on Parallel Processing,* IEEE Computer Society, Washington, DC, pp. 146-53.

Aho, A., Hopcroft, J., and Ullman, J. (1974). *The Design and Analysis of Computer Algorithms.* Addison-Wesley, Reading, Mass.

Akl, S. G. (1989). *The Design and Analysis of Parallel Algorithms.* Prentice Hall, Englewood Cliffs, NJ.

Arlazarov, V. L., Dinic, E. A., Kronrod, M. A., and Faradzev, I. A. (1970). On economical construction of the transitive closure of a directed graph. *Soviet Math. Dokl.* 11, 1209-10.

Atkinson, M. D., and Santoro, N. (1988). A practical algorithm for Boolean matrix multiplication. *Inform. Process. Lett.* 29, 37-8.

Borodin, A., von zur Gathen, J., and Hopcroft, J. (1982). Fast parallel matrix and GCD computations. *Information and Control* 52, 241-56.

Cannon, L. E. (1969). A cellular computer to implement the Kalman filter algorithm. Ph.D. dissertation, Montana State University, Mont.

Chandra, A. K. (1976). *Maximal parallelism in matrix multiplication.* IBM Tech. Rep. RC6193, Thomas J. Watson Research Center, Yorktown Heights, NY.

Chaudhuri, P., and Ghosh, R. K. (1986). Parallel algorithms for analyzing activity networks. *BIT* 26, 418-29.

Chaudhuri, P. (1987). Efficient Boolean matrix and graph algorithms on a bounded parallel computation model. *J. Instn. Electronics & Telecom. Engrs.* 33, 48-52.

Cheng, K. H., and Sahni, S., (1987). VLSI systems for band matrix multiplication. *Parallel Computing* 4, 239-58.

Dekel, E., Nassimi, D., and Sahni, S. (1981). Parallel matrix and graph algorithms. *SIAM J. Computing* 10, 657-75.

Flynn, M. J., and Kosaraju, S. R. (1976). Processes and their interactions. *Kybernetics* 5, 159-63.

Fox, G. C., Otto, S. W., and Hey, A. J. G. (1987). Matrix algorithms on a hypercube I: Matrix multiplication. *Parallel Computing* 4, 17-31.

Fox, G. C., Johnson, M. A., Lyzenga, G. A., Otto, S. W., Salmon, J. K., and Walker, D. W. (1988). *Solving Problems on Concurrent Processors vol. 1: General Techniques and Regular Problems.* Prentice Hall, Englewood Cliffs, NJ.

Geist, G. A., Heath, M. T., and Ng, E. (1987). Parallel algorithms for matrix computations. In *The Characteristics of Parallel Algorithms,* L. H. Jamieson, D. B. Gannon, and R. J. Douglass, eds. MIT Press, Mass., pp. 233-51.

Gentleman, W. M. (1978). Some complexity results for matrix computations on parallel processors. *J. ACM* 25, 112-15.

Horowitz, E. (1979). VLSI architectures for matrix computations. *Proceedings of the 1979 International Conference on Parallel Processing,* IEEE Computer Society, Washington, DC, pp. 124-7.

Horowitz, E., and Zorat, A. (1983). Divide-and-conquer for parallel processing. *IEEE Transactions on Computers* C-32, 582-5.

Hwang, K., and Cheng, Y. H. (1982). Partitioned matrix algorithms for VLSI arithmetic systems. *IEEE Transactions on Computers* C-31, 1215-24.

Kung, H. T. (1979). *Let's design algorithms for VLSI systems.* Tech. Rep. CMU-CS-79-151, Dept. of Computer Science, Carnegie-Mellon University, Pittsburgh, Pa.

Kung, H. T., and Leiserson, C. E. (1978). Systolic arrays (for VLSI). In Sparse Matrix Symposium, *SIAM,* pp. 256-82.

Manber, U. (1989). *Introduction to Algorithms: A Creative Approach.* Addison-Wesley, Reading, Mass.

Mead, C. A., and Conway, L. A. (1980). *Introduction to VLSI Systems.* Addison-Wesley, Reading, Mass.

Nath, D., Maheshwari, S. N., and Bhatt, P. C. P. (1983). Efficient VLSI networks for parallel processing based on orthogonal trees. *IEEE Transactions on Computers* C-32, 569-81.

Pease, M. C. (1967). Matrix inversion using parallel processing. *J. ACM* 14, 757-64.

Preparata, F. P., and Vuillemin, J. (1980). Area-time optimal VLSI networks for multiplying matrices. *Inform. Process. Lett.* 11, 77-80.

Quinn, M. J. (1987). *Designing Efficient Algorithms for Parallel Computers.* McGraw-Hill, NY.

Ramakrishnan, I. V., and Varman, P. (1984). Modular matrix multiplication on a linear array. *IEEE Transactions on Computers* C-33, 952-8.

Santoro, N. (1981). Four $O(n^2)$ multiplication methods for sparse and dense Boolean matrices. *Proceedings of the 10th Conference on Numerical Mathematics and Computing.* In *Congressus Numerantium* vol. 31 (Utilitas Mathematica, Winnipeg), pp. 241-52.

Stone, H. S. (1971). Parallel processing with the perfect shuffle. *IEEE Transactions on Computers* C-20, 153-61.

Stone, H. S. (1980). Parallel computers. In *Introduction to Computer Architecture*, H. S. Stone, ed. Science Research Associates Chicago, Chap. 8.

Strassen, V. (1969). Gaussian elimination is not optimal. *Numerische Mathematik* 13, 354-6.

Strassen, V. (1986). The asymptotic spectrum of tensors and the exponent of matrix multiplication. *Proceedings of the 27th Annual IEEE Symposium on Foundations of Computer Science,* IEEE Computer Society, Washington, DC, pp. 49-54.

Ullman, J. (1984). *Computational Aspects of VLSI.* Computer Science Press, Rockville, Md.

Varman, P., Ramakrishnan, I. V., and Fussell, D. S. (1984). A robust matrix-multiplication array. *IEEE Transactions on Computers* C-33, 919-22.

Vyskoc, J. (1984). A note on Boolean matrix multiplication. *Inform. Process. Lett.* 19, 249-51.

Wilf, H. S. (1986). *Algorithms and Complexity.* Prentice Hall, Englewood Cliffs, NJ.

# CHAPTER 7

# Algorithms for Unweighted Graphs

## 7.1 INTRODUCTION

Graphs are essential tools for understanding and solving a wide range of problems in diverse disciplines. For example, graph theoretic models are conveniently used for parsing diagram analysis in linguistics, chemical structure matching and structural isomer prediction in chemistry, planning and scheduling in operations research, analysis of markov chains in probability theory, analysis of networks in electrical engineering, and representing computational concepts in computer science. As a result the design of graph theory algorithms has been studied for a long time and there are efficient serial algorithms for the solution of various graph theory problems. This is not the case for parallel graph algorithms; however, a great deal of research in this area has been reported in the literature over the past twenty years.

The last three chapters of this book are devoted to a discussion of parallel graph algorithms. This chapter addresses a number of basic graph problems for unweighted graphs and presents the design and analysis of fast and efficient parallel algorithms for them. The next two chapters deal, respectively, with parallel algorithms for weighted graphs, and parallel updating algorithms for graphs.

The organization of this chapter is as follows. Section 2 covers parallel algorithms for the solution of tree-related problems. Parallel algorithms for searching graphs are considered in Section 3. Connectivity problems, i.e., problems related to connectedness, biconnectedness, and triconnectedness are addressed in Section 4. Parallel algorithms for the solution of other important connectivity-related problems, e.g., finding a set of fundamental cycles, bridges and bridge-connected components, and centers and medians are presented in Section 5. A brief discussion on the complexity results of other parallel algorithms for unweighted graphs together with the relevant references are given in Section 6.

# 7.2 ALGORITHMS ON TREES

The tree is undoubtedly one of the most important fundamental concepts in graph theory. There are many useful operations which are often performed on trees. The most common operation is traversal, i.e., visiting each node of the tree exactly once in some order. Three frequently used traversal methods for a binary tree are preorder, inorder, and postorder traversals. There are two principal ways to traverse a general ordered tree. These are the preorder traversal and the postorder traversal. In the preorder traversal a node of the tree is visited before any of its children are visited and in the postorder traversal a node is visited after visiting all its children. After completion of the traversal, every node of the tree is assigned with a number (or rank) which gives the order of its traversal. Formally, the preorder and the postorder traversals of a tree are defined as the traversal of the corresponding binary tree in the following way:

*Preorder traversal*

> Process the root node;
> Traverse the left subtree in preorder;
> Traverse the right subtree in preorder.

*Postorder traversal*

> Traverse the left subtree in postorder;
> Traverse the right subtree in postorder;
> Process the root node.

The lower bound for the serial computation time for traversing a tree consisting of n nodes is $\Omega(n)$, since, by definition, each node has to be visited once. There exist optimal serial algorithms for these traversal problems (see e.g., Horowitz and Sahni 1977). There are two ways to perform the traversal of a general ordered tree. One is by converting the general ordered tree into the equivalent binary tree and then applying the corresponding traversal algorithm for binary trees. The other is to obtain a traversal list without converting it into its equivalent binary tree. In this section, we study both approaches. We begin by presenting a parallel algorithm for generating the binary tree representation of general ordered trees in Section 7.2.1. Then, in Section 7.2.2, parallel traversal of binary trees is discussed. The traversal of general ordered trees is considered in Section 7.2.3. Other basic tree functions including the nearest common ancestor for every pair of nodes of a tree, centers and medians of trees are discussed in Sections 7.2.4 and 7.2.5, respectively. Finally, in Section 7.2.6 we discuss the Euler tour technique which is of great use when designing parallel algorithms for tree-related problems. The computational model used for all of the algorithms in this section is an unbounded CREW PRAM, unless otherwise specified.

## 7.2.1 Binary Tree Representation of Trees

The terminology used in this section is standard. A tree in which one node is distinguished from all others is called a rooted tree — denoted by T(r). The distinguished node r is called the root of the tree. It is assumed that all the nodes of the given general ordered tree are arbitrarily numbered from 1 through n and we shall not distinguish between a node and its number. Since a tree is a special case of a graph, we sometimes denote a tree T(r) as T(r) =

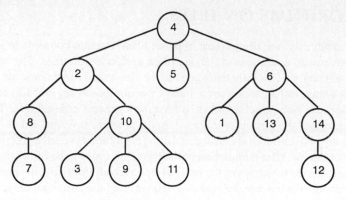

**Figure 7.1**  An arbitrary general ordered tree T(4) rooted at node 4.

<N, E>, where N is the set of |N| = n nodes and E is the set of |E| = e = n − 1 edges. Let us assume that the general ordered tree T(r) = <N, E> be represented by the "parent-of" relation. That is, for each node i ∈ N its parent or immediate predecessor, denoted by parent(i), is given. It is assumed that parent(r) = r. Each node j of the set of nodes denoted by child(i) is a child or son of a node i, i.e., parent(j) = i. To obtain an equivalent binary tree representation for a general ordered tree, we need a relationship between the nodes, which can be characterized by at most two quantities. One such relationship is the leftmost-child-next-right-sibling relationship. Every node has at most one leftmost-child and at most one next-right-sibling. For example, consider the tree in Figure 7.1. In this tree, the leftmost-child of node 2 is node 8 and the corresponding next-right-sibling is node 5. Since the leftmost-child and the next-right-sibling of any node depends on how the tree is drawn, in drawing a tree, the children of each node i ∈ N are assumed to be sorted in ascending order. Thus, the lowest-numbered child becomes the leftmost-child for each node i. The next-right-sibling of i is a node j ∈ child(parent(i)) having the next higher number. Using this relationship between the nodes, the tree in Figure 7.1 can be transformed into an equivalent binary tree shown in Figure 7.2.

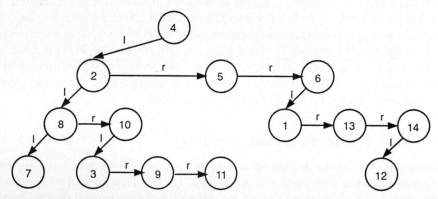

**Figure 7.2**  The binary tree representation of the tree T(4) in Figure 7.1. The leftmost child and the next-right-sibling relations are shown by the labeled arrows $\underset{\rightarrow}{l}$ and $\underset{\rightarrow}{r}$, respectively.

Without loss of generality, let us call the leftmost-child and the next-right-sibling of every node of the general ordered tree the leftchild and the rightchild, respectively, in the equivalent binary tree.

**Definition 7.1:** Three functions *leftchild*, *rightchild*, and *father* are defined on the set of nodes of a general ordered tree as follows:

(i) leftchild(i)    = j,  if j = min{k | parent(k) = i}
                    = $\emptyset$, otherwise;

(ii) rightchild(i)  = j,  if j = min{k | k > i AND parent(k) = parent(i)}
                    = $\emptyset$, otherwise;

(iii) father(i)     = parent(i),   if rightchild(i) = $\emptyset$
                    = $\emptyset$,          otherwise.

The parallel algorithm given below, which generates the binary tree representation of a general ordered tree, computes the values of the functions leftchild, rightchild, and father for each node of the tree. The algorithm is obtained by straightforward parallelization of the corresponding serial method for obtaining the binary tree representation of general ordered trees (see Horowitz and Sahni 1977).

### *Algorithm* **CREW_EQUIVALENT_BINARY**

Input: parent(i) for each node i $\in$ N in T(r) = <N, E>.

Output: leftchild(i), rightchild(i), and father(i) for each node i$\in$N in T(r).

*for* i = 1 *to* n *dopar*
   *if* parent(i) $\neq$ i
   *then* k(i) := n × parent(i) + n − i
   *else* k(i) := 0
   *fi*
*odpar*
sort the nodes i $\in$ N of the tree with k(i) as the key and store them in an
      array NODE(1 : n) in ascending order;
*for* i = 1 *to* n *dopar*
   leftchild(NODE(i)) := rightchild(NODE(i)) := father(NODE(i)) := $\emptyset$;
   *if* i = 1 AND parent(NODE(i)) $\neq$ i
   *then* leftchild(parent(NODE(i))):= NODE(i)
   *fi*
   *if* i < n AND parent(NODE(i)) = parent(NODE(i + 1))
   *then* rightchild(NODE(i)) := NODE(i + 1)
   *else if* i < n AND parent(NODE(i + 1)) $\neq$ NODE(i)
      *then* leftchild(parent(NODE(i + 1))) := NODE(i + 1)
      *fi*
   *fi*
   *if* rightchild(NODE(i)) = $\emptyset$
   *then* father(NODE(i)) := parent(NODE(i))
   *fi*
*odpar*

**Table 7.1**

| Node, i | parent(i) | leftchild(i) | rightchild(i) | father(i) |
|---------|-----------|--------------|---------------|-----------|
| 1 | 6 | ∅ | 13 | ∅ |
| 2 | 4 | 8 | 5 | ∅ |
| 3 | 10 | ∅ | 9 | ∅ |
| 4 | 4 | 2 | ∅ | ∅ |
| 5 | 4 | ∅ | 6 | ∅ |
| 6 | 4 | 1 | ∅ | 4 |
| 7 | 8 | ∅ | ∅ | 8 |
| 8 | 2 | 7 | 10 | ∅ |
| 9 | 10 | ∅ | 11 | ∅ |
| 10 | 2 | 3 | ∅ | 2 |
| 11 | 10 | ∅ | ∅ | 10 |
| 12 | 14 | ∅ | ∅ | 14 |
| 13 | 6 | ∅ | 14 | ∅ |
| 14 | 6 | 12 | ∅ | 6 |

The leftchild, rightchild, and father for each node of the tree T(4) in Figure 7.1, computed by algorithm CREW_EQUIVALENT_BINARY, are shown in Table 7.1.

**Complexity Analysis**

To obtain the complexity of algorithm CREW_EQUIVALENT_BINARY, we observe that each of the two parallel for-loops requires $O(1)$ time when $O(n)$ processors are employed. Thus, the complexity of the parallel sorting algorithm is the determining factor in the computational complexity of the algorithm. For this purpose, we may use the CREW sorting algorithm discussed in Chapter 4. However, in order to obtain a better time bound, let us use a recent result on parallel sorting due to Cole (1988). Cole showed that it is possible to sort n elements on an n processor CREW PRAM in $O(\log n)$ time. Using this parallel sorting algorithm, we can implement algorithm CREW_EQUIVALENT_BINARY in $O(\log n)$ time with $O(n)$ processors.

## 7.2.2  Traversal of Binary Trees

In this section, we consider the problem of traversing a binary tree in preorder and design a parallel algorithm for this task. Similar algorithms for other types of traversal can be designed quite easily. We assume here that the binary tree is represented by leftchild, rightchild, and father relations. If only the leftchild and rightchild for each node are available then the father relation can easily be obtained by examining the rightchild of every node i ∈ N and by setting father(i) to parent(i) when rightchild(i) is empty, and setting to ∅ otherwise. In the case of general ordered trees, we first apply algorithm CREW_EQUIVALENT_BINARY to obtain the corresponding binary tree represented by the leftchild, rightchild, and father relations. Given a binary tree, the basic idea underlying preorder traversal is as follows. The leftchild of a node i, if it exists, should appear as the next node to i in the preorder list. Otherwise, the rightchild of i, if it exists, appears as the next node to i. If node i has neither a leftchild nor a rightchild then, to obtain the next node to be visited in preorder, the nearest ancestor of node i (say, it is node j) in the tree having a rightchild is located. The rightchild of node j is then made the next node of i in the preorder traversal. Thus, if a node has either a leftchild or a rightchild the task is very simple. But if it has neither, then the task of locating the nearest ancestor having a rightchild is not so simple. For this purpose, we exploit the father relations for the nodes. More precisely, we apply folding on father relations, i.e., the father relations are propagated towards the root of the tree, by using the "growing by doubling" technique, so that the nonempty father relations of the nodes are updated to nodes having a rightchild or, if there is none, to the root of the tree. A complete description of the algorithm is given below.

### Algorithm CREW_PREORDER_BINARY

Input: leftchild(i), rightchild(i), and father(i) for each node $i \in N$ in $T(r) = <N, E>$.

Output: The preorder traversal list of the nodes of $T(r)$ and the preorder traversal rank for each node $i \in N$ denoted by pre(i).

```
construct the array NODE(1 : n) according to
        algorithm CREW_EQUIVALENT_BINARY;
for i = 1 to n dopar
    next(NODE(i)) := ∅
    for j = 1 to ⌈log n⌉ do
        if father(NODE(i)) ≠ ∅ AND father(father(NODE(i))) ≠ ∅
        then father(NODE(i)) := father(father(NODE(i)))
        fi
    od
    if leftchild(i) ≠ ∅
    then next(NODE(i)) := leftchild(NODE(i))
    else if rightchild(NODE(i)) ≠ ∅
        then next(NODE(i)) := rightchild(NODE(i))
        else if father(NODE(i)) ≠ ∅
            then next(NODE(i)) := rightchild(father(NODE(i)))
            fi
        fi
    fi
    pre(NODE(i)) := 1;
    far(NODE(i)) := ∅;
    if next(NODE(i)) ≠ ∅
    then far(next(NODE(i))) := NODE(i)
    fi
    for j = 1 to ⌈log n⌉ do
        if far(NODE(i)) ≠ ∅
        then do
                pre(NODE(i)) := pre(NODE(i)) + pre(far(NODE(i)));
                far(NODE(i)) := far(far(NODE(i)))
            od
        fi
    od
odpar
```

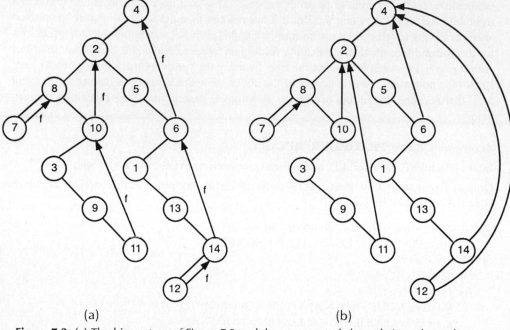

**Figure 7.3** (a) The binary tree of Figure 7.2 and the nonempty father relations shown by labeled arrows $\underset{\rightarrow}{f}$ (e.g., father(6) = 4 but father(5) = $\emptyset$); (b) the effect of folding on the father relations.

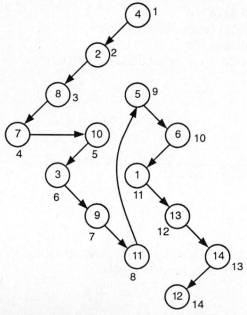

**Figure 7.4** The preorder traversal list of the binary tree in Figure 7.3a along with the preorder ranks of nodes.

The algorithm consists of a single parallel for-loop. Observe that the first serial for-loop within the parallel for-loop performs the folding on the father relations mentioned earlier. The binary tree of Figure 7.2 is repeated in Figure 7.3a together with the nonempty father relations. Figure 7.3b shows the effect of folding on the father relations. The preorder traversal list of the binary tree of Figure 7.3a along with the preorder rank of each node is shown in Figure 7.4.

**Complexity Analysis**

The construction of the array NODE($1:n$) takes $O(\log n)$ time using $O(n)$ processors as has been shown in Section 7.2.1. Each of the two serial for-loops within the parallel for-loop requires $O(\log n)$ time and all other assignments take constant time. Thus, the overall time complexity of algorithm CREW_PREORDER_BINARY is $O(\log n)$ when $O(n)$ processors are available. The cost of this algorithm is $O(n \log n)$ which is, of course, close to but not optimal.

## 7.2.3 Traversal of General Ordered Trees

The traversal list for a general ordered tree can be obtained by first converting it into the equivalent binary tree using algorithm CREW_EQUIVALENT_BINARY and then applying the corresponding binary tree traversal algorithm to this equivalent binary tree. In this section, we consider the problem of traversing a general ordered tree without converting it into the equivalent binary form. As before, we shall concentrate only on the preorder traversal of a general ordered tree $T(r) = <N, E>$ and design a parallel algorithm for the solution of this problem. Parallel algorithms for other traversal methods are left as exercises.

The tree traversal algorithm given below uses an array denoted by $A^j(i)$, $1 \le i \le n$, $0 \le j \le n-1$, in which each row i contains a path from the root to node i in $T(r)$ so that each entry of $A^j(i)$ (i.e., row i and column j) gives the node number of the jth ancestor of i. The concept of such an array was first introduced by Savage and Ja' Ja' (1981). An arbitrary rooted tree $T(5)$ and the corresponding array $A^j(i)$, $1 \le i \le n$, $0 \le j \le n-1$, for $n = 10$ are shown in Figure 7.5.

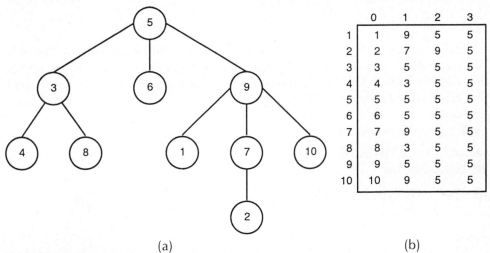

|    | 0  | 1 | 2 | 3 |
|----|----|---|---|---|
| 1  | 1  | 9 | 5 | 5 |
| 2  | 2  | 7 | 9 | 5 |
| 3  | 3  | 5 | 5 | 5 |
| 4  | 4  | 3 | 5 | 5 |
| 5  | 5  | 5 | 5 | 5 |
| 6  | 6  | 5 | 5 | 5 |
| 7  | 7  | 9 | 5 | 5 |
| 8  | 8  | 3 | 5 | 5 |
| 9  | 9  | 5 | 5 | 5 |
| 10 | 10 | 9 | 5 | 5 |

(a)                                                      (b)

**Figure 7.5** (a) An arbitrary rooted tree $T(5)$ with $n = 10$; (b) the array $A^j(i)$, $1 \le i \le 10$, $0 \le j \le 9$, corresponding to the rooted tree $T(5)$. The entries not shown are all 5.

**Definition 7.2**: Define on the set of nodes of a rooted tree $T(r) = <N, E>$ a function "A" as follows:

$$A(i) = parent(i), \forall\ i \in N\ AND\ i \neq r$$
$$= r, \qquad otherwise.$$

**Definition 7.3**: Define on the set of nodes of a rooted tree $T(r) = <N, E>$ a recursive function "$A^j$", $0 \leq j \leq n - 1$ as follows:

$$A^j(i) = A(A^{j-1}(i)), \forall\ i \in N\ AND\ j > 0$$
$$= i, \qquad otherwise.$$

Now the level of each node $i \in N$, denoted by level(i), is given by

$$level(i) = min\{j\ |\ A^j(i) = r\ AND\ 0 \leq j \leq n - 1\}.$$

A simple parallel algorithm, based on the "growing by doubling" paradigm, which constructs the array $A^j(i)$, $1 \leq i \leq n$, $0 \leq j \leq n - 1$, in O(log n) time is given below.

### Algorithm ANCESTOR_ARRAY

Input: parent(i) for each node $i \in N$ of tree $T(r)$.

Output: The array $A^j(i)$, $1 \leq i \leq n$, $0 \leq j \leq n - 1$.

*for* i = 1 *to* n *dopar*
  $A^0(i) := i;$
  $A^1(i) := parent(i)$
*odpar*
*for* w = 0 *to* $\lceil \log (n - 1) \rceil$ *do*
  *for* x = 1 *to* $2^w$ *dopar*
    *for* i = 1 *to* n *dopar*
      $k := 2^w;$
      $A^{k+x}(i) := A^k(A^x(i))$
    *odpar*
  *odpar*
*od*

It is clear that the first parallel for-loop runs in O(1) time with O(n) processors. The body of the second for-loop consists of two nested parallel for-loops which can be executed in O(1) time with O($n^2$) processors. Since the body of this for-loop is repeated log n times, the overall time complexity of algorithm ANCESTOR_ARRAY is O(log n) when O($n^2$) processors are employed.

The preorder traversal algorithm is based on the following lemma whose proof is trivial.

**Lemma 7.1:** Let $T(r)$ be a rooted tree. The preorder rank corresponding to each node $i \in N$ can be computed as

$$pre(i) = \sum_{u \in ANC(i) - \{r\}} NDES(parent(u), rank(u) - 1) + level(i) + 1,$$

where

NDES(i, j)  is the number of descendants of the first j children of $i \in N$ (a node is a descendant of itself);

rank(i)      is the rank of node $i \in N$, i.e., its position among all its brothers (nodes having the same parent are said to be brothers);

ANC(i)     is the set of ancestors of $i \in N$ (a node is an ancestor of itself).

An informal description of the preorder traversal algorithm is now given.

### *Algorithm* CREW_PREORDER_TRAVERSAL

Input: parent(i) for each node $i \in N$ in tree $T(r) = <N, E>$.

Output: The preorder traversal rank, pre(i) for each node $i \in N$.

construct the array $A^j(i)$, $1 \leq i \leq n$, $0 \leq j \leq n - 1$, using
        algorithm ANCESTOR_ARRAY;

```
for i = 1 to n dopar
    for j = 0 to n - 1 dopar
        if Aʲ(i) = r
        then B[i, j] := 1
        else B[i, j] := 0
        fi
    odpar
odpar
for i = 1 to n dopar
    for j = 0 to n - 1 dopar
        if j = 0
        then C[i, 0] := B[i, 0]
        else C[i, j] := B[i, j] - B[i, j - 1]
        fi
    odpar
odpar
for i = 1 to n dopar
    for j = 0 to n - 1 dopar
        if C[i, j] = 1
        then level(i) := j
        fi
    odpar
odpar
obtain the maximum level L from level(i), ∀ i ∈ N;
for i = 1 to n dopar
    for j = 0 to L dopar
        DEPTH[i, level(i) - j] := 0
    odpar
odpar
for i = 1 to n dopar
    for j = 0 to L dopar
        DEPTH[i, level(i) - j] := Aʲ(i)
    odpar
odpar
```

compute the number of descendants ND(i), for each i ∈ N by counting the number of
  occurrences of i in column level(i) of array DEPTH[1 : n, 0 : L];
compute rank(i), ∀ i ∈ N;
compute the number of children NS(i), for each node i ∈ N;
*for* i = 1 *to* n *dopar*
  *for* j = 1 *to* NS(i) *dopar*

  compute NDES(i, j) using the relation $NDES(i, j) = \sum_{1 \le p \le j} ND(s_p),$

  where $s_p$ is the pth child of i in T(r)
  *odpar*
*odpar*
*for* i = 1 *to* n *dopar*
  compute pre(i) using the expression in Lemma 7.1
*odpar*

The results of performing the computations in the various steps of algorithm
CREW_PREORDER_TRAVERSAL with respect to the tree shown in Figure 7.5a are given
in Table 7.2.

**Complexity Analysis**

The construction of the array $A^j(i)$, $1 \le i \le n$, $0 \le j \le n - 1$, requires O(log n) time with $O(n^2)$
processors — see the complexity analysis of algorithm ANCESTOR_ARRAY. Computa-
tion of level(i), ∀ i ∈ N of the tree T(r), performed by the first three parallel for-loops requires
only O(1) time using $O(n^2)$ processors. The maximum of level(i), ∀ i ∈ N can be obtained
in O(log n) time with O(n) processors. Next the construction of array DEPTH[1 : n, 0 : L] by
the fourth and fifth parallel for-loops takes O(1) time when O(nL) processors are employed.
It can be verified that for each node i ∈ N, the computation of the number of descendants
ND(i), the rank rank(i), and the number of children NS(i) require O(log n) time with O(n)
processors. Considering all the nodes, these three can be computed in O(log n) time with
$O(n^2)$ processors. The partial sum of the form $s_1 + s_2 + \ldots + s_j$, $1 \le j \le n$, can be computed
in O(log n) time with O(n) processors (see algorithm PARTIAL_SUMS of Section 5.3.3).

**Table 7.2**

| Node, i | parent(i) | level(i) | ND(i) | NS(i) | pre(i) |
|---------|-----------|----------|-------|-------|--------|
| 1 | 9 | 2 | 1 | 0 | 7 |
| 2 | 7 | 3 | 1 | 0 | 9 |
| 3 | 5 | 1 | 3 | 2 | 2 |
| 4 | 3 | 2 | 1 | 0 | 3 |
| 5 | 5 | 0 | 10 | 3 | 1 |
| 6 | 5 | 1 | 1 | 0 | 5 |
| 7 | 9 | 2 | 2 | 1 | 8 |
| 8 | 3 | 2 | 1 | 0 | 4 |
| 9 | 5 | 1 | 5 | 3 | 6 |
| 10 | 9 | 2 | 1 | 0 | 10 |

Since each node i has NS(i) children, the time needed to compute NDES(i, j), $1 \leq j \leq$ NS(i), is O(log NS(i)) if NS(i) processors are employed. As a result, all of the partial sums, NDES(i, j), $1 < j <$ NS(i), can be computed in parallel in max$\{$O(log (NS(i))) $| i \in N\} \equiv$ O(log n) time with $\Sigma_{i \in N}$ NS(i) = n − 1 processors. Therefore, the parallel for-loop for computing NDES(i, j), $1 \leq i \leq$ n, $1 \leq j \leq$ NS(i), takes O(log n) time with $O(n^2)$ processors, using algorithm PARTIAL_SUMS. Finally, the last parallel for-loop runs in O(log n) time using $O(n^2)$ processors to compute pre(i), $\forall$ i $\in$ N, according to Lemma 7.1. Thus, combining the computational complexities of all of the steps, we find that the time complexity of algorithm CREW_PREORDER_TRAVERSAL is O(log n) when $O(n^2)$ processors are used.

The cost of this algorithm is $O(n^2 \log n)$ which is far from being optimal. We can perform the same computation in O(log n) time using only O(n) processors if we convert T(r) into its equivalent binary form first and then apply the preorder traversal algorithm for binary trees. Thus it seems that the parent-of relation is not a good representation for general ordered trees — at least for the purpose of traversing the tree in parallel. The better representation is, of course, the leftmost-child-next-right-sibling relation which is equivalent to the leftchild and rightchild relations on the corresponding binary tree.

## 7.2.4 Nearest Common Ancestors

One of the most useful functions on trees is the *nearest common ancestor* (NCA) which is defined for every pair of nodes of a rooted tree. The notion of the NCA for every pair of nodes has applications in solving other graph theory problems such as finding the centers and medians of trees and the set of fundamental cycles of undirected graphs. We begin this section by giving formal definitions of *common ancestors* and NCAs for a pair of nodes of the tree. Finally, we present a CREW PRAM algorithm for solving the all-pairs NCA problem.

**Definition 7.4:** For a pair of nodes y and z in a rooted tree T(r) = <N, E>, the collection of nodes $\{x_i | i = 1, 2, \ldots, k\}$ is defined to be the set of common ancestors if and only if there exists tree-paths $x_i$ to y and $x_i$ to z, for each i = 1, 2, . . . , k. That is, $x_i$ is an ancestor of both y and z. It is obvious that the root of the tree r $\in$ $\{x_i | i = 1, 2, \ldots, k\}$.

**Definition 7.5:** A common ancestor x of a pair of nodes y and z in a rooted tree T(r) is defined to be the nearest common ancestor, denoted by NCA(y, z), if and only if in the preorder traversal of T(r) every common ancestor u $\neq$ x of y and z is visited before visiting x, i.e., every common ancestor u $\in$ $\{x_i | i = 1, 2, \ldots, k\}$ − $\{x\}$ of y and z is an ancestor of x.

For example, with reference to the tree of Figure 7.1, NCA(7, 3) = 2, NCA(7, 12) = 4 and NCA(7, 8) = 8. The underlying idea of the parallel algorithm for finding the NCA(y, z), $\forall$ y, z $\in$ N is as follows. First the array DEPTH[1 : n, 0 : L] (as used by algorithm CREW_PREORDER_TRAVERSAL ) is computed for the given tree T(r). Then, for every pair of nodes y, z $\in$ N, NCA(y, z) is computed using the following relation:

NCA(y, z) = {DEPTH(y, k) | k = max{p | DEPTH(y, p) = DEPTH(z, p), $0 \leq p \leq$ L}.

The details of the algorithm are given on the next page.

*Algorithm*  **CREW_NC_ANCESTORS**

Input: parent(i) for each node i ∈ N in T(r) = <N, E>.

Output: The nearest common ancestor NCA(y, z), for each pair of nodes y, z ∈ N.

construct the array DEPTH[1 : n, 0 : L] as in
                algorithm CREW_PREORDER_TRAVERSAL;
*for* y = 1 *to* n *dopar*
    *for* z = 1 *to* n *dopar*
        l(y, z) := 0;
        h(y, z) := L + 1;
        flag(y, z) := FALSE;
        *while* not flag(y, z) *do*
            m(y, z) := ⌊(l(y, z) + h(y, z))/2⌋;
            *if* DEPTH[y, m(y, z)] ≠ DEPTH[z, m(y, z)]
            *then* h(y, z) := m(y, z)
            *else if* DEPTH[y, m(y, z)] = 0
                *then* h(y, z) := m(y, z)
                *else if* DEPTH[y, m(y, z) + 1] = DEPTH[z, m(y, z) + 1]
                    *then* l(y, z) := m(y, z)
                    *else do*
                            NCA(y, z) := DEPTH[y, m(y, z)];
                            flag(y, z) := TRUE
                        *od*
                *fi*
            *fi*
        *fi*
    *od*
    *odpar*
*odpar*

**Complexity Analysis**

The complexity analysis for algorithm CREW_NC_ANCESTORS is straightforward. The construction of the array DEPTH[1 : n, 0 : L] requires $O(\log n)$ time using $O(n^2)$ processors, as has been discussed earlier. The while-loop within the nested parallel for-loops implements a modified binary search algorithm and, for a particular pair of nodes, this step requires $O(\log L)$ time using a single processor. Thus, the parallel for-loop runs in $O(\log L)$ time with $O(n^2)$ processors. Therefore, the overall time complexity of algorithm CREW_NC_ANCESTORS is $O(\log n)$ when $O(n^2)$ processors are used. The lower bound to the serial computing time for this problem is $\Omega(n^2)$, since this amount of time is required simply to output NCAs for $n^2$ pairs of nodes. The cost of algorithm CREW_NC_ANCESTORS is $O(n^2 \log n)$ which exceeds the optimal cost by a factor of only $\log n$.

## 7.2.5  Centers and Medians of Trees

Centers and medians of a tree provide useful topological information about the tree. Intuitively, if node x is given as the center of a tree, then it means that node x is located more centrally than any of the other nodes of the tree. Before giving the formal definitions of centers and medians of a tree, we first introduce some notation.

The distance between two nodes i and j, $i, j \in N$ in a rooted tree $T(r) = <N, E>$ is the number of edges between i and j and is denoted by $d(i, j)$. Obviously, $d(i, i) = 0$. The separation number, denoted by $s(i)$, of a node i in a tree is the distance from i to the node farthest from i in $T(r)$. That is

$$s(i) = \max\{d(i, j) \mid j = 1, 2, \ldots, n\}.$$

The transmission number $t(i)$ of a node $i \in N$, is the sum of the distances between i and all other nodes $j \in N$. Thus,

$$t(i) = \sum_{1 \le j \le n} d(i, j)$$

**Definition 7.6:** A node $c \in N$ for which $s(c)$ is minimum, i.e., c satisfies

$$\max\{d(c, j) \mid j = 1, 2, \ldots, n\} \le \max\{d(k, j) \mid j = 1, 2, \ldots, n\}, 1 \le k \le n,$$

is defined to be the center of $T(r)$. A tree can have either one or two centers (see e.g., Deo 1974).

**Definition 7.7:** A node $m \in N$ for which $t(m)$ is minimum, i.e., m satisfies

$$\sum_{1 \le j \le n} d(m, j) \le \sum_{1 \le j \le n} d(k, j), \quad 1 \le k \le n,$$

is defined to be the median of $T(r)$.

The CREW PRAM algorithm for computing the centers and medians of trees presented below uses the nearest common ancestor, $NCA(i, j)$, for every pair of nodes $i, j \in N$.

## *Algorithm* **CREW_CM_TREE**

Input: parent(i), for each node $i \in N$ of $T(r)$.

Output: Centers and medians of $T(r)$.

find for each pair of nodes $i, j \in N$, $NCA(i, j)$, using algorithm **CREW_NC_ANCESTORS**;
*for* i = 1 *to* n *dopar*
   *for* j = 1 *to* n *dopar*
      $d(i, j) := level(i) + level(j) - 2 \times level(NCA(i, j))$
   *odpar*
*odpar*
*for* i = 1 *to* n *dopar*
   compute $s(i) := \max\{d(i, j) \mid j = 1, 2, \ldots, n\}$
*odpar*
obtain the minimum of all $s(i)$'s and denote it by C;
*for* i = 1 *to* n *dopar*
   *if* $s(i) = C$
   *then* mark i as a center of $T(r)$
   *fi*
*odpar*

*for* i = 1 *to* n *dopar*

$$t(i) := \sum_{1 \le j \le n} d(i, j)$$

*odpar*
obtain the minimum of all t(i)'s and denote it by M;
*for* i = 1 *to* n *dopar*
   *if* t(i) = M
   *then* mark i as a median of T(r)
   *fi*
*odpar*

The results of an illustrative computation using algorithm CREW_CM_TREE and the tree in Figure 7.5a is shown in Table 7.3.

**Table 7.3**

| Node, i | s(i) | set of centers of T(5) | t(i) | set of medians of T(5) |
|---------|------|------------------------|------|------------------------|
| 1 | 4 | | 24 | |
| 2 | 5 | | 30 | |
| 3 | 4 | | 20 | |
| 4 | 5 | | 28 | |
| 5 | 3 | {5, 9} | 16 | {5, 9} |
| 6 | 4 | | 24 | |
| 7 | 4 | | 22 | |
| 8 | 5 | | 28 | |
| 9 | 3 | | 16 | |
| 10 | 4 | | 24 | |

## Complexity Analysis

The computation of the NCAs for all pairs of nodes using algorithm CREW_NC_ANCESTORS requires $O(\log n)$ time with $O(n^2)$ processors. The computation of the distance functions for all pairs of nodes, performed by the first parallel for-loop of algorithm CREW_CM_TREE, takes $O(1)$ time using $O(n^2)$ processors. The second parallel for-loop, which computes the separation numbers s(i), $i \in N$, can be implemented in $O(\log n)$ time with $O(n^2)$ processors. The computation of the minimum of all s(i)'s requires $O(\log n)$ time with $O(n)$ processors and the identification of the centers of the tree T(r) takes $O(1)$ time with $O(n)$ processors. Similarly, the computation of t(i), for all $i \in N$, and finding the minimum of all t(i)'s require $O(\log n)$ time with $O(n^2)$ processors. Finally, the set of medians of T(r) can be identified, by the last parallel for-loop, in $O(1)$ time using $O(n)$ processors. Therefore, considering the computational complexities of the individual steps, the overall time complexity of algorithm CREW_CM_TREE is $O(\log n)$ when $O(n^2)$ processors are employed.

## 7.2.6 The Euler Tour Technique

The Euler tour technique on trees, introduced by Tarjan and Vishkin (1984), is a very powerful tool when designing parallel algorithms for trees. The key idea behind this technique is the construction of a list of edges of the tree which forms a Euler tour of the directed version of the tree. The directed version of the tree is obtained simply by replacing each undirected edge (i, j) by two directed edges (i, j) and (j, i), respectively. We shall see that, once the Euler tour in the corresponding directed tree is obtained, a large class of tree functions can be computed in O(log n) time using O(n) processors on the PRAM model. In this section, we give an informal and high-level description of this technique for computing various tree functions.

If we assume that a rooted tree $T(r) = <N, E>$ has n nodes, then the number of edges in the directed version of the tree is obviously $2n - 2$. Suppose, now, that E contains all of these directed edges. Each node $i \in N$ has a list of its outgoing edges, where *tadj(i)* points to the first such edge and *tnext((i, j))* points to the edge after (i, j) on node i's list. If there is no such edge, then tnext(i, j)) = $\emptyset$. Each edge (i, j) has an extra pointer which points to its inverse (j, i). We need this extra pointer to find the edge (j, i) quickly when dealing with edge (i, j).

The Euler tour of the directed version of T(r) can easily be obtained, in a serial environment, by traversing the tree using depth-first search. In order to find the tour in parallel, let us denote the edge following edge (i, j) in the tour by *tournext((i, j))*. Now, a circular list corresponding to a Euler tour of the directed version of T(r) can be computed in parallel as follows. For each edge (i, j), the next edge tournext((i, j)) in the tour is tnext((j, i)) if tnext((j, i)) is not $\emptyset$ (null), and is tadj(j) otherwise. When this list has been constructed, we break the Eulerian tour at an edge which makes edge (r, u) the first edge on the list, where, as usual, r is the root and u is a child of r in T(r). This broken list is called the *traversal list*. We call an edge (i, j) an *advance edge* if it points away from the root, and a *retreat edge* otherwise. The directed version of a rooted tree T(1) with n = 5, its list representation with tadj and tnext pointers, and the traversal list are shown in Figure 7.6. It is assumed that the edges incident on each node are ordered in a clockwise fashion.

Now, we number the edges of the traversal list from 1 to $2n - 2$ according to their position in the list, using the list-ranking technique. The *rank* of an element i in a linked list, denoted by *rank(i)*, is defined here as the distance of the element from the end of the list. Thus the first element has rank n, if there are n elements in the list, and the last element has rank 1. We can compute the rank for every element in the list by using the doubling technique in time O(log n) using O(n) processors (see Section 3.5.2).

After the numbering phase of the edges in the traversal list using the list-ranking algorithm, we can easily identify the two classes of edges, namely, the advance edges and the retreat edges. Assuming that rank(i, j) denotes the rank of the edge in the traversal list, an edge (i, j) is an advance edge if rank(i, j) > rank(j, i). Using these values, we can mark each directed edge either as an advance edge or a retreat edge. Now, to show some representative applications of the Euler tour technique we describe how to compute: (a) the preorder traversal rank; and (b) the number of descendants, for every node of a rooted tree T(r).

The advance edges occur in preorder in the traversal list constructed using the Euler tour on the directed version of the tree T(r). Let (i, j) be the advance edge leading to j, i.e., parent(j) = i. If num(i, j) denotes the number of advance edges following (i, j) in the traversal list, then the preorder traversal rank of j, pre(j) = n − num(i, j). There is no advance edge leading to the

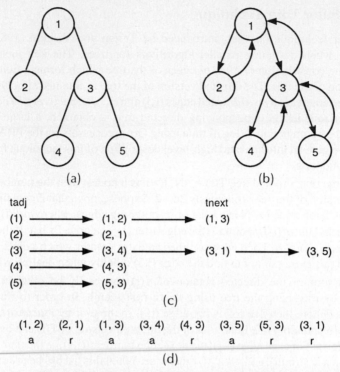

(a)                                                    (b)

tadj                                                  tnext
(1) ——————▶ (1, 2) ——————▶ (1, 3)
(2) ——————▶ (2, 1)
(3) ——————▶ (3, 4) ——————▶ (3, 1) ——————▶ (3, 5)
(4) ——————▶ (4, 3)
(5) ——————▶ (5, 3)

(c)

(1, 2)   (2, 1)   (1, 3)   (3, 4)   (4, 3)   (3, 5)   (5, 3)   (3, 1)
  a        r        a        a        r        a        r        r

(d)

**Figure 7.6**   (a) An arbitrary rooted tree T(1) with n = 5; (b) the directed version of T(1) obtained by replacing each undirected edge (i, j) in T(1) by two directed edges (i, j) and (j, i), respectively; (c) the list representation of T(1) in which the tadj and tnext pointers are shown but not the pointer connecting each edge with its inverse; (d) the traversal list for T(1), where "a" and "r" stand for advance edge and retreat edge, respectively.

root r, and its preorder traversal rank is assumed to be 1. The computation of num(i, j) for every advance edge (i, j) ∈ E can be obtained by initializing num(i, j) to 1 if (i, j) is an advance edge and 0 otherwise, and then applying the doubling technique similar to that used for list-ranking.

Thus, preorder traversal ranks for all the nodes of a tree can be obtained in $O(\log (2n - 2)) \equiv O(\log n)$ time using $2n - 2 \equiv O(n)$ processors on the EREW PRAM model.

In order to compute the number of descendants of node j ∈ N of a tree T(r) = <N, E>, we need to compute both the number of advance edges from (parent(j), j) to the end of the traversal list, i.e., num(parent(j), j), and the number of advance edges from (j, parent(j)) to the end of the list, denoted by rnum(j, parent(j)). Again, calculation of these two values for all edges of T(r) requires $O(\log n)$ time with $O(n)$ processors. It can easily be verified that the number of descendants of node j, NDES(j) is equal to num(parent(j), j) − rnum(j, parent(j)) + 1. Clearly, the computation of the number of descendants for all nodes of T(r) can be performed in $O(\log n)$ time using $O(n)$ processors on the EREW PRAM model.

**Table 7.4**

| Node, i | advance edge (i, j) | num(i, j) | rnum(i, j) | pre(i) | NDES(i) |
|---------|---------------------|-----------|------------|--------|---------|
| 1 | — | — | — | 1 | 5 |
| 2 | (1, 2) | 3 | 3 | 2 | 1 |
| 3 | (1, 3) | 2 | 0 | 3 | 3 |
| 4 | (3, 4) | 1 | 1 | 4 | 1 |
| 5 | (3, 5) | 0 | 0 | 5 | 1 |

The computation, by the algorithms discussed above, of the preorder traversal rank and the number of descendants of each node of the tree T(1) of Figure 7.6 are shown in Table 7.4.

## 7.3  GRAPH SEARCHING

Graph searching is of fundamental importance and it is the basis of a large number of other graph theory algorithms. Three basic graph search techniques are: the depth-first search (DFS), the breadth-first search (BFS), and the breadth-depth search (BDS).

For DFS, the search begins by visiting an arbitrary node of a given graph. In general, if u is the most recently visited node then the search is continued by selecting an unexplored edge (u, v) and visiting v, if v has not been visited earlier; on the other hand, if v has been visited already, the search is continued at u with other unexplored edges. After completing the search through all the edges involving u, the search is renewed at a node w from which u was visited. Keeping track of the edges which lead to a new node during the search yields a spanning tree, rooted at the start node, which is called the DFS spanning tree (DFST, for short).

The BFS of a graph also proceeds by first visiting an arbitrary node, say, r. After visiting r all the nodes at a distance of 1 from r are visited. Next, all the nodes at a distance of 2 from r are visited, and so on, until the entire graph is processed. Thus, the search started at a node u continues until all the unexplored edges involving u have been examined. After completing the examination of all the edges involving u the search is started at an adjacent node at the same level, if there is any. Otherwise, the search proceeds with a node at the next level. Keeping track of the edges that lead to a new node during the search yields a spanning tree rooted at the start node r, which is referred to as the BFS spanning tree (BFST).

In BDS, the search proceeds in the same way as for BFS in the sense that the search, started at a node u, continues until all the unexplored edges involving u have been examined. But, as in DFS, the next node to be searched from is the node most recently labeled as visited. The spanning tree created during searching of a graph using BDS is referred to as the BDS spanning tree (BDST).

The spanning trees obtained by applying these three search techniques on the graph of Figure 7.7a are shown in Figures 7.7b-d. There are standard serial algorithms for each of these three search techniques with time complexity O(n + e). This time complexity is apparent, since by denoting the degree of a node i as deg(i), we can express the upper bound to the serial computation time as

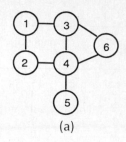

(a)

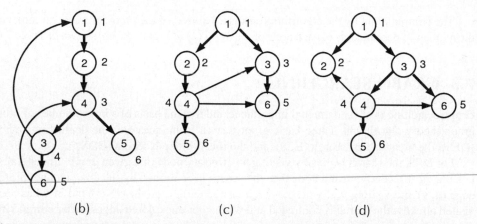

(b)                          (c)                          (d)

**Figure 7.7** (a) A graph G with n = 6 and e = 7; (b)–(d) the DFS, BFS, and BDS spanning trees of G taking node 1 as the start node. The bold arrows indicate the tree edges and the direction of traversal. The normal arrows are the nontree edges pointing towards nodes which have already been visited. The numbers alongside the nodes give their order of traversal.

$$T_s = \sum_{1 \le i \le n} (\deg(i) + 1) = 2e + n.$$

In the following sections, we investigate each of the three graph search techniques in the context of parallel processing. We shall see that all the algorithms developed are based on the "growing by doubling" paradigm and hence have a similar structure.

## 7.3.1 Depth-First Search

Depth-first search (DFS) is probably the most useful search technique and has many applications (Tarjan 1972). But DFS seems to be inherently serial because searching occurs along a single edge from a single node thereby restricting the possibility of parallel processing. The DFS problem has been investigated by Eckstein and Alton (1977), and Reghbati and Corneil (1978) on the CREW PRAM model without much success. As a consequence, DFS was suspected of being unsuitable for parallel processing. Recent work by Reif (1985) also strengthens the argument in favor of the earlier suspicions about the DFS. More precisely, Reif's work gives strong evidence that the DFS of graphs cannot be accomplished in deterministic polylogarithmic parallel time, i.e., in time $O(\log^c n)$, for any constant $c \geq 1$. Although this is the case with DFS of general graphs, we shall show that it is possible to design a fast parallel algorithm for DFS of directed acyclic graphs (DAGs). DAGs are a special class of digraphs which have no cycles. Below, we present a fast parallel algorithm for the DFS of DAGs on the CREW PRAM model. The technique we shall use for the DFS of DAGs is a type of "growing by doubling" and we will refer to it as the "partial spanning tree doubling" technique. This technique has been introduced in Section 3.5.2 as a useful paradigm for designing parallel algorithms.

Let $G = <N, E>$ be a DAG with a set N of n nodes and a set E of e edges. As before, without loss of generality, the set of nodes N is assumed to be $\{1, 2, \ldots, n\}$. If $(i, j) \in E$, then i is said to be the immediate predecessor of j in G. If there is a directed path from i to j, then j is said to be reachable from i; alternatively i can reach j.

**Definition 7.8:** Given a DAG $G = <N, E>$, a tree rooted at a node x ($x \in N$) containing all nodes reachable from x through a directed path of length less than or equal to $2^k$, where k is an integer satisfying $0 \leq k \leq \lceil \log n \rceil$, is called a *k-tree* and is denoted by $T(x, k)$.

It is clear that the adjacency list for each node $x \in N$ of G represents the 0-tree $T(x, 0)$. A k-tree is called a *k-dfs-tree* if and only if it preserves the DFS property defined below.

**Definition 7.9:** Given a pair of nodes y and z ($y \neq z$) in a k-tree $T(x, k)$ such that $(y, z)$ is an edge in DAG G but $(y, z)$ does not belong to $T(x, k)$, then the k-tree $T(x, k)$ is said to preserve the DFS property if one of the following conditions is satisfied:

(i) $post(y \mid T(x, k)) > post(z \mid T(x, k))$,

(ii) the path x to y in $T(x, k)$ consists of $2^k$ edges;

where $post(y \mid T(x, k))$ denotes the postorder rank of node y in the k-tree $T(x, k)$.

The definitions above are illustrated by an example in Figure 7.8. When constructing a DFS spanning tree we assume that the children of each node of a tree are ordered in ascending order of their indices (i.e., node numbers).

The parent and preorder rank of a node y in a k-tree $T(x, k)$ are denoted by $parent(y \mid T(x, k))$ and $pre(y \mid T(x, k))$, respectively. It is assumed that the trees $T(x, 0)$, $x = 1, 2, \ldots, n$, are available as input and that there exists a node $s \in N$ such that there is a path from s to every other node of the DAG. The algorithm is based on the following idea. Initially, for each $x \in N$, all of the trees $T(y, 0)$, $y \in T(x, 0)$, are merged with the tree $T(x, 0)$ to produce a new tree $T(x, 1)$. The process of tree-merging is repeated $\lceil \log n \rceil$ times, to produce, finally, a tree $T(x, \lceil \log n \rceil)$ for each $x \in N$ so that $T(s, \lceil \log n \rceil)$ is the desired DFST of G. The tree merging is carried out in such a manner that at any stage k, the tree $T(x, k)$ obtained from the trees $T(x, k - 1)$ and the trees $T(y, k - 1)$, $y \in T(x, k - 1)$, $0 < k \leq \lceil \log n \rceil$ preserves the DFS property. A detailed description of the algorithm is given below.

*Algorithm* **CREW_DFS**

Input: The tree $T(x, 0)$ for each $x \in N$, specified by $parent(y \mid T(x, 0))$ for each $y \in N$.

Output: The $\lceil \log n \rceil$-dfs-trees $T(x, \lceil \log n \rceil)$, $\forall x \in N$, specified by $parent(y \mid T(x, \lceil \log n \rceil))$ and $pre(y \mid T(x, \lceil \log n \rceil))$, $\forall y \in N$, of which $T(s, \lceil \log n \rceil)$ is the DFST of DAG G.

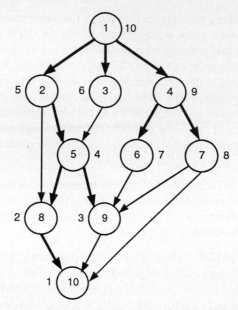

**Figure 7.8** An arbitrary DAG, G, with n = 10, in which node 1 can reach any other node, and the 2-dfs-tree T(1, 2). The edges of T(1, 2) are shown by bold lines. The numbers alongside the nodes are the corresponding postorder traversal ranks.

```
k := 0
while k < ⌈log n⌉ do
    for x = 1 to n dopar
        compute post(y | T(x, k)) for all y ∈ N
    odpar
    p := 0
    while p < ⌈log n⌉ do
        for x = 1 to n dopar
            for y = 1 to n dopar
                for z = (p⌈n/log n⌉ + 1) to ((p + 1)⌈n/log n⌉) dopar
                    if (z = x) AND (parent(y | T(x, k)) ≠ ∅)
                    then Mₓᵏ(y, z) := post(y | T(x, k))
                    else if (z ∈ T(x, k)) AND (parent(y | T(z, k)) ≠ ∅)
                        then Mₓᵏ(y, z):= post(z | T(x, k))
                        else Mₓᵏ(y, z) := ∞
                        fi
                    fi
                odpar
            odpar
        odpar
        p := p + 1
    od
```

*for* x = 1 *to* n *dopar*
    *for* y = 1 *to* n *dopar*
        find $z_m$ such that $M_x^k(y, z_m) - \min\{M_x^k(y, z) \mid z = 1, 2, \ldots, n\}$
        *if* $M_x^k(y, z_m) \neq \infty$
        *then* parent(y | T(x, k + 1)) := parent(y | T($z_m$, k))
        *fi*
    *odpar*
    *odpar*
    k := k + 1
*od*
*for* x = 1 *to* n *dopar*
    compute pre(y | T(x, $\lceil \log n \rceil$)) for y $\in$ N
*odpar*

Execution of algorithm CREW_DFS is illustrated in Figure 7.9 with reference to the DAG of Figure 7.8.

## Complexity Analysis

Algorithm CREW_DFS consists mainly of a while-loop followed by a parallel for-loop. The body of this while-loop again consists of a parallel for-loop, another while-loop followed by a nested parallel for-loop.

Now, the first parallel for-loop within the main while-loop computes the postorder traversal ranks for each node of n trees; each tree consists of at most n nodes. For this purpose, we may use a parallel algorithm, similar to that for finding the preorder traversal ranks for the nodes of a tree, described in the previous section, having the same time and processor bounds. The details of the parallel postorder traversal rank algorithm is left as an exercise. Thus, the implementation of this parallel for-loop requires O(log n) time when O($n^2$) processors are available.

It is easy to verify that execution of the body of the inner while-loop requires O(1) time when O($n^2 \lceil n/\log n \rceil$) processors are available. Since the inner while-loop is repeated $\lceil \log n \rceil$ times to initialize n matrices, each of size n × n, this loop runs in O(log n) time with O($n^2 \lceil n/\log n \rceil$) processors. Now we need to analyze the complexity of the parallel for-loop appearing after the inner while-loop.

This parallel for-loop consists of another nested for-loop within which it is mainly required to compute the minimum of n numbers. In Section 5.2.2, we have shown how to compute the maximum of n numbers in O(log n) time with O($\lceil n/\log n \rceil$) processors. Finding the minimum of n numbers is a logically equivalent problem to that of finding the maximum. Hence the abovementioned parallel for-loop which mainly computes the minimum of each of the $n^2$ rows, each having n numbers, can be implemented in O(log n) time using O($n^2 \lceil n/\log n \rceil$) processors. Therefore, the time complexity of the body of the main while-loop is O(log n) using O($n^2 \lceil n/\log n \rceil$) processors. Since this loop is repeated $\lceil \log n \rceil$ times, the overall time complexity of the loop is O($\log^2 n$) with O($n^2 \lceil n/\log n \rceil$) processors.

The last parallel for-loop computes the preorder traversal rank for each node of n trees, each tree consisting of at most n nodes (in fact, much less than n for most of the trees). For this purpose, we may use the traversal algorithm of the previous section that implements this

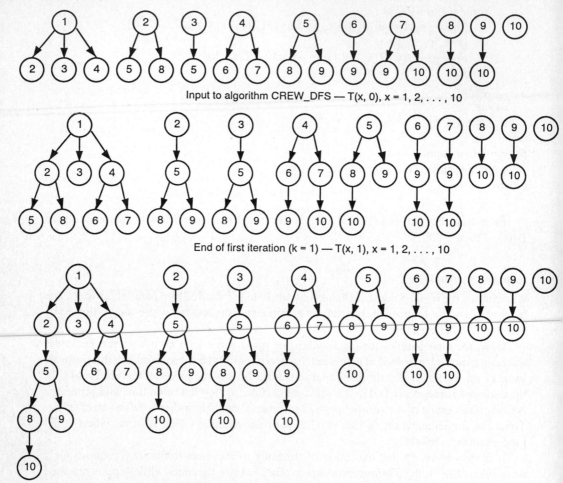

Input to algorithm CREW_DFS — T(x, 0), x = 1, 2, . . . , 10

End of first iteration (k = 1) — T(x, 1), x = 1, 2, . . . , 10

End of second iteration (k = 2) — T(x, 2), x = 1, 2, . . . , 10

**Figure 7.9** The trees T(x, 1) and T(x, 2) obtained from T(x, 0), x = 1, 2, . . . , 10, of the DAG G of Figure 7.8 using algorithm CREW_DFS.

for-loop in $O(\log n)$ time with $O(n^2)$ processors. All other assignment statements of algorithm CREW_DFS require $O(1)$ time using a single processor.

Therefore, the overall time complexity of algorithm CREW_DFS is $O(\log^2 n)$ when $O(n^2 \lceil n/\log n \rceil)$ processors are used. This result shows that, although the DFS of general graphs seems to be inherently serial, it is possible to find a fast parallel DFS algorithm for DAGs. However, the cost of this algorithm is $O(n^3 \log n)$ which is more than the time complexity of the best-known serial algorithm for the DFS problem by a factor of no less than $n \log n$.

## Correctness of the algorithm

Correctness of the algorithm CREW_DFS is established using the following lemmas:

**Lemma 7.2:** A k-tree $T(x, k), x \in N$ obtained at the end of k successive iterations of the body of the main while-loop of algorithm CREW_DFS contains all nodes $y \in N$ reachable from x by a path of length $\leq 2^k$ units.

**Proof:** The lemma holds trivially for a 0-tree $T(x, 0), x \in N$, since, by definition, $T(x, 0)$ contains only the nodes $y \in N$ such that $(x, y) \in E$.

Assume as induction hypothesis that the lemma is true for every i-tree $T(x, i), x \in N$, where $i < k$. Consider a node $y \in N$ which does not belong to $T(x, i + 1)$ but is such that there exists a path of length $\leq 2^{i+1}$ units from x to y in the DAG G. From the body of the main while-loop of algorithm CREW_DFS, we observe that $y \notin T(x, i + 1)$ implies that there is no node $u \in T(x, i)$ with $y \in T(u, i)$. By the induction hypothesis $T(u, i)$ contains all nodes v reachable from u by a path of length $\leq 2^i$ units in G. Consequently, if $y \notin T(x, i)$ and in addition, $y \notin T(u, i)$ for any node $u \in T(x, i)$, then every path from x to y in G is of length $> 2^i + 2^i = 2^{i+1}$ units. This contradicts the initial assumption about node y. Therefore, every node $y \in N$ reachable from x by a path of length $\leq 2^{i+1}$ belongs to $T(x, i + 1)$. Hence, the lemma holds.

**Lemma 7.3:** A k-tree $T(x, k), x \in N$ obtained at the end of k successive iterations of the body of the main while-loop of algorithm CREW_DFS does not contain any node $y \in N$, for which the length of every path from x to y in the DAG G is $> 2^k$ units.

**Proof:** The lemma trivially holds for 0-trees $T(x, 0), \forall x \in N$, since, by definition $T(x, 0)$ consists of only nodes y for which $(x, y) \in E$. This proves the base step of the inductive proof. Following a similar line of reasoning as that used for Lemma 7.2, one can prove by induction that the lemma holds for any k-tree $T(x, k), x \in N$.

**Lemma 7.4:** The k-tree $T(x, k), x \in N$, formed from the $(k - 1)$-trees $T(x, k - 1)$ and all $T(y, k - 1), y \in T(x, k - 1)$, at the end of the kth iteration of the body of the main while-loop of algorithm CREW_DFS, preserves the DFS property (i.e., $T(x, k)$ is a k-dfs-tree).

**Proof:** The lemma is trivially true for $k = 0$, since by definition $T(x, 0), x \in N$, preserves the DFS property.

We now assume as induction hypothesis that the lemma holds for every i-tree $T(x, i)$, $x \in N$, where i is an integer satisfying $i < k$. Consider the $(i + 1)$-tree $T(x, i + 1)$. This tree is obtained by merging the i-trees $T(z_j, i), j = 1, 2, \ldots, r$, such that $z_j \in T(x, i)$, with the i-tree $T(x, i)$. For each node y a unique immediate predecessor is selected to define the new $(i + 1)$-tree $T(x, i + 1)$. Let us assume that $(z_j, y) \in E$, for $j = 1, 2, \ldots, r$. There are two cases to consider.

Case I: $y \in T(x, i)$ and $y \in T(z_j, i), j = 1, 2, \ldots, r$, such that $z_j \in T(x, i)$.

Case II: $y \notin T(x, i)$ but $y \in T(z_j, i), j = 1, 2, \ldots, r$, such that $z_j \in T(x, i)$.

Selection of the parent of y in $T(x, i + 1)$ proceeds (cf. the body of the main while-loop) by computing the minimum of $post(y \mid T(x, i))$ and $post(z_j \mid T(x, i))$, $j = 1, 2, \ldots, r$ (if $y \notin T(x, i)$ then it is assumed that $post(y \mid T(x, i)) = \infty$). This implies that, for any pair of nodes $y, z \in T(x, i + 1)$, there is no edge $(y, z)$ in G such that $post(y \mid T(x, i + 1)) < post(z \mid T(x, i + 1))$, provided that $T(x, i)$ and $T(z_j, i)$, $j = 1, 2, \ldots, r$, preserve the DFS property. Thus, from the base step and the induction hypothesis it follows that $T(x, k)$, $\forall x \in N$, preserves the DFS property. Hence $T(x, k)$ is a k-dfs-tree, where k is a nonzero integer. Therefore, the lemma holds.

**Theorem 7.1:** The tree $T(s, \lceil \log n \rceil)$, $s \in N$ is a DFST of the DAG $G = <N, E>$.

**Proof:** By Lemma 7.2 it follows that the tree $T(s, \lceil \log n \rceil)$, $s \in N$, consists of every node of DAG G that is reachable from s by a path consisting of $n + 1$ edges or less. Since every path between a pair of nodes in G contains at most $n - 1$ edges and we have assumed that the node s can reach every other node of the DAG G, the $\lceil \log n \rceil$-tree $T(s, \lceil \log n \rceil)$ consists of all the nodes of G. Finally, from Lemma 7.4 it follows that the tree $T(s, \lceil \log n \rceil)$, $s \in N$, also preserves the DFS property. Hence, the theorem follows.

## 7.3.2 Breadth-First Search

Breadth-first search (BFS) is a good search technique in the context of parallel processing. A simple observation which suggests the possibility that there might be fast parallel BFS algorithms is that, unlike DFS, the searching of a graph using BFS can be carried out along all of the edges of a node by visiting all the children of the node simultaneously. Below, we shall see that the BFS of general graphs can be performed in logarithmic parallel time on the CREW PRAM model. The algorithm is developed by characterizing the BFS property in a similar manner, as has been done for the DFS property in the previous section.

For convenience, let us assume that $G = <N, E>$ is a digraph. An undirected graph may be considered to be an equivalent digraph with each edge $(i, j)$ of the undirected graph replaced by two oppositely directed edges $(i, j)$ and $(j, i)$. We define here a k-tree in relation to a digraph G rather than to a DAG. For this definition we need to replace only "DAG" with "digraph" in Definition 7.8. A k-tree is now called a *k-bfs-tree* if and only if it preserves the BFS property defined as follows:

**Definition 7.10:** Let y and z $(y \neq z)$ be a pair of nodes in a k-tree $T(x, k)$, $x \in N$. Also, let the BFS traversal rank of z in $T(x, k)$ be denoted by $bfs(z \mid T(x, k))$. Now assuming that $parent(z \mid T(x, k)) \neq y$ and $bfs(parent(z \mid T(x, k))) > bfs(y \mid T(x, k))$, the tree $T(x, k)$ is said to preserve the BFS property if there is no edge $(y, z) \in E$ in G.

A digraph G with $n = 6$ nodes and the 2-bfs-tree $T(1, 2)$ are shown in Figure 7.10.

It is assumed that the trees $T(x, 0)$, $\forall x \in N$ are available as input. The algorithm is based on an idea similar to that of tree merging as used for DFS of DAGs. In this case, at every stage $k$, $0 < k \leq \lceil \log n \rceil$, of the tree-merging process, we have to ensure that the BFS property is preserved in the k-trees $T(x, k)$ obtained from the $(k - 1)$-trees $T(x, k - 1)$ and all $T(y, k - 1)$, $y \in T(x, k - 1)$, for all $x \in N$. The parallel BFS algorithm based on the above idea appears on the facing page.

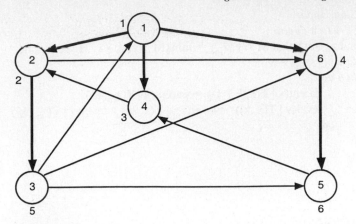

**Figure 7.10** An arbitrary digraph G with n = 6 and the 2-bfs-tree T(1, 2). The edges of T(1, 2) are shown by bold lines. The numbers alongside the nodes are the corresponding BFS traversal ranks.

*Algorithm* **CREW_BFS**

Input: The tree T(x, 0), for each x ∈ N, specified by parent(y | T(x, 0)) and the level denoted by level(y | T(x, 0)), for each node y ∈ N.

Output: The BFS spanning trees each rooted at a node x ∈ N, T(x, $\lceil \log n \rceil$) specified by parent(y | T(x, $\lceil \log n \rceil$)) and bfs(y | T(x, $\lceil \log n \rceil$)), for each y ∈ N.

k := 0
*while* k < $\lceil \log n \rceil$ *do*
   *for* x = 1 *to* n *dopar*
      compute bfs(y | T(x, k)) for all y ∈ N
   *odpar*
   p := 0
   *while* p < $\lceil \log n \rceil$ *do*
     *for* x = 1 *to* n *dopar*
       *for* y = 1 *to* n *dopar*
         *for* z = (p $\lceil n/\log n \rceil$ + 1) *to* ((p + 1) $\lceil n/\log n \rceil$ ) *dopar*
           *if* (z = x) AND (parent(y | T(x, k)) ≠ ∅ )
           *then* $M_x^k(y, z)$ := 0
           *else if* (z ∈ T(x, k) AND (parent (y | T(z, k)) ≠ ∅ )
              *then* $M_x^k(y, z)$ := n × (level(z | T(x, k)) +
                            level(y | T(z, k))) + bfs(z | T(x, k))
              *else* $M_x^k(y, z)$ := ∞
              *fi*
           *fi*
         *odpar*
       *odpar*
     *odpar*
     p := p + 1
  *od*

*for* x = 1 *to* n *dopar*

 *for* y = 1 *to* n *dopar*

  find $z_m$ such that $M_x^k(y, z_m) := \min\{M_x^k(y, z) \mid z = 1, 2, \ldots, n\}$

  *if* $M_x^k(y, z_m) \neq \infty$

  *then do*

   parent(y | T(x, k + 1)) := parent(y | T($z_m$, k))

   level(y | T(x, k)) := level($z_m$ | T(x, k)) + level(y | T($z_m$, k))

   *od*

  *fi*

 *odpar*

*odpar*

k := k + 1

*od*

*for* x = 1 *to* n *dopar*

compute bfs(y | T(x, ⌈log n⌉)) for all y ∈ N

*odpar*

The construction of the k-bfs-trees, for k = 1 and 2, for the digraph of Figure 7.10 is shown in Figure 7.11.

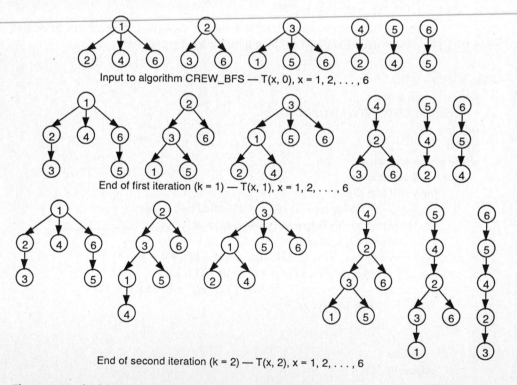

Input to algorithm CREW_BFS — T(x, 0), x = 1, 2, . . . , 6

End of first iteration (k = 1) — T(x, 1), x = 1, 2, . . . , 6

End of second iteration (k = 2) — T(x, 2), x = 1, 2, . . . , 6

**Figure 7.11** The k-bfs-trees T(x, 1) and T(x, 2) obtained from T(x, 0), x = 1, 2, . . . , 6, of the digraph of Figure 7.10, by algorithm CREW_BFS.

The arguments regarding the correctness of algorithm CREW_BFS are as follows. Since every path between a pair of nodes in G consists of at most $n - 1$ edges, the tree $T(x, \lceil \log n \rceil)$, for each node $x \in N$, obtained as the output of algorithm CREW_BFS must consist of all nodes of G. Finally, it can be proved by induction that the tree $T(x, \lceil \log n \rceil)$, for each $x \in N$, preserves the BFS property.

**Complexity Analysis**

The complexity of algorithm CREW_BFS can be analyzed in a manner similar to that for algorithm CREW_DFS; we need only discuss how the BFS traversal ranks for each node can be computed. For the purpose of computing the BFS traversal ranks for each node $i$ of a rooted tree $T(r) = <N, E>$ we use the following facts.

**Fact 7.1:** If $level(i \mid T(r)) > level(j \mid T(r))$ for a pair of nodes $i, j \in N$, then $bfs(i \mid T(r)) > bfs(j \mid T(r))$.

**Fact 7.2:** If $level(i \mid T(r)) = level(j \mid T(r))$ and $pre(i \mid T(r)) > pre(j \mid T(r))$, for a pair of nodes $i, j \in N$, then $bfs(i \mid T(r)) > bfs(j \mid T(r))$.

As a consequence of these facts, we have the following lemma.

**Lemma 7.5:** Let $T(r) = <N, E>$ be a rooted tree. Then, the BFS rank for each node $i \in N$ can be computed as

$$bfs(i) = \sum_h N(h) + LN(level(i \mid T(r)), i), \forall\ i \in N \text{ AND } i \neq r,$$
$$= 1, \text{ else};$$

taking the summation over $0 \le h \le level(i \mid T(r)) - 1$, where $N(h)$ is the number of nodes at level $h$ in $T(r)$, and $LN(level(i \mid T(r)), i)$ is the number of nodes at level $level(i \mid T(r))$ with preorder ranks less than or equal to that of $i$.

A parallel BFS ranking algorithm for rooted trees, based on the above lemma, can easily be obtained, by making some minor modifications to algorithm CREW_PREORDER_TRAVERSAL. The details of the modifications required are left as an exercise. Clearly, such a parallel BFS ranking algorithm for general ordered rooted trees requires $O(\log n)$ time when $O(n^2)$ processors are used.

An analysis similar to that of algorithm CREW_DFS shows that algorithm CREW_BFS has time complexity of $O(\log^2 n)$ when $O(n^3)$ processors are employed.

## 7.3.3 Breadth-Depth Search

In this section, we present a fast parallel algorithm for the breadth-depth search (BDS) of DAGs on the CREW PRAM model using the same partial tree-merging technique as is used in the previous sections. First, we characterize the BDS property in terms of the preorder and the reverse postorder traversal ranks of the nodes of a spanning tree of the given DAG G = <N, E>. The reverse postorder traversal of a tree is defined as the traversal of the corresponding binary tree in the following way, starting with the root:

Visit the root;

Traverse the right subtree in reverse postorder;

Traverse the left subtree in reverse postorder.

The definition of a k-tree with reference to a DAG G is given in Section 7.2.1 (Definition 7.8).

**Definition 7.11:** Given a pair of nodes y and z in a k-tree $T(x, k)$ such that $(y, z)$ is an edge in DAG $G = <N, E>$, but $(y, z)$ does not belong to $T(x, k)$, then, the tree, $T(x, k)$, is said to preserve the BDS property if one of the following conditions is satisfied:

   (i) $pre(y \mid T(x, k)) < pre(z \mid T(x, k))$ AND $rpost(y \mid T(x, k)) > rpost(z \mid T(x, k))$;

  (ii) there exists a path from $parent(z \mid T(x, k))$ to y in $T(x, k)$;

 (iii) the path x to y in $T(x, k)$ consists of $2^k$ edges;

where $rpost(y \mid T(x, k))$ represents the reverse postorder traversal rank of node y in tree $T(x, k)$. If a k-tree $T(x, k)$ preserves the BDS property then we call it a *k-bds-tree*.

It is assumed that initially the DAG is available in the form of its adjacency relations, which in fact define the 0-trees $T(x, 0)$, $\forall x \in N$. We also assume that the node $s \in N$ from which the search is to be initiated can reach every other node $i \in N - \{s\}$ by a path of length one or more. An arbitrary DAG G with $n = 6$ and $s = 1$, along with the 2-bds-tree $T(1, 2)$ are shown in Figure 7.12. The algorithm is based on a tree-merging technique similar to that used in other search methods in the previous sections. In this case, we have to ensure that during merging of the $(k - 1)$-trees $T(x, k - 1)$, and all $T(y, k - 1)$ such that $y \in T(x, k - 1)$ to produce the k-tree $T(x, k)$, the BDS property is preserved. A complete description of the algorithm on the CREW PRAM model follows.

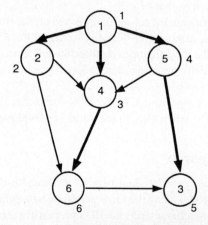

**Figure 7.12** An arbitrary DAG G with $n = 6$ and $s = 1$, and the 2-bds-tree $T(1, 2)$. The edges of $T(1, 2)$ are shown by bold lines. The numbers alongside the nodes are the corresponding BDS traversal ranks.

## Algorithm CREW_BDS

Input: The tree $T(x, 0)$ for each $x \in N$, specified by parent$(y \mid T(x, 0))$ for each $y \in N$.

Output: The $\lceil \log n \rceil$-bds-trees $T(x, \lceil \log n \rceil)$, $\forall x \in N$, specified by parent$(y \mid T(x, \lceil \log n \rceil))$ and the BDS traversal rank for each node denoted by bdr$(y \mid T(x, \lceil \log n \rceil))$, $\forall y \in T(x, \lceil \log n \rceil)$, of which $T(s, \lceil \log n \rceil)$ is the BDST of DAG G.

$k := 0$
*while* $k < \lceil \log n \rceil$ *do*
    *for* $x = 1$ *to* n *dopar*
        compute pre$(y \mid T(x, k))$ and rpost$(y \mid T(x, k))$ for all $y \in N$
    *odpar*
    $p := 0$
    *while* $p < \lceil \log n \rceil$ *do*
        *for* $x = 1$ *to* n *dopar*
            *for* $y = 1$ *to* n *dopar*
                *for* $z = (p \lceil n/\log n \rceil + 1)$ *to* $((p + 1) \lceil n/\log n \rceil)$ *dopar*
                    *if* $(z = x)$ AND (parent$(y \mid T(x, k)) \neq \emptyset$)
                    *then if* (pre(parent$(y \mid T(x, k)) \mid T(x, k)) <$ pre$(z \mid T(x, k))$)
                            AND (rpost(parent$(y \mid T(x, k)) \mid T(x, k)) <$ rpost$(z \mid T(x, k))$)
                      *then* $M_x^k(y, z) := -\infty$
                      *else* $M_x^k(y, z) :=$ pre$(z \mid T(x, k))$
                      *fi*
                  *else* $M_x^k(y, z) := -\infty$
                  *fi*
                *odpar*
            *odpar*
        *odpar*
        $p := p + 1$
    *od*
    *for* $x = 1$ *to* n *dopar*
        *for* $y = 1$ *to* n *dopar*
            find $z_m$ such that $M_x^k(y, z_m) := \max\{M_x^k(y, z) \mid z = 1, 2, \ldots, n\}$
            *if* $M_x^k(y, z_m) \neq \infty$
            *then* parent$(y \mid T(x, k + 1)) :=$ parent$(y \mid T(z_m, k))\}$
            *fi*
        *odpar*
    *odpar*
    $k := k + 1$
*od*
*for* $x = 1$ *to* n *dopar*
    compute bdr$(y \mid T(x, \lceil \log n \rceil))$ for all $y \in N$
*odpar*

Figure 7.13 shows the construction of the k-bds-trees using algorithm CREW_BDS, for $k = 1$ and 2, for the DAG G shown in Figure 7.12.

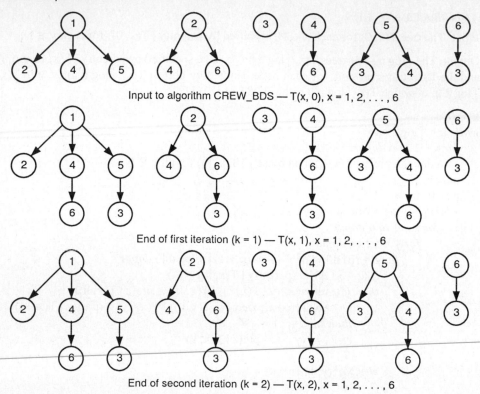

Input to algorithm CREW_BDS — T(x, 0), x = 1, 2, . . . , 6

End of first iteration (k = 1) — T(x, 1), x = 1, 2, . . . , 6

End of second iteration (k = 2) — T(x, 2), x = 1, 2, . . . , 6

**Figure 7.13** The k-bds-trees T(x, k), for k =1 and 2, obtained from T(x, 0), x = 1, 2, . . . , 6, by algorithm CREW_BDS.

Observe that since every path between a pair of nodes in G consists of at most $n - 1$ edges, and node s can reach every other node $i \in N - \{s\}$ by a path of length one or more, the tree $T(s, \lceil \log n \rceil)$, obtained as one of the outputs of algorithm CREW_BDS, must consist of all nodes of G. Finally, it can be shown by induction that the tree $T(x, \lceil \log n \rceil)$, for each $x \in N$, preserves the BDS property. Complete proof of correctness of the algorithm is left as an exercise.

The problem of BDS for general graphs cannot always be solved using tree-merging technique of the type just described since the presence of cycles, in some cases, can create difficulties with regard to the selection of the correct parents of some nodes in the BDST. More precisely, when merging $T(x, k)$ and $T(z, k), z \in T(x, k)$, it may happen that there exists a path $x, \ldots, z_a, \ldots, z$ in $T(x, k)$, and that $T(z, k)$ contains a path $z, \ldots, z_a, z_1, z_2, \ldots, y$, so that according to algorithm CREW_BDS, $z_a$ will be deleted from the path $z, \ldots, z_a, z_1, z_2, \ldots, y$ during merging. In this case, the parallel selection of the parents of the nodes $z_1, z_2, \ldots, y$ in $T(x, k + 1)$ may be incorrect, i.e., $T(x, k + 1)$ cannot be ensured to preserve the BDS property. This problem is similar to that encountered while trying to process a general graph in parallel in depth-first order. From these observations and because of the fact that the DFS is inherently serial, it appears that the BDS of general graphs is also inherently serial.

**Complexity Analysis**

The complexity analysis of algorithm CREW_BDS is straightforward and is similar to that for algorithm CREW_DFS. The only difference is that in this case we also need, in addition to both the preorder and reverse postorder traversal algorithms for rooted general ordered trees, a BDS tree traversal algorithm to implement the last parallel for-loop which computes bdr(y | T(x, $\lceil \log n \rceil$)), for all x, y ∈ N. To this end, we may design a parallel algorithm based on the following lemma whose proof is trivial.

**Lemma 7.6:** Let T(r) = <N, E> be a rooted general ordered tree. Then, the breadth-depth order rank corresponding to each node i ∈ N can be computed as

$$\text{bdr}(i \mid T(r)) = \sum_j [\text{NS}(\text{parent}(j \mid T(r))) + \sum_k \text{ND}(k)] + \text{rank}(i) + 1$$

where the summations over j ∈ ANC(i) − {r} and k ∈ {S(parent(j | T(r))) AND rank(k) > rank(j)}, and s(i) is the set of children of node i ∈ N (i exclusive); other notation is the same as that introduced in Section 7.2.

A parallel algorithm for computing the BDS traversal ranks of the nodes of a tree T(r) having n nodes, based on Lemma 7.6, can be obtained by modifying algorithm CREW_PREORDER_TRAVERSAL and has same time and processor bounds.

Finally, an analysis similar to that for algorithm CREW_DFS shows that algorithm CREW_BDS requires $O(\log^2 n)$ time when $O(n^2 \lceil n/\log n \rceil)$ processors are available.

# 7.4 PARALLEL CONNECTIVITY ALGORITHMS

This section deals with three different connectivity problems. These are:

(i) finding the connected components of an undirected graph;
(ii) finding the biconnected components of an undirected connected graph; and
(iii) finding the triconnected components of an undirected biconnected graph.

All of the algorithms discussed are primarily based on the CREW PRAM model of computation.

## 7.4.1 Connected Components

Let G = <N, E> be an (undirected) graph. A connected component of G is a maximal connected subgraph of G. A graph G is connected if it has a single connected component, otherwise it is disconnected. Given a graph G, one can determine, in parallel, whether or not it is connected simply by making a call to algorithm CREW_BFS. After applying the parallel BFS algorithm, we need to concentrate on the BFS tree rooted at an arbitrary node of G and determine whether there exists any node in G which is not included in the BFS tree. Clearly, both the time and processor complexities of this algorithm will be determined by those of algorithm CREW_BFS. These are $O(\log^2 n)$ and $O(n^3)$, respectively. A more interesting problem, however, is to determine all of the connected components of G, instead of merely testing G for connectedness.

The parallel algorithms available in the literature for determining the connected components of undirected graphs can broadly be classified according to two major criteria. One criterion is the basic technique employed and the other is the format used for the input. There are three basic techniques employed for designing such algorithms. These are based on (i) BFS; (ii) transitive closure; and (iii) node collapse strategy. The most common form of input is either adjacency lists or an adjacency matrix. The adjacency matrix is perhaps more popular, since it allows the connected components problem to be formulated in terms of a matrix manipulation problem. However, for sparse graphs, the adjacency matrix representation may lead to inefficient algorithms and in such cases adjacency lists are quite often used. In the following sections, we discuss parallel connected components algorithms based on the three basic techniques mentioned above.

### 7.4.1.1  Connected Components Using BFS

The technique for finding the connected components of a dense graph based on the BFS of the given graph was first proposed by Reghbati and Corneil (1978). They used a parallel BFS algorithm having time complexity $(T/k) + L\lceil \log n \rceil + 2n$ with k processors, where T is the complexity of the optimal serial BFS algorithm and L is the distance of the farthest node from the start node. Consequently, the time complexity of their algorithm cannot be reduced beyond $O(n)$. Here, we present a fast parallel connected components algorithm on the CREW PRAM model based on algorithm CREW_BFS, which was proposed in the previous section. It may be noted that algorithm CREW_BFS can also be used for a disconnected undirected graph. In this case, it generates a BFS spanning forest consisting of n partial BFS trees, each rooted at a node $i \in N$ of the graph $G = \langle N, E \rangle$ instead of n BFSTs. However, we are only interested here in the $\lceil \log n \rceil$-bfs-trees $T(i, \lceil \log n \rceil)$, $\forall i \in N$, produced by algorithm CREW_BFS.

### *Algorithm* **CREW_BF_CCOMP**

Input: The trees $T(i, 0)$, specified by parent$(j \mid T(i, 0))$ and level$(j \mid T(i, 0))$, for all $i, j \in N$ of the given graph G.

Output: For each node i its component number, denoted by comp(i), $i \in N$, where each component is identified by its lowest-numbered member node.

construct $n \lceil \log n \rceil$-bfs-trees, $T(i, \lceil \log n \rceil)$, $i = 1, 2, \ldots, n$, of G;
*for* i = 1 *to* n *dopar*
    *for* j = 1 *to* n *dopar*
        *if* parent$(j \mid T(i, \lceil \log n \rceil)) \neq \emptyset$
        *then* C[i, j] := i
        *else* C[i, j] := $\infty$
        *fi*
    *odpar*
*odpar*
compute the minimum of each column
    j = 1, 2, \ldots, n of C and denote it by m(j);
*for* j = 1 *to* n *dopar*
    comp(j) := m(j)
*odpar*

Algorithm CREW_BF_CCOMP constructs the connectivity matrix C[1 : n, 1 : n] from the n ⌈log n⌉-bfs-trees, each rooted at a node i ∈ N of G, such that

C[i, j] = i,  if there is a path of length 0 or more from i to j in G,
     = ∞,  otherwise.

The construction of this matrix is performed by the first parallel for-loop. Finally, the component number is assigned to each node j as the smallest number in each column j of matrix C. This is carried out by the rest of the algorithm. An example illustrating the execution of this algorithm is shown in Figure 7.14.

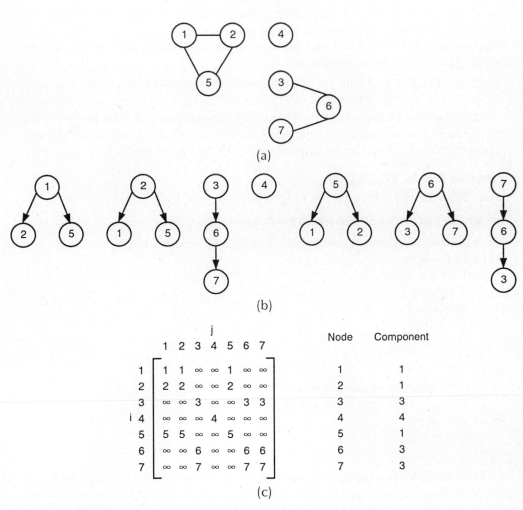

(a)

(b)

(c)

**Figure 7.14** (a) An arbitrary undirected graph G with n = 7 nodes; (b) the 3-bfs-trees T(i, 3), i = 1, 2, . . . , 7; (c) the connectivity matrix C[1 : 7,1 : 7] and the component numbers for each node i = 1, 2, . . . , 7, of G.

**Complexity Analysis**

The construction of the n $\lceil \log n \rceil$-bfs-trees T(i, $\lceil \log n \rceil$), $\forall$ i $\in$ N, of G using algorithm CREW_BFS requires $O(\log^2 n)$ time with $O(n^3)$ processors (see Section 7.3.2). The time complexity of the three remaining steps of algorithm CREW_BF_CCOMP are O(1), O(log n) and O(1), respectively. The first two steps require $O(n^2)$ processors while the last step requires O(n) processors only. Therefore, the overall time complexity of algorithm CREW_BF_CCOMP is $O(\log^2 n)$ when $O(n^3)$ processors are available. This complexity result is independent of whether the graph is sparse or dense. There is no doubt that this algorithm is fast compared to that due to Reghbati and Corneil (1978), but its cost $O(n^3 \log^2 n)$ is far from being optimal.

### 7.4.1.2  Connected Components Using Transitive Closure

The solution of the connected components problem using the transitive closure matrix is based on the following idea. Assuming that the graph G = <N, E> is given in the form of its adjacency matrix A[1 : n, 1 : n], its transitive closure matrix (also called the reachability matrix) R[1 : n, 1 : n] is computed so that

$$R[i, j] = 1, \quad \text{if there is a path of length 0 or more from i to j in G,}$$
$$= 0, \quad \text{otherwise.}$$

The component number of a node i $\in$ N is then just the smallest j such that R[i, j] = 1. We first present a general parallel algorithm for connected components based on this idea and then analyze its complexity under different variants of the PRAM model.

---

*Algorithm* **PRAM_TC_CCOMP**

Input: The adjacency matrix A[1 : n, 1 : n] of graph G = <N, E>.

Output: For each node i, its component number comp(i), i $\in$ N.

obtain the transitive closure matrix R from the adjacency matrix A of G;
*for* i = 1 *to* n *dopar*
    *for* j = 1 *to* n *dopar*
        *if* R[i, j] = 1
        *then* C[i, j] := i
        *else* C[i, j] := $\infty$
        *fi*
    *odpar*
*odpar*
compute the minimum of each column
    j = 1, 2, . . . , n of C and denote it by m(j);
*for* j = 1 *to* n *dopar*
    comp(j) := m(j)
*odpar*

---

The only difference between the connected components algorithms using BFS and transitive closure is that in the first case we obtain the reachability information (i.e., whether a node i can reach to another node j, i, j $\in$ N, in G or not) from the n $\lceil \log n \rceil$-bfs-trees while in the second case this is done by computing the transitive closure matrix R through Boolean matrix manipulation.

**Complexity Analysis**

It is clear that the dominating factor in the computational complexity of algorithm PRAM_TC_CCOMP is the computation of the transitive closure matrix. The complexity of computing the transitive closure matrix depends on the type of PRAM model used. It can be seen that each of the two parallel for-loops can be executed on any PRAM model in O(1) time with $O(n^2)$ and $O(n)$ processors. The computation of the minimum of n numbers can also be computed on any PRAM model in $O(\log n)$ time with $O(n)$ processors. We will consider two different implementations of algorithm PRAM_TC_CCOMP, the first on the CRCW PRAM and the other on the CREW PRAM model.

(a) CRCW PRAM implementation: The transitive closure matrix R of G can be obtained from its adjacency matrix A using the repeated squares method, i.e., $R = (A + I)^n = (\ldots (((A + I)^2)^2)^2 \ldots)$. Thus, the computation of R requires $O(\log n)$ Boolean matrix multiplications. On a CRCW PRAM, we have seen that two Boolean matrices, each of size $n \times n$, can be multiplied in constant time with $O(n^3)$ processors. Thus, R can be computed on the CRCW PRAM in $O(\log n)$ time using $O(n^3)$ processors. Consideration of the complexities of the other statements of algorithm PRAM_TC_CCOMP, allows us to conclude that the connected components algorithm using the transitive closure matrix requires $O(\log n)$ time with $O(n^3)$ processors on the CRCW PRAM model.

(b) CREW PRAM implementation: Since two Boolean matrices can be multiplied in $O(\log n)$ time using $O(n^3)$ processors on a CREW PRAM model, the computation of the transitive closure matrix on this model requires $O(\log^2 n)$ time with $O(n^3)$ processors. Therefore, the overall time complexity of the algorithm PRAM_TC_CCOMP when implemented on an unbounded CREW PRAM model is $O(\log^2 n)$ when $O(n^3)$ processors are employed.

### 7.4.1.3 *Connected Components Based on Node Collapse Method*

A third approach to solving the connected components problem is by using the node collapse method first used by Hirschberg (Hirschberg 1976; Hirschberg et al. 1979). The key idea underlying this method is as follows. Given the graph G = <N, E> in the form of its adjacency matrix, adjacent nodes are combined into "supernodes," which are then themselves combined until each remaining supernode represents a connected component of G. Each node is always a member of exactly one supernode, and each supernode is identified by its lowest-numbered member, which is also called its *root*. We now present a parallel algorithm for finding the connected components, following Hirschberg's idea, on the CREW PRAM model.

In essence the algorithm consists of the repetition of three stages. First, the lowest-numbered neighboring supernode of each node is obtained. Second, each supernode root is connected to the root of the lowest-numbered neighboring supernode. Finally, all newly connected supernodes are collapsed into larger supernodes. This process is continued until all the nodes in a connected component have been merged into a single supernode. This supernode has no edges connecting it to any other supernode and the algorithm terminates. Since the number of supernodes is reduced by a factor of at least two in each repetition, $\lceil \log n \rceil$, such iterations are sufficient to collapse each connected component into a single supernode. The execution of this algorithm is shown in Figure 7.15, and its details are given below. Each node belongs to exactly one connected component. We use a vector V[1 : n] to specify the connected components as follows. If $G_c = <N_c, E_c>$ is any connected component of G, then for all $i \in N_c$, V[i] is the lowest-numbered element of $N_c$.

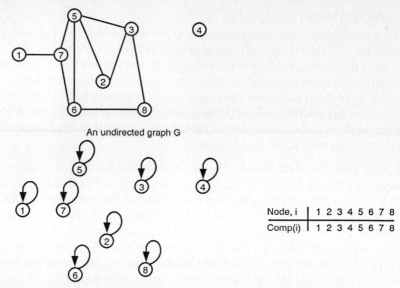

An undirected graph G

lowest-numbered node which is in the same connected component at the beginning

| Node, i | 1 2 3 4 5 6 7 8 |
|---|---|
| Comp(i) | 1 2 3 4 5 6 7 8 |

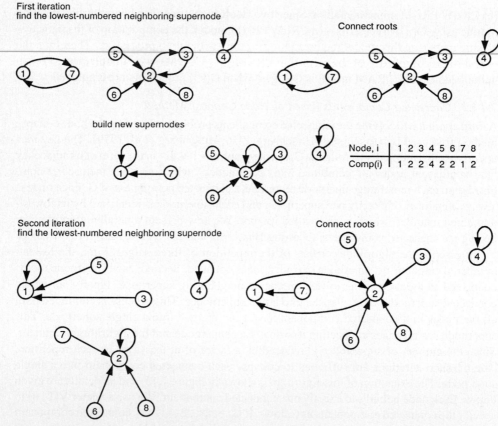

**First iteration**
find the lowest-numbered neighboring supernode

Connect roots

build new supernodes

| Node, i | 1 2 3 4 5 6 7 8 |
|---|---|
| Comp(i) | 1 2 2 4 2 2 1 2 |

**Second iteration**
find the lowest-numbered neighboring supernode

Connect roots

**Figure 7.15** continued on the facing page.

**build new supernodes**

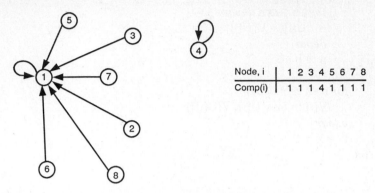

| Node, i | 1 | 2 | 3 | 4 | 5 | 6 | 7 | 8 |
|---------|---|---|---|---|---|---|---|---|
| Comp(i) | 1 | 1 | 1 | 4 | 1 | 1 | 1 | 1 |

**Figure 7.15** The different iterative stages of the parallel connected components algorithm based on node collapse method.

*Algorithm* **CREW_NC_CCOMP**

Input: The adjacency matrix $A[1 : n, 1 : n]$ of an undirected graph G.

Output: The vector $V[1 : n]$, in which $V[i]$ is the lowest-numbered node j reachable from node i.

*for* $i = 1$ *to* n *dopar*
$\quad$ $V[i] := i$
*odpar*
$k := 0$
*while* $k < \lceil \log n \rceil$ *do*
$\quad$ *for* $i = 1$ *to* n *dopar*
$\quad\quad$ compute the minimum of $\{V[j] \mid A[i, j] = 1 \text{ AND } V[j] \neq V[i]\}$ and call it $x_i$
$\quad\quad$ *if* $x_i$ exists
$\quad\quad$ *then* $U[i] := x_i$
$\quad\quad$ *else* $U[i] := V[i]$
$\quad\quad$ *fi*
$\quad$ *odpar*
$\quad$ *for* $i = 1$ *to* n *dopar*
$\quad\quad$ compute the minimum of $\{U[j] \mid V[j] = i \text{ AND } U[j] \neq i\}$ and call it $y_i$
$\quad\quad$ *if* $y_i$ exists
$\quad\quad$ *then* $U[i] := y_i$
$\quad\quad$ *else* $U[i] := V[i]$
$\quad\quad$ *fi*
$\quad$ *odpar*
$\quad$ *for* $i = 1$ *to* n *dopar*
$\quad\quad$ $V[i] := U[i]$
$\quad$ *odpar*

```
    p := 0
    while p < ⌈log n⌉ do
        for i = 1 to n dopar
            U[i] := U[U[i]]
        odpar
        p := p + 1
    od
    for i = 1 to n dopar
        V[i] := min{U[i], V[U[i]]}
    odpar
    k := k + 1
od
```

## Complexity Analysis

Algorithm CREW_NC_CCOMP consists of a parallel for-loop (for initialization) and a while-loop. This parallel for-loop takes only $O(1)$ time using $O(n)$ processors. The body of the while-loop consists of four parallel for-loops and another while-loop. This inner while-loop is repeated $\lceil \log n \rceil$ times and each iteration takes $O(1)$ time with $O(n)$ processors. Thus, the inner while-loop runs in $O(\log n)$ time using $O(n)$ processors. Each of the first two for-loops within the main while-loop takes $O(\log n)$ time with $O(n^2)$ processors to compute the n minimum values of n lists each of size n. The other two parallel for-loops clearly require $O(1)$ time with $O(n)$ processors. Combining the complexities of each of these statements we find that a single execution of the body of the main while-loop requires $O(\log n)$ time with $O(n^2)$ processors. Since the while-loop is repeated $\lceil \log n \rceil$ times, the overall time complexity of algorithm CREW_NC_CCOMP is $O(\log^2 n)$ with $O(n^2)$ processors.

## 7.4.2  Biconnected Components

Given a connected undirected graph $G = \langle N, E \rangle$, a node $a \in N$ is said to be an *articulation node* of G if there exist nodes i and j in N such that i, j and a are all distinct, and every path between i and j contains a. Alternatively, a is an articulation node of G if deletion of a splits G into two or more components. The graph G is *biconnected* if $G - \{i\}$ is connected for every $i \in N$. Thus, an undirected connected graph is biconnected if and only if it has no articulation nodes. A *biconnected component* (bcc) of an undirected graph $G = \langle N, E \rangle$ is a maximal biconnected subgraph of G. These definitions are illustrated in Figure 7.16. In this section, we present a parallel algorithm which tests a graph for biconnectedness and we also describe how to obtain bccs, in parallel, on the CREW PRAM model.

Let us denote by $G_i$ the graph obtained from G by removing $i \in N$. The idea underlying the parallel algorithm for testing a graph for biconnectedness is simple. We simply test $G_i$ for connectedness for all $i \in N$. If for some $j \in N$ we find that $G_i$ is not connected, then j is an articulation node. If we find that no $i \in N$ is an articulation node of G, then G is biconnected. The details of the algorithm are shown on the facing page.

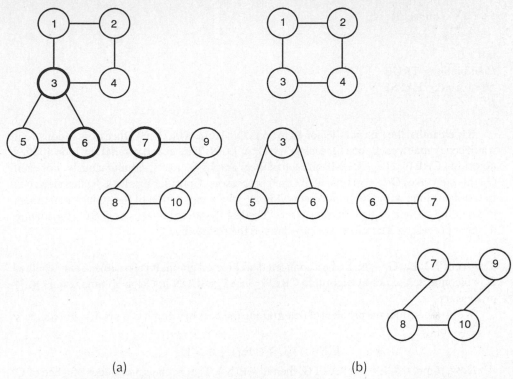

(a)                                    (b)

**Figure 7.16** (a) An undirected graph G in which the articulation nodes are shown by bold circles; (b) the biconnected components of G.

*Algorithm* **CREW_TEST_BICON**

Input: The adjacency matrix A[1 : n, 1 : n] of the given undirected graph G = <N, E>.

Output: If the graph is biconnected, then the algorithm sets the Boolean variable "bicon" to "TRUE"; "FALSE" otherwise.

*for* i = 1 *to* n *dopar*
    construct $A_i$[1 : n – 1, 1 : n – 1] from A by deleting the ith row
        and the jth column of A, i.e., $A_i$ represents the adjacency matrix of graph $G_i$
*odpar*
*for* i = 1 *to* n *dopar*
    determine from $A_i$ whether $G_i$ is connected or not
        using algorithm CREW_NC_CCOMP
    *if* $G_i$ is connected
    *then* connect(i) := 0
    *else* connect(i) := 1
    *fi*
*odpar*

$$s := \sum_{1 \le i \le n} \text{connect}(i)$$

*if* s = 0
*then* bicon := TRUE
*else* bicon := FALSE
*fi*

It is clear that the first parallel for-loop takes $O(1)$ time with $O(n^3)$ processors to construct n adjacency matrices $A_i$, one for each graph $G_i$, $\forall$ i $\in$ N. The second parallel for-loop applies algorithm CREW_NC_CCOMP on each of the n graphs $G_i$, i $\in$ N, simultaneously. For each $G_i$, this step takes $O(\log^2 n)$ time with $O(n^2)$ processors. Considering all i $\in$ N, this step runs in $O(\log^2 n)$ time with $O(n^3)$ processors. Finally, the computation of the sum of n numbers takes $O(\log n)$ time using $O(n)$ processors. The last if-statement takes only $O(1)$ time using a single processor. Therefore, we have proved the following.

**Theorem 7.2:** Let G = <N, E> be a connected undirected graph. It is possible to test whether G is biconnected or not by algorithm CREW_TEST_BICON in $O(\log^2 n)$ time using $O(n^3)$ processors.

We now consider the problem of determining the bccs of a graph G = <N, E>. For a subset N' of N, let

$$E(N') = \{(i, j) \in E \mid i, j \in N'\}.$$

Now, if g = <N', E'> is a bcc of G, then E' = E(N'). That is, the set of nodes of a bcc of G determines it completely. Let us define a relation R on N × N by iRj iff i and j are in a common bcc of G. Stated otherwise, iRj iff, for all x $\in$ N distinct from i and j, there is a path between i and j in $G_x$. We can state this fact in the form of a lemma.

**Lemma 7.7:** Let $G_x$ = <$N_x$, $E_x$> be the graph obtained from G = <N, E> by removing node x $\in$ N and all edges incident on x. Also, let $G_x^*$ be the transitive closure of $G_x$. Then, for distinct nodes i and j in N, iRj if (i, j) is an edge in $G_x^*$ for all x $\in$ N distinct from i and j.

A simple modification to algorithm CREW_NC_CCOMP yields a parallel algorithm that computes $G_x^*$ from $G_x$, x $\in$ N. Let $A_x$ be the adjacency matrix of $G_x$. Then the transitive closure matrix of $A_x$, denoted by $A_x^*$, is simply the adjacency matrix for $G_x^*$. Clearly, the elements of $A_x^*$ satisfy $A_x^*[i, j] = 1$ iff i and j are in the same biconnected component of G. Thus, we can obtain an algorithm for computing $A_x^*$, each element of which is initially assumed to be zero, by adding the following step at the end of algorithm CREW_NC_CCOMP:

*for* i = 1 *to* n *dopar*
　*for* j = 1 *to* n *dopar*
　　*if* comp(i) = comp(j)
　　*then* $A_x^*[i, j]$ := 1
　　*fi*
　*odpar*
*odpar*

Since this step takes constant time with $O(n^2)$ processors, the overall time complexity of the CREW PRAM algorithm for computing the transitive closure matrix remains $O(\log^2 n)$ using $O(n^2)$ processors. Therefore, the graph $G_x^*$ can be computed from $G_x$ in time $O(\log^2 n)$ using $O(n^2)$ processors. The computation of all such $G_x^*$ from $G_x$, $x \in N$, requires $O(\log^2 n)$ time and $O(n^3)$ processors. That is, the relation R can be obtained in $O(\log^2 n)$ time using $O(n^3)$ processors. Once the relation R has been constructed, the computation of the bccs is fairly simple and makes use of the following lemma.

**Lemma 7.8:** Let $(i, j)$ be an edge of the graph $G = <N, E>$. Then, the set of nodes of the bcc of G which contains edge $(i, j)$ is given by $N_{(i, j)} = \{k \in N \mid iRj \text{ AND } kRj\}$.

Using Lemma 7.8, we can find the nodes of the bccs containing the edge $(i, j) \in E$ in constant time using $O(n)$ processors. Finally, the distinct bccs, from $N_{(i, j)}$, $(i, j) \in E$ can be obtained in $O(\log n)$ time using $O(n^3)$ processors. Thus we have proved the following theorem.

**Theorem 7.3:** Given a connected undirected graph $G = <N, E>$, it is possible to find the bccs of G in $O(\log^2 n)$ time using $O(n^3)$ processors on the CREW PRAM model.

## 7.4.3 Triconnected Components

The problems of testing an undirected biconnected graph for *triconnectedness*, and finding the *triconnected components* (tccs) on the CREW PRAM model are considered in this section. Let us first define precisely what we mean by a triconnected graph and the tccs of an undirected biconnected graph.

Let $G = <N, E>$ be an undirected biconnected graph. Also, let $g_1 = <N_1, E_1>$ and $g_2 = <N_2, E_2>$ be two subgraphs of G. Then, $g_1 + g_2$ defines a subgraph $<N_1 \cup N_2, E_1 \cup E_2>$. Let $\{i, j\}$ be a pair of nodes in N. If the removal of the pair $\{i, j\}$ splits the graph G into a pair of subgraphs $g_1 = <N_1, E_1>$ and $g_2 = <N_2, E_2>$ such that

$$G = g_1 + g_2,$$
$$E_1 \cap E_2 = \emptyset,$$
and $\quad N_1 \cap N_2 = \{i, j\}$

then $g_1$ and $g_2$ are said to be a *split* of G at $\{i, j\}$. If a split exists at $\{i, j\}$, then $\{i, j\}$ is called a *separation pair*. We now define the *blocks*, which are associated with the subgraphs of a split. Corresponding to a split $[g_1, g_2]$ of G at $\{i, j\}$, the blocks $b_1$ and $b_2$ associated with $g_1$ and $g_2$ are defined as follows:

$$\begin{aligned} b_1 &= <N_1, E_1 \cup \{(i, j)\}>, \text{ if } g_1 \text{ is not a path} \\ &= \emptyset, \qquad\qquad\qquad \text{otherwise;} \\ b_2 &= <N_2, E_2 \cup \{(i, j)\}>, \text{ if } g_2 \text{ is not a path} \\ &= \emptyset, \qquad\qquad\qquad \text{otherwise.} \end{aligned}$$

The edge $(i, j)$ is called a virtual edge. A graph $G = <N, E>$ is triconnected if it is biconnected and has no split. A tcc of an undirected biconnected graph G is a maximal triconnected block of G. Informally, if a biconnected graph G splits into two blocks, then G may be further decomposed by splitting one of these blocks if it is not triconnected (i.e., there is a split in it). This process is continued until no further splitting is possible. The resulting triconnected blocks then correspond to the tccs of G. We now present some basic properties about triconnected graphs in the form of lemmas.

**Lemma 7.9:** If an undirected graph $G = <N, E>$ is triconnected, then for each node $i \in N$ its degree, denoted by $\deg(i)$, is greater than or equal to 3.

**Proof:** Assume the contrary, i.e., there exists a node $i \in N$ such that $\deg(i) = 2$ and the graph G is triconnected. Let $(i, j)$ and $(i, k)$ be the two edges incident on i. Obviously, a split at $\{j, k\}$ is possible which contradicts the initial assumption. Hence, the lemma follows.

**Lemma 7.10:** An undirected graph is triconnected iff for all pairs $\{i, j\}$ of nodes in N, there exist three, node disjoint, paths between i and j.

**Proof:** The "if" part of the proof is straightforward. Because, if there exist three node disjoint paths between every pair of nodes i and j in N, then there exists no separation pair, the removal of which disconnects i and j. Therefore, the graph is triconnected.

For the "only if" part of the proof, assume that G has a split $[g_1, g_2]$ at $\{i, j\}$, with $g_1 = <N_1, E_1>$ and $g_2 = <N_2, E_2>$. Consider any nodes $u \in N_1$ and $v \in N_2$. Clearly, we cannot have three node disjoint paths between u and v.

Let us now define a relation R on $N \times N$ by $iRj$ iff i and j are in the same triconnected component of G. Also let $G_{ab} = <N_{ab}, E_{ab}>$ denote the subgraph of $G = <N, E>$ obtained by removing a and b, a, $b \in N$, and all edges incident on a and b. The relation R can be computed using the following lemma whose proof is omitted.

**Lemma 7.11:** Let $G_{ab}^* = <N_{ab}, E_{ab}^*>$ be the transitive closure of $G_{ab} = <N_{ab}, E_{ab}>$. Then, $iRj$ iff for all $\{a, b\}$ such that a, $b \notin \{i, j\}$, $(i, j) \in E_{ab}^*$.

The basic idea underlying the parallel algorithm for testing a graph for triconnectedness is to test all $G_{ij}$ for connectedness for every pair of nodes i and j, i, $j \in N$. If $G_{ij}$ is connected for all pairs of i and j, i, $j \in N$, then the graph G is triconnected. If $G_{ij}$ is not connected for some i, $j \in N$, then G is not triconnected and $\{i, j\}$ is a separation pair. The CREW PRAM algorithm based on this idea is given below.

*Algorithm* **CREW_TEST_TRICON**

Input: The adjacency matrix $A[1 : n, 1 : n]$ of the given undirected biconnected graph $G = <N, E>$.

Output: The algorithm sets a Boolean variable "tricon" to "TRUE" if G is triconnected; otherwise it is set to "FALSE."

*for* i = 1 *to* n *dopar*
    *for* j = 1 *to* n *dopar*
            construct $A_{ij}[1 : n - 2, 1 : n - 2]$ from A by deleting the ith and jth
                rows and the ith and jth columns of A, i.e.,
                $A_{ij}$ represents the adjacency matrix of graph $G_{ij}$
    *odpar*
*odpar*

*for* i = 1 *to* n *dopar*
   *for* j = 1 *to* n *dopar*
        determine from $A_{ij}$ whether $G_{ij}$ is connected or not
            using algorithm CREW_NC_CCOMP
      *if* $G_{ij}$ is connected
      *then* connect(i, j) := 0
      *else* connect(i, j) := 1
      *fi*
   *odpar*
*odpar*
*for* i= 1 *to* n *dopar*

$$s(i) := \sum_{1 \le j \le n} \text{connect}(i, j)$$

*odpar*

$$s := \sum_{1 \le i \le n} s(i)$$

*if* s = 0
*then* tricon := TRUE
*else* tricon := FALSE
*fi*

The first parallel for-loop takes $O(1)$ time using $O(n^4)$ processors to construct $n^2$ adjacency matrices each of size $(n-2) \times (n-2)$. The second parallel for-loop runs in $O(\log^2 n)$ time with $O(n^4)$ processors, since algorithm CREW_NC_CCOMP is executed in parallel for $n^2$ graphs $G_{ij}$, for all pairs of nodes, $i, j \in N$. The third parallel for-loop requires $O(\log n)$ time with $O(n^2)$ processors. The computation of s takes $O(\log n)$ time with $O(n)$ processors. The last if-statement assigns the Boolean variable "tricon" either a TRUE or a FALSE value in constant time with a single processor. Hence, we have the following theorem.

**Theorem 7.4:** Given an undirected biconnected graph $G = \langle N, E \rangle$, it is possible to test whether G is triconnected or not in $O(\log^2 n)$ time when $O(n^4)$ processors are available.

We now show how the tccs of G can be obtained within the same time and processor bounds as those of algorithm CREW_TEST_TRICON. In the second parallel for-loop, algorithm CREW_TEST_TRICON computes the connected components of $G_{ij}$, $i, j \in N$, to determine whether $G_{ij}$ is connected or not. Now, with minor modifications of this algorithm we can compute the transitive closure matrix $A_{ij}^*$ for every $G_{ij}$, $i, j \in N$, as shown in the previous section. Once the transitive closure matrices $A_{ij}^*$ are available, we can compute iRj easily using Lemma 7.11. Thus, computation of the relation R takes $O(\log^2 n)$ time using $O(n^4)$ processors. In order to compute the tccs, we note that two tccs can intersect at most at two nodes. From this fact, it follows that every set of three nodes of a tcc determines that tcc uniquely. Let S be a relation on $N \times N \times N$ such that $(i, j, k) \in S$ if (iRj AND jRk AND iRk). Since the relation R is not transitive, we require all three relations. The computation of the tccs uses the following lemma.

**Lemma 7.12:** Three nodes i, j, and k of G belong to the same tcc of G if (i, j, k) ∈ S, and the set of nodes of the tcc of G which contains the nodes i, j and k is given by $N_{(i,j,k)}$ = {x ∈ N | xRi AND xRj AND xRk}.

It is easy to verify that, once the relation R is available, we can compute the relation S in constant time using $O(n^3)$ processors. Finally, from R and S, we can find the tccs of G in $O(\log^2 n)$ time when $O(n^3)$ processors are employed. Thus, we have the following theorem.

**Theorem 7.5:** Given an undirected biconnected graph G = <N, E>, it is possible to find the tccs of G in $O(\log^2 n)$ time when $O(n^4)$ processors are available on the CREW PRAM model.

# 7.5 ALGORITHMS FOR OTHER CONNECTIVITY-RELATED PROBLEMS

In addition to the algorithms for finding connected, biconnected and triconnected components, there are parallel algorithms for solving several other connectivity-related problems. Examples of such problems include: finding a set of fundamental cycles, bridges and bridge-connected components, and centers and medians. A set of fundamental cycles, bridges, centers etc. provide useful topological information about the concerned graph and have applications in real-life problems. In this section, we present parallel algorithms for these problems on the CREW PRAM model.

## 7.5.1 Set of Fundamental Cycles

Let $g_1$ = <$N_1$, $E_1$> and $g_2$ = <$N_2$, $E_2$> be the two subgraphs of an undirected graph G = < N, E >. Then the symmetric difference of $g_1$ and $g_2$, written $g_1 \oplus g_2$, is the subgraph $g_{12}$ = <$N_{12}$, $E_{12}$> of G such that

$E_{12}$ = {e ∈ $E_1$ ∪ $E_2$ | e ∉ $E_1$ ∩ $E_2$}, and

$N_{12}$ = {i ∈ N | some edge of $E_{12}$ is incident on i}.

A set of fundamental cycles, SFC, of a graph, G = <N, E> is a collection X of cycles of G with the property that any cycle C of G can be written as C = $C_1 \oplus C_2 \oplus \ldots \oplus C_k$ for some sub-collection of cycles $C_1, C_2, \ldots, C_k$ ∈ X. SFC is defined with respect to a spanning tree of the graph G. Let T = <N, E'> be a spanning tree of a graph G. Every nontree edge e of G, i.e., e ∈ E − E', creates a cycle if it is added to T. The collection of cycles {$C_{(i, j)}$ | (i, j) ∈ E − E'} is an SFC of G (Reingold et al. 1977). This fact is used as a basis for designing the parallel SFC algorithm. Figure 7.17 shows an SFC of an example graph G with n = 6 nodes with respect to a BFS spanning tree of G.

The idea underlying the parallel SFC algorithm presented here is simple. First a spanning tree of G = < N, E > rooted at a node, say r ∈ N, denoted by T(r) = <N, E'> is constructed, and then the nontree edges of G are identified. If an edge (i, j) ∈ E − E', then the nearest common ancestor (NCA) of i and j, i.e., NCA(i, j) is computed. Finally, for each (i, j) ∈ E − E', the fundamental cycle $C_{(i, j)}$ is constructed by the two paths joining i and j to NCA(i, j) in T(r). A detailed description of the algorithm is given on the facing page.

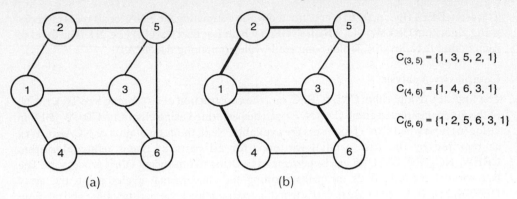

$C_{(3, 5)} = \{1, 3, 5, 2, 1\}$

$C_{(4, 6)} = \{1, 4, 6, 3, 1\}$

$C_{(5, 6)} = \{1, 2, 5, 6, 3, 1\}$

**Figure 7.17** (a) An undirected graph G with n = 6 nodes; (b) a BFST of G rooted at node 1, shown by bold lines; the nontree edges of G, and the SFC with respect to this BFST.

*Algorithm* **CREW_SFC**

Input: The adjacency matrix A[1 : n, 1 : n ] of the given undirected graph G = <N, E>.

Output: The SFC, i.e., the set $\{C_{(i, j)} \mid (i, j) \in E - E'\}$ with respect to a spanning tree T(r) = <N, E'> of G.

construct a spanning tree T(r) of G;
*for* i = 1 *to* n *dopar*
   *for* j = 1 *to* n *dopar*
       find NCA(i, j) using algorithms CREW_NC_ANCESTORS
   *odpar*
*odpar*
*for* i = 1 *to* n *dopar*
   *for* j = 1 *to* n *dopar*
      *if* (i, j) ∈ E
      *then if* (i, j) ∉ E'
         *then do*
             x := level(NCA(i, j));
             y := level(i) + level(j) − 2 × level(NCA(i, j));
             construct a vector $C_{(i, j)}$[1 : y] by copying
             DEPTH[i , x : level(i)] followed by
             DEPTH[j, x : level(j)] in reverse order into
             locations $C_{(i, j)}$[1 : level(i) − x + 1] and
             $C_{(i, j)}$[level(i) − x + 2 : y + 2], respectively
        *od*
      *fi*
    *fi*
   *odpar*
*odpar*

The array DEPTH[1 : n, 0 : L] is constructed while computing the NCA for all pairs of nodes using algorithm CREW_NC_ANCESTORS, where L = max{level(i) | i ∈ N}. The level of each node i ∈ N, level(i), is also computed while computing the NCAs.

**Complexity Analysis**

The first step of algorithm CREW_SFC, i.e., the construction of a spanning tree T(r), r ∈ N, of the given undirected graph G = <N, E> can be performed using algorithm CREW_BFS in $O(\log^2 n)$ time when $O(n^3)$ processors are available. Next, the computation of NCAs in T(r), as required by the first parallel for-loop, for all pairs of nodes using algorithm CREW_NC_ANCESTORS can be performed in O(log n) time using $O(n^2)$ processors. The last parallel for-loop finds the paths forming the fundamental cycles using the array DEPTH[1 : n, 0 : L]. It is easy to verify that this computation takes constant time and no more than $O(n(e - n + 1)) \equiv O(n^3)$ processors. Thus, the overall time complexity of algorithm CREW_SFC is $O(\log^2 n)$ when $O(n^3)$ processors are employed.

## 7.5.2  Bridges and Bridge-connected Components

An edge of an undirected connected graph G = <N, E> is *a bridge* if the removal of this edge disconnects G. Since a spanning tree T(r) = <N, E'>, rooted at r ∈ N, of G is a connected subgraph of G containing all the nodes of G, any edge of G which is a bridge must appear in T(r). Therefore, in order to find the bridges of G, it is sufficient to test only the edges of T(r). Assuming that T(r) is available in the form of the "parent-of" relation — i.e., for every node r ∈ N, parent(i) is specified in T(r) — the following lemma provides a way of determining whether or not an edge (i, parent(i)) ∈ E', where i ∈ N and i ≠ r, is a bridge of G.

**Lemma 7.13:** Given a node i ∈ N of G = <N, E> and a rooted spanning tree T(r) such that i ≠ r, the edge (i, parent(i)) is a bridge of G iff it is the only edge of G which joins a descendant of i, including i, in T(r) with a nondescendant of i in T(r).

   A formal proof of this lemma is given in Savage (1977) and Tarjan (1972) and is omitted here. An undirected graph G and its bridges are shown in Figure 7.18.

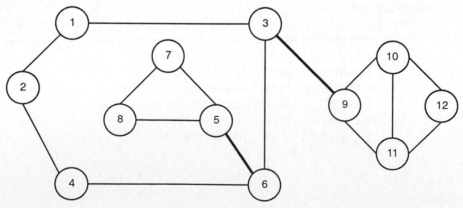

**Figure 7.18**  An undirected connected graph G. The bridges of G are shown by bold lines.

A straightforward method of determining whether for a given $i \in N$ any descendant of $i$ is joined to a nondescendant of $i$ through the edge $(i, parent(i))$, is to use $n^2$ processors to examine all edges joining descendants of $i$ to nondescendants of $i$. Taking all edges of $T(r)$ into account, this process for finding all bridges can be performed in constant time using $O(n^3)$ processors. The construction of a spanning tree using algorithm CREW_BFS takes $O(\log^2 n)$ time when $O(n^3)$ processors are available. Thus, the time complexity of the parallel algorithm based on the above idea is $O(\log^2 n)$ time using $O(n^3)$ processors. We shall now describe a parallel algorithm which also achieves the time bound of $O(\log^2 n)$ but uses only $O(n^2)$ processors.

**Definition 7.12:** For a node $i \in N$ and a spanning tree $T(r) = <N, E'>$ of $G = <N, E>$, the common ancestor (CA) $j$ of the collection $\{i\} \cup \{k \mid (i, k) \in E - E'\}$ is defined to be the *farthest common ancestor* at $i$, denoted by $FCA(i)$, iff in the preorder traversal of $T(r)$ every CA, $c \neq j$, is visited before visiting $j$.

Let the set of descendants of $i \in N$ in $T(r)$ be denoted by $DES(i)$. Then, we denote by $DNTE(k)$ the set of nontree edges $(i, j) \in E - E'$ such that at least one of $i$ and $j$ belongs to $DES(k)$. Thus,

$$DNTE(k) = \{(i, j) \in E - E' \mid i \in DES(k) \text{ OR } j \in DES(k)\}.$$

Following these definitions, we now propose a lemma which is the basis of the parallel bridge-finding algorithm.

**Lemma 7.14:** For a node $i \in N$ with $i \neq r$, where $T(r) = <N, E'>$ is a spanning tree of a graph $G = <N, E>$, let $(i, j) \in DNTE(k)$ be such that $pre(NCA(i, j)) = \min\{pre(NCA(p, q)) \mid (p, q) \in DNTE(k)\}$. Then, the edge $(k, parent(k))$ is a bridge of $G$ iff $pre(k) \leq pre(NCA(i, j))$.

**Proof** (Ghosh 1986): Since $(i, j) \in DNTE(k)$ implies either that $i \in DES(k)$ or $j \in DES(k)$ or both $i, j \in DES(k)$, then $NCA(i, j)$ must either be an ancestor or a descendant of $k$. But $pre(k) \leq pre(NCA(i, j))$ implies that $NCA(i, j)$ is a descendant of $k$ in $T(r)$. Thus, $(k, parent(k))$ is the only edge of $G$ that joins $k$ to a nondescendant of $k$ in $T(r)$. The rest follows by Lemma 7.13.

The algorithm based on the above discussion appears below.

### Algorithm CREW_BRIDGES

Input: The adjacency matrix $A[1 : n, 1 : n]$ of the given undirected graph $G = <N, E>$.

Output: The set of edges $\{(i, j) \mid (i, j) \text{ is a bridge of } G\}$.

```
construct a spanning tree T(r) of G;
for i = 1 to n dopar
    for j = 1 to n dopar
        find NCA(i, j) using algorithm CREW_NC_ANCESTORS;
        ADES[i, j] := 0;
        if j is a descendant of i
        then ADES[i, j] := 1
        fi
    odpar
odpar
```

```
for i = 1 to n dopar
    compute pre(i) in T(r) using algorithm CREW_PREORDER_TRAVERSAL
odpar
for i = 1 to n dopar
    for j = 1 to n dopar
        N[i, j] := 0
        if (i, j) ∈ E
        then if (i, j) ∉ E'
            then N[i, j] := 1
            fi
        fi
    odpar
odpar
for i = 1 to n dopar
    for j = 1 to n dopar
        if N[i, j] = 1
        then ANCA[i, j] := pre(NCA(i, j))
        else ANCA[i, j] := ∞
        fi
    odpar
odpar
for i = 1 to n dopar
    find x such that ANCA(i, x) = min{ANCA(i, y) | y = 1, 2, . . . , n}
    if ANCA[i, x] ≤ n
    then FCA(i) := NCA(i, x)
    else FCA(i) := ∞
    fi
odpar
for i = 1 to n dopar
    for j = 1 to n dopar
        if ADES[i, j] = 1 AND FCA(j) ≤ n
        then AFCA[i, j] := pre(FCA(j))
        else AFCA[i, j] := ∞
        fi
    odpar
odpar
for i = 1 to n dopar
    find x such that AFCA[i, x] = min {AFCA[i, y] | y = 1, 2, . . . , n};
    NUM(i) := AFCA[i, x]
odpar
for i = 1 to n dopar
    if i ≠ r
    then if pre(i) ≤ NUM(i)
        then mark (i, parent(i)) as bridge
        fi
    fi
odpar
```

The complexity of algorithm CREW_BRIDGES can be obtained by analyzing the complexity of the first statement and the complexity of each parallel for-loop separately and then combining these complexities. A spanning tree T(r) of G can be constructed in $O(\log^2 n)$ time using $O(n^2)$ processors using a modified version of algorithm CREW_NC_CCOMP. The modifications required are simple in nature and are left as an exercise. The first parallel for-loop which computes the NCAs for all pairs of nodes and constructs the descendant array ADES[1 : n, 1 : n] takes $O(\log n)$ time with $O(n^2)$ processors. The computation of pre(i), for all i ∈ N, using algorithm CREW_PREORDER_TRAVERSAL requires $O(\log n)$ time with $O(n^2)$ processors. The third parallel for-loop, which computes the nontree edge matrix N[1 : n, 1 : n] and constructs the array ANCA[1 : n, 1 : n] runs in constant time when $O(n^2)$ processors are available. Both the fifth and seventh parallel for-loops require $O(\log n)$ time and O(n) processors for each i. Thus, considering all i ∈ N, they take $O(\log n)$ time with $O(n^2)$ processors. The sixth parallel for-loop runs in constant time using $O(n^2)$ processors. Finally, the parallel for-loop which marks the bridges of G takes only O(1) time when O(n) processors are used. Combining the complexities of individual steps we have the following theorem.

**Theorem 7.6:** Algorithm CREW_BRIDGES requires $O(\log^2 n)$ time using $O(n^2)$ processors to find all of the bridges of a connected undirected graph G = <N, E> on the CREW PRAM model.

The problem of finding the maximal connected subgraphs of a given undirected connected graph G = <N, E> so that none of the subgraphs contains a bridge — i.e., finding the bridge-connected components — is easy when the bridges of G are available. Specifically, we first eliminate all the bridges in G and then use algorithm CREW_NC_CCOMP to find the connected components of the resulting graph. Each of the connected components thus obtained is a bridge-connected component of G. The algorithm obviously runs in $O(\log^2 n)$ time on the CREW PRAM model when $O(n^2)$ processors are employed.

## 7.5.3 Centers and Medians of Graphs

The centers and medians of graphs are defined in the same manner as for trees in Section 7.2.5. Thus, if l(i, j) denotes the length of the shortest path between nodes i and j, i, j ∈ N in graph G = <N, E> then the separation number for i ∈ N is defined as s(i) = max{l(i, j) | j ∈ N} and the centers of G are the nodes of G with the minimum separation number. The transmission number for i ∈ N is defined as t(i) = $\Sigma_{j \in N}$ l(i, j), and the medians of G are the nodes of G having the minimum transmission number. An undirected graph G can have k centers and m medians, where $1 \le k, m \le n$.

The most important task in finding the centers and medians of a graph G is the computation of l(i, j), for all i, j ∈ N. For this purpose, we may use algorithm CREW_BFS which generates n BFSTs T(i, ⌈log n⌉) of G rooted at a node i, for all i ∈ N. It is a property of the BFS spanning trees of a graph G that the level of a node j ∈ N in a BFST rooted at a node i ∈ N is the length of the shortest path from i to j, i.e., l(i, j). Once l(i, j), for all i, j ∈ N is available, the remaining computation required to find the centers and medians of G is straightforward. An informal description of the parallel algorithm is presented on the next page.

*Algorithm* **CREW_CM_GRAPH**

Input: T(i, 0), for all x ∈ N, specified by parent(j | T(i, 0)) and level(j | T(i, 0)), for all j ∈ N.

Output: Centers and medians of G.

construct n BFSTs T(i, ⌈log n⌉) each rooted
    at a node i using algorithm CREW_BFS;
l(i, j) := level(j | T(i, ⌈log n⌉));
*for* i = 1 *to* n *dopar*
    compute s(i) = max{l(i, j) | j = 1, 2, . . . , n};
    obtain the minimum of all s(i)'s and denote it by C;
    *if* s(i) = C
    *then* mark i as a center of G
    *fi*
*odpar*
*for* i = 1 *to* n *dopar*

$$t(i) := \sum_{1 \leq j \leq n} l(i, j);$$

    obtain the minimum of all t(i)'s and denote it by M;
    *if* t(i) = M
    *then* mark i as a median of G
    *fi*
*odpar*

Figure 7.19, on page 245, illustrates the execution of algorithm CREW_CM_GRAPH with the help of an example.

**Complexity Analysis**

The construction of n BFSTs using algorithm CREW_BFS requires $O(\log^2 n)$ time with $O(n^3)$ processors. It is easy to verify that each of the two parallel for-loops can be implemented in $O(\log n)$ time with $O(n^2)$ processors. Therefore, the overall time complexity of algorithm CREW_CM_ GRAPH is $O(\log^2 n)$ when $O(n^3)$ processors are employed.

Observe that, even if we use the CRCW PRAM model, we cannot improve the time bound of algorithm CREW_CM_GRAPH because of the bottleneck in computing the n BFSTs using algorithm CREW_BFS. In fact, if we can generate n minimum-depth spanning trees of G, each rooted at a node i ∈ N, in less time than $O(\log^2 n)$ on the CRCW PRAM model, then it is possible to find the centers and medians in less time than that required by algorithm CREW_CM_GRAPH. We now show that it is possible, by defining the minimum-depth (MD) property using only the level information to obtain an $O(\log n \log \log n)$ time algorithm for finding n minimum-depth spanning trees on a CRCW PRAM. The basis is that only the level of a node is important in the minimum-depth spanning tree but not its order. The MD property can be defined as follows.

**Definition 7.13:** Let i, j be a pair of nodes in the k-tree T(x, k) such that (i, j) ∈ E but (i, j) does not belong to T(x, k). Then the tree T(x, k) is said to possess the MD property if

either            (i) level(j | T(x, k)) ≥ level(j | T(x, k)) − 1;
or               (ii) level(j | T(x, k)) = $2^k$.

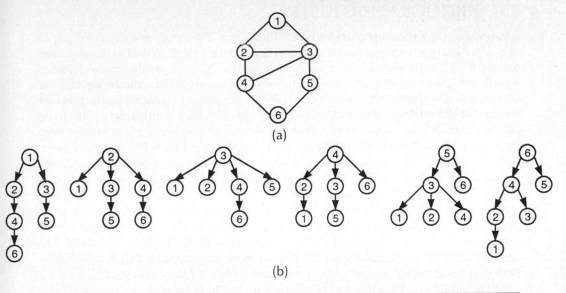

(a)

(b)

| Node i | s(i) | set of centers of G | t(i) | set of medians of G |
|--------|------|---------------------|------|---------------------|
| 1 | 3 | | 9 | |
| 2 | 2 | | 7 | |
| 3 | 2 | {2, 3, 4, 5} | 6 | {3} |
| 4 | 2 | | 7 | |
| 5 | 2 | | 8 | |
| 6 | 3 | | 9 | |

(c)

**Figure 7.19** (a) A graph G; (b) BFSTs of G, each rooted at a node i = 1, 2, . . . , 6; (c) centers and medians of G.

Using a similar tree-merging technique as that employed in algorithm CREW_BFS, it is possible to compute n minimum-depth spanning trees. During each iteration, we need, in this case, to ensure that the partial trees generated preserve the MD property. This algorithm is simpler than algorithm CREW_BFS and can be implemented in $O(\log n \log \log n)$ time using $O(n^3)$ processors if the maximum (minimum) finding algorithm of time complexity $O(\log \log n)$ with $O(n)$ processors (see Section 5.2.1) is used. In this case, the centers and medians of a graph can be obtained in $O(\log n \log \log n)$ time with $O(n^3)$ processors on the CRCW PRAM model.

# 7.6 BIBLIOGRAPHIC NOTES

Every tree can be represented as an equivalent binary tree. The transformations necessary to obtain the binary tree representation of general ordered trees are described in Horowitz and Sahni (1977). The parallel algorithm presented in Section 7.2.1 is a parallelization of a serial algorithm based on the ideas presented in Horowitz and Sahni (1977); a similar algorithm is also presented in Ghosh and Bhattacharjee (1984a). The parallel algorithm for the preorder traversal of binary trees presented in Section 7.2.2 is based on the algorithm due to Ghosh and Bhattacharjee (1984a). There is an O(log n) time preorder traversal algorithm for trees (represented in the form of their equivalent binary trees) on the EREW PRAM model due to Kalra and Bhatt (1985) that requires O(n) processors. The traversal of general ordered trees is considered in Tsin and Chin (1984), and Chaudhuri (1987a); the results presented in Section 7.2.3 are based mainly on those of Savage and Ja' Ja' (1981), Tsin and Chin (1984), and Chaudhuri (1987a). The parallel NCAs algorithm of Section 7.2.4 is based on ideas presented in Tsin and Chin (1984). The problems of finding the centers and medians of trees in parallel is discussed in Chaudhuri (1987b) with reference to the CREW PRAM model. The section on the use of the Euler tour technique on trees, introduced by Tarjan and Vishkin (1984), is based mainly on their original work and on that of Manber (1989).

DFS and BFS, in the context of parallel processing, have been studied extensively by many researchers. Important references include Alton and Eckstein (1979), Chaudhuri (1988, 1990), Dekel et al. (1981), Eckstein and Alton (1977), Ghosh and Bhattacharjee (1984a, 1984b), Kim and Chwa (1986), Reghbati and Corneil (1978), Reif (1985), and Zhang (1986). Reif showed that the DFS problem is P-complete with respect to deterministic log space reductions (Reif 1985). The parallel computation thesis states that the notion of time on an unbounded parallel computation model is polynomially equivalent to the notion of space on a serial model of computation (Chandra and Stockmeyer 1976; Goldschlager 1978, 1982). It is not known whether all members of P, the problems solvable in deterministic polynomial time, are solvable in $O(\log^c n)$ space, for some c independent of n. A problem X in P is *log space complete* for P if every other problem in P is reducible in log space to X. It has been conjectured by Cook (1974) that the problems that are log space complete for P require polynomial space. If this conjecture is true, then it follows clearly from the parallel computation thesis that problems that are log space complete for P cannot be solved in deterministic logarithmic parallel time. Therefore, Reif's work gives strong evidence that the DFS of general graphs cannot be performed in deterministic parallel time of $O(\log^c n)$, for any constant $c \geq 1$. In Section 7.3.1 we have presented a deterministic logarithmic time parallel algorithm for the DFS of DAGs, a subclass of general graphs, following Chaudhuri (1990). A parallel DFS algorithm for DAGs that takes $O(\log^2 n)$ time with $O(n^{2.81}/\log n)$ processors has been proposed by Ghosh and Bhattacharjee (1984a). Later Zhang (1986) presented a counter-example and found the necessary and sufficient condition under which Ghosh and Bhattacharjee's algorithm would fail. Another DFS algorithm for DAGs which requires $O(\log^2 n)$ time and $O(n^3/\log n)$ processors is due to Kim and Chwa (1986). Kim and Chwa's algorithm is based on the shortest-path algorithm of Dekel et al. (1981), whereas the algorithm presented in this chapter for the same problem is based on a tree merging technique. In a recent paper, Hagerup (1990) has shown that for the class of undirected embedded planar graphs, the DFS is no more difficult than the BFS problem on the CREW PRAM model. More precisely, Hagerup's algorithm constructs the DFST in O(log n) time with $O(n^3)$ processors for this special class of graphs.

A number of algorithms are available for BFS on different models of computation. Dekel et al. (1981) proposed $O(\log^2 n)$ time parallel BFS algorithms for both cube connected and perfect shuffle computers. On the CREW PRAM model parallel BFS algorithms have been proposed by Ghosh and Bhattacharjee (1984b) and Kim and Chwa (1986). Both of these algorithms require $O(\log^2 n)$ time; the first one needs $O(n^3)$ processors and the second one $O(n^3/\log n)$ processors. The parallel BFS algorithm presented in Section 7.3.2 is based on the ideas presented by Gosh and Bhattacharjee (1984b).

BDS of graphs has not been studied extensively. The early work on this problem is due to Reghbati and Corneil (1978). They proposed a parallel BDS algorithm on a k-bounded CREW PRAM which has time complexity $O(n \log k + (e/k))$. This algorithm is not very attractive from the speedup point of view as its time complexity cannot be reduced beyond $O(n \log n)$. BDS of general graphs is suspected to be inherently serial and a deterministic parallel algorithm has been presented for the BDS of DAGs on the CREW PRAM model by Chaudhuri (1988). The parallel BDS algorithm for DAGs presented in Section 7.2.3 is based on this work.

A good deal of work has been reported in the literature on the connected components and connectivity related problems. Parallel algorithms for the connectivity problem based on BFS was first proposed by Arjomandi (Reghbati) and Corneil (1975, 1978). However, a much faster parallel algorithm has been presented in Section 7.4.1.1. A number of papers which use the transitive closure approach have been published for the solution of the connected components problem. These include Reghbati and Corneil (1978), Chandra (1976), and Kucera (1982). The algorithm of Reghbati and Corneil requires $O(\log^2 n)$ time with $O(n^3)$ processors, whereas Chandra's matrix-multiplication-based algorithm takes $O(\log^2 n)$ time using only $O(n^{2.81}/\log n)$ processors. Both of these algorithms work on the CREW PRAM model. Kucera (1982), on the other hand, obtained an $O(\log n)$ time parallel algorithm on the CRCW PRAM model that uses $O(n^4)$ processors. Note that the parallel algorithm presented in Section 7.4.1.2 has been shown to work on the CRCW PRAM in $O(\log n)$ time but with $O(n^3)$ processors only.

The third approach for the connected components problem is perhaps more attractive, since the node collapse method gives rise to fast as well as efficient parallel algorithms for this problem. As a consequence, many papers have been published for the parallel solution of the connectivity problem based on the node collapse method. These include Hirschberg (1976), Hirschberg et al. (1979), Nassimi and Sahni (1980), Chin et al. (1982), Savage and Ja' Ja' (1981), Nath and Maheswari (1982), Shiloach and Vishkin (1982a), Awerbuch and Shiloach (1983), and Vishkin (1984).

The algorithm presented in Section 7.4.1.3 is based on Hirschberg (1976). Hirschberg et al. (1979) have improved their result by reducing the number of processors to $O(n \lceil n/\log n \rceil)$ without increasing the time complexity. These algorithms work on the CREW PRAM model. Nassimi and Sahni (1980) propose a parallel connected component algorithm using the node collapse method that takes $O(n^{0.5} \log n)$ time with n processors on a mesh connected computer. The algorithm of Chin et al. takes $O(\log^2 n)$ time but requires only $O(n \lceil n/\log^2 n \rceil)$ processors on the CREW PRAM model. Savage and Ja' Ja''s algorithm runs in $O(\log d \log n)$ time with $O(n^3/\log n)$ processors on the CREW PRAM model, where d is the diameter of the graph. Nath and Maheswari (1982) have shown that, on the EREW PRAM model, this problem can be solved in $O(\log^2 n)$ time using $O(e + n \log n)$ processors. The algorithm due to Shiloach and Vishkin (1982a) runs in $O(\log n)$ time on the CRCW PRAM using n + 2e processors. Awerbuch and Shiloach (1983) have improved the results of Shiloach and Vishkin (1982a) to obtain an O(log n) time connected components algorithm on the same model using 2e processors. The time complexity of Vishkin's algorithm is $O(n^2/P)$, on a CRCW PRAM with P ($\leq n^2/\log^2 n$) processors. Han and Wagner (1990) have recently proposed yet another efficient parallel connected component algorithm on the CREW PRAM model which runs in $O((e/k) + (n \log n/k) + \log^2 n)$ time with k processors.

The parallel biconnected components algorithm presented in Section 7.4.2 is based on the work of Savage and Ja' Ja' (1981). Other references for the solution of this problem include Eckstein (1979), Tsin and Chin (1984), and Tarjan and Vishkin (1984). Eckstein's algorithm takes $O(d \log^2 n)$ time and $O((n + e)/d)$ processors on the CREW PRAM model. Savage and Ja' Ja' have proposed two parallel algorithms, both of which work on the CREW PRAM model. The first algorithm uses $O(\log^2 n)$ with $O(n^3/\log n)$ processors, while the second algorithm runs in $O(\log^2 n \log k)$ time with $O(n e + n^2 \log n)$ processors, where k is the number of bccs. Tsin and Chin's algorithm requires $O(\log^2 n)$ time and $O(n \lceil n/\log^2 n \rceil)$ processors on the CREW PRAM model. Tarjan and Vishkin proposed a CRCW PRAM bccs algorithm that takes O(log n) time with only O(n + e) processors. Tarjan and Vishkin's algorithm can also be implemented on the CREW PRAM model which, in general, takes $O(n^2/p)$ time with $p \leq n^2/\log^2 n$ processors. The work on the triconnected components problem in the context of parallel processing is due to Ja' Ja' and Simon (1982). Section 7.4.3 owes much to their work.

References on the SFC problem include Savage and Ja' Ja' (1981), Tsin and Chin (1984), and Ghosh (1986). The algorithm presented in Section 7.5.1 follows the ideas of Savage and Ja' Ja'. Tsin and Chin proposed a better algorithm than that due to Savage and Ja' Ja' that runs in $O(\log^2 n)$ time but requires only $O(n \lceil n/\log n \rceil)$ processors. Ghosh's algorithm also runs in $O(\log^2 n)$ time but uses $O(n (e - n + 1))$ processors, and hence performs efficiently only when the graph is sparse. All these algorithms work on the CREW PRAM model.

The problems of finding the bridges and the bridge-connected components have been studied by Tsin and Chin (1984), Tarjan and Vishkin (1983), and Ghosh (1986). Tsin and Chin's algorithm takes $O(\log^2 n)$ time with $O(n \lceil n/\log n \rceil)$ processors on the CREW PRAM model. Tarjan and Vishkin proposed an O(log n) time algorithm on the CRCW PRAM model that requires O(n + e) processors. Ghosh's algorithm runs in $O(\log^2 n)$ time and requires $O(n (e - n + 1))$ processors on the CREW PRAM model. The algorithm presented in Section 7.5.2 is based on the ideas of Ghosh (1986) but its implementation has been shown to require only $O(n^2)$ processors. Atallah and Kosaraju (1984) have studied the bridge-finding problem on a mesh connected computer with $n^2$ processors. Their algorithm runs in O(n) time. Dekel et al. (1981) showed that, on both cube connected and perfect shuffle computers, the median of a graph can be obtained in time $O(\log^2 n)$ with $O(n^3)$ processors. On the CRCW PRAM model, $O(\log n \log \log n)$ time algorithms with $O(n^2 \lceil n/\log \log n \rceil)$ processors for finding the centers and medians of graphs have been presented by Chaudhuri (1987b).

Other important parallel algorithms for unweighted graphs which have not been discussed in this book include the problems relating to maximum matching, maximum independent set, planarity testing, strong orientation, strong connectivity augmentation, Euler circuits, etc. A parallel algorithm for maximum matching was investigated by Shiloach and Vishkin on the CRCW PRAM model (Shiloach and Vishkin 1982b). They showed that a maximum matching in bipartite graphs can be obtained in $O(n^{1.5} \log n)$ time using O(e/n) processors. Kim and Chwa (1987) later showed that this problem can be solved in time $O(n \log n \log \log n)$ using $O(n^2 \lceil n/\log n \rceil)$ processors on the CREW PRAM model. Dekel and

Sahni (1982) have proposed an algorithm to find the maximum matching of a convex bipartite graph on the CREW PRAM model. Their algorithm has time complexity $O(\log^2 n)$ with $O(n)$ processors. They used this algorithm to derive parallel algorithms for scheduling problems. For the maximum independent set problem, Karp and Wigderson (1985) have proposed a parallel algorithm that runs in $O(\log^4 n)$ with $O(n^3/\log^3 n)$ processors on the EREW PRAM model. On the same model Luby's algorithm (Luby 1985) runs in $O(\log^2 n)$ time with $O(n^2 e)$ processors. Ja' Ja' and Simon (1982) presented two parallel algorithms for testing the planarity of a graph. The first algorithm has time complexity $O(\log^2 n)$ with $O(n^4)$ processors; the second also takes $O(\log^2 n)$ time but uses $O(n^{3.29}/\log^2 n)$ processors. Both of these algorithms use the parallel triconnected components algorithm. A parallel algorithm for the strong orientation problem due to Atallah (1984) requires $O(\log^2 n)$ time with $O(n^3)$ processors on the EREW PRAM model. Tsin (1985) has improved this result and obtained a CREW PRAM algorithm that requires $O(\log^2 n)$ time with only $O(n \lceil n/\log^2 n \rceil)$ processors. This algorithm can also be implemented on the CRCW PRAM in $O(\log n)$ time using $O(n + e)$ processors. The strong connectivity augmentation problem on the CRCW PRAM model has been considered by Chaudhuri (1987c). His parallel algorithm requires $O(\log n)$ time with $O(n^3)$ processors. Awerbuch et al. (1984) and Atallah and Vishkin (1984) present parallel algorithms for finding Euler circuits for directed and undirected graphs. The time complexity of the first algorithm is $O(\log e)$ with $O(e)$ processors on the CRCW PRAM model. The algorithm due to Atallah and Vishkin, on the other hand, requires $O(\log n)$ time with $O(n + e)$ processors on the same model.

## 7.7 EXERCISES

7.7.1  Design an $O(\log n)$ time algorithm for postorder traversal of a binary tree on the CREW PRAM model.

7.7.2  Design an $O(\log n)$ time algorithm for postorder traversal of a general ordered tree without converting it into its equivalent binary tree.

7.7.3  The reverse postorder traversal of a tree is defined in Section 7.3.3. Show how you can modify the algorithm designed for Exercise 7.7.2 to compute the reverse postorder traversal rank of each node of a tree.

7.7.4  Will there be any improvement in the complexity of algorithm CREW_CM_TREE of Section 7.2.5 that finds the centers and medians of trees, if implemented on a CRCW PRAM?

7.7.5  Develop complete algorithms for traversing a tree in (i) preorder, and (ii) postorder on the EREW PRAM model based on the Euler tour technique introduced in Section 7.2.6.

7.7.6  Study Reif's work which showed that the depth-first search problem is complete in deterministic polynomial time with respect to deterministic log-space reduction (Reif 1985).

7.7.7   Design a parallel algorithm for the depth-first search of general graphs on a TSC. Analyze the complexity of your algorithm.

7.7.8   Repeat Exercise 7.7.7 for the breadth-first search problem.

7.7.9   Repeat Exercise 7.7.7 for the breadth-depth search problem.

7.7.10  Develop CREW PRAM algorithms for computing (i) the BFS, and (ii) the BDS traversal ranks for each node of a general ordered rooted tree. Use Lemmas 7.5 and 7.6, respectively, as the basis for each of these algorithms. Analyze the complexities of your algorithms.

7.7.11  Give a formal proof of correctness of algorithm CREW_BFS of Section 7.3.2.

7.7.12  Repeat Exercise 7.7.11 for algorithm CREW_BDS of Section 7.3.3.

7.7.13  Design a parallel algorithm for the connected components problem on a cube connected SIMD computer with $n^3$ processors. What is the time complexity of your algorithm?

7.7.14  Design a parallel connected components algorithm on the CRCW PRAM model that runs in $O(n^2/P)$ time with $P$ ( $\leq n^2/\log^2 n$) processors (Vishkin 1984).

7.7.15  Modify algorithm CREW_NC_CCOMP of Section 7.4.1.3 to obtain a spanning tree of a graph. What is the complexity of the modified algorithm?

7.7.16  Design a connected components algorithm on a TSC with $O(n)$ PEs (Yeh and Lee 1984).

7.7.17  Modify the algorithm obtained in Exercise 7.7.15 to compute the transitive closure of an undirected graph. Analyze the complexity of your algorithm.

7.7.18  Design an algorithm for computing the strongly connected components of a directed graph on a CREW PRAM model. Analyze its complexity. What will be the complexity of your algorithm if it is implemented on a CRCW PRAM?

7.7.19  Completely develop a CREW PRAM algorithm for computing the biconnected components based on the ideas presented in Section 7.4.2.

7.7.20  Study Tarjan and Vishkin's algorithm for computing the biconnected components of a connected undirected graph (Tarjan and Vishkin 1984). Compare this algorithm with that due to Tsin and Chin (1984).

7.7.21  Develop completely a CREW PRAM algorithm for computing the triconnected components of an undirected biconnected graph based on the ideas presented in Section 7.4.3.

7.7.22 Design a parallel algorithm to find all triangles of a directed graph (a triangle is a directed cycle of length three) on the CREW PRAM model. Analyze its complexity. What will be the complexity of your algorithm if implemented on the CRCW PRAM model?

7.7.23 Show that the bridges of an undirected connected graph can be computed in $O(\log n)$ time on a CRCW PRAM.

7.7.24 Show that the bridge-finding problem can be solved on a two-dimensional mesh connected SIMD computer with $n^2$ processors in $O(n)$ time (Atallah and Kosaraju 1984).

7.7.25 Design a parallel algorithm for computing the medians of a graph on a cube connected SIMD computer with $O(n^3)$ processors. What is the time complexity of your algorithm?

7.7.26 Repeat Exercise 7.7.24 for the perfect shuffle computer.

7.7.27 The strong connectivity augmentation problem is defined as follows. Given a directed graph $G = \langle N, E \rangle$, find a set $E_a$ of minimum number of edges such that the directed graph $G_a = \langle N, E \cup E_a \rangle$ is strongly connected.

Design an $O(\log n)$ time parallel algorithm for this problem on a CRCW PRAM. What is its processor complexity?

7.7.28 The strong orientation problem is defined as follows. Given a connected, bridgeless undirected graph $G = \langle N, E \rangle$, assign directions to the edges of $G$ so that the resulting directed graph is strongly connected.

Design an algorithm for the strong orientation problem on the CREW PRAM model. Analyze the complexity of your algorithm.

# 7.8 BIBLIOGRAPHY

Alton, D. A., and Eckstein, D. M. (1979). Parallel breadth-first search of p-sparse graphs. *Proceedings of the West Coast Conference on Combinatorics, Graph Theory and Computing,* Arcata, Calif. 79-93.

Arjomandi, E., and Corneil, D. G. (1975). Parallel computations in graph theory. *Proceedings of the 16th Annual Symposium on Foundations of Computer Science,* IEEE Computer Society, Washington, DC, pp. 13-18.

Atallah, M. J. (1984). Parallel strong orientation of an undirected graph. *Inform. Process. Lett.* 18, 37-9.

Atallah, M. J., and Kosaraju, S. R. (1984). Graph Problems on a mesh-connected processor array. *J. ACM* 31, 649-67.

Atallah, M. J., and Vishkin, U. (1984). Finding Euler tours in parallel. *J. Computer and System Sci.* 29, 330-7.

Awerbuch, B., and Shiloach, Y. (1983). New connectivity and MSF algorithms for ultracomputer and PRAM. *Proceedings of the 1983 International Conference on Parallel Processing,* IEEE Computer Society, Washington, DC, pp. 175-9.

Awerbuch, B., Israeli, A., and Shiloach, Y. (1984). Finding Euler circuits in logarithmic parallel time. *Proceedings of the 16th Annual ACM Symposium on Theory of Computing,* ACM, NY, pp. 249-57.

Chandra, A. K. (1976). *Maximal parallelism in matrix multiplication.* IBM Tech. Rep. RC 6193, Thomas J. Watson Research Center, Yorktown Heights, NY.

Chandra, A. K., and Stockmeyer, L. J. (1976). Alternation. *Proceedings of the 17th Annual Symposium on Foundations of Computer Science,* IEEE Computer Society, Washington, DC, pp. 98-108.

Chaudhuri, P. (1987a). Finding basic tree functions in parallel. *Proceedings of the International Symposium on Electronic devices, Circuits and Systems,* Kharagpur, India, pp. 252-5.

Chaudhuri, P. (1987b). Algorithms for finding centers and medians of trees and graphs on a parallel computation model. *J. Indian Inst. Sci.* 67, 429-38.

Chaudhuri, P. (1987c). An O(log n) parallel algorithm for strong connectivity augmentation problem. *Intern. J. Computer Math.* 22, 187-97.

Chaudhuri, P. (1988). Fast parallel graph searching with applications. *BIT* 28, 2-18.

Chaudhuri, P. (1990). Finding and updating depth first spanning trees of acyclic digraphs in parallel. *Computer Journal* 33, 247-51.

Chin, F. Y., Lam, J., and Chen, I. -N. (1982). Efficient parallel algorithms for some graph problems. *Comm. ACM* 25, 659-65.

Cook, S. A. (1974). An observation on time-storage trade-off. *J. Computer and System Sci.* 9, 308-16.

Dekel, E., and Sahni, S. (1982). A parallel matching algorithm for convex bipartite graphs. *Proceedings of the 1982 International Conference on Parallel Processing,* IEEE Computer Society, Washington, DC, pp. 178-84.

Dekel, E., Nassimi, D., and Sahni, S. (1981). Parallel matrix and graph algorithms. *SIAM J. Computing* 10, 657-75.

Deo, N. (1974). *Graph Theory with Applications to Engineering and Computer Science.* Prentice Hall, Englewood Cliffs, NJ.

Eckstein, D. M. (1979). *BFS and biconnectivity.* Tech. Rep. 79-11, Dept. of Computer Science, Iowa State University, Ames, Iowa.

Eckstein, D. M., and Alton, D. A. (1977). Parallel graph processing using depth-first search. *Proceedings of the Conference on Theoretical Computer Science,* Waterloo, Ont., pp. 21-9.

Ghosh, R. K. (1986). Parallel algorithms for connectivity problems in graph theory. *Intern. J. Computer Math.* 18, 193-218.

Ghosh, R. K., and Bhattacharjee, G. P. (1984a). A parallel search algorithm for directed acyclic graphs. *BIT* 24, 134-50.

Ghosh, R. K., and Bhattacharjee, G. P. (1984b). Parallel breadth-first search algorithms for trees and graphs. *Intern. J. Computer Math.* 15, 255-68.

Goldschlager, L. M. (1978). *A unified approach to models of synchronous parallel computation.* Tech. Rep. 114, Computer Science Dept., University of Toronto, Ontario.

Goldschlager, L. M. (1982). A universal interconnection pattern for parallel computers. *J. ACM* 29, 1073-86.

Hagerup, T. (1990). Planar depth-first search in O(log n) parallel time. *SIAM J. Computing* 19, 678-704.

Han, Y., and Wagner, R. A. (1990). An efficient and fast connected component algorithm. *J. ACM* 37, 626-42.

Hirschberg, D. S. (1976). Parallel algorithms for the transitive closure and the connected component problems. *Proceedings of the 8th Annual Symposium on the Theory of Computing,* ACM, NY, pp. 55-7.

Hirschberg, D. S., Chandra, A. K., and Sarwate, D. V. (1979). Computing connected components on parallel computers. *Comm. ACM* 22, 461-4.

Horowitz, E, and Sahni, S. (1977). *Fundamentals of Data Structures.* Computer Science Press, Potomac, Md.

Ja' Ja', J., and Simon, J. (1982). Parallel algorithms in graph theory: Planarity testing. *SIAM J. Computing* 11, 314-28.

Kalra, N. C., and Bhatt, P. C. P. (1985). Parallel algorithms for tree traversals. *Parallel Computing* 2, 163-71.

Karp, R. M., and Wigderson, A. (1985). A fast parallel algorithm for the maximal independent set problem. *J. ACM* 32, 762-73.

Kim, T., and Chwa, K. (1986). Parallel algorithms for a depth first search and a breadth first search. *Intern. J. Computer Math.* 19, 39-54.

Kim, T., and Chwa, K. (1987). An O(n log n log log n) parallel maximum matching algorithm for bipartite graphs. *Inform. Process. Lett.* 24, 15-17.

Kucera, L. (1982). Parallel computation and conflicts in memory access. *Inform. Process. Lett.* 14, 93-6.

Luby, M. (1985). A simple parallel algorithm for the maximal independent set problem. *Proceedings of the 17th Annual Symposium on Theory of Computing,* ACM, NY, pp. 1-10.

Manber, U. (1989). *Introduction to Algorithms: A Creative Approach.* Addison-Wesley, Reading, Mass.

Nassimi, D., and Sahni, S. (1980). Finding connected components and connected ones on a mesh-connected parallel computer. *SIAM J. Computing* 9, 744-57.

Nath, D., and Maheswari, S. N. (1982). Parallel algorithms for the connected components and minimal spanning tree problems. *Inform. Process. Lett.* 14, 7-11.

Reghbati, E., and Corneil, D. G. (1978). Parallel computations in graph theory. *SIAM J. Computing* 2, 230-7.

Reif, J. H. (1985). Depth-first search is inherently sequential. *Inform. Process. Lett.* 20, 229-34.

Reingold, E. M., Nievergelt, J., and Deo, N. (1977). *Combinatorial Algorithms: Theory and Practice.* Prentice Hall, Englewood Cliffs, NJ.

Savage, C. (1977). Parallel algorithms for graph theoretic problems. Ph.D. dissertation, Dept. of Mathematics, University of Illinois, Urbana-Champaign, Ill.

Savage, C., and Ja' Ja', J. (1981). Fast, efficient parallel algorithms for some graph problems. *SIAM J. Computing* 10, 682-91.

Shiloach, Y., and Vishkin, U. (1982a). An O(log n) parallel connectivity algorithm. *J. Algorithms* 3, 57-67.

Shiloach, Y., and Vishkin, U. (1982b). An O(n² log n) parallel MAX-FLOW algorithm. *J. Algorithms* 3, 128-46.

Tarjan, R. E. (1972). Depth-first search and linear graph algorithms. *SIAM J. Computing* 1, 146-60.

Tarjan, R. E., and Vishkin, U. (1983). *An efficient parallel biconnectivity algorithm.* Tech. Rep. TR-69, Ultracomputer Note-51, Courant Institute of Mathematical Sciences, NY.

Tarjan, R. E., and Vishkin, U. (1984). Finding biconnected components and computing tree functions in logarithmic parallel time. *Proceedings of the 23rd Annual Symposium on Foundations of Computer Science,* IEEE Computer Society, Washington, DC, pp. 12-20.

Tsin, Y. H. (1985). An optimal parallel processor bound in strong orientation of an undirected graph. *Inform. Process. Lett.* 20, 143-6.

Tsin, Y. H., and Chin, F. Y. (1984). Efficient parallel algorithms for a class of graph theoretic problems. *SIAM J. Computing* 13, 580-99.

Vishkin, U. (1984). An optimal parallel connectivity algorithm. *Discrete App. Math.* 9, 197-207.

Zhang, Y. (1986). A note on parallel depth first search. *BIT* 26, 195-8.

# Algorithms for Weighted Graphs

## 8.1 INTRODUCTION

We may often need to model problems which occur in practice using graphs in which weights or costs are associated with each edge. For example, graphs may be used to represent the road map of a country, with nodes representing the cities and weighted edges representing the highways connecting them. The weights of the edges may represent the distances between the cities or the bus fares from one city to another. Similarly, route maps for airways may be represented by weighted graphs. Several questions relating to minimum weight or cost naturally arise for such structures. For example, one may be interested to know (a) whether it is possible to find a set of edges of the graph which connects all nodes and whose total weight is minimum; and (b) if there is more than one path between two nodes, what is the minimum weighted path (shortest path) between these two nodes? The weight or the length of a path is the sum of the weights of the edges on the path.

In this chapter, we will consider the solutions to these problems using various parallel computational models. The first problem described above is called the minimum spanning tree problem; the second is called the shortest paths problem. Two variants of the shortest paths problem are frequently encountered — one is the single-source shortest paths problem, in which we find all the shortest paths between a single source and all other nodes of the graph; and the other is the all-pairs shortest paths problem in which the shortest path between every pair of nodes is of interest.

An arbitrary weighted undirected graph is shown in Figure 8.1. In order to represent weighted graphs we may use the weighted adjacency matrix which is obtained by replacing each entry (i, j) of the adjacency matrix by the corresponding weight or cost. If there is no edge between two nodes i and j or i = j, then the corresponding entry in the cost adjacency matrix

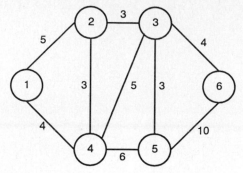

**Figure 8.1** An arbitrary weighted undirected graph.

is filled with some large number, say ∞. In the adjacency lists representation, a field can be added to each list element for the weight. It is assumed that all weights are positive real numbers. In Section 2 we will investigate the minimum spanning tree problem on different computational models. Sections 3 and 4 deal with the two variants of the shortest paths problem.

One of the most important applications of weighted directed acyclic graphs is in the modeling of large complicated projects. Graphs used for this application are called activity networks. The analysis of activity networks is considered in Section 5. A discussion of other parallel algorithms for weighted graphs and relevant references are included in Section 6.

## 8.2 MINIMUM SPANNING TREE ALGORITHMS

Given a weighted, connected, and undirected graph G = <N, E>, a minimum spanning tree (MST) of G is a tree connecting all the nodes of N with edges of E such that the sum of its edge weights is minimum. When all the edges in E have distinct weights, the MST is unique. There are many different methods for constructing an MST, all of which are based on the following two lemmas whose proofs are given in texts such as Aho et al. (1974), and Goodman and Hedetniemi (1977).

**Lemma 8.1:** Let G = <N, E> be an undirected connected graph and T = <N, E'> be a spanning tree for G. Then, the following hold:

(i) for all i, j ∈ N, the path between i and j in T is unique; and

(ii) if any edge (i, j) ∈ E − E' is added to T, a unique cycle results.

**Lemma 8.2:** Let G = <N, E> be a connected, weighted, undirected graph and let X be some proper subset of the set of nodes N. If (i, j) is an edge of minimum weight such that i ∈ X and j ∈ N − X, then there exists an MST that includes (i, j) as an edge.

Primarily, there are three classes of algorithms for computing an MST of a weighted graph in a serial computing environment. These are: Sollin's algorithm (Sollin 1977) which is based on the minimum weighted edge from each node method; Prim-Dijkstra's algorithm (Prim 1957; Dijkstra 1959) based on the nearest neighbor method; and Kruskal's algorithm based on the minimum weighted edge first method (Kruskal 1956). Among these MST algorithms, the algorithm due to Sollin is probably the most suitable for parallelization. In this section, we shall present parallel MST algorithms on the CREW PRAM, EREW PRAM and TSC, respectively.

## 8.2.1 CREW PRAM Algorithm

Several MST algorithms exist on the CREW PRAM model. They are basically parallelizations of Sollin's serial MST algorithm on the CREW PRAM model. We will first describe briefly the algorithm due to Sollin. The algorithm starts with a forest F(0) obtained by forming a tree from each node of the given graph and omitting all edges. A collection of trees is called a forest. At each step, the minimum weighted edge incident on each tree is selected. All these edges are added to the current forest F(k) to form the new forest F(k + 1). This process is continued until the forest collapses to a single tree which gives an MST of the given undirected weighted, connected graph G = <N, E>. The algorithm based on this idea is given below.

*Algorithm* **SERIAL_MST(S)**

Input: An undirected, connected graph G = <N, E> given by its weight adjacency matrix W.

Output: An MST of G.

F(0) := <N, $\emptyset$ >;
k := 0;
*while* there is more than one tree in F(k) *do*
    *for* each tree $T_i$ in forest F(k) *do*
        select a minimum weighted edge (x, y) such that x is in $T_i$ and
            y is in any other tree $T_j$ in forest F(k)
    *od*
    form the forest F(k + 1) by joining all $T_i$ and $T_j$ of F(k)
        with the corresponding selected edges;
    k := k + 1
*od*

In the worst case this algorithm requires $\lceil \log n \rceil$ iterations of the while-loop. It can be verified that a straightforward implementation of algorithm SERIAL_MST(S) requires $O(n^2 \log^2 n)$ time. Execution of the algorithm is illustrated in Figure 8.2.

There are several implementations of the above algorithm on different variants of the PRAM model. Following Savage and Ja' Ja' (1981) we shall describe a parallel version on the CREW PRAM model. In order to parallelize algorithm SERIAL_MST(S), a suitable parallel implementation of the body of the while-loop is required. We shall show that this computation can be performed in $O(\log n)$ time using $O(n^2)$ processors. The details of the algorithm are given below.

*Algorithm* **CREW_MST(S)**

Input: The weight adjacency matrix W of G.

Output: An MST of G.

*for* i = 1 *to* n *dopar*
    R[i] := i
*odpar*

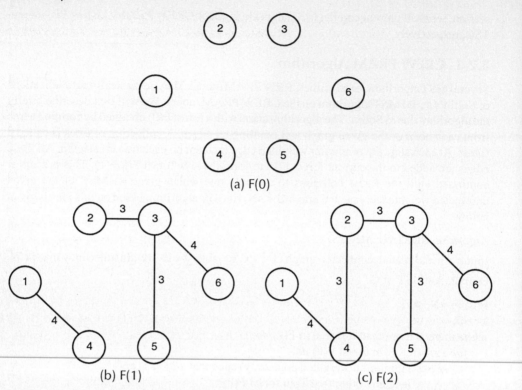

(a) F(0)

(b) F(1)                                            (c) F(2)

**Figure 8.2** The iterative steps of algorithm SERIAL_MST(S) during the construction of an MST of the weighted undirected graph of Figure 8.1.

```
completed := FALSE;
while not completed do
    for i = 1 to n dopar
        for j = 1 to n dopar
            if R[i] ≠ R[j]
            then X[j] := W[i, j]
            else X[j] := ∞
            fi
            find k such that X[k] = min{X[j] | j = 1, 2, . . . , n};
            N[i] := k
        odpar
    odpar
    for each component Tₓ of the forest (say, F(t)) do
        select a node i such that W[i, N[i]] is minimal over all nodes of Tₓ;
        add all of the edges (i, N[i]) to create a new forest F(t + 1)
    od
```

*for* i = 1 *to* n *dopar*
    find the corresponding R[i], i.e., the component
        where node i belongs
*odpar*
*for* i = 1 *to* n *dopar*
  *for* j = 1 *to* n *dopar*
    *if* R[i] = R[j]
    *then* completed := TRUE
    *fi*
  *odpar*
  *odpar*
*od*

### Complexity Analysis

The first parallel for-loop, which represents each node as a single tree (whose root is itself) through the assignment statement R[i] := i, for all $i \in N$, takes constant time using $O(n)$ processors. The first parallel for-loop within the while-loop has to find the minimum of n numbers for each i = 1, 2, . . . , n, in addition to a single assignment statement. Thus, this parallel for-loop requires $O(\log n)$ time using $O(n^2)$ processors. The second parallel for-loop within the while-loop finds, for each component $T_x$ of the existing forest, say F(t), a node i with minimum value W[i, N[i]]. Then, the edge (i, N[i]) is added to the existing forest to create a new forest. This process requires $O(\log n)$ time using $O(n^2)$ processors. The third parallel for-loop within the while-loop finds, for each node i, a representative component where node i belongs, namely, R[i]. For each node, this can be done in time $O(\log n)$ with $O(n)$ processors, using the same technique as that in the connected components algorithm in Section 7.4.1.3. Therefore, considering all nodes, this for-loop requires $O(\log n)$ time with $O(n^2)$ processors. The last parallel for-loop can be implemented in $O(\log n)$ time with $O(n^2)$ processors. It requires $O(\log n)$ time to fan-in all the test results in order to assign a truth value to the Boolean variable "completed" because concurrent write is not allowed by the computational model assumed. Thus, combining the complexities of all the individual statements of the while-loop, we find that it requires $O(\log n)$ time when $O(n^2)$ processors are used. Since this while-loop is repeated $\lceil \log n \rceil$ times in the worst case, the overall time complexity of algorithm CREW_MST(S) is $O(\log^2 n)$ when $O(n^2)$ processors are available.

## 8.2.2 EREW PRAM Algorithm

The parallel MST algorithm on the EREW PRAM model presented in this section is a parallel implementation of Prim's MST algorithm (Prim 1957). An efficient computer implementation of Prim's serial algorithm was given by Dijkstra (Dijkstra 1959). The algorithm begins execution with a forest consisting of n isolated nodes. A node is then chosen arbitrarily from the forest to be the first node in the partially constructed MST. This partial tree is grown successively by selecting and including the nearest neighbor from the set of isolated nodes. Alternatively, at an intermediate step an edge (i, j) is added to the partially formed tree T' if T' $\cup$ {(i, j)} is also a tree and (i, j) is the minimum weighted edge which guarantees this property (with ties broken arbitrarily). The algorithm based on this idea, attributed to Prim and Dijkstra, is as follows.

*Algorithm* **SERIAL_MST(P-D)**

Input: The weight adjacency matrix W of G = <N, E>.

Output: An MST of G denoted by T = <N, E'> and the weight (cost) of T, i.e., the sum of the weights of all the edges of T — denoted by TW.

```
E' := ∅;
TW := 0;
N[1] := 0;
for i = 2 to n do
    N[i] := 1;
    D[i] := W[1, i]
od
while |E'| < n − 1 do
    select j such that D[j] = min{D[i] | N[i] ≠0};
    E' := E' ∪ {(j, N[j])};
    TW := TW + D[j];
    for i = 1 to n do
        if (N[i] ≠ 0) AND (W[i, j] < W[i, N[i]])
        then do
                N[i] := j;
                D[i] := W[i, j]
            od
        fi
    od
od
```

Algorithm SERIAL_MST(P-D) uses two auxiliary arrays N and D, in addition to the cost adjacency matrix W. These arrays hold, for each node, the nearest neighbor and the weight associated with the edge between these two nodes. This algorithm requires $n - 1$ iterations of its while-loop. At each iteration a new edge is added to the partially built tree and its total weight is incremented. The selection of the required edge can be performed in $O(n)$ time. Thus, algorithm SERIAL_MST(P-D) requires $O(n^2)$ time to find an MST of a weighted, connected graph G. Execution of the algorithm is illustrated in Figure 8.3.

We now present a parallel implementation of Prim-Dijkstra's serial algorithm on the EREW PRAM model. The version given here is adapted from Akl (1986, 1989). The algorithm is adaptive or self-reconfiguring in that the same algorithm works for a defined range of available processors for which the product of the parallel running time and the number of processors used remains constant. This product is $O(n^2)$ implying that the algorithm is cost-optimal, since the cost is the same as that for the best-known serial algorithm for this problem.

It is assumed that there are K processors denoted by $p_1, p_2, \ldots, p_K$ in the EREW PRAM, where $K = n^{1-a}$, for $0 < a < 1$. Each processor $p_i$ is assigned a distinct subset $N_i$ — of size $n^a$ — of the set of nodes N. The weight adjacency matrix W is stored in the shared memory. We have seen that algorithm SERIAL_MST(P-D) proceeds in $n - 1$ stages and that at each stage a new node — and hence a new edge — is added to the existing partial tree. The parallel version of this algorithm selects a new node as follows. Each processor selects from among

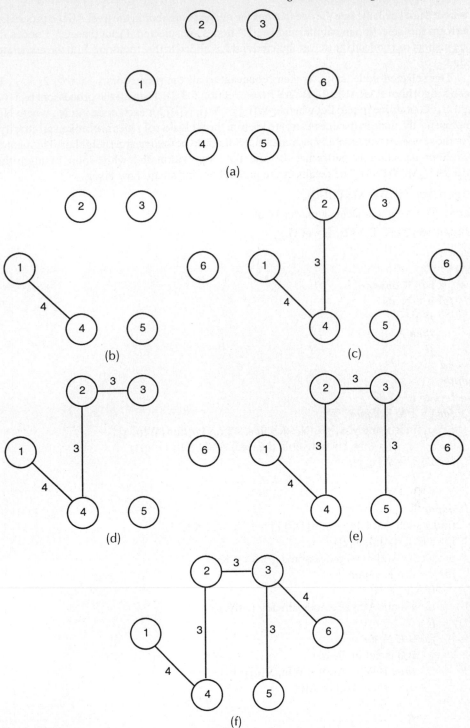

**Figure 8.3** The steps in the construction of an MST of the undirected weighted graph of Figure 8.1, using algorithm SERIAL_MST(P-D).

its nodes not yet in the tree the one that has the nearest neighbor in the tree. All the processors perform this selection in parallel and so $n^{1-a}$ nodes are selected. From these $n^{1-a}$ nodes the one nearest to a node in the tree is obtained and it is added to the tree along with the associated edge.

The selected node, say j, is then broadcast to all the processors $p_i$, i = 1, 2, . . . , K, using algorithm PARALLEL_BCAST (see Section 5.3.2). Then all the processors $p_i$, i = 1, 2, . . . , K, examine in parallel whether W[i, j] < W[i, N[i]] for each node i in $N_i$, where N[i] represents the node in the tree nearest to i before the inclusion of j (ties are broken arbitrarily). For those nodes i which satisfy the relation, j is made to be their nearest neighbor. This nearest neighbor selection is performed by the for-loop within the while-loop in algorithm SERIAL_MST(P-D). The details of the parallel algorithm are now given.

*Algorithm* **EREW_MST(P-D)**

Input: The weight adjacency matrix W of G = <N, E>.

Output: An MST T = <N, E'> of G.

E' := ∅;
N[1] := 0;
*for* j = 1 *to* K *dopar*
    *for* u ∈ $N_j$ *do*
        *if* u ≠ 1
        *then* N[u] := 1
        *fi*
    *od*
*odpar*
*for* i =1 *to* n − 1 *do*
    *for* j = 1 *to* K *dopar*
        $p_j$ finds x and y, x, y ∈ $N_j$ such that W[x, y] = min{W[p, q] |
            (p ∈ $N_j$ but not yet in the tree) AND (N[p] = q)};
        D[j] := W[x, y];
        A[j] := x;
        B[j] := y
    *odpar*
    find z such that D[z] = min{D[j] | j = 1, 2, . . . , K};
    E' := E' ∪ {A[z], B[z]};
    broadcast A[z] to all processors $p_i$, 1 ≤ i ≤ K;
    *for* j = 1 *to* K *dopar*
        *if* A[z] ∈ $N_j$
        *then* mark A[z] as a node already in the tree
        *fi*
        *for* u ∈ $N_j$ *do*
            *if* u is not in the tree
            *then if* W[u, A[z]] < W[u, N[u]]
                *then* N[u] := A[z]
                *fi*
            *fi*
        *od*
    *odpar*
*od*

## Complexity Analysis

The first parallel for-loop runs in $O(n^a)$ time since each processor $p_j$ performs $n^a$ assignments. The first parallel for-loop within the serial for-loop requires $O(n^a)$ time, since each processor performs $n^a - 1$ comparisons to obtain the minimum of $n^a$ numbers. The computation of the maximum of K numbers can be performed using algorithm EREW_MAXIMUM (see Section 5.2.2). We can modify this algorithm in order to find the minimum of K numbers within the same time and processor bounds. Thus, to compute the minimum of D[j], j = 1, 2, . . . , K, to determine the edge to be added to the partial tree requires $O(\log K) = O(\log n^{1-a}) \equiv O(\log n)$ time. To broadcast A[z] to all K processors, we use algorithm PARALLEL_BCAST (see Section 5.3.2). This also requires $O(\log K) \equiv O(\log n)$ time. The last parallel for-loop again takes $O(n^a)$ time when K processors are used in parallel. All other statements of the algorithm take constant time. Combining the complexities of all the steps, we find that the execution of the body of the main serial for-loop takes $O(n^a)$ time. Thus, the overall time complexity of algorithm EREW_MST(P-D) is $O(n^{1+a})$. Since the algorithm uses $K = n^{1-a}$ processors, its cost is $O(n^2)$.

## 8.2.3 TSC Algorithm

A parallel version of algorithm SERIAL_MST(P-D) on the TSC is presented in this section. It was originally proposed by Bentley (1980). Let us assume that there are n square processors in the TSC. We shall see later that the same time bound as for n square processors can also be achieved by using n/log n square processors. The n square processors assumption is made to simplify the presentation. The initialization is performed on the driver computer of the TSC. The values are transmitted to the square processors by pipelining. The time required to perform this step is $O(n)$.

On each iteration of the parallel algorithm, the triangle processors compute the next edge to be added to the partially built MST. Thus, each iterative step determines the minimum of n numbers in $O(\log n)$ time. To perform this computation, each triangle processor computes the minimum of the two numbers it receives from the previous level and broadcasts the result to the next level. During each iteration, the node nearest to the current partial MST is propagated down to the square processors in $O(\log n)$ steps. If W[i, j] < W[i, N[i]], then the square processor i updates N[i] to j and D[i] to W[i, j]. A complete description of the algorithm is given below. In the algorithm, we have shown explicitly the processes to be executed on the driver, square, and triangle processors. The processes to be executed on the circle processors simply broadcast the data they receive to the next level, and are not shown in the algorithm.

*Algorithm* **TSC_MST(P-D)**

Input: The weight adjacency matrix W of G = <N, E> on the driver computer.

Output: An MST T = <N, E'> of G stored on the driver computer.

```
start all processes;
process driver(d) is
    E' := ∅;
    count := 0;
```

```
    for each node i do
        if i = 1
        then do
                N[i] := 0;
                D[i] := ∞
            od
        else  do
                N[i] := 1;
                D[i] := W[1, i]
            od
        fi
        send (i, N[i], D[i]) to the topmost circle
    od
    loop
        receive (i, N[i], D[i]);
        E' := E' ∪ {i, N[i]};
        count := count + 1;
        if count < n − 1
        then send (i, N[i], D[i]) to the topmost circle
        else exit loop
        fi
    end
    terminate the algorithm
process square (p) is
    loop
        receive (i, N[i], D[i]);
        if N[i] ≠ 0
        then if i = p
            then do
                    N[p] := 0;
                    D[p] := ∞
                od
            else if W[p, i] < D[i]
                then do
                        N[p] := i;
                        D[p] := W[p, x]
                    od
                fi
            fi
        fi
        send (p, N[p], D[p]) to triangle processor
    end
process triangle (t) is
    loop
        (receive (i, N[i], D[i]) from left) // (receive (j, N[j], D[j]) from right);
```

*if* D[i] < D[j]
    *then* send (i, N[i], D[i])
    *else* send (j, N[j], D[j])
    *fi*
*end*

## Complexity Analysis

It is easy to verify that each iteration of algorithm TSC_MST(P-D) takes O(log n) time. O(log n) time is required to transmit data from the driver to the square processors through the circle processors. In addition, another O(log n) time is required to transmit data from the square processors back to the driver through the triangle processors. Every square and triangle processor takes constant time to execute its process. Since n − 1 iterations are required to obtain all the n − 1 edges of the MST, the algorithm requires O(n log n) time. Therefore, algorithm TSC_MST(P-D) runs in O(n log n) time using O(n) processors. The cost of the algorithm is O(n² log n), which is not optimal. However, we may use the technique introduced in Section 3.6.1 to reduce the number of processors without increasing its running time. Thus, algorithm TSC_MST(P-D) can be implemented within the time bound given above using only O(n/log n) processors. Clearly, this implementation leads to a cost optimal parallel MST algorithm on the TSC. The important features of this optimal implementation are as follows.

Instead of assigning a single node to each square processor, assign log n nodes to each of n/log n processors. Thus, during each iteration, every square processor now finds the minimum of log n nodes. This takes O(log n) time. The triangle processors find the minimum of O(n/log n) numbers. Thus, each iteration still takes O(log n) time and the overall time complexity of algorithm TSC_MST(P-D) when implemented on a TSC with O(n/log n) processors remains O(log n).

# 8.3 SINGLE-SOURCE SHORTEST PATHS

In this section we consider the single-source shortest paths problem, in which it is required to find the shortest or the minimum weighted paths from a specified node, called the source, to all other nodes in a weighted graph. We present parallel algorithms for the solution of this problem on the EREW PRAM model as well as on the TSC. Both parallel algorithms are obtained by parallelizing the well-known algorithm for the single-source shortest paths problem due to Dijkstra (1959). For convenience, we first briefly outline Dijkstra's serial algorithm.

The algorithm proceeds by setting labels to the nodes of the given graph. At each stage in the algorithm some nodes have permanent labels and others have temporary labels. The labels of the nodes are simply the weights of the minimum weighted paths from the source to the nodes concerned. Initially, a permanent label 0 is assigned to the source node, say s, and a temporary label ∞ to the remaining n − 1 nodes. Then in each stage another node is assigned a permanent label according to the following rules:

(a) Every node j which has not yet been permanently labeled is given a new temporary label with value

$$\min\{\text{old label of } j, \text{ old label of } i + W[i, j]\},$$

where i is the node which has been permanently labeled in the previous iteration, and W[i, j] is the weight associated with edge (i, j). If there is no edge (i, j), then W[i, j] is set to ∞, as usual.

(b) The minimum value among all the temporary labels is found, and this value is assigned as the permanent label of the corresponding node. In the case of a number of temporary labels being equal an arbitrary node is selected for permanent labeling.

These steps are repeated until all the nodes of the digraph have been assigned permanent labels. A more formal description of the algorithm is given below.

### Algorithm SERIAL_SSP

Input: A graph G = <N, E>, a source s ∈ N, and the non-negative weight associated with edge (i, j) as W[i, j], for all (i, j) ∈ E.

Output: The weight W[i] of the minimum weighted (or shortest) path from the source to every other node i ∈ N.

*for* i = 1 *to* n *do*
    S[i] := 0;
    D[i] := W[s, i]
*od*
*for* j = 2 *to* n − 1 *do*
    select x such that W[x] = min{D[y] | S[y] = 0};
    S[x] := 1;
    *for* i = 1 *to* n *do*
        *if* S[i] = 0
        *then* W[i] := min{D[i], D[x] + W[x, i]}
        *fi*
    *od*
*od*

The time taken by algorithm SERIAL_SSP is $O(n^2)$. Its execution is illustrated using an example in Figure 8.4. In the following two sections, we show efficient parallel implementations of this algorithm on both EREW PRAM and TSC.

## 8.3.1 EREW PRAM Algorithm

As in the previous section, let us assume that there are $K = n^{1-a}$ processors available in the EREW PRAM, where $0 < a < 1$. In the parallel version of the single-source shortest paths algorithm, each processor $p_i$ is assumed to be responsible for a subset $N_i$ of N, where $|N_i| = n^a$. That is, $N_i$ is assigned to processor $p_i$, $1 \leq i \leq K$. Clearly, $\cup_{1 \leq i \leq K} N_i = N$. It is assumed that the weight adjacency matrix W[i, j], i, j ∈ N is stored in the shared memory. Two arrays A and B are used to store the temporary labels. During each iteration, each processor $p_i$, $1 \leq i \leq K$, uses the array A and all K processors together use the array B. The details of the algorithm are presented on page 267-8.

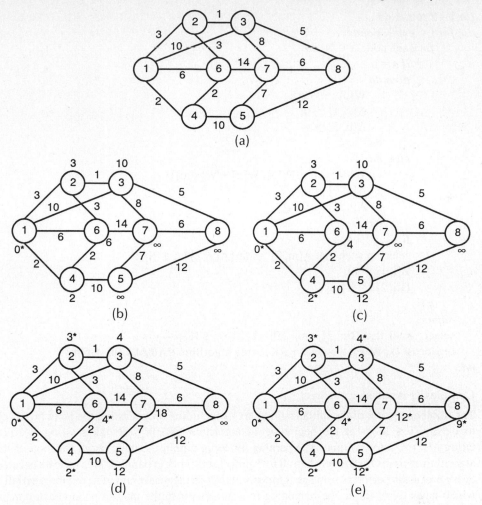

**Figure 8.4** (a) An arbitrary undirected weighted graph G; (b)–(e) the different stages in the execution of algorithm SERIAL_SSP which computes the single-source shortest paths of G with node 1 as the source node. The numbers beside the nodes are their labels. Labels with asterisks are permanent labels.

*Algorithm* **EREW_SSP**

Input: A positively edge-weighted graph $G = <N, E>$ with n nodes given in the form of its weight adjacency matrix W.

Output: The weight W[i] of the minimum weighted path from source s to node i for each node $i \in N$.

x := s;

W[x] := W[s] := 0;

broadcast (x, W[x]) to $p_i$, $1 \le i \le K$, using algorithm PARALLEL_BCAST;

*for* j = 2 *to* n-1 *do*

    *for* i = 1 *to* K *dopar*

        *for* each node u ∈ $N_i$ *do*

            *if* x = u

            *then do*

                    W[u] := W[x];

                    A[u, 1] := 0;

                    A[u, 2] := ∞

                *od*

            *else do*

                    W[u] := min{W[u], W[x] + W[x, u]};

                    A[u, 1] := u;

                    A[u, 2] := W[u]

                *od*

            *fi*

            select m such that A[m, 2] = min{A[u, 2] | u ∈ $N_i$};

            B[i, 1] := m;

            B[i, 2] := W[m]

    *od*

    *odpar*

    select x such that B[x, 2] = min{B[i, 2] | 1 ≤ i ≤ K};

    broadcast (x, W[x]) to $p_i$, 1 ≤ i ≤ K, using algorithm PARALLEL_BCAST

*od*

### Complexity Analysis

The implementation of the initialization part — including broadcasting the pairs (x, W[x]) to $p_i$, 1 ≤ i ≤ K — at the beginning of algorithm EREW_SSP takes O(log K), i.e., $O(\log n^{1-a}) \equiv O(\log n)$ time. The parallel for-loop, within the main serial for-loop of the algorithm, runs in $O(n^a)$ time when all $n^{1-a}$ processors work in parallel. This follows because every processor performs some assignments and finds the maximum of $n^a$ numbers serially, which takes $O(n^a)$ time. The remaining two statements in the main for-loop each require $O(n^{1-a})$, i.e., O(log n) time, using an EREW minimum finding algorithm and algorithm PARALLEL_BCAST of Chapter 5. Thus each execution of the body of the main for-loop requires $O(n^a)$ time. Since the for-loop is repeated O(n) times, the overall time complexity of algorithm EREW_SSP is $O(n^{1+a})$.

The cost of the algorithm is $O(n^2)$ which matches the time complexity of algorithm SERIAL_SSP. Also, this algorithm is adaptive in the sense that the time complexity depends on the number of processes available — which can vary within a certain range — while the cost of the algorithm remains unchanged.

## 8.3.2  TSC Algorithm

It is assumed that the TSC consists of P, 1 < P ≤ n square processors. In this algorithm, each square processor $p_i$, 1 ≤ i ≤ P is assigned a distinct subset $N_i$ of N of size n/P, such that $\cup_{1 \le i \le P} N_i = N$. It is assumed that n is divisible by P. More precisely, the data related to the nodes with indices in the range 1 to n/P are assigned to square processor $p_1$, the data related to the nodes with indices in the range $(n/P) + 1$ to $2(n/P)$ are assigned to processor $p_2$, and so on. As before, we denote the weight associated with an edge $(i, j) \in E$ of the given weighted graph $G = <N, E>$ by $W[i, j]$ and the weight of the minimum weighted path (shortest path) from source s to any node $i \in N$ by $W[i]$. It is assumed that, in each square processor $p_i$, for each node $u \in N_i$, the list $W[x, u]$, $\forall(x, u) \in E$ is available in the form of a sorted list $W[x_1, u], W[x_2, u], \ldots, W[x_a, u]$ satisfying $W[x_1, u] \geq W[x_2, u] \geq \ldots \geq W[x_a, u]$. When the algorithm terminates, the result $W[i]$, for all $i \in N$, is available on the driver computer.

### Algorithm TSC_SSP

Input: On each square processor $p_i$, $1 < i \leq P$, the weight $W[x, u]$, $\forall(x, u) \in E$ is available in the form of a sorted list such that $u \in N_i$.

Output: $W[i]$, $\forall x \in N$ on the driver computer.

```
start all processes;
process driver (d) is
    W[s] := 0;
    count := 0;
    send (s, 0) to the topmost circle;
    loop
        receive (i, W[i]);
        count := count + 1;
        if count < n − 1
        then send (i, W[i]) to the topmost circle
        else exit loop
        fi
    end
    terminate the algorithm
process square (pi) is
    loop
        receive (j, W[j]);
        for each node u ∈ Ni do
            if j = u
            then do
                    W(u) := ∞;
                    remove j from Ni
                od
            fi
            if Ni ≠ ∅
            then do
                    find a node u ∈ Ni such that
                        W[u] = min{W[u], W[j] + W[j, u]};
                    send (u, W[u]) to triangle processor
                od
            else send (0, ∞)
            fi
        od
    end
```

*process* triangle (t) *is*
   **loop**
      (receive (i, W[i]) from left) // (receive (j, W[j]) from right);
      *if* W[i] < W[j]
      *then* send (i, W[i])
      *else* send (j, W[j])
      *fi*
   **end**

### Complexity Analysis

From the description of algorithm TSC_SSP we see that, at each iteration the pairs (i, W[i]), $i \in N$, are broadcast by the driver (d), through the circle s to the computation nodes (square processors). This process takes $O(\log P)$ time since the TSC has P square processors. Each square processor requires $O(n/P)$ time in the worst case to execute the corresponding process which is performed in parallel by all of them. Finally, the triangle processors take $O(\log P)$ time to select the pair (i, W[i]), $i \in N$, which is then broadcast to the driver computer. Thus, the driver (d) receives (i, W[i]) for each $i \in N$ at time $O(n/P + \log P)$ after it initiates the computation. Since $(n - 1)$ iterations are required, the overall complexity of algorithm TSC_SSP is $O(n^2/P + n \log P)$ when p $(1 < P \leq n)$ square processors are employed.

The cost of algorithm TSC_SSP is $O(n^2)$ which is the same as the time complexity of algorithm SERIAL_SSP. The algorithm is also adaptive since it works for P, $1 < P \leq n$, square processors without any change in its cost.

## 8.4  ALL-PAIRS SHORTEST PATHS

This section deals with the problem of computing the shortest or the minimum weighted paths between all pairs of nodes of a graph. There are $n^2$ different pairs of nodes. However, the simple approach of applying a parallel single-source shortest paths algorithm n times, choosing a different source on each occasion, does not lead to an efficient parallel algorithm. The cost of such an algorithm is obviously n times that of EREW_SSP or TSC_SSP. Fast parallel algorithms have been developed for the all-pairs shortest paths problem using different models of parallel computation. In the following sections, we shall design and analyze parallel algorithms for this problem using the PRAM model as well as cube connected and perfect shuffle SIMD computers.

### 8.4.1  Algorithm for PRAM Models

We will first develop a general algorithm for solving the all-pairs shortest paths problem on the shared memory SIMD (PRAM) model and then analyze its complexity under two different memory access restrictions which give the complexities of the algorithm when implemented on a CREW PRAM and a CRCW PRAM. The algorithm is developed using a similar tree-merging technique to the one used in designing parallel algorithms for the graph search problems in Chapter 7.

Without loss of generality, we assume that G = <N, E> is a positive edge-weighted digraph without parallel edges and self-loops. An undirected weighted graph may be considered to be an equivalent weighted digraph if each edge $(i, j)$ of the undirected graph is replaced by two oppositely directed edges $(i, j)$ and $(j, i)$, and the same weight is assigned to each of these two edges as that of the replaced undirected edge. A k-tree is defined with reference to digraph G in a manner similar to that in Definition 7.8. For convenience, let us denote the weight associated with each edge $(x, y) \in E$ in G by $W(y \mid T(x, 0))$. The sum of the weights associated with each of the paths from x to y in tree $T(x, k)$ is denoted by $W(y \mid T(x, k))$. As for parallel graph search algorithms in Chapter 7, the parallel shortest paths algorithm begins with the 0-trees $T(x, 0)$, $\forall x \in N$, and, at the end of the tree-merging process, produces a tree $T(x, \lceil \log n \rceil)$ for each $x \in N$, with each tree being a shortest or minimum weighted path tree rooted at x, and containing all nodes of G reachable from x. The tree merging is carried out in such a manner that, at any stage k, the tree $T(x, k)$ obtained from the trees $T(x, k-1)$ and all $T(y, k-1)$, $y \in T(x, k-1)$, $0 < k \leq \lceil \log n \rceil$, must preserve the shortest path property defined as follows.

**Definition 8.1:** Given a pair of nodes y and z in a tree $T(x, k)$ such that $(y, z)$ is an edge in $G = <N, E>$ but $(y, z)$ does not belong to $T(x, k)$, then the tree $T(x, k)$ is said to preserve the shortest paths property if one of the following holds:

(i) $W(y \mid T(x, k)) + W(z \mid T(y, 0)) \geq W(z \mid T(x, k))$;

(ii) The path x to y in $T(x, k)$ consists of $2^k$ edges.

A k-tree that satisfies the shortest paths property is said to be a *k-spp-tree*. The algorithm given below has a structure similar to that of the algorithms developed for the graph searching problems.

*Algorithm* **ALL_PAIRS_SP**

Input: The tree $T(x, 0)$ for each $x \in N$, specified by parent$(y \mid T(x, 0))$ and $W(y \mid T(x, 0))$ for each $y \in N$.

Output: The shortest path tree $T(x, \lceil \log n \rceil)$ for each $x \in N$, specified by parent$(y \mid T(x, \lceil \log n \rceil))$ and $W(y \mid T(x, \lceil \log n \rceil))$ for each $y \in N$.

```
k := 0;
while k < ⌈log n⌉ do
    p := 0;
    while p < ⌈log log n⌉ do
        for x = 1 to n dopar
            for y = 1 to n dopar
                for z = (p⌈n/log log n⌉ + 1) to (p + 1)⌈n/log log n⌉ dopar
                    if (z = x) AND (parent(y | T(x, k)) ≠ ∅)
                    then Mₓᵏ(y, z) := W(y | T(x, k))
                    else if (z ∈ T(x, k)) AND (parent(y | T(z, k)) ≠ ∅)
                            then Mₓᵏ(y, z) := W(z | T(x, k)) + W(y | T(z, k))
                            else Mₓᵏ(y, z) := ∞
                            fi
                    fi
                odpar
            odpar
        odpar
```

            p := p + 1
    *od*
    *for* x = 1 *to* n *dopar*
        *for* y = 1 *to* n *dopar*
                find $z_m$ such that $M_x{}^k(y, z_m)$ = min$\{M_x{}^k(y, z) \mid z = 1, 2, \ldots, n\}$
                *if* $M_x{}^k(y, z_m) \neq \infty$
                *then do*
                            parent(y | T(x, k + 1)) := parent(y | T($z_m$, k));
                            W(y | T(x, k)) := $M_x{}^k(y, z_m)$
                    *od*
            *fi*
        *odpar*
    *odpar*
    k : = k + 1
*od*

As far as the correctness of algorithm ALL_PAIRS_SP is concerned, observe that, since every path between a pair of nodes of G consists of at most n − 1 edges, the tree T(x, $\lceil \log n \rceil$), for each node x ∈ N, produced by the algorithm must contain all nodes of G reachable from x. Finally, it can easily be shown by induction that the tree T(x, $\lceil \log n \rceil$), ∀ x ∈ N, preserves the shortest paths property. The execution of algorithm ALL_PAIRS_SP is illustrated using an example in Figure 8.5.

## Complexity Analysis

**(i) CREW PRAM:** The body of the main while-loop of algorithm ALL_PAIRS_SP consists of another while-loop for initializing n matrices each of size n × n, and a nested parallel for-loop. Assuming that the computational model is a CREW PRAM, we can easily verify that the inner while-loop runs in O(log log n) time when O($n^2 \lceil n/\log \log n \rceil$) processors are employed. Using the parallel algorithm for finding the minimum of n elements which requires O(log n) time using n processors, the nested for-loop can be implemented in O(log n) time using O($n^3$) processors. Thus, a single execution of the body of the main while-loop requires O(log n) time when O($n^3$) processors are used. Since this while-loop is repeated $\lceil \log n \rceil$ times the overall time complexity of the shortest paths algorithm on the CREW PRAM is O($\log^2 n$) when O($n^3$) processors are employed.

**(ii) CRCW PRAM:** If we consider the computational model to be a CRCW PRAM, then the implementation of all steps of algorithm ALL_PAIRS_SP, except the nested for-loop, will remain the same as those for the CREW PRAM. The nested for-loop can be implemented using the fast and efficient minimum finding algorithm on the CRCW PRAM due to Shiloach and Vishkin (1981). This algorithm runs in O(log log n) time when O($\lceil n/\log \log n \rceil$) processors are employed. Thus, on the CRCW PRAM, a single execution of the body of the main while-loop requires O(log log n) time when O($n^2 \lceil n/\log \log n \rceil$) processors are used. Therefore, the overall time complexity of algorithm ALL_PAIRS_SP, when implemented on the CRCW PRAM, is O(log n log log n) with O($n^2 \lceil n/\log \log n \rceil$) processors. Using the constant time algorithm for finding the minimum (maximum), algorithm ALL_PAIRS_SP can even be implemented in O(log n) time. However, this implementation requires O($n^4$) processors.

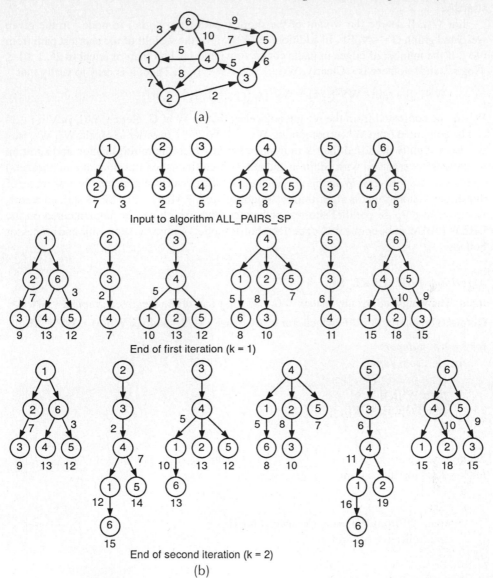

**Figure 8.5** (a) An arbitrary weighted directed graph G with n = 6 nodes; (b) construction of the trees T(x, 1) and T(x, 2) from the trees T(x, 0), x = 1, 2, . . . , 6, using algorithm ALL_PAIRS_SP.

## 8.4.2 Algorithms for Other Parallel Models

In this section, we will show that the matrix multiplication algorithm can be suitably modified to construct a parallel algorithm for solving the all-pairs shortest paths problem. The parallel algorithm discussed here follows the work of Dekel et al. (1981). It is based on the following strategy.

Let $W(i, j)$ denote the weight of the shortest path from node i to node j in the given weighted graph $G = <N, E>$. In addition, let $W^k[i, j]$ be the weight of the shortest path from i to j, if the number of edges in paths connecting i and j is less than or equal to $2^k$, $1 \le k \le \lceil \log n \rceil$, and $\infty$ otherwise. Clearly, $W(i, j) = W^{\lceil \log n \rceil}[i, j]$. Then, it is easy to verify that

$$W^k[i, j] = \min\{ W^{k/2}[i, x] + W^{k/2}[x, j] \mid x = 1, 2, \ldots, n\}.$$

$W^1$ can be computed from the weight adjacency matrix W of G. Hence, $W(i, j)$, $\forall i, j \in N$ can be computed from $W^1$ by computing $W^2, \ldots, W^{\lceil \log n \rceil}$. In order to obtain $W^2$, $W^4$, etc., we use a slightly modified matrix multiplication in which the multiplication and addition operations are replaced with addition and min (which finds the minimum of two numbers) operations, respectively. With this special matrix multiplication algorithm, the remainder of the all-pairs shortest paths algorithm is straightforward. PARALLEL_SP, described below, is a general-purpose parallel shortest paths algorithm which can be implemented on the CREW PRAM, cube connected, or perfect shuffle models within the same time and processor bounds.

### *Algorithm* PARALLEL_SP

Input: The weight adjacency matrix $W[i, j]$, $1 \le i, j \le n$, of the weighted graph $G = <N, E>$.

Output: The matrix $W^{\lceil \log n \rceil}$ which, for every pair $i, j \in N$, satisfies $W(i, j) = W^{\lceil \log n \rceil}[i, j]$.

*for* i = 1 *to* n *dopar*
   *for* j = 1 *to* n *dopar*
      *if* i ≠ j AND $W[i, j] = 0$
      *then* $W^1[i, j] := \infty$
      *else* $W^1[i, j] := W[i, j]$
      *fi*
   *odpar*
*odpar*
*for* k = 1 *to* $\lceil \log (n - 1) \rceil$ *do*
   $q := 2^{k-1}$;
   $r := 2^k$;
   compute $W^r$ from $W^q$ using the special matrix
      multiplication algorithm
*od*

### Complexity Analysis

In order to analyze the complexity of this algorithm, we need to specify the particular parallel model of computation to be used in the implementation of algorithm PARALLEL_SP. Observe that the complexity of this algorithm is primarily dependent on the complexity of the special matrix multiplication algorithm. Incidentally, this algorithm can be implemented on each of the CREW PRAM, cube connected and perfect shuffle models in $O(\log n)$ time using $O(n^3)$ processors (see Chapter 6). Thus, algorithm PARALLEL_SP runs on each of these computational models in $O(\log^2 n)$ time when $O(n^3)$ processors are employed.

# 8.5 ANALYZING ACTIVITY NETWORKS

Activity networks represent one of the most successful applications of directed acyclic graphs (DAGs) in the planning and scheduling of large complicated projects. A project can be viewed as a collection of well-defined, nonoverlapping individual jobs or tasks called activities. Because of technological restrictions some activities must be completed before initiation of some other activities, i.e., there is a precedence relationship among the various activities. Moreover, each activity also requires a certain amount of time which is referred to as the duration of the activity. A weighted DAG $G = <N, E>$ can be used to represent an activity network in which each edge represents an activity and the weight associated with that edge represents the duration of the activity. The nodes represent the beginning and end of activities and are called the events of the project. Such an activity network is referred to as an activity-on-edge (AOE) network. An AOE network consists of a single source event (or node) denoted by s (say) and a single destination or terminal event (or node) denoted by f, representing the project initiation and the project completion, respectively. AOE networks are sometimes called PERT (Program Evaluation and Review Technique), project, or event networks (Deo 1974; Gillett 1976).

In order to analyze an AOE network we need to perform the following:

(a) Check for directed circuits in the AOE network. The presence of a directed circuit implies that the AOE network is infeasible because, in this case, a situation arises in which at least one pair of activities have precedence over each other and neither of the activities can be initiated. When it has been established that the AOE network is feasible, its events are arranged in topological order.

(b) Compute the earliest and latest start times for each activity represented by an edge of the AOE network, and identify the critical activities.

The earliest start time (EST) of an activity $(i, j) \in E$ in an AOE network $G = <N, E>$ is the earliest possible time at which that activity can be initiated. This is simply the weight of the longest path from the source event s to the event i. The latest start time (LST) of an activity is the latest allowable time at which that activity can be initiated without affecting the project duration. The difference between the LST and EST for each activity $(i, j) \in E$ gives the maximum amount of time by which the activity $(i, j)$ can be delayed without affecting the project and is referred to as the slack time (ST) for activity $(i, j)$. The activities for which the slack time is zero, i.e., the activities which must be initiated at the earliest possible time, are called the critical activities. A delay in initiating a critical activity affects the project by increasing its duration.

In Section 8.5.1 we consider the problem of the topological ordering of the events of an AOE network on an unbounded CRCW PRAM model. Then, in Sections 8.5.2 and 8.5.3 respectively, we analyze AOE networks in the context of both unbounded and bounded PRAM models.

## 8.5.1 Topological Ordering Algorithm

The standard serial topological ordering algorithm, which has time complexity $O(n + e)$ terminates when a directed circuit, if there is one, is detected during the ordering process; otherwise it returns the topological order for each event (node) of the AOE network (DAG) (see, e.g., Horowitz and Sahni 1978). However, the parallel algorithm we are designing assumes that the given digraph for which the topological ordering is to be performed is a DAG. In order to ensure that the given digraph is a DAG before proceeding to the topological ordering of its nodes, we check, as a preprocessing step, whether there is a directed circuit in the digraph or not. An outline of the algorithm is given below where we assume that the computational model is a CRCW PRAM.

The algorithm uses the reachability matrix $R[1 : n, 1 : n]$ of the digraph which can be obtained from its adjacency matrix $A[1 : n, 1 : n]$ using the repeated squares method (see Section 7.4.1.2). The computation of the reachability matrix requires $O(\log n)$ Boolean matrix multiplications and can be performed in $O(\log n)$ time using $O(n^3)$ processors on the CRCW PRAM. We also compute the transpose $A^T[1 : n, 1 : n]$ of the adjacency matrix $A[1 : n, 1 : n]$, which takes $O(1)$ time with $O(n^2)$ processors.

After obtaining both R and $A^T$ for the given digraph G, we examine for each pair of i and j, i, j $\in$ N, the entries $R[i, j]$ and $A^T[i, j]$. If both $R[i, j]$ and $A^T[i, j]$ are unity for a pair i, j $\in$ N then there is a circuit of length $\geq 2$ with i and j as two of its nodes. Thus, a digraph G is a DAG if for each pair of i and j, i, j $\in$ N, at least one of $R[i, j]$, or $A^T[i, j]$ is zero. From this discussion, we have the following theorem.

**Theorem 8.1:** A digraph G = <N, E> can be tested for the occurrence of circuits in time $O(\log n)$ with $O(n^3)$ processors on the CRCW PRAM model.

Assuming that the given digraph G = <N, E> is a DAG, we now design a parallel topological ordering algorithm on the CRCW PRAM model. A topological ordering of the nodes of a DAG is a linear ordering of the nodes with the property that if i is a predecessor of j in the DAG, then i precedes j in the linear ordering. The idea on which our parallel algorithm is based is to find the number of nodes that are reachable from each node of G. These nodes are then sorted into n buckets so that a node i $\in$ N is placed in cell i of bucket j if j nodes are reachable from node i. The buckets can be implemented easily in a two-dimensional array $B[1 : n, 1 : n]$, where each column represents a unique bucket. Moreover, each of the n elements of a bucket represents a unique cell. Thus, cell i of bucket j can be referred to as $B[i, j]$. Initially, a score 0 is assigned to each cell of each of the n buckets. Placing a node in a cell is indicated by assigning a score 1 to the cell. Finally, the scores assigned to the cells of a bucket are updated in parallel to the partial sum of the scores in all preceding buckets and all preceding cells in the same bucket including the one being updated. That is, for each pair i and j, $1 \leq i, j \leq n$, $B[i, j]$ is updated as

$$B[i, j] = \sum_{1 \leq y \leq j-1} \sum_{1 \leq x \leq n} B[x, y] + \sum_{1 \leq z \leq i} B[z, j].$$

The topological order for each node i $\in$ N is then computed from the updated score of the corresponding cell. An outline of the complete algorithm is given below.

*Algorithm* **CRCW_TOP_ORDER**

Input: The adjacency matrix $A[1 : n, 1 : n]$ of the given DAG G = <N, E>.

Output: Topological order TOP[i] for each node i $\in$ N in G.

obtain the reachability matrix R[1 : n, 1 : n] of G;
*for* i = 1 *to* n *dopar*

$$count(i) := \sum_{1 \le j \le n} R[i, j]$$

*odpar*
*for* i = 1 *to* n *dopar*
   *for* j = 1 *to* n *dopar*
      B[i, j] := 0
   *odpar*
*odpar*
*for* i = 1 *to* n *dopar*
   *if* count(i) = j
   *then* B[i, j] := 1
   *fi*
*odpar*
*for* j = 1 *to* n *dopar*
   *for* i = 1 *to* n *dopar*

$$B[i, j] := \sum_{1 \le x \le i} B[x, j]$$

   *odpar*
*odpar*
*for* j = 1 *to* n *dopar*

$$C[j] := \sum_{1 \le y \le j} B[n, y]$$

*odpar*
*for* i = 1 *to* n *dopar*
   *for* j = 1 *to* n *dopar*
      B[i, j] := C[j − 1] + B[i, j]
   *odpar*
*odpar*
*for* i = 1 *to* n *dopar*
   PSUM[i] := B[i, count(i)];
   TOP[i] := n − PSUM[i] +1
*odpar*

The following argument is the basis for the correctness of the algorithm. If node i precedes node j in the DAG G, then it is clear that count(i) > count(j) which implies that PSUM[i] > PSUM[j] and hence TOP[i] < TOP[j]. This agrees exactly with the definition of the topological ordering of the nodes of a DAG. An arbitrary DAG with n = 10, and the corresponding array B before and after the updating process are shown in Figure 8.6.

### Complexity Analysis

We have seen that the reachability matrix R[1 : n, 1 : n] of a DAG G can be obtained in $O(\log n)$ time using $O(n^3)$ processors. Each of the first and fifth parallel for-loops takes

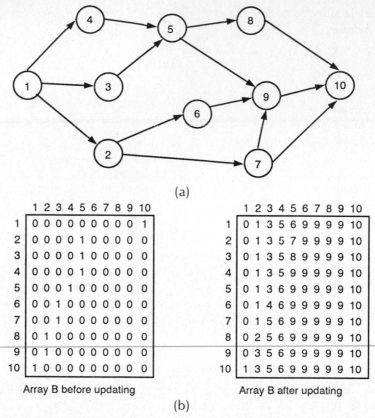

(a)

|   | 1 2 3 4 5 6 7 8 9 10 |
|---|---|
| 1 | 0 0 0 0 0 0 0 0 0 1 |
| 2 | 0 0 0 0 1 0 0 0 0 0 |
| 3 | 0 0 0 0 1 0 0 0 0 0 |
| 4 | 0 0 0 0 1 0 0 0 0 0 |
| 5 | 0 0 0 1 0 0 0 0 0 0 |
| 6 | 0 0 1 0 0 0 0 0 0 0 |
| 7 | 0 0 1 0 0 0 0 0 0 0 |
| 8 | 0 1 0 0 0 0 0 0 0 0 |
| 9 | 0 1 0 0 0 0 0 0 0 0 |
| 10 | 1 0 0 0 0 0 0 0 0 0 |

Array B before updating

|   | 1 2 3 4 5 6 7 8 9 10 |
|---|---|
| 1 | 0 1 3 5 6 9 9 9 9 10 |
| 2 | 0 1 3 5 7 9 9 9 9 10 |
| 3 | 0 1 3 5 8 9 9 9 9 10 |
| 4 | 0 1 3 5 9 9 9 9 9 10 |
| 5 | 0 1 3 6 9 9 9 9 9 10 |
| 6 | 0 1 4 6 9 9 9 9 9 10 |
| 7 | 0 1 5 6 9 9 9 9 9 10 |
| 8 | 0 2 5 6 9 9 9 9 9 10 |
| 9 | 0 3 5 6 9 9 9 9 9 10 |
| 10 | 1 3 5 6 9 9 9 9 9 10 |

Array B after updating

(b)

**Figure 8.6** (a) An arbitrary DAG with n = 10 nodes; (b) array B[1 : 10, 1 : 10] corresponding to DAG G before and after updating.

$O(\log n)$ time with $O(n^2)$ processors. The second and the sixth parallel for-loops require $O(1)$ time when $O(n^2)$ processors are employed. Each of the third and seventh parallel for-loops runs in $O(1)$ time with $O(n)$ processors. The fourth parallel for-loop for updating the scores of all $n^2$ cells requires $O(\log n)$ time and $O(n^3)$ processors. Therefore, the overall time complexity of algorithm CRCW_TOP_ORDER is $O(\log n)$ when $O(n^3)$ processors are used.

## 8.5.2 Analyzing Activity Networks on Unbounded PRAM Models

Analysis of an activity (AOE) network consists in finding (i) the project duration; (ii) the earliest start time EST(i, j); (iii) the latest start time LST(i, j); and (iv) the slack time ST(i, j), for each activity (i, j) ∈ E of the AOE network G = <N, E>. Finally, each activity (i, j) ∈ E for which ST(i, j) is zero is identified as a critical activity. The serial algorithm for this problem requires $O(n + e)$ time. For illustrative purposes, let us consider the AOE network of Figure 8.7 representing a hypothetical project. The project duration is 18 units, which is the maximum weighted, or the longest path, from the source node s to the terminal node f. The earliest start time EST(i, j), for each activity (i, j) ∈ E, is the weight of the maximum weighted path from node s to node i of the AOE network. Thus, to obtain the project duration

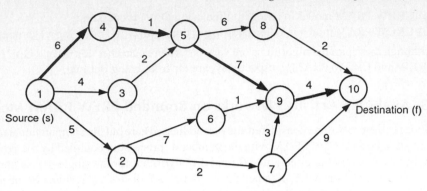

**Figure 8.7**  AOE network of a hypothetical project. The critical activities are shown by bold lines.

and the EST(i, j), $\forall$ (i, j) $\in$ E, we modify the all-pairs shortest paths algorithm of Section 8.4.1 to compute the weights of the maximum weighted or longest paths between every pair of nodes. The modifications necessary are straightforward and hence omitted. Thus, as an extension of results of Section 8.4.1, we have the following results:

   (i) computation of the all-pairs longest paths on the CREW PRAM requires $O(\log^2 n)$ time when $O(n^3)$ processors are employed;

   (ii) the all-pairs longest paths algorithm can be implemented to run on the CRCW PRAM in $O(\log n \log \log n)$ time with $O(n^2 \lceil n/\log \log n \rceil)$ processors.

Thus, both the project duration and EST(i, j), $\forall$ (i, j) $\in$ E, can be obtained in $O(\log^2 n)$ (resp. $O(\log n \log \log n)$) time with $O(n^3)$ (resp. $O(n^2 \lceil n/\log \log n \rceil)$) processors on the CREW PRAM (resp. CRCW PRAM) model.

When EST(i, j) is available for each activity (i, j) $\in$ E, the latest start time LST(i, j), (i, j) $\in$ E, can readily be computed using the following relation

$$LST(i, j) = MWP(s, f) - MWP(j, f) - W[i, j],$$

where MWP(i, j) denotes the weight of the maximum weighted path from event i to event j of the AOE network. Thus, LST(i, j), (i, j) $\in$ E, can be computed in constant time using O(e) processors on both CREW and CRCW PRAM models using the relation above, when the other parameters are known. It now remains only to identify the critical activities of the AOE network. This is easily done by computing the slack times ST(i, j), for each activity (i, j) $\in$ E using the following relation

$$ST(i, j) = LST(i, j) - EST(i, j).$$

Thus, the critical activities of the AOE network can be identified in O(1) time with O(e) processors on both CREW and CRCW models when both EST(i, j) and LST(i, j), for each (i, j) $\in$ E, are known. Therefore, the parallel algorithm described above for analyzing the AOE network has the same time and processor bounds as those for the all-pairs longest paths problem. In summary, an AOE network can be analyzed on an unbounded

(i) CREW PRAM model in $O(\log^2 n)$ time using $O(n^3)$ processors;

(ii) CRCW PRAM model in $O(\log n \log \log n)$ time with $O(n^2 \lceil n/\log \log n \rceil)$ processors.

Although these parallel algorithms are very fast, their costs $O(n^3 \log^2 n)$ and $O(n^3 \log n)$ for CREW and CRCW PRAMs, respectively, are far from being optimal.

### 8.5.3  Analyzing Activity Networks on Bounded EREW PRAM Model

The same problem as the one considered above is addressed here but the computational model is assumed to be an EREW PRAM with the number of processors bounded by the problem size n. For this we turn our attention to the parallel algorithm for the single-source shortest paths problem of Section 8.3.1, obtained by parallelizing Dijkstra's algorithm. Some minor modifications to this algorithm produce the single-source longest paths algorithm which has the same time and processor bounds, i.e., $O(n^{1+a})$ time with $K = n^{1-a}$ processors, where $0 < a < 1$.

The project duration and the earliest start time EST(i, j), for each activity $(i, j) \in E$ can be obtained on a bounded EREW PRAM in $O(n^{1+a})$ time using $n^{1-a}$ processors, where $0 < a < 1$. When EST(i, j) is available for each activity $(i, j) \in E$, the latest start time LST(i, j), $\forall (i, j) \in E$, can be computed using an algorithm similar to the one for solving the single-source longest paths problem. In this case, unlike the single-source shortest (longest) paths algorithm, computation starts at the destination event f and proceeds towards the source event s. More precisely, this algorithm computes LST(i, j) for each activity $(i, j) \in E$ using the following relation.

$$\text{LST}(i, j) = \begin{cases} W[f] - W[i, f], & \text{for } j = f, \\ \min\{\text{LST}(j, k) - W[i, j]) \mid (j, k) \in E\}, & \text{for } j \neq f. \end{cases}$$

The details of the algorithm are left as an exercise. It is easy to see that this algorithm also achieves the same time bound, using an identical number of processors, as the single-source longest paths algorithm. Thus, AOE networks can be analyzed on a bounded EREW PRAM model in $O(n^{1+a})$ time with $K = n^{1-a}$ processors, where $0 < a < 1$. Although the parallel algorithm on the bounded EREW PRAM described above is not very fast, its cost is close to being optimal.

## 8.6  BIBLIOGRAPHIC NOTES

Several parallel algorithms for computing a minimum spanning tree of a weighted, connected, undirected graph have been reported in the literature. These are obtained by parallelizing one or other of the three classical algorithms: Sollin's algorithm (Sollin 1977), Prim-Dijkstra's algorithm (Prim 1957; Dijkstra 1959), and Kruskal's algorithm (Kruskal 1956). In Section 2, we presented the parallelized versions of the algorithms of Sollin and Prim-Dijkstra using Savage and Ja' Ja' (1981), Akl (1986, 1989), and Bentley (1980). Other important references to parallel minimum spanning tree algorithms include Hirschberg (1982), Chin et al. (1982), Nath and Maheswari (1982), Yeh and Lee (1984), Kucera (1982), Levitt and Kautz (1972), Deo and Yoo (1981), and Kwan and Ruzzo (1984). In particular, the algorithms of Hirschberg, Chin et al., Nath and Maheswari, and Yeh and Lee are obtained by parallelizing Sollin's minimum spanning tree algorithm. The parallel algorithms of

Kucera, and Levitt and Kautz are based on the ideas of Kruskal's serial algorithm. Deo and Yoo have given parallelizations of the Sollin and Prim-Dijkstra algorithms. The algorithms of Kwan and Ruzzo are obtained by parallelizing all three classical serial algorithms.

Savage and Ja' Ja' (1981), and Nath and Maheswari (1982) based their parallel minimum spanning tree algorithms on the connected components algorithm of Hirschberg (1976). On the CREW PRAM model, Savage and Ja' Ja''s algorithm achieves a time complexity of $O(\log^2 n)$ using $O(n^2)$ processors (see Section 8.2.1) while, on the EREW PRAM model, Nath and Maheswari showed that the minimum spanning tree can be computed in $O(\log^2 n)$ time with $O(n^2/\log n)$ processors. Chin et al. (1982) modified Hirschberg's connected components algorithm to run in $O(\log^2 n)$ time using $O(n\lceil n/\log^2 n\rceil)$ processors. This finally leads to a parallel minimum spanning tree algorithm having the same time and processor bounds as those for the modified connected components algorithm.

On the CRCW PRAM model, Kucera's parallel minimum spanning tree algorithm (Kucera 1982) runs in $O(\log n)$ time but requires $O(n^5)$ processors. However, on the same model Hirschberg (1982) presented an $O(\log n)$ time parallel algorithm for the same problem using only $O(n^3)$ processors.

Parallel minimum spanning tree algorithms on the TSC have been developed by Bentley (1980), and Yeh and Lee (1984). Bentley's algorithm takes $O(\log n)$ time when $O(n/\log n)$ processors are available, while the algorithm due to Yeh and Lee runs in $O(n^2/P)$ time with $P$ $(1 \le P \le n)$ processing elements. Section 8.2.3 is based on the ideas presented in Bentley (1980).

Levitt and Kautz (1972) implemented Kruskal's algorithm, which has time complexity of $O(n^2)$ with $O(n^2)$ processors on a systolic array. Deo and Yoo (1981) present two parallel algorithms for the minimum spanning tree problem on an MIMD machine. The algorithm obtained by parallelizing Sollin's algorithm requires $O(n^2 \log n/P)$ time with $P \le n$ processors whereas that obtained by parallelizing the Prim-Dijkstra algorithm runs in $O(n^{1.5})$ time using $O(n^{0.5})$ processors.

Kwan and Ruzzo (1984) have developed parallel algorithms for finding minimum spanning trees using the three different schemes on the CREW PRAM model. The time complexities of all three algorithms have been shown to be $O((e \log n)/P)$, where the constraints on the number of processors $P$ for the three different cases are, respectively, as follows: $P \log P \le (e \log n)/n$; $P \le \log n$; and $P \le e/\log n$. Additional references on parallel minimum spanning tree algorithms include Atallah and Kosaraju (1984), Awerbuch and Shiloach (1983), Doshi and Varman (1987), Reif (1982), and Savage (1977).

Parallel algorithms for the single-source shortest paths problem reported in the literature are based on the parallelization of one or other of two classical serial algorithms: one due to Dijkstra (1959), and the other due to Moore (1957). The parallel algorithms on the EREW PRAM and the TSC for this problem, presented in Section 8.3, are obtained by parallelizing Dijkstra's serial algorithm. The presentation is based on Mateti and Deo (1982), and Chaudhuri (1990a). Mateti and Deo have presented the parallelized versions of both Dijkstra's and Moore's algorithms on machines as varied as array processors, MIMD machines and TSC. The time complexities of the parallel algorithms range from $O(n \log n)$ to $O(n)$ when unbounded parallelism is assumed. Other references to the parallel single-source shortest paths algorithms include Paige and Kruskal (1985), and Yoo (1983).

The all-pairs shortest paths problem has been investigated by Dekel et al. (1981), Kucera (1982), Hirschberg (1982), Levitt and Kautz (1972), Ghosh and Bhattacharjee (1984), and

Chaudhuri (1988). In particular, Dekel et al. have proposed parallel algorithms for the solution of this problem on both cube connected and perfect shuffle computers. All of these algorithms achieve $O(\log^2 n)$ time bound with $O(n^3)$ processors. Section 8.4.2 is based on the ideas presented in Dekel et al. (1981). The parallel algorithm in Kucera (1982) uses the CRCW PRAM model and computes the all-pairs shortest paths in $O(\log n)$ time when $O(n^4)$ processors are available. The same result has also been obtained by Hirschberg (Hirschberg 1982). Levitt and Kautz (1972) have developed a parallel algorithm for the same problem which runs in $O(n)$ time on the systolic array model. On the CREW PRAM model, Ghosh and Bhattacharjee proposed an $O(\log^2 n)$ time parallel algorithm with $O(n^3)$ processors for the all-pairs shortest paths problem. It has been shown by Chaudhuri (1988), using a similar idea to that of Ghosh and Bhattacharjee (1984), that the all-pairs shortest paths problem can be solved on the CRCW PRAM model in $O(\log d \log \log n)$ time using $O(n^2 \lceil n/\log \log n \rceil)$ processors, where $d \le n - 1$ is the graph diameter. Section 8.4.1 is based on the ideas presented by Ghosh and Bhattacharjee (1984), and Chaudhuri (1988).

Other references to all-pairs shortest paths algorithms in the literature include Arjomandi (1975), Savage (1977), Deo et al. (1980), and Paige and Kruskal (1985). The reader is also referred to Quinn and Deo (1984), and Moitra and Iyengar (1987) each of which includes a survey of parallel minimum spanning tree and shortest paths algorithms.

Parallel algorithms for analyzing AOE networks on a number of different models of computation are described in Dekel et al. (1981), Chaudhuri and Ghosh (1986), and Chaudhuri (1988, 1990a, 1990b). Dekel et al. have proposed parallel algorithms for the solution of this problem which works on both perfect shuffle and cube connected computers. The time complexity of their algorithm is $O(\log^2 n)$ with $O(n^3)$ processors. Chaudhuri and Ghosh proposed a parallel algorithm for the same problem on the CRCW PRAM model that requires $O(\log d \log \log n)$ time with $O(n^3)$ processors. In Chaudhuri (1988), it has been shown that the same time bound can also be achieved by using $O(n^2 \lceil n/\log \log n \rceil)$ processors on the CRCW PRAM model. In Section 8.5.1, we presented a parallel algorithm to test the feasibility of an AOE network. This parallel algorithm and the parallel algorithm for topological ordering of the events of the AOE network are adapted from Chaudhuri and Ghosh (1986). Both of these algorithms run in $O(\log n)$ time using $O(n^3)$ processors on the CRCW PRAM model. On the same model, another parallel topological ordering algorithm due to Kucera (1982) also runs in $O(\log n)$ time but requires $O(n^4)$ processors. A parallel algorithm for analyzing AOE networks is described in Chaudhuri (1990a) that runs in $O(n^{1+a})$ time with $O(n^{1-a})$ processors on a bounded EREW PRAM model, where a $(0 < a < 1)$ depends on the number of processors available. An algorithm for the same problem on the TSC is presented in Chaudhuri (1990b). Sections 8.5.2 and 8.5.3 are based on the ideas in Chaudhuri and Ghosh (1986), and Chaudhuri (1988, 1990a).

A parallel algorithm for finding maximum flow in a directed, weighted graph is presented in Shiloach and Vishkin (1982). The time complexity of this algorithm is $O(n^3(\log n)/P)$, where $P$ $(P \le n)$ is the number of processors used on the CRCW PRAM model. It has been shown in Goldschlager et al. (1982) that the maximum flow problem is log-space complete for $P$ which gives strong evidence that a polylogarithmic time parallel algorithm for this problem is not possible. Parallel algorithms for the maximum capacity path problem are presented in Chen and Feng (1973), and Chen (1975). Quinn and Deo (1984) contains a number of references to parallel algorithms for a related problem — the traveling salesman problem.

# 8.7 EXERCISES

8.7.1 Design an O(log n) time parallel algorithm for the minimum spanning tree problem on a CRCW PRAM. What is its processor complexity?

8.7.2 Design a minimum spanning tree algorithm for a TSC with P square processors, where $1 < P \leq n$.

8.7.3 Show that the minimum spanning tree of a weighted undirected graph can be obtained in O(n) time on a two-dimensional mesh connected SIMD computer having $n^2$ processors (Atallah and Kosaraju 1984).

8.7.4 Give an example of a weighted undirected graph in which Sollin's algorithm requires only a single iteration to find a minimum spanning tree. Also give an example in which $\lceil \log n \rceil$ iterations are required.

8.7.5 Discuss how Kruskal's minimum spanning tree algorithm can be implemented on a systolic array (Levitt and Kautz 1972).

8.7.6 Design a single-source shortest paths algorithm on an MIMD computer by parallelizing Dijkstra's algorithm (Mateti and Deo 1982).

8.7.7 Modify algorithm PARALLEL_SP of Section 8.4.2 to provide not only the weight of the shortest path between every pair of nodes but also a list of the edges on the shortest path.

8.7.8 Design a systolic algorithm for the all-pairs shortest paths problem.

8.7.9 Design a CREW PRAM algorithm for computing weights of the longest paths between every pair of nodes in a weighted directed acyclic graph. Analyze its complexity. What would be the complexity if the same algorithm is implemented on a CRCW PRAM model using the same number of processors?

8.7.10 Develop an efficient algorithm for the single-source longest paths problem on an EREW PRAM model as suggested in Section 8.5.3.

8.7.11 Completely develop the algorithm for computing the latest start time (LST) for each activity of an AOE network based on the ideas presented in Section 8.5.3.

8.7.12 Design a parallel algorithm for analyzing AOE networks on a TSC having P ($1 < P \leq n$) square processors. What is the time complexity of your algorithm?

# 8.8 BIBLIOGRAPHY

Aho, A., Hopcroft, J., and Ullman, J. (1974). *The Design and Analysis of Computer Algorithms.* Addison-Wesley, Reading, Mass.

Akl, S. G. (1986). An adaptive and cost-optimal parallel algorithm for minimum spanning trees. *Computing* 36, 271-7.

Akl, S. G. (1989). *The Design and Analysis of Parallel Algorithms.* Prentice Hall, Englewood Cliffs, NJ.

Arjomandi, E. (1975). A study of parallelism in graph theory. Ph.D. dissertation, Dept. of Computer Science, University of Toronto, Ontario.

Atallah, M. J., and Kosaraju, S. R. (1984). Graph problems on a mesh-connected processor array. *J. ACM* 31, 649-67.

Awerbuch, B., and Shiloach, Y. (1983). New connectivity and MSF algorithms for ultracomputer and PRAM. *Proceedings of the 1983 International Conference on Parallel Processing,* IEEE Computer Society, Washington, DC, pp. 175-9.

Bentley, J. L. (1980). A parallel algorithm for constructing minimum spanning trees. *J. Algorithms* 1, 51-9.

Chaudhuri, P. (1988). Fast parallel graph searching with applications. *BIT* 28, 2-18.

Chaudhuri, P. (1990a). An adaptive parallel algorithm for analyzing activity networks. *Operations Research Lett.* 9, 31-4.

Chaudhuri, P. (1990b). Parallel algorithm for analyzing activity networks on a tree-structured computer. *Intern. J. Electronics* 68, 925-30.

Chaudhuri, P., and Ghosh, R. K. (1986). Parallel algorithms for analyzing activity networks. *BIT* 26, 418-29.

Chen, I. -N. (1975). A new parallel algorithm for network flow problems. *Lecture Notes in Computer Science,* vol. 24, Springer-Verlag, NY, pp. 306-7.

Chen, Y. K., and Feng, T. Y. (1973). A parallel algorithm for maximum flow problem. *Proceedings of the 1973 Computer Conference on Parallel Processing,* IEEE Computer Society, Washington, DC, p. 60.

Chin, F. Y., Lam, J., and Chen, I. -N. (1982). Efficient parallel algorithms for some graph problems. *Comm. ACM* 25, 659-65.

Dekel, E., Nassimi, D., and Sahni, S. (1981). Parallel matrix and graph algorithms. *SIAM J. Computing* 10, 657-75.

Deo, N. (1974). *Graph Theory with Applications to Engineering and Computer Science.* Prentice Hall, Englewood Cliffs, NJ.

Deo, N., and Yoo, Y. B. (1981). Parallel algorithms for the minimum spanning tree problem. *Proceedings of the 1981 International Conference on Parallel Processing,* IEEE Computer Society, Washington, DC, pp. 188-9.

Deo, N., Pang, C. Y., and Lord, P. E. (1980). Two parallel algorithms for shortest path problems. *Proceedings of the 1980 International Conference on Parallel Processing,* IEEE Computer Society, Washington, DC, pp. 244-53.

Dijkstra, E. (1959). A note on two problems in connexion with graphs. *Numer. Math.* 1, 269-71.

Doshi, K., and Varman, P. (1987). Optimal graph algorithms on a fixed size linear array. *IEEE Transactions on Computers* C-36, 460-70.

Ghosh, R. K., and Bhattacharjee, G. P. (1984). Parallel algorithm for shortest paths. *IEE Proceedings* 133 Pt. E, 87-93.

Gillett, B. E. (1976). *Introduction to Operations Research — A Computer Oriented Algorithmic Approach.* McGraw-Hill, NY.

Goldschlager, L. M., Shaw, R. A., and Staples, J. (1982). The maximum flow problem is log space complete for P. *Theoretical Comput. Sci.* 21, 105-11.

Goodman, S. E., and Hedetniemi, S. T. (1977). *Introduction to the Design and Analysis of Algorithms.* McGraw-Hill, NY.

Hirschberg, D. S. (1976). Parallel algorithms for the transitive closure and the connected component problem. *Proceedings of the 8th Annual ACM Symposium on the Theory of Computing,* ACM, NY, pp. 55-7.

Hirschberg, D. S. (1982). Parallel graph algorithms without memory conflicts. *Proceedings of the 20th Allerton Conference,* University of Illinois, Urbana-Champaign, Ill., pp. 257-63.

Horowitz, E., and Sahni, S. (1978). *Fundamentals of Computer Algorithms.* Computer Science Press, Potomac, Md.

Kruskal, J. B. (1956). On the shortest subtree of a graph and the traveling salesman problem. *Proceedings of the American Mathematical Society,* pp. 48-50.

Kucera, L. (1982). Parallel computation and conflicts in memory access. *Inform. Process. Lett.* 14, 93-6.

Kwan, S. C., and Ruzzo, W. L. (1984). Adaptive parallel algorithms for finding minimum spanning trees. *Proceedings of the 1984 International Conference on Parallel Processing,* IEEE Computer Society, Washington, DC, pp. 439-43.

Levitt, K. N., and Kautz, W. T. (1972). Cellular arrays for the solution of graph problems. *Comm. ACM* 15, 789-801.

Mateti, P., and Deo, N. (1982). Parallel algorithms for the single source shortest path problem. *Computing* 29, 31-49.

Moitra, A., and Iyengar, S. S. (1987). Parallel algorithms for some computational problems. In *Advances in Computers*, vol. 26, M. Yovits, ed. Academic Press, NY, pp. 93-153.

Moore, E. F. (1957). The shortest path through a maze. *Proceedings of the International Symposium on the Theory of Switching,* vol. 2, pp. 285-92.

Nath, D., and Maheswari, S. N. (1982). Parallel algorithms for the connected components and minimal spanning tree problems. *Inform. Process. Lett.* 14, 7-11.

Paige, R. C., and Kruskal, C. P. (1985). Parallel algorithms for shortest path problems. *Proceedings of the 1985 International Conference on Parallel Processing,* IEEE Computer Society, Washington, DC, pp. 14-20.

Prim, R. C. (1957). Shortest connection networks and some generalizations. *Bell Syst. Tech. J.* 36, 1389-401.

Quinn, M. J., and Deo, N. (1984). Parallel graph algorithms. *Computing Surveys* 16, 319-48.

Reif, J. H. (1982). Symmetric complementation. *Proceedings of the 14th Annual ACM Symposium on Theory of Computing,* ACM, NY, pp. 201-14.

Savage, C. (1977). Parallel algorithms for graph theoretic problems. Ph.D. dissertation, Mathematics Dept., University of Illinois, Urbana-Champaign, Ill.

Savage, C., and Ja' Ja', J. (1981). Fast, efficient parallel algorithms for some graph problems. *SIAM J. Computing* 10, 682-90.

Shiloach, Y., and Vishkin, U. (1981). Finding the maximum, merging, and sorting in a parallel computation model. *J. Algorithms* 2, 88-102.

Shiloach, Y., and Vishkin, U. (1982). An $O(n^2\log n)$ parallel MAX-FLOW algorithm. *J. Algorithms* 3, 128-46.

Sollin, M. (1977). An algorithm attributed to Sollin. In *Introduction to the Design and Analysis of Algorithms,* Authors: S. E. Goodman and S. T. Hedetniemi, McGraw-Hill, NY, Section 5.5.

Yeh, D. Y., and Lee, D. T. (1984). Graph algorithms on a tree-structured parallel computer. *BIT* 24, 333-40.

Yoo, Y. B. (1983). Parallel processing for some network optimization problems. Ph.D. dissertation, Dept. of Computer Science, Washington State University, Pullman.

# CHAPTER
# 9

# Updating
# Algorithms for
# Graphs

## 9.1 INTRODUCTION

Updating or incremental graph algorithms are used to recompute (update) properties of a graph after a minor modification has been made to it. These modifications may be as follows: (a) a node and edges from it incident upon other nodes in the graph may be added or deleted; (b) an edge joining two nodes may be added to the graph or an edge may be deleted; and (c) for weighted graphs, a change in the weight or cost associated with an edge.

Let S be a solution to a problem P on graph G obtained using algorithm A. Algorithm A is referred to as the start-over or the main algorithm for P. Let G' be the graph obtained after a minor modification is made to G, and S' be the corresponding solution for P on G'. Now an updating algorithm A' for this problem P finds S' from S. In order to be a useful updating algorithm A' must have a low cost compared to that of A. When seeking updating algorithms for serial models of computation one mainly attempts to reduce their time complexities with respect to their corresponding start-over algorithms. In the case of parallel updating algorithms, the aim is to reduce time and/or processor complexities with respect to their corresponding start-over algorithms.

Serial updating algorithms for graphs have received some attention in the past while the interest in the same for parallel computational models is relatively of more recent origin. In this chapter, we investigate parallel updating algorithms for some fundamental graph theory problems which include finding the minimum spanning tree (MST), graph searching, computing connected components, and finding fundamental sets of cycles. These problems are considered in Sections 2 through 5. Finally, the Bibliographic Notes provide some important references for both serial and parallel graph updating algorithms.

# 9.2 PARALLEL UPDATE OF MINIMUM SPANNING TREES

The problem of updating a minimum spanning tree (MST) involves reconstruction of the new MST from a given MST when the weight associated with an edge of the graph has changed or a node along with all of the edges incident upon it is added to or deleted from the graph. We shall consider these problems separately and call them the edge update and node update problems, respectively. In the development of the parallel updating algorithms in this section, we will assume the computational model to be a CRCW PRAM with the equality resolution rule for write conflicts. Later, we shall see that the proposed algorithms can easily be adapted to work on the other variants of the PRAM model.

The parallel MST algorithm of Section 8.2.1 is considered as the start-over algorithm. The time and processor complexities of this algorithm are $O(\log^2 n)$ and $O(n^2)$, respectively. Important features of updating algorithms are the data structures which are used to store the previous solution and auxiliary information generated by the start-over algorithms. Such data structures should permit fast access to the required information in order to facilitate the construction of efficient updating algorithms. In the following section, we discuss suitable data structures and present some basic algorithms which will be used later.

## 9.2.1 Data Structures and Basic Algorithms

An $n \times n$ array is used to store a spanning tree (forest) of the graph G. Each row i of the array contains the tree-path from i to r, where r is the root of the tree to which i belongs. Such an array was used in Section 7.2.3 and a parallel algorithm (algorithm ANCESTOR_ARRAY) was given for constructing such an array A for a general ordered rooted tree. The time complexity of this algorithm is $O(\log^2 n)$ with $O(n^2)$ processors on both CREW PRAM and CRCW PRAM models. In addition to the array A, i.e., $A^j(i)$, $1 \le i \le n$, $0 \le j \le n - 1$, we use a linear array LEN of size n which contains the lengths of all the paths for each node. The construction of LEN is straightforward and can be obtained by computing the level of each node as shown in algorithm CREW_PREORDER_TRAVERSAL of Section 7.2.3. Entries in row i of A beyond column LEN[i] are assumed to be invalid. When the graph undergoes a minor change, the algorithm to be presented recomputes the MST of the updated graph and also updates the contents of A and LEN. We now present a set of basic algorithms which operate on the arrays A and LEN to extract useful information and update them appropriately.

### 9.2.1.1 Nearest Common Ancestor and Maximum Weighted Edge Selection

The first algorithm in this section computes from A the nearest common ancestor denoted by NCA(i, j), for a pair of nodes i and j in a tree T rooted at a node r. We have given a nearest common ancestors algorithm in Section 7.2.4 which works on the CREW PRAM model. This algorithm computes all-pairs NCAs in $O(\log n)$ time when $O(n^2)$ processors are available. However, if the array A is available, it is possible to compute the NCAs in constant time. A detailed description of this fast nearest common ancestor algorithm follows.

### Algorithm NCA

Input: The array $A^j(i)$, $1 \le i \le n$, $0 \le j \le n - 1$, and the array LEN[i], $1 \le i \le n$.

Output: For a given pair of nodes p, q $\in$ N, the nearest common ancestor NCA(p, q).

```
for k = 0 to n - 1 dopar
    P[k] := Q[k] := ∞
odpar
for k = 0 to n - 1 dopar
    P[LEN[p] - k] := Aᵏ(p);
    Q[LEN[q] - k] := Aᵏ(q)
odpar
for k = 0 to n - 1 dopar
    if P[k] = Q[k] AND P[k] ≠ ∞
    then X[k] := 0
    else X[k] := 1
    fi
odpar
for k = 0 to n - 2 dopar
    if x[k] = 0 AND X[k + 1] = 1
    then NCA(p, q) := P[k]
    fi
odpar
```

Each parallel for-loop of algorithm NCA runs in constant time with n processors. Therefore, the overall time complexity for the computation of NCA(p, q), for a pair of nodes p, q ∈ N in a rooted tree represented by A and LEN, is O(1) using O(n) processors.

In order to find the maximum weighted edge on any path i to j in the MST T, we use the following simple algorithm. Observe that any path from i to j in T passes through NCA(i, j) (in a special case NCA(i, j) may be identical either to i or j).

### *Algorithm* MAX_WEIGHTED_EDGE

Input: Arrays A and LEN; and the weight adjacency matrix W corresponding to the MST T.

Output: An edge (p, q) in the path i to j in T with weight W[p, q] which is maximum among the weights of all the edges in path i to j.

```
compute NCA(i, j) using algorithm NCA;
obtain the tree-paths from NCA(i, j) to i and
            from NCA(i, j) to j using the array A;
determine the edge (p, q) in the path from i to j in T such that
        W[p, q] = max{W[x, y] | (x, y) ∈ {(tree-path NCA(i, j) to i)
                ∪ (tree-path NCA(i, j) to j)}};
```

Clearly the first two statements of this algorithm can be implemented in O(1) time with O(n) processors. To determine the maximum weighted edge in the path from i to j in T, we use the maximum finding algorithm of Section 5.2.1 which runs in constant time with $O(n^2)$ processors on the CRCW PRAM model to find the maximum of n elements. Thus, the overall time complexity of algorithm MAX_WEIGHTED_EDGE is O(1) when $O(n^2)$ processors are used.

*9.2.1.2   Deletion and Insertion of Edges*

Assume that the spanning forest/tree of G is stored in array A and that an edge $(x, y)$ is deleted from the spanning forest. Clearly, the tree T originally containing the edge $(x, y)$ is now split into two trees. If y is the parent of x in T and T is rooted at r, then the deletion of $(x, y)$ splits T into two trees one of which is rooted at x and the other at r. The following algorithm replaces T by these two new trees and updates A and LEN accordingly.

*Algorithm* **EDGE_DELETION**

Input: Arrays A and LEN corresponding to the forest/tree of G and an edge $(x, y)$ such that y is the parent of x in the concerned tree.

Output: Updated versions of A and LEN after the deletion of edge $(x, y)$.

*for* i = 1 *to* n *dopar*
    d := LEN[i] − LEN[x];
    *if* $A^d(i) = x$
    *then* LEN[i] := d
    *fi*
*odpar*

---

The assignment of each of the n processors to a unique node for the purpose of detecting whether it is a descendant of x followed by updating of LEN takes constant time. Therefore, algorithm EDGE_DELETION can be implemented in O(1) time using O(n) processors.

A second deletion algorithm is now presented which deletes multiple tree edges from the spanning forest/tree of G.

*Algorithm* **MULTIPLE_EDGE_DELETION**

Input: Arrays A and LEN of the corresponding spanning forest/tree of G together with the tree edges $(x_1, y_1), (x_2, y_2), \ldots, (x_k, y_k)$ to be deleted. A Boolean array $R[1 : n]$ is used to indicate whether or not a node becomes the root of a tree upon deletion of these tree edges. It is assumed that $y_i$ is the parent of $x_i$, $1 \leq i \leq k$.

Output: Updated A and LEN.

*for* each $(x, y) \in \{(x_1, y_1), (x_2, y_2), \ldots, (x_k, y_k)\}$ *dopar*
    R[x] := 1
*odpar*
*for* i = 1 *to* n *dopar*
    *for* j = 1 *to* n *dopar*
        d := LEN[i] − LEN[j];
        *if* $A^d(i) = j$ *then*
            *if* R[j] = 1 *then*
                *for* m = 1 *to* n *dopar*
                    *if* m ≤ LEN[i] *then*
                        *if* m > LEN[j] *then*

$$A^m(i) := 0$$
$$fi$$
$$fi$$
*odpar*
$$fi$$
$$fi$$
*odpar*
*odpar*
*for* i = 1 *to* n *dopar*
    *for* j = 0 *to* n − 1 *dopar*
        *if* $A^j(i) \neq 0$ AND $A^{j+1}(i) = 0$ *then*
            LEN[i] := j
        *fi*
    *odpar*
*odpar*

The first parallel for-loop of algorithm MULTIPLE_EDGE_DELETION requires constant time using at most $O(n)$ processors. The second nested parallel for-loop also runs in constant time but requires $O(n^3)$ processors. The last parallel for-loop again takes constant time but uses $O(n^2)$ processors. Thus, the overall time complexity of algorithm MULTIPLE_EDGE_DELETION is $O(1)$ when $O(n^3)$ processors are employed.

Finally in this section, we describe another simple algorithm which will be used frequently in some of the updating algorithms presented later in this chapter. This algorithm updates the arrays A and LEN appropriately when two trees in the spanning forest of G are merged by adding an edge. The algorithm is presented below.

*Algorithm* **EDGE_INSERTION**

Input: Arrays A and LEN in which the spanning forest of G is stored. An edge (x, y) which joins two trees denoted by $T_x$ and $T_y$ with $x \in T_x$ and $y \in T_y$.

Output: Updated versions of A and LEN in which the tree obtained by merging $T_x$ and $T_y$ replaces $T_x$ and $T_y$ in the spanning forest of G. Assume that $r_y$ is the root of the new tree.

row x of A := x followed by the path y to $r_y$;
*for* each ancestor z of x in $T_x$ *dopar*
    row z of A := the reverse of the path x to z in $T_x$
                followed by the new path of x
*odpar*
*for* each node $z \in T_x$ not processed in the previous step *dopar*
    compute NCA(x, z) in $T_x$ using algorithm NCA;
    row z of A := path z to NCA(x, z) followed by
                the new path NCA(x, z) to $r_y$
*odpar*

Each of the three main steps in algorithm EDGE_INSERTION runs in $O(1)$ time and requires at most $O(n^2)$ processors.

## 9.2.2  Updating Algorithms for MST

In order to investigate parallel updates for the MST T of a weighted graph G, we assume that T is available in terms of the arrays A and LEN, as discussed in the previous section. To create these, we use algorithm CREW_MST(S) from Section 8.2.1 as the start-over algorithm and then transform its output to obtain A and LEN by using the methods described in Section 7.2.3.

### 9.2.2.1  Edge Update

The edge update problem involves constructing a new MST when the weight of an edge in the given graph is changed. The problems of edge deletion and edge insertion in an MST can be subsumed within the problems arising from increasing or decreasing the weight of an edge where it is assumed that nonexistent edges are of infinite weights. There are several cases to be considered when the weight of an edge of G is changed. The weight of an edge may either increase or decrease and this edge may or may not be in the given MST of G. If the weight of a nontree edge increases or that of a tree edge decreases then there will be no change in the MST T. The MST T may change if the weight of a nontree edge decreases or the weight of a tree edge increases; in either case at most one edge of T becomes a nontree edge in the updated MST T' and a nontree edge for T becomes a tree edge in T'. A parallel algorithm for updating MST T to obtain a new MST T' is given below.

*Algorithm*  **MST_EDGE_UPDATE**

Input: Arrays A and LEN corresponding to the MST T of G, and the weight matrix W. In addition, the edge $(i, j) \in E$ in G whose weight is changed from $W[i, j]$ to $W'[i, j]$ is given.

Output: The updated MST T'.

*if* $(i, j) \in T$
*then if* $W'[i, j] > W[i, j]$
    *then do*
           delete $(i, j)$ using algorithm EDGE_DELETION assuming that j
              is the parent of i in T which splits T into two trees —
              one rooted at r and the other at i;
           compute the minimum weight edge $(u, v)$
              connecting the two trees;
           add edge $(u, v)$ to merge these two trees using
              algorithm EDGE_INSERTION
       *od*
    *fi*
*else do*
    *if* $W'[i, j] < W[i, j]$
    *then do*
           find the maximum weighted edge $(u,v)$ on the path from
              i to j in T assuming i to be closer to root r using
              algorithm MAX_WEIGHTED_EDGE
           *if* $W[u, v] > W'[i, j]$
           *then do*
               delete $(u, v)$ from T using algorithm EDGE_DELETION

> splitting T into two trees — one rooted
> at r and the other at u or v;
>     add edge (i, j) to merge these two trees using
> algorithm EDGE_INSERTION

        *od*
    *fi*
      *od*
   *fi*
    *od*
*fi*


## Complexity Analysis

The complexity analysis of algorithm MST_EDGE_UPDATE is straightforward and depends primarily on the complexities of algorithms EDGE_DELETION, EDGE_INSERTION, and MAX_WEIGHTED_EDGE. The only step whose implementation we need to discuss is the one which computes the minimum weight edge (u, v) connecting two trees. This can be implemented in $O(1)$ time with $O(n^3)$ processors, by first identifying all of the edges (x, y) such that x and y belong to the two different trees and then selecting the minimum weighted edge from among all such edges. Thus, considering the complexities of all other steps of the algorithm, we obtain its time complexity to be $O(1)$ when $O(n^3)$ processors are employed on the CRCW PRAM model.

It can be shown that if the algorithms EDGE_DELETION, EDGE_INSERTION, and MAX_WEIGHTED_EDGE are implemented on a CREW PRAM model, then the time complexities of all three algorithms will be increased by a factor of log n while the processor complexities will be reduced by a factor of n. Using these adapted algorithms on the CREW PRAM, we find that algorithm MST_EDGE_UPDATE can be implemented in time $O(\log n)$ with $O(n^2)$ processors. The details of the implementations are left as an exercise.


### 9.2.2.2 *Node Update*

The node update problem involves reconstructing a new MST T' from T when a node is either inserted or deleted from the underlying graph G. In this section, we present a node update algorithm which updates T when a new node along with the edges incident upon it are inserted in G. The update algorithm for MST when a node and the edges incident on it are deleted from G is left as an exercise.

When a node x is inserted in G along with a set of edges incident on it, a set of cycles is introduced into its MST. Each of these cycles results from a pair of edges incident on the new node. There can be at most n such incident edges and so at most $O(n^2)$ cycles may be induced in T. The updating algorithm breaks all of these cycles simultaneously by deleting the maximum weighted edge on each cycle. It is important to note that although $O(n^2)$ cycles are simultaneously broken, only n − 1 edges, not $O(n^2)$ edges are deleted. The following lemmas ensure that, after breaking all $O(n^2)$ cycles we are left with a tree which is an MST of the modified graph.

**Lemma 9.1:** Let T = <N, $E_T$> be an MST of G = <N, E>. Suppose that G' = <N, E ∪ {e'}> is the graph obtained by adding a new edge e' to G. Then, an MST T' of G' is obtained by adding e' to T and deleting the maximum weighted edge in the cycle created.

**Proof:** Assume, to the contrary, that T′ is not an MST of G′. Then there exists an edge e″ which, when added to T′, can create a cycle in which there is an edge with weight greater than that of e″. This contradicts the minimality of T in G and hence the lemma follows.

**Lemma 9.2:** Let $G_x$ be the graph obtained by adding a new node x and all the edges incident on x to the MST T of G. If all the cycles created by every pair of edges incident on x are broken by removing the maximum weighted edge on each cycle, then a tree T′ is obtained which is the desired updated MST of $G_x$.

**Proof:** Lemma 9.2 implies that in order to update the MST of a graph G, after a node x has been added, it is necessary to consider only the edges of the updated graph $G_x$. To prove this lemma, we need to show that T′ obtained by breaking all the cycles in the way stated in this lemma is indeed a tree and, in addition, that it is an MST of $G_x$.

First, it is obvious that T′ is acyclic since it is obtained by breaking all the cycles of $G_x$. Let us assume that T′ is not connected, i.e., it has several components. Consider the set of edges $E_c$ = {e | e is an edge deleted from $G_x$ whose end nodes belong to different components of T′}. Also, let e′ be the minimum weighted edge in the set $E_c$. Now any cycle in $G_x$ that contains e′ must pass through at least two components of T′. That is, it must have at least two edges that are in $E_c$. Clearly e′ cannot be deleted since it is not a maximum weighted edge on this cycle. Thus, there cannot be more than one component in T′ and so T′ is a tree.

Second, to prove the last part of the lemma, we note that every nontree edge is the maximum weighted edge on the cycle it induces in the MST. Since all the cycles are broken by removing the maximum weighted edge in each cycle induced by x, the tree T′ thus obtained is an MST.

A detailed description of the algorithm based on the ideas above is given below.

*Algorithm* **NODE_INSERTION**

Input: Arrays A and LEN corresponding to the current MST T, the new node x to be inserted, and the edges connecting x to nodes $\{i_1, i_2, \ldots, i_k\}$.

Output: The updated MST T′.

*for* each distinct pair (s, t), s, t ∈ $\{i_1, i_2, \ldots, i_k\}$ *dopar*
    find the maximum weighted edge in the tree paths s to t in T using
          algorithm MAX_WEIGHTED_EDGE and let it be (u, v)
*odpar*
select the maximum weighted edge among the edges (x, s), (t, x) and (u, v);
remove the edge selected in the above step using
    algorithm MULTIPLE_EDGE_DELETION;
*for* each new edge $(i_m, x)$, $1 \leq m \leq k$ not deleted in the above step *dopar*
    add edge $(i_m, x)$ to T′ using algorithm EDGE_INSERTION
*odpar*

**Complexity Analysis**
Each cycle contains at most n edges. Thus the computation of the maximum weighted edge on each cycle requires $O(1)$ time with $O(n^2)$ processors on the CRCW PRAM model. Since there are at most $O(n^2)$ cycles, the first parallel for-loop takes $O(1)$ time with $O(n^4)$ processors. It is easily seen that the implementation of the other statements of algorithm NODE_INSERTION requires no more than $O(1)$ time and $O(n^4)$ processors on the CRCW

PRAM model. Therefore, algorithm NODE_INSERTION has time complexity O(1) when $O(n^4)$ processors are employed.

## 9.3 UPDATING ALGORITHMS FOR GRAPH SEARCHING PROBLEMS

In this section we will consider the problem of updating a DFS spanning tree (DFST) of a DAG when a new node along with all its incident edges is inserted or when an edge is inserted in the underlying graph. It is interesting to note that, since all three search techniques discussed in Chapter 7 are based on the "growing by doubling" paradigm, the updating algorithms presented in this section can be modified suitably to handle the corresponding cases of BFS for general graphs and BDS for DAGs. Similar updating algorithms can be designed for the all-pairs shortest paths problem, since the parallel algorithm for this problem given in Chapter 8 also has a similar structure to those of the searching algorithms of Chapter 7. Thus, the unified approach used to solve these problems not only produces fast parallel algorithms for their solutions but also results in the development of efficient parallel algorithms for updating the current solution when the underlying graph is modified in the ways mentioned earlier. The rest of this section deals with updating algorithms for the DFST of a DAG for node and edge insertions.

It is assumed that all the $\lceil \log n \rceil$-dfs-trees $T(x, \lceil \log n \rceil)$, $\forall x \in N$ of G, specified by parent$(y \mid T(x, \lceil \log n \rceil))$ and pre$(y \mid T(x, \lceil \log n \rceil))$, $\forall y \in N$, of which $T(s, \lceil \log n \rceil)$ is the DFST of DAG G are available (see Section 7.3.1). Assume that the indegree (i.e., the number of edges incident upon a node) of the new node to be inserted, say u, is greater than zero, i.e., it cannot be a new source node in G. Also assume that there are edges from each of $x_1$, $x_2$, $\ldots, x_p$ to u and from u to $y_1, y_2, \ldots, y_q$. The basic idea underlying the algorithm is to initialize a new 0-dfs-tree $T(u, 0)$ and to select a unique parent of u in each of the $\lceil \log n \rceil$-dfs-trees. Then, by means of a single iteration of a tree-merging process, similar to that used by the parallel DFST algorithm (see algorithm CREW_DFS), all $\lceil \log (n+1) \rceil$-dfs-trees are obtained, where $T(s, \lceil \log (n+1) \rceil)$ is the updated DFST. The following algorithm illustrates the construction of a DFST for the augmented DAG from the $\lceil \log n \rceil$-dfs-trees of G. Without loss of generality we assume u to be n + 1.

### Algorithm DFS_NODE_INSERTION

Input: The trees $T(x, \lceil \log n \rceil)$ specified by parent$(y \mid T(x, \lceil \log n \rceil))$ and pre$(y \mid T(x, \lceil \log n \rceil))$, for all x, y = 1, 2, . . . , n and the new node n + 1 together with the edges $(x_1, n + 1)$, $(x_2, n + 1), \ldots, (x_p, n + 1), (n + 1, y_1), (n + 1, y_2), \ldots, (n + 1, y_q)$.

Output: The reconstructed trees denoted by $T(x, \lceil \log (n + 1) \rceil)$, specified by parent$(y \mid T(x, \lceil \log (n + 1) \rceil))$ and pre$(y \mid T(x, \lceil \log (n + 1) \rceil))$, for all x, y = 1, 2, . . . , n + 1. The tree $T(s, \lceil \log (n + 1) \rceil)$ is the updated DFST.

*for* x = 1 *to* n *dopar*
    compute post$(y \mid T(x, \lceil \log n \rceil))$ for all $y \in N$
*odpar*
*for* x = 1 *to* n *dopar*
    find $x_a$ such that post$(x_a \mid T(x, \lceil \log n \rceil)) = \min\{$post$(x_i \mid T(x, \lceil \log n \rceil)) \mid$
                              i = 1, 2, . . . , p$\}$;

parent(n+1 | T(x, ⌈log n⌉)) := $x_a$
*odpar*
*for* j = 1 *to* q *dopar*
    parent($y_j$ | T(n + 1, 0)) := n + 1
*odpar*
merge T(n + 1, 0) and all T($y_j$, ⌈log n⌉), j = 1, 2, . . . , q as in algorithm
        CREW_DFS so that all the trees produced preserve the DFS
        property and denote the resulting tree by T(n + 1, ⌈log (n + 1)⌉);
*for* x = 1 *to* n *dopar*
    merge T(n + 1, ⌈log n⌉) with T(x, ⌈log n⌉) and
            denote the resulting tree by T(x, ⌈log (n + 1)⌉)
*odpar*
*for* x = 1 *to* n + 1 *dopar*
    compute pre(y | T(x, ⌈log (n + 1)⌉) for y = 1, 2, . . . , n + 1
*odpar*

Computing the postorder and preorder traversal ranks required by the first and the last parallel for-loops of algorithm DFS_NODE_INSERTION can be implemented in O(log n) time with O($n^2$) processors (see Section 7.3.1). The second parallel for-loop can be implemented in O(log n) time with O(np/log n) ≡ O($n^2$/log n) processors using the minimum (maximum) finding algorithm of Section 5.2.2. The third parallel for-loop runs in O(1) time with q ≡ O(n) processors. Finally, the merging of the partial spanning trees can be implemented in a similar manner to that specified by the nested parallel for-loop in the inner while-loop of algorithm CREW_DFS. Clearly, this takes O(log n) time with O($n^2$ ⌈n/log n⌉) processors. Therefore, the overall time complexity of algorithm CREW_DFS is O(log n) when O($n^2$ ⌈n/log n⌉) processors are employed. Thus, this updating algorithm is efficient when compared to that of the corresponding start-over algorithm and the improvement is by a factor of log n.

Consider now the edge update problem where a new edge (u, v) is inserted in the DAG G. We recompute the DFST and the other ⌈log n⌉-dfs-trees denoted by T'(s, ⌈log n⌉) and T'(x, ⌈log n⌉), x ∈ N − {s}, respectively, as follows.

### *Algorithm* DFS_EDGE_INSERTION

Input: The trees T(x, ⌈log n⌉) specified by parent(y | T(x, ⌈log n⌉)) and pre(y | T(x, ⌈log n⌉)), for all x, y = 1, 2, . . . , n, and the new edge (u, v) of G.

Output: The recomputed trees T'(x, ⌈log n⌉), for all x = 1, 2 , . . . , n.

*for* x = 1 *to* n *dopar*
    compute post(y | T(x, ⌈log n⌉)) for all y ∈ N
*odpar*
*for* x = 1 *to* n *dopar*
    *if* post(u | T(x, ⌈log n⌉)) < post(v | T(x, ⌈log n⌉))
    *then* parent(v | T(x, ⌈log n⌉)) := u
    *fi*
*odpar*

*for* x = 1 *to* n *dopar*

    compute post(y | T(x, $\lceil \log n \rceil$)) for all y ∈ N

*odpar*

*for* x = 1 *to* n *dopar*

    merge all T(y, $\lceil \log n \rceil$) with T(x, $\lceil \log n \rceil$), y ∈ T(x, $\lceil \log n \rceil$) so that the

             recomputed tree T'(x, $\lceil \log n \rceil$) preserves the DFS property

*odpar*

*for* x = 1 *to* n *dopar*

    compute pre(y | T'(x, $\lceil \log n \rceil$)) for all y ∈ N

*odpar*

Each of the first, third, and last parallel for-loops requires $O(\log n)$ time with $O(n^2)$ processors while the second for-loop requires only $O(1)$ time when $O(n)$ processors are employed. Finally, the fourth parallel for-loop can be implemented in $O(\log n)$ time with $O(n^2 \lceil n / \log n \rceil)$ processors — see algorithm DFS_NODE_INSERTION. Therefore, algorithm DFS_EDGE_INSERTION also runs in $O(\log n)$ time when $O(n^2 \lceil n / \log n \rceil)$ processors are available.

## 9.4  UPDATING THE CONNECTED COMPONENTS

Given an undirected graph G and its connected components, we consider in this section the problems of recomputing the connected components after a new edge or node is inserted in G or an edge of G is deleted. The general conventions we observe with regard to the output of the start-over algorithms, which are initially used to compute the connected components of G, are as follows. We shall label each connected component by a representative node in that component. For each node in G the algorithm outputs the label of the component to which it belongs. These are fairly standard conventions for all the different connected components algorithms presented in Section 7.4.1. We also assume that the connected components are available as trees in the spanning forest of G. However, with the exception of the algorithm in Section 7.4.1.1, this last assumption is not true for the outputs of all the algorithms of Section 7.4.1. Thus, for every tree in the spanning forest of G, its root represents the corresponding component of G. The updating algorithms developed in this section assume the existence of the arrays A and LEN corresponding to the spanning forest of G prior to changing it. If the connected components are originally obtained using the BFS technique — as in Section 7.4.1.1 — then the spanning forest of G is available. The arrays A and LEN can be obtained in $O(\log n)$ time with $O(n^2)$ processors using algorithm ANCESTOR_ARRAY of Section 7.2.3. However, if the connected components of G are initially computed using the transitive closure or node collapse method as in Sections 7.4.1.2 and 7.4.1.3, respectively, then we can use an algorithm due to Tarjan and Vishkin (1984) that computes an arbitrary spanning forest of G in $O(\log n)$ time using $O(n + e)$ processors on both CRCW and CREW PRAM models. Finally, we apply algorithm ANCESTOR_ARRAY to obtain the arrays A and LEN. In this section, we will also need to use the algorithms EDGE_DELETION and EDGE_INSERTION presented in Section 9.2.1.2.

Consider first the case of edge insertion. Let the edge (i, j) be inserted in G. Now, if i and j belong to the same connected component of G, then the connected components and the arrays A and LEN remain unchanged. Alternatively, if i and j belong to two different components of G, then the edge (i, j) merges two components into one and as a result A and LEN have to be updated. The updating algorithm in this case simply consists of a call to algorithm EDGE_INSERTION to merge two trees (components) which also updates A and LEN.

Consider now the case where an edge (i, j) is deleted from G. Again there are two distinct cases. One arises when (i, j) is a nontree edge in which case there will be no change either in the connected components or the arrays A and LEN. On the other hand, if (i, j) is a tree edge, the tree to which it belongs is first split by removing the edge (i, j). The two resulting trees are then merged if there is an edge joining them. The details are shown in the following algorithm.

### Algorithm CCOMP_EDGE_DELETION

Input: Arrays A and LEN storing the spanning forest of G, and the edge (i, j) to be deleted from G.

Output: Updated A and LEN corresponding to the updated connected components, thus giving the spanning forest of G.

*if* (i, j) is an edge in a tree rooted at r
*then* split the tree into two trees one rooted either at i or j
           and the other rooted at r using algorithm EDGE_DELETION
*fi*
*for* each nontree edge (x, y) *dopar*
     *if* x and y are in two different trees
     *then* insert (x, y) to merge the two trees
               using algorithm EDGE_INSERTION
     *fi*
*odpar*

The if-statement requires $O(1)$ time with $O(n)$ processors. Observe that in the parallel for-loop of algorithm CCOMP_EDGE_DELETION at most one edge (x, y) will succeed in the test. Thus this step also requires $O(1)$ time but $O(n^2)$ processors. Therefore, the overall time complexity of algorithm CCOMP_EDGE_DELETION is $O(1)$ with $O(n^2)$ processors.

If a new node x together with the edges $(x, y_1), (x, y_2), \ldots, (x, y_k)$ are added to G, then components containing the nodes $y_1, y_2, \ldots, y_k$ are merged into one. All the trees corresponding to the components which are to be merged in this process are replaced with a single tree rooted at x. The details of the algorithm are shown below.

### Algorithm CCOMP_NODE_INSERTION

Input: Arrays A and LEN, together with node x and edges $(x, y_1), (x, y_2), \ldots, (x, y_k)$ to be inserted in G.

Output: Updated connected components in arrays A and LEN.

*for* each tree rooted at some i *dopar*
    *for* each node $y \in \{y_1, y_2, \ldots, y_k\}$ *dopar*
        *if* y is a node in the tree rooted at i
        *then* S(i) := y
        *fi*
    *odpar*
*odpar*

add a new row to array A corresponding to x
>    with x as the root of a tree without any edges;
*for* each node i that is a root of some tree *dopar*
>    *if* S(i) = y
>    *then* insert edge (x, y) to merge the trees rooted
>                        at i and x using algorithm EDGE_INSERTION
>    *fi*
*odpar*

    The first parallel for-loop can be implemented in constant time with $O(n^2)$ processors. Note that the assignment statement in this for-loop may be executed concurrently by several processors for the same values of i and y, and that this is permitted by our computational model. The last for-loop can also be executed in time $O(1)$ with at most $O(n^2)$ processors. Thus, the overall time and processor complexities of algorithm CCOMP_NODE_ INSERTION are $O(1)$ and $O(n^2)$, respectively.

    All the updating algorithms presented above for the connected components problem require $O(1)$ time with $O(n^2)$ processors, provided the original connected components of G are available in the arrays A and LEN. It can be verified that each of these algorithms can be implemented on the CREW PRAM in $O(\log n)$ time with $O(n^2)$ processors.

## 9.5 PARALLEL UPDATES FOR THE SET OF FUNDAMENTAL CYCLES

This section deals with updating algorithms for the set of fundamental cycles (SFC) when a new edge is inserted or deleted, or a new node and all edges incident upon it are inserted into a graph G. To construct these algorithms, we assume that the start-over algorithm, in addition to SFC, also produces the spanning forest of the graph G in the form of the arrays A and LEN discussed earlier. It can be verified that this additional output requirement does not affect the time and processor complexities of the start-over algorithm. The basic idea of all the updating algorithms in this section is to modify arrays A and LEN when the graph G undergoes a change and then to recompute the fundamental cycles by identifying the current nontree edges. The updating process often requires the following algorithm which constructs the fundamental cycles for a given set of nontree edges from arrays A and LEN and stores them in an array called FCARRAY. Every row of FCARRAY corresponds to an edge of G, and stores the fundamental cycle corresponding to that edge (if there is one).

*Algorithm* **FCYCLE**

Input: Arrays A and LEN, and a set of edges $(x_i, y_i)$, $1 \leq i \leq k$, which are nontree edges with respect to the spanning forest of G.

Output: The cycle formed by each $(x_i, y_i)$ in FCARRAY$[(x_i, y_i)]$, $1 \leq i \leq k$.

*for* each edge $(u, v) \in \{(x_i, y_i) \mid 1 \leq i \leq k\}$ *dopar*
>    obtain NCA(u, v) using algorithm NCA;
>    FCARRAY$[(u, v)]$ := cycle formed by edge (u, v) and
>                        tree-paths u to NCA(u, v), NCA(u, v) to v
*odpar*

For each nontree edge, algorithm FCYCLE takes $O(1)$ time with $O(n)$ processors. Therefore, for all k nontree edges this algorithm runs in $O(1)$ time when $O(nk) \equiv O(n^2)$ processors are employed.

Consider now the case of edge insertion. If the edge $(x, y)$ inserted in G is such that it merges two connected components of G, then the SFC remains unchanged. However, A and LEN have to be updated and this can be done by using algorithm EDGE_INSERTION (see Section 9.2.1.2). On the other hand, if the new edge $(x, y)$ is such that i and j belong to the same component, then the corresponding cycle is added to the SFC. The details are given in the following algorithm.

### Algorithm SFC_EDGE_INSERTION

Input: Arrays A and LEN, and the edge $(x, y)$ to be inserted in G.

Output: The updated SFC of G or the updated version of A and LEN.

*if* $A^{LEN[x]}(x) = A^{LEN[y]}(y)$
*then* samecomp := 1
*else* samecomp := 0
*fi*
*if* samecomp = 1
*then* obtain the cycle induced by edge $(x, y)$ using algorithm FCYCLE
*else* update A and LEN using algorithm EDGE_INSERTION
*fi*

The first if-statement can be executed in $O(1)$ time with a single processor while the second if-statement also takes $O(1)$ time but requires $O(n^2)$ processors. Therefore, the overall time and processor complexities of algorithm SFC_EDGE_INSERTION are $O(1)$ and $O(n^2)$, respectively.

Two cases have to be considered in the event of the deletion of an edge $(x, y)$ from G. If $(x, y)$ is a tree edge with respect to the given forest of G but is not a bridge then it is necessary to compute all fundamental cycles. If $(x, y)$ is a nontree edge, then only the corresponding row of FCARRAY is deleted and both A and LEN remain unchanged. The following is an algorithmic description of the update for the edge deletion problem.

### Algorithm SFC_EDGE_DELETION

Input: Arrays A and LEN, and the edge $(x, y)$ to be deleted from G.

Output: The updated SFC, and arrays A and LEN.

*if* $(x, y)$ is a nontree edge
*then* remove the row corresponding to the edge $(x, y)$ in FCARRAY
*else* update A, LEN and connected components
            using algorithm CCOMP_EDGE_DELETION
*fi*
*if* $A^{LEN[x]}(x) = A^{LEN[y]}(y)$
*then* samecomp := 1
*else* samecomp := 0
*fi*

*if* samecomp = 1 *then*

    *for* each nontree edge (u, v) *dopar*

        find the fundamental cycle induced by (u, v)

            using algorithm FCYCLE

    *odpar*

*fi*

The first if-statement has time complexity $O(1)$ when $O(n^2)$ processors are used. The second if-statement can be executed in $O(1)$ time with a single processor. Since, in the worst case, $O(n^2)$ fundamental cycles are to be computed, the last if-statement of algorithm SFC_EDGE_DELETION can be implemented in $O(1)$ time using $O(n^3)$ processors. Combining the complexities of the individual statements the time and processor complexities of algorithm SFC_EDGE_DELETION are $O(1)$ and $O(n^3)$, respectively.

Finally, we consider the case of inserting a node x with edges incident upon $y_1$, $y_2$, $\ldots$, $y_k$ in G. When node x and its associated edge are added to G, the connected components and spanning forest of G are first updated. Clearly, some of the edges incident on x become new nontree edges. Each of these new nontree edges induce a unique fundamental cycle. All these fundamental cycles are added to the old SFC to give the updated SFC. This procedure correctly updates the SFC, since the addition of x and all its associated edges to G merges the connected components of G without affecting any of the previously computed fundamental cycles. The details of the algorithm are shown below.

### *Algorithm* SFC_NODE_INSERTION

Input: Arrays A and LEN. Node x and edges $(x, y_1), (x, y_2), \ldots, (x, y_k)$ to be inserted in G.

Output: The updated SFC, and arrays A and LEN.

update the connected components, and arrays A and LEN

    using algorithm CCOMP_NODE_INSERTION;

*for* each nontree edge (u, v) *dopar*

    find the fundamental cycle induced by (u, v)

        using algorithm FCYCLE and add to array FCARRAY

*odpar*

The time and processor complexities of algorithm CCOMP_NODE_ INSERTION are $O(1)$ and $O(n^2)$, respectively, and this determines the complexity of the first statement of algorithm SFC_NODE_INSERTION. Since, in the parallel for-loop, a maximum of $O(n)$ new fundamental cycles may be induced by the new nontree edges, this step requires $O(1)$ time with $O(n^2)$ processors. Therefore, the overall time complexity of algorithm SFC_NODE_INSERTION becomes $O(1)$ when $O(n^2)$ processors are employed on the CRCW PRAM model.

## 9.6 BIBLIOGRAPHIC NOTES

Serial algorithms for updating minimum spanning trees have been investigated by Spira and Pan (1975), Chin and Houck (1978), and Frederickson (1983). In particular, Frederickson presented an $O(\sqrt{e})$ serial algorithm for the edge update problem. Spira and Pan, and Chin and

Houck have proposed O(n) serial algorithms for updating the minimum spanning tree when a new node is inserted into the graph. Clearly, these algorithms are efficient when compared to the known start-over algorithms for the minimum spanning tree problem. The serial start-over algorithms for this problem require $O(n^2)$ time for dense graphs and O(e log n) time for sparse graphs. Any serial updating algorithm for the node insertion problem must examine, in the worst case, at least n − 1 edges of the existing minimum spanning tree and n edges incident upon the new node. Hence, the lower bound to the computational time of the node insertion problem is $\Omega(n)$. The algorithms presented in Spira and Pan (1975) and in Chin and Houck (1978) for the node insertion problem require O(n) time which is the same as the lower bound to the computational time for this problem. Hence these algorithms are optimal.

Serial updating algorithms for the shortest-path problem have been described in Cheston (1976), and Spira and Pan (1975). Serial updating of connected components have been investigated in Even and Shiloach (1982) under the operation of edge deletion. Updating algorithms for the transitive closure of directed graphs have been studied in Ibaraki and Katoh (1983).

Parallel updating algorithms for minimum spanning trees have been investigated in Pawagi and Ramakrishnan (1986), Sherlekar et al. (1985), Varman and Doshi (1986), Tsin (1988), Jung and Mehlhorn (1988), and Pawagi (1989). Pawagi and Ramakrishnan investigated the edge and node update problems on the CREW PRAM model and gave O(log n) time algorithms using $O(n^2)$ processors. Later, Tsin extended Pawagi and Ramakrishnan's work to include the node deletion problem. Varman and Doshi solved the node update problem efficiently using O(n) processors. The product of the parallel time and the number of processors used in Varman and Doshi's algorithm is O(n log n), which differs by a factor of only log n from the optimal cost. Sherlekar et al. have proposed O(1) time updating algorithms for minimum spanning trees on the CRCW PRAM model. The algorithms presented in Section 2 of this chapter are based on the works reported in Pawagi and Ramakrishnan (1986), and Sherlekar et al. (1985). Jung and Mehlhorn (1988) reported an optimal parallel updating algorithm for the node insertion problem on the CRCW PRAM model. More specifically, their algorithm has time complexity of O(log n) when O(n/log n) processors are employed. In a recent paper, Pawagi investigated the multiple update problem for minimum spanning trees (Pawagi 1989). This problem involves more than one change in the underlying graph as opposed to the usual updating problem. Pawagi proposed a parallel algorithm for updating a minimum spanning tree when k new nodes are inserted in the original graph. His algorithm achieves the time and processor bounds of O(log n log k) and O(nk), respectively, on the CREW PRAM model.

Updating the depth-first spanning trees of acyclic digraphs in parallel is addressed in Chaudhuri (1990), where O(log n) time parallel updating algorithms for the node insertion and edge insertion problems are presented on the CREW PRAM model. Section 3 is based on the ideas presented there. An efficient parallel algorithm for shifting the root of a depth-first spanning tree is presented in Tiwari (1986). Tiwari's algorithm runs in O(log n) time with $O(n^3)$ processors on the CREW PRAM model.

The problems of updating the connected components, set of fundamental cycles, bridges and bridge-connected components have been studied in Sherlekar et al. (1985) on the CRCW PRAM model. They have reported O(1) time parallel algorithms for all these problems. Sections 4 and 5 of this chapter are mainly based on their ideas.

## 9.7 EXERCISES

9.7.1 Discuss in detail how algorithms EDGE_DELETION, EDGE_INSERTION, and MAX_WEIGHTED_EDGE of Section 9.2.1 can be implemented on the CREW PRAM model.

9.7.2 Show how algorithm MST_EDGE_UPDATE of Section 9.2.2.1 can be executed in $O(\log n)$ time with $O(n^2)$ processors when implemented on a CREW PRAM.

9.7.3 Show that the problem of node deletion in updating minimum spanning trees can be solved in $O(\log n)$ time on a CREW PRAM model (Tsin 1988).

9.7.4 Show that algorithm NODE_INSERTION of Section 9.2.2.2 can be implemented on a CREW PRAM model in $O(\log n)$ time when $O(n^2)$ processors are available.

9.7.5 Study both the node and edge deletion problems in updating a DFS spanning tree of a DAG. Is it possible to design a fast algorithm for each of these problems on a CREW PRAM model?

9.7.6 Design parallel algorithms for the node and edge insertion problems in updating the BFS spanning tree of a graph on the CREW PRAM model.

9.7.7 Repeat Exercise 9.5.6 with reference to the updating of the BDS spanning tree of a DAG.

9.7.8 Consider the root-shifting problem for DFS spanning trees which is defined below. Given a connected, undirected graph G and a DFS spanning tree T with root r, find a DFS spanning tree S of G with a specified root s.

Design an $O(\log n)$ time parallel algorithm for solving this problem on a CREW PRAM model with $O(n^3)$ processors (Tiwari 1986).

9.7.9 Show how each of the algorithms CCOMP_EDGE_DELETION and CCOMP_NODE_INSERTION of Section 9.4 can be implemented on a CREW PRAM model in $O(\log n)$ time without any increase in the processor complexity.

## 9.8 BIBLIOGRAPHY

Chaudhuri, P. (1990). Finding and updating depth first spanning trees of acyclic digraphs in parallel. *Computer Journal* 33, 247-51.

Cheston, G. (1976). *Incremental algorithms in graph theory.* Tech. Rep. TR-91, Dept. of Computer Science, University of Toronto, Ontario.

Chin, F. Y., and Houck, D. (1978). Algorithms for updating minimum spanning trees. *J. Computer and System Sci.* 16, 333-44.

Even, S., and Shiloach, Y. (1982). An on-line edge deletion problem. *J. ACM* 28, 1-4.

Frederickson, G. (1983). Data structures for on-line updating of minimum spanning trees. *Proceedings of the 15th ACM Symposium on Theory of Computing,* ACM, NY, pp. 252-7.

Ibaraki, T., and Katoh, N. (1983). On-line computation of transitive closure of graphs. *Inform. Process. Lett.* 16, 95-7.

Jung, H., and Mehlhorn, K. (1988). Parallel algorithms for computing maximal independent sets in trees and for updating minimum spanning trees. *Inform. Process. Lett.* 27, 227-36.

Pawagi, S. (1989). A parallel algorithm for multiple updates of minimum spanning trees. *Proceedings of the 1989 International Conference on Parallel Processing,* IEEE Computer Society, Washington, DC, pp. III-9-15.

Pawagi, S., and Ramakrishnan, I. V. (1986). An O(log n) algorithm for parallel update of minimum spanning trees. *Inform. Process. Lett.* 22, 223-9.

Sherlekar, D. D., Pawagi, S., and Ramakrishnan, I. V. (1985). O(1) parallel time incremental graph algorithms. *Proceedings of the 5th Conference on the Foundations of Software Technology and Theoretical Computer Science,* New Delhi, India (*Lecture Notes in Computer Science,* Springer-Verlag, NY, vol. 206; eds. G. Goos and J. Hartmanis), pp. 477-93.

Spira, P. M., and Pan, A. (1975). On finding and updating spanning trees and shortest paths. *SIAM J. Computing* 4, 375-80.

Tiwari, P. (1986). An efficient parallel algorithm for shifting the root of a depth first spanning tree. *J. Algorithms* 7, 105-19.

Tsin, Y. H. (1988). On handling vertex deletion in updating minimum spanning trees. *Inform. Process. Lett.* 27, 167-8.

Varman, P., and Doshi, K. (1986). A parallel vertex insertion algorithm for minimum spanning trees. *Proceedings of the 13th Colloquium on Automata Languages and Programming* (*Lecture Notes in Computer Science,* Springer-Verlag, NY, vol. 226; eds. G. Goos and J. Hartmanis), pp. 424-33.

# Author Index

# Subject Index